Database Design and Relational Theory

Normal Forms and All That Jazz

Second Edition

C. J. Date

Apress®

Database Design and Relational Theory: Normal Forms and All That Jazz

C. J. Date
Healdsburg, California, USA

ISBN-13 (pbk): 978-1-4842-5539-1   ISBN-13 (electronic): 978-1-4842-5540-7
https://doi.org/10.1007/978-1-4842-5540-7

Managing Director, Apress Media LLC: Welmoed Spahr
Acquisitions Editor: Jonathan Gennick
Development Editor: Laura Berendson
Coordinating Editor: Jill Balzano

Cover image designed by Freepik (www.freepik.com)

Distributed to the book trade worldwide by Springer Science+Business Media New York, 233 Spring Street, 6th Floor, New York, NY 10013. Phone 1-800-SPRINGER, fax (201) 348-4505, e-mail orders-ny@springer-sbm.com, or visit www.springeronline.com. Apress Media, LLC is a California LLC and the sole member (owner) is Springer Science + Business Media Finance Inc (SSBM Finance Inc). SSBM Finance Inc is a **Delaware** corporation.

For information on translations, please e-mail rights@apress.com, or visit http://www.apress.com/rights-permissions.

Apress titles may be purchased in bulk for academic, corporate, or promotional use. eBook versions and licenses are also available for most titles. For more information, reference our Print and eBook Bulk Sales web page at http://www.apress.com/bulk-sales.

Any source code or other supplementary material referenced by the author in this book is available to readers on GitHub via the book's product page, located at www.apress.com/9781484255391. For more detailed information, please visit http://www.apress.com/source-code.

Printed on acid-free paper

*In computing, elegance is not a dispensable luxury
but a quality that decides between success and failure.*

—Edsger W. Dijkstra

The ill design is most ill for the designer.

—Hesiod

*It is to be noted that when any part of this paper is dull
there is design in it.*

—Sir Richard Steele

*The idea of a formal design discipline is often rejected on account of
vague cultural / philosophical condemnations such as "stifling
creativity"; this is more pronounced … where a romantic vision of
"the humanities" in fact idealizes technical incompetence …*

*[We] know that for the sake of reliability and intellectual control
we have to keep the design simple and disentangled.*

—Edsger W. Dijkstra

My designs are strictly honorable.

—Anon.

——— ♦♦♦♦♦ ———

**To my wife Lindy
and my daughters Sarah and Jennie
with all my love**

Table of Contents

About the Author

C. J. Date is an independent author, lecturer, researcher, and consultant, specializing in relational database technology. He is best known for his book *An Introduction to Database Systems* (8th edition, Addison-Wesley, 2004), which has sold some 900,000 copies at the time of writing and is used by several hundred colleges and universities worldwide. He is also the author of numerous other books on database management, including most recently:

- From Ventus: *Go Faster! The TransRelational™ Approach to DBMS Implementation* (2002, 2011)

- From Addison-Wesley: *Databases, Types, and the Relational Model: The Third Manifesto* (3rd edition, with Hugh Darwen, 2007)

- From Trafford: *Logic and Databases: The Roots of Relational Theory* (2007) and *Database Explorations: Essays on The Third Manifesto and Related Topics* (with Hugh Darwen, 2010)

- From Apress: *Date on Database: Writings 2000-2006* (2006)

- From Morgan Kaufmann: *Time and Relational Theory: Temporal Databases in the Relational Model and SQL* (with Hugh Darwen and Nikos A. Lorentzos, 2014)

- From O'Reilly: *Relational Theory for Computer Professionals: What Relational Databases Are Really All About* (2013); *View Updating and Relational Theory: Solving the View Update Problem* (2013); *SQL and Relational Theory: How to Write Accurate SQL Code* (3rd edition, 2015); *The **New** Relational Database Dictionary* (2016); and *Type Inheritance and Relational Theory: Subtypes, Supertypes, and Substitutability* (2016)

- From Lulu: *E. F. Codd and Relational Theory: A Detailed Review and Analysis of Codd's Major Database Writings* (2019)

Mr Date was inducted into the Computing Industry Hall of Fame in 2004. He enjoys a reputation that is second to none for his ability to explain complex technical subjects in a clear and understandable fashion.

Preface to the First Edition

This book began life as a comparatively short chapter in a book called *Database in Depth: Relational Theory for Practitioners* (O'Reilly, 2005). That book was superseded by a greatly expanded version called *SQL and Relational Theory: How to Write Accurate SQL Code* (O'Reilly, 2009), where the design material, since it was somewhat tangential to the main theme of the book, ceased to be a chapter as such and became a (somewhat longer) appendix instead. I subsequently began work on a second edition of this latter book.[1] During the course of that work, I found there was so much that needed to be said on the subject of database design in general that the appendix threatened to grow out of all proportion to the rest of the book. Since the topic was, as I've indicated, rather out of line with the major emphasis of that book anyway, I decided to cut the Gordian knot and separate the material out into a book of its own: the one you're looking at right now.

Three points arise immediately from the foregoing:

- First, the present book does assume you're familiar with material covered in the *SQL and Relational Theory* book (in particular, it assumes you know exactly what *relations*, *attributes*, and *tuples* are). I make no apology for this state of affairs, however, since the present book is aimed at database professionals and database professionals ought really to be familiar with most of what's in that earlier book, anyway.

- Second, the previous point notwithstanding, there's unavoidably a small amount of overlap between this book and that earlier book. I've done my best to keep that overlap to a minimum, however.

---

[1]That second edition was published by O'Reilly in 2012. It was followed in 2015 by a third. Thus, all references to that book in what follows should be understood as referring to that third edition specifically (where it makes any difference).

- Third, there are, again unavoidably, many references in this book to that earlier one. Now, most references in this book to other publications are given in full, as in this example:

  > Ronald Fagin: "Normal Forms and Relational Database Operators," Proc. 1979 ACM SIGMOD International Conference on Management of Data, Boston, Mass. (May/June 1979)

  In the case of references to the *SQL and Relational Theory* book in particular, however, from this point forward I'll give them in the form of that abbreviated title alone.

Actually I've published several short pieces over the years, in one place or another, on various aspects of design theory, and the present book is intended among other things to preserve the good parts of those earlier writings. But it's not just a cobbling together of previously published material, and I sincerely hope it won't be seen as such. For one thing, it contains much new material. For another, it presents a more coherent, and I think much better, perspective on the subject as a whole (I've learned a lot myself over the years!). Indeed, even when a portion of the text is based on some earlier publication, the material in question has been totally rewritten and, I trust, improved.

Now, there's no shortage of books on database design—so what makes this one different? In fact I don't think there's a book on the market that's quite like this one. There are many books (of considerably varying quality, in my not unbiased opinion) on design practice, but those books (again, in my own opinion) usually don't do a very good job of explaining the underlying theory. And there are a few books on design theory, too, but they tend to be aimed at theoreticians, not practitioners, and to be rather academic in tone. What I want to do is bridge the gap; in other words, I want to explain the theory in a way that practitioners should be able to understand, and I want to show why that theory is of considerable practical importance. What I'm not trying to do is be exhaustive; I don't want to discuss the theory in every last detail, I want to concentrate on what seem to me the important parts (though, naturally, my treatment of the parts I do cover is meant to be precise and accurate, as far as it goes). Also, I'm aiming at a judicious blend of the formal and the informal; in other words, I'm trying to provide a gentle introduction to the theory, so that:

a. You can use important theoretical results to help you actually do design, and

b. You'll be able, if you're so inclined, to go to the more academic texts and understand them.

In the interest of readability, I've deliberately written a fairly short book, and I've deliberately made each chapter fairly short, too.[2] (I'm a great believer in doling out information in small and digestible chunks.) Also, every chapter includes a set of exercises (answers to most of which are given in Appendix D at the back of the book),[3] and I do recommend that you have a go at some of those exercises if not all. Some of them are intended to show how to apply the theoretical ideas in practice; others provide (in the answers if not in the exercises as such) additional information on the subject matter, over and above what's covered in the main body of the text; and still others are meant—for example, by asking you to prove some simple theoretical result—to get you to gain some understanding as to what's involved in "thinking like a theoretician." Overall, I've tried to give some insight into what design theory is and why it is the way it is.

Prerequisites

My target audience is database professionals: more specifically, database professionals with a more than passing interest in database design. In particular, therefore, I assume you're reasonably familiar with the relational model, or at least with certain aspects of that model (Chapter 2 goes into more detail on these matters). As already indicated, familiarity with the *SQL and Relational Theory* book would be helpful.

Logical vs. Physical Design

This book is about design *theory*; by definition, therefore, it's about logical design, not physical design. Of course, I'm not saying physical design is unimportant (of course not); but I am saying it's a distinct activity, separate from and subsequent to logical design. To spell the point out, the "right" way to design a database is as follows:

1. Do a clean logical design first. Then, as a separate and subsequent step:

---

[2]Sadly, the second edition is somewhat larger than its predecessor. That always happens with new editions, of course, though in the present case the increase is due in part to the fact that—in response to reader requests—I've increased the font size. In any case, at least the individual chapters are still fairly short. Mostly.

[3]In response to reader requests again, in this second edition I've moved the answers that are specific to a given chapter to the end of the chapter in question and deleted the old Appendix D.

2. Map that logical design into whatever physical structures the target DBMS happens to support.[4]

Note, therefore, that the physical design should be derived from the logical design and not the other way around. (Ideally, in fact, the system should be able to derive the physical design "automatically" from the logical design, without the need for human involvement in the process at all.)[5]

To repeat, the book is about design theory. So another thing it's not about is the various ad hoc design methodologies—entity / relationship modeling and the like—that have been proposed over the years, at one time or another. Of course, I realize that certain of those methodologies are fairly widely used in practice, but the fact remains that they enjoy comparatively little by way of a solid theoretical basis. As a result, they're mostly beyond the scope of a book like this one. However, I do have a few remarks here and there on such "nontheoretical" matters (especially in Chapters 8 and 17, also in Appendix C).

Acknowledgments

I'd like to thank Hugh Darwen, Ron Fagin, David McGoveran, and Andy Oram for their meticulous reviews of earlier drafts of this book. Each of these reviewers helped correct a number of misconceptions on my part (rather more such, in fact, than I like to think). Of course, it goes without saying that any remaining errors are my responsibility. I'd also like to thank Chris Adamson for help with certain technical questions, and my wife Lindy for her support throughout the production of this book, as well as all of its predecessors.

C. J. Date
Healdsburg, California
2012 (minor revisions 2019)

---

[4]DBMS = database management system. Note that there's a logical difference between a DBMS and a database! Unfortunately, the industry very commonly uses the term *database* when it means either some DBMS product, such as Oracle, or the particular copy of such a product that happens to be installed on some particular computer. I do *not* follow that usage in this book. The problem is, if you call the DBMS a database, then what do you call the database?

[5]This idea isn't as farfetched as it might seem. See my book *Go Faster! The TransRelational*™ *Approach to DBMS Implementation* (Ventus, 2002, 2011), available as a free download from *http://bookboon.com*.

Preface to the Second Edition

This edition differs from its predecessor in many ways. The overall objective remains the same, of course—I'm still trying to provide a gentle introduction to design theory—but the text has been revised throughout to reflect, among other things, experience gained from teaching live classes based on the first edition. Quite a lot of new material has been added (including new chapters on sixth normal form and the various normal forms between fourth and fifth, and a couple of new appendixes on database design in general). Examples, exercises, and answers have been expanded and improved in various respects, and the text has been subjected to a thorough overhaul throughout. Numerous cosmetic improvements and a variety of technical corrections—an embarrassingly large number of these, I'm sorry to have to report—have also been made. The net effect is to make the text rather more comprehensive (but, sadly, some 50% bigger) than its predecessor.

My thanks to O'Reilly Media Inc. (publisher of the first edition) for permission to place this second edition with a different publisher.

C. J. Date
Healdsburg, California
2019

PART I

Setting the Scene

This part of the book consists of two introductory chapters, the titles of which ("Preliminaries" and "Prerequisites," respectively) are more or less self-explanatory.

CHAPTER 1

Preliminaries

(On being asked what jazz is:)
Man, if you gotta ask, you'll never know.

—Louis Armstrong (attrib.)

This book has as its subtitle *Normal Forms and All That Jazz.* Clearly some explanation is needed! First of all, of course, I'm talking about design theory—database design theory, that is—and everybody knows that normal forms are a major component of that theory; hence the first part of the subtitle. But there's more to that theory than just normal forms, and that fact accounts for that subtitle's second part. Third, it's unfortunately the case that—from the practitioner's point of view, at any rate—design theory seems to be riddled with terms and concepts that are hard to understand and don't seem to have much to do with design as actually done in practice. That's why I framed the latter part of my subtitle in colloquial (not to say slangy) terms; I wanted to convey the idea that, although we'd necessarily be dealing with "difficult" material on occasion, the treatment of that material would be as undaunting and unintimidating as I could make it. But whether I've succeeded in that aim is for you to judge, of course.

I'd also like to say a little more on the question of whether design theory has anything to do with design as carried out in practice. Let me be clear: Nobody could, or should, claim that database design is easy. But a sound knowledge of the theory can only help. In fact, if you want to do design properly—if you want to build databases that are as robust, flexible, and accurate as they're supposed to be—then you simply have to come to grips with the theory. There's just no alternative: at least, not if you want to claim to be a design professional. Design theory is the scientific foundation for database design, just as the relational model is the scientific foundation for database technology in general. And just as anyone professionally involved in database technology in general needs to be familiar with the relational model, so anyone involved in database design in particular needs to be familiar with design theory. Proper design is so important! After all, the

© C. J. Date 2019
C. J. Date, *Database Design and Relational Theory*, https://doi.org/10.1007/978-1-4842-5540-7_1

database lies at the heart of so much of what we do in the computing world; so if it's badly designed, the negative impacts can be extraordinarily widespread.

Some Quotes from the Literature

Since we're going to be talking quite a lot about normal forms, I thought it might be—well, not exactly enlightening, but entertaining, possibly (?)—to begin with a few quotes from the literature. The starting point for the whole concept of normal forms is, of course, *first normal form* (1NF), and so an obvious question is: *Do you know what 1NF is?* As the following quotes demonstrate (sources omitted to protect the guilty), a lot of people don't:

- To achieve first normal form, each field in a table must convey unique information.

- An entity is said to be in the first normal form (1NF) when all attributes are single valued.

- A relation is in 1NF if and only if all underlying domains contain atomic values only.

- If there are no repeating groups of attributes, then [the table] is in 1NF.

Now, it might be argued that some if not all of these quotes are at least vaguely correct—but they're all hopelessly sloppy, even when they're generally on the right lines. *Note:* In case you're wondering, I'll be giving a precise and accurate definition of 1NF in Chapter 4.

Let's take a closer look at what's going on here. Here again is the first of the foregoing quotes, now given in full:

- To achieve first normal form, each field in a table must convey unique information. For example, if you had a Customer table with two columns for the telephone number, your design would violate first normal form. First normal form is fairly easy to achieve, since few folks would see a need for duplicate information in a table.

    OK, so apparently we're talking about a design that looks something like this:

CUSTNO	PHONENO1	PHONENO2	. . .

Now, I can't say whether this is a good design or not, but it certainly doesn't violate 1NF. (I can't say whether it's a good design because I don't know exactly what "two columns for the telephone number" means—the phrase "duplicate information in a table" suggests we're recording the same phone number twice, but such an interpretation is absurd on its face. But even if that interpretation is correct, it still wouldn't constitute a violation of 1NF as such.)

Here's another quote:

- First Normal Form ... means the table should have no "repeating groups" of fields ... A repeating group is when you repeat the same basic attribute (field) over and over again. A good example of this is when you wish to store the items you buy at a grocery store ... [*and the writer goes on to give an example, presumably meant to illustrate the concept of a repeating group, of a table called Item Table, with columns called Customer, Item1, Item2, Item3, and Item4*]:

CUSTOMER	ITEM1	ITEM2	ITEM3	ITEM4

Well, this design is almost certainly bad—what happens if the customer doesn't purchase exactly four items?—but the reason it's bad isn't that it violates 1NF; like the previous example, in fact, it's a 1NF design. So, while it might perhaps be claimed—indeed, it often is claimed—that 1NF does mean, loosely, "no repeating groups," a repeating group is *not* "when you repeat the same basic attribute over and over again."[1]

How about this one (a cry for help found on the Internet)? I'm quoting it absolutely verbatim, except that I've added some boldface:

- I have been trying to find the correct way of normalizing tables in Access. From what I understand, it goes from the 1st normal form to 2nd, then 3rd. Usually, that's as far as it goes, but sometimes to the 5th and 6th. Then, there's also the Cobb 3rd. This all makes sense to me. **I am supposed to teach a class in this starting next week,** and I just got the textbook. It says something entirely different. It says 2nd normal form is only for tables with a multiple-field primary key, 3rd normal form is only for tables with a single-field key. 4th normal form

---

[1]At the same time it's not as easy as you might think to say exactly what it is! See further discussion in Chapter 4.

can go from 1st to 4th, where there are no independent one-to-many relationships between primary key and non-key fields. Can someone clear this up for me please?

And one more (this time with a "helpful" response):

- *It's not clear to me what "normalized" means. Can you be specific about what normalization rules you are referring to? In what way is my schema not normalized?*

  Normalization: The process of replacing duplicate things with a reference to the original thing.

  For example, given "john is-a person" and "john obeys army," one observes that the "john" in the second sentence is a duplicate of "john" in the first sentence. Using the means provided by your system, the second sentence should be stored as "->john obeys army."

A Note on Terminology

As I'm sure you noticed, the quotes in the previous section were expressed for the most part in the familiar "user friendly" terminology of tables, rows, and columns (or fields). In this book, by contrast, I'll favor the more formal terms *relation, tuple* (usually pronounced to rhyme with *couple*), and *attribute*. I apologize if this decision on my part makes the text a little harder to follow, but I do have my reasons. As I said in *SQL and Relational Theory*:[2]

> I'm generally sympathetic to the idea of using more user friendly terms, if they can help make the ideas more palatable. In the case at hand, however, it seems to me that, regrettably, they don't make the ideas more palatable; instead, they distort them, and in fact do the cause of genuine understanding a grave disservice.

---

[2]I remind you from the preface that throughout this book I use *SQL and Relational Theory* as an abbreviated form of reference to my book *SQL and Relational Theory: How to Write Accurate SQL Code* (3rd edition, O'Reilly, 2015).

The truth is, a relation is *not* a table, a tuple is *not* a row, and an attribute is *not* a column. And while it might be acceptable to pretend otherwise in informal contexts—indeed, I often do so myself—I would argue that it's acceptable only if all parties involved understand that those more user friendly terms are just an approximation to the truth and fail overall to capture the essence of what's really going on. To put it another way: If you do understand the true state of affairs, then judicious use of the user friendly terms can be a good idea; but in order to learn and appreciate that true state of affairs in the first place, you really do need to come to grips with the formal terms.

To the foregoing, let me add that (as I said in the preface) I do assume you know exactly what *relations*, *attributes*, and *tuples* are—though in fact formal definitions of these constructs can be found in Chapter 5.

There's another terminological matter I need to get out of the way, too. The relational model is, of course, a data model. Unfortunately, however, this latter term has two quite distinct meanings in the database world.[3] The first and more fundamental one is this:

> **Definition (data model, first sense):** An abstract, self-contained, logical definition of the data structures, data operators, and so forth, that together make up the abstract machine with which users interact.

This is the meaning we have in mind when we talk about the relational model in particular: The data structures in the relational model are relations, of course, and the data operators are the relational operators projection, join, and all the rest. (As for that "and so forth" in the definition, it covers such matters as keys, foreign keys, and various related concepts.)

The second meaning of the term *data model* is as follows:

> **Definition (data model, second sense):** A model of the data (especially the persistent data) of some particular enterprise.

---

[3]This observation is undeniably correct. However, one reviewer wanted me to add that the two meanings can be thought of as essentially the same concept at different levels of abstraction. I hope that helps!

In other words, a data model in the second sense is just a (logical, and possibly somewhat abstract) database design. For example, we might speak of the data model for some bank, or some hospital, or some government department.

Having explained these two different meanings, I'd like to draw your attention to an analogy that I think nicely illuminates the relationship between them:

- A data model in the first sense is like a programming language, whose constructs can be used to solve many specific problems but in and of themselves have no direct connection with any such specific problem.

- A data model in the second sense is like a specific program written in that language—it uses the facilities provided by the model, in the first sense of that term, to solve some specific problem.

It follows from all of the above that if we're talking about data models in the second sense, then we might reasonably speak of "relational models" in the plural, or "a" relational model, with an indefinite article. But if we're talking about data models in the first sense, then *there's only one relational model*, and it's *the* relational model, with the definite article.

Now, as you are probably aware, most writings on database design, especially if their focus is on pragma rather than the underlying theory, use the term "model," or the term "data model," exclusively in the second sense. But—*please note very carefully!*—I don't follow this practice in the present book; in fact, I don't use the term "model" at all, except occasionally to refer to the relational model as such.

The Running Example

Now let me introduce the example I'll be using as a basis for most of the discussions in the rest of the book: the familiar—not to say hackneyed—suppliers-and-parts database. (I apologize for dragging out this old warhorse yet one more time, but I do believe that using essentially the same example in a variety of different books and publications can help, not hinder, the learning process.) Sample values are shown in Figure 1-1 on the next page.[4] To elaborate:

---

[4]For reasons that might or might not become clear later, the values shown in Fig. 1.1 differ in two small respects from those in other books of mine: First, the status for supplier S2 is shown as 30 instead of 10; second, the city for part P3 is shown as Paris instead of Oslo.

- *Suppliers:* Relvar S denotes suppliers.[5] Each supplier has one supplier number (SNO), unique to that supplier; one name (SNAME), not necessarily unique (though the SNAME values in Figure 1-1 do happen to be unique); one status value (STATUS), representing some kind of ranking or preference level among suppliers; and one location (CITY).

- *Parts:* Relvar P denotes parts (more accurately, kinds of parts). Each kind of part has one part number (PNO), which is unique; one name (PNAME), not necessarily unique; one color (COLOR); one weight (WEIGHT); and one location where parts of that kind are stored (CITY).

- *Shipments:* Relvar SP denotes shipments—it shows which parts are supplied, or shipped, by which suppliers. Each shipment has one supplier number (SNO), one part number (PNO), and one quantity (QTY). Also, I assume for the sake of the example that there's at most one shipment at any given time for a given supplier and a given part, and so each shipment has a supplier-number / part-number combination that's unique.

S

SNO	SNAME	STATUS	CITY
S1	Smith	20	London
S2	Jones	30	Paris
S3	Blake	30	Paris
S4	Clark	20	London
S5	Adams	30	Athens

P

PNO	PNAME	COLOR	WEIGHT	CITY
P1	Nut	Red	12.0	London
P2	Bolt	Green	17.0	Paris
P3	Screw	Blue	17.0	Paris
P4	Screw	Red	14.0	London
P5	Cam	Blue	12.0	Paris
P6	Cog	Red	19.0	London

SP

SNO	PNO	QTY
S1	P1	300
S1	P2	200
S1	P3	400
S1	P4	200
S1	P5	100
S1	P6	100
S2	P1	300
S2	P2	400
S3	P2	200
S4	P2	200
S4	P4	300
S4	P5	400

Figure 1-1. *The suppliers-and-parts database—sample values*

[5]If you don't know what a relvar is, for now you can just take it to be a table in the usual database sense. See Chapter 2 for further explanation.

Keys

Before going any further, I need to review the familiar concept of *keys,* in the relational sense of that term. First of all, as I'm sure you know, every relvar has at least one *candidate* key. A candidate key is basically just a unique identifier; in other words, it's a combination of attributes—often but not always a "combination" consisting of just a single attribute—such that every tuple in the relvar has a unique value for the combination in question. For example, with respect to the database of Figure 1-1:

- Every supplier has a unique supplier number and every part has a unique part number, so {SNO} is a candidate key for S and {PNO} is a candidate key for P.

- As for shipments, given the assumption that there's at most one shipment at any given time for a given supplier and a given part, {SNO,PNO} is a candidate key for SP.

Note the braces, by the way; to repeat, candidate keys are always combinations, or *sets,* of attributes (even when the set in question contains just one attribute), and the conventional representation of a set on paper is as a commalist of elements enclosed in braces.

This is the first time I've mentioned the term *commalist,* which I'll be using from time to time in the pages ahead. It can be defined as follows. Let *xyz* be some syntactic construct (for example, "attribute name"); then the term *xyz commalist* denotes a sequence of zero or more *xyz*'s in which each pair of adjacent *xyz*'s is separated by a comma (blank spaces appearing immediately before or after any comma are ignored). For example, if *A, B,* and *C* are attribute names, then the following are all attribute name commalists:

A , B , C

C , A , B

B

A , C

So too is the empty sequence of attribute names.

Moreover, when some commalist is enclosed in braces and thereby denotes a set, then (a) blank spaces appearing immediately after the opening brace or immediately before the closing brace are ignored, (b) the order in which the elements appear within the commalist is immaterial (because sets have no ordering to their elements), and (c) if an element appears more than once, it's treated as if it appeared just once (because sets don't contain duplicate elements).

Next, as I'm sure you also know, a *primary* key is a candidate key that's been singled out in some way for some kind of special treatment. Now, if the relvar in question has just one candidate key, then it doesn't make any real difference if we call that key primary. But if the relvar has two or more candidate keys, then it's usual to choose one of them to be primary, meaning it's somehow "more equal than the others." Suppose, for example, that suppliers always have both a unique supplier number and a unique supplier name, so that {SNO} and {SNAME} are both candidate keys. Then we might choose {SNO}, say, to be the primary key.

Observe now that I said it's *usual* to choose a primary key. Indeed it is usual—but it's *not* 100% necessary. If there's just one candidate key, then there's no choice and no problem; but if there are two or more, then having to choose one and make it primary smacks a little bit of arbitrariness, at least to me. (Certainly there are situations where there don't seem to be any really good reasons for making such a choice. There might even be good reasons for not doing so. Appendix C elaborates on such matters.) For reasons of familiarity, I'll usually follow the primary key discipline myself in this book—and in pictures like Figure 1-1 I'll indicate primary key attributes by double underlining—but I want to stress the fact that it's really candidate keys, not primary keys, that are significant from a relational point of view, and indeed from a design theory point of view as well. Partly for such reasons, from this point forward I'll use the term *key*, unqualified, to mean any candidate key, regardless of whether the candidate key in question has additionally been designated as primary. (In case you were wondering, the special treatment enjoyed by primary keys over other candidate keys is mainly syntactic in nature, anyway; it isn't fundamental, and it isn't very important.)

More terminology: First, a key involving two or more attributes is said to be *composite* (and a noncomposite key is sometimes said to be *simple*). Second, if a given relvar has two or more keys and one is chosen as primary, then the others are sometimes said to be *alternate* keys (see Appendix C). Third, a *foreign* key is a combination, or set, of attributes *FK* in some relvar *R2* such that each *FK* value is required to be equal to some value of some key *K* in some relvar *R1* (*R1* and *R2* not necessarily distinct).[6] With reference to Figure 1-1, for example, {SNO} and {PNO} are both foreign keys in relvar SP, corresponding to keys {SNO} and {PNO} in relvars S and P, respectively.

The Place of Design Theory

As I said in the preface, by the term *design* I mean logical design, not physical design. Logical design is concerned with what the database looks like to the user (which means, loosely, what relvars exist and what constraints apply to those relvars); physical design, by contrast, is concerned with how a given logical design maps to physical storage.[7] And the term *design theory* refers specifically to logical design, not physical design—the point being that physical design is necessarily dependent on aspects (performance aspects in particular) of the target DBMS, whereas logical design is, or should be, DBMS independent. Throughout this book, then, the unqualified term *design* should be understood to mean logical design specifically, unless the context demands otherwise.

Now, design theory as such isn't part of the relational model; rather, it's a separate theory that builds on top of that model. (It's appropriate to think of it as part of relational theory in general, but it's not, to repeat, part of the relational model per se.) Thus, design concepts such as further normalization are themselves based on more fundamental notions—e.g., the projection and join operators of the relational algebra—that *are* part of the relational model. (All of that being said, however, it could certainly be argued that design theory is a *logical consequence* of the relational model, in a sense. In other words, I think it would be inconsistent to agree with the relational model in general but not to agree with the design theory that's based on it.)

The overall objective of logical design is to achieve a design that's (a) hardware independent, for obvious reasons; (b) operating system and DBMS independent, again for obvious reasons; and finally, and perhaps a little controversially, (c) *application* independent (in other words, we're concerned primarily with what the data is, rather than with how it's going to be used). Application independence in this sense is desirable

---

[6]This definition is deliberately a little simplified (though it's good enough for present purposes). A better one can be found in Chapter 3, also in *SQL and Relational Theory*.

[7]Be aware, however, that other writers (a) use those terms *logical design* and *physical design* to mean something else and (b) use other terms to mean what I mean by those terms. *Caveat lector.*

for the very good reason that it's normally—perhaps always—the case that not all uses to which the data will be put are known at design time; thus, we want a design that'll be robust, in the sense that it won't be invalidated by the advent of application requirements that weren't foreseen at the time of the original design. Observe that one important consequence of this state of affairs is that we aren't (or at least shouldn't be) interested in making design compromises for physical performance reasons. Design theory in general, and individual database designs in particular, should never be driven by mere performance considerations.

Back to design theory as such. As we'll see, that theory includes a number of formal theorems, theorems that provide practical guidelines for designers to follow. So if you're a designer, you need to be familiar with those theorems. Let me quickly add that I don't mean you need to know how to prove the theorems in question (though in fact the proofs are often quite simple); what I mean is, you need to know what the theorems say—i.e., you need to know the results—and you need to be prepared to apply those results. That's the nice thing about theorems: Once somebody's proved them, then their results become available for anybody to use whenever they need to.

Now, it's sometimes claimed, not entirely unreasonably, that all design theory really does is *bolster up your intuition*. What do I mean by this remark? Well, consider the suppliers-and-parts database. The obvious design for that database is the one illustrated in Figure 1-1; I mean, it's "obvious" that three relvars are necessary, that attribute STATUS belongs in relvar S, that attribute COLOR belongs in relvar P, that attribute QTY belongs in relvar SP, and so on. But why exactly are these things obvious? Well, suppose we try a different design; for example, suppose we move the STATUS attribute out of relvar S and into relvar SP (intuitively the wrong place for it, of course, since status is a property of suppliers, not shipments). Figure 1-2 on the next page shows a sample value for this revised shipments relvar, which I'll call STP to avoid confusion:[8]

---

[8]For obvious reasons, throughout this book I use T, not S, as an abbreviation for STATUS.

STP

SNO	STATUS	PNO	QTY
S1	20	P1	300
S1	20	P2	200
S1	20	P3	400
S1	20	P4	200
S1	20	P5	100
S1	20	P6	100
S2	30	P1	300
S2	30	P2	400
S3	30	P2	200
S4	20	P2	200
S4	20	P4	300
S4	20	P5	400

Figure 1-2. *Relvar STP—sample value*

A glance at the figure is sufficient to show what's wrong with this design: It's
redundant, in the sense that every tuple for supplier S1 tells us S1 has status 20, every
tuple for supplier S2 tells us S2 has status 30, and so on.[9] And design theory tells us that
not designing the database in the obvious way will lead to such redundancy, and tells
us also (albeit implicitly, perhaps) what the consequences of such redundancy will
be. In other words, design theory is largely—though not exclusively—about reducing
redundancy, as we'll see. (As an aside, I remark that partly for such reasons, the theory
has been described, perhaps a little unkindly, as *a good source of bad examples.*)

Now, if design theory really does just bolster up your intuition, then it might be (and
indeed has been) criticized on the grounds that it's really all just common sense anyway.
By way of example, consider relvar STP again. As I've said, that relvar is obviously badly
designed; the redundancies are obvious, the consequences are obvious too, and any
competent human designer would "naturally" avoid such a design, even if that designer
had no explicit knowledge of design theory at all. But what does "naturally" mean here?
What principles are being applied by that human designer in opting for a more "natural"
(and better) design?

The answer is: They're exactly the principles that design theory talks about (the
principles of normalization, for example). In other words, competent designers already
have those principles in their brain, as it were, even if they've never studied them
formally and can't put a name to them or articulate them precisely. So yes, the principles
are common sense—but they're *formalized* common sense. (Common sense might be

---

[9]You might notice another problem, too: The design can't properly represent suppliers like supplier
S5 who currently supply no parts at all. This problem and others like it are discussed in Chapter 3.

common, but it's not always easy to say exactly what it is!) What design theory does is state *in a precise way* what certain aspects of common sense consist of. In my opinion, that's the real achievement—or one of the real achievements, anyway—of the theory: It formalizes certain commonsense principles, thereby opening the door to the possibility of mechanizing those principles (that is, incorporating them into computerized design tools). Critics of the theory often miss this point; they claim, quite rightly, that the ideas are mostly just common sense, but they don't seem to realize it's a significant achievement to state what common sense means in a precise and formal way.

As a kind of postscript to the foregoing, I note that common sense might not always be that common anyway. The following lightly edited extract from a paper by Robert R. Brown[10] illustrates the point. Brown begins by giving "a simplified real example"—his words—involving an employee file (with fields for employee number, employee name, phone number, department number, and manager name) and a department file (with fields for department number, department name, manager name, and manager's phone number), where everything has the intuitively obvious meaning. Then he continues:

> The actual database on which this example is based had many
> more files and fields and much more redundancy. When the
> designer was asked his reasons for such a design, he cited
> performance and the difficulty of doing joins. Even though the
> redundancy should be clear to you in my example, it was not that
> evident in the design documentation. In large databases with
> many more files and fields, it is impossible to find the duplications
> without doing extensive information analysis and without having
> extended discussions with the experts in the user organizations.

Incidentally, there's another quote I like a lot—in fact, I used it as an epigraph in *SQL and Relational Theory*—that supports my contention that practitioners really do need to know the theoretical foundations of their field. It's from Leonardo da Vinci (and is thus some 500 years old!), and it goes like this (I've added the boldface):

> Those who are enamored of practice without theory are like a pilot
> who goes into a ship without rudder or compass and never has
> any certainty where he is going. **Practice should always be based
> upon a sound knowledge of theory.**

---

[10]Robert R. Brown: "Database Systems in Engineering: Key Problems, and Potential Solutions," in the proceedings of a database symposium held in Sydney, Australia (November 15th-17th, 1984).

Aims of this Book

If you're like me, you'll have encountered lots of design theory terms in the literature and live presentations and the like—terms such as *projection-join normal form, the chase, join dependency, FD preservation,* and many others—and I'm sure you've wondered from time to time exactly what they all mean. Thus, it's one of my aims in this book to explain such terms: to define them carefully and accurately, to explain their relevance and applicability, and generally to remove any air of mystery that might seem to surround them. And if I'm successful in that aim, I'll have gone a good way to explaining what design theory is and why it's important (indeed, a possible alternative title for the book could well be *Database Design Theory: What It Is and Why You Should Care*). Overall, it's my goal to provide a painless introduction to design theory for database professionals. More specifically, what I want to do is the following:

- Review, albeit from a possibly unfamiliar perspective, aspects of design you should already be familiar with

- Explore in depth aspects you're probably not already familiar with

- Provide clear and accurate explanations and definitions (with plenty of examples) of all pertinent concepts

- *Not* spend too much time on material that's widely understood already, such as second and third normal form (2NF and 3NF)[11]

All of that being said, I should say too that database design is *not* my favorite subject. The reason it's not is that much of that subject is still somewhat ... well, subjective. As I said earlier, design theory is the scientific foundation for database design. Sadly, however, there are numerous design issues that the theory simply doesn't address at all (at least, not yet). Thus, while the formal principles I'll be describing in this book do represent the scientific part of design, there are other parts that, as I've put it elsewhere, are still much more in the nature of an artistic endeavor. Indeed, one message of the book is precisely that we need more science in this field (see Chapter 17).

---

[11]However, I will at least give precise definitions of those familiar concepts for reasons of completeness. Since I'm sure they really are familiar, however, I'll take the liberty of appealing to them from time to time even before we get to those definitions.

To put a more positive spin on matters, I'd like to draw your attention to the following. Design theory is, at least in part, about capturing the meaning of data, and as Codd himself once said in connection with that notion:[12]

> [The] task of capturing the meaning of data (in a reasonably formal way) is never ending ... The goal is nevertheless an extremely important one because *even small successes can bring understanding and order into the field of database design.*

In fact, I'll go further: If your design violates any of the known science, then, as I've written elsewhere (in a slightly different context), the one thing you can be sure of is that things will go wrong. And though it might be hard to say exactly what will go wrong, and it might be hard to say whether things will go wrong in a major or minor way, you *know*—it's guaranteed—that they will go wrong. Theory is important.

Concluding Remarks

This book grew in the writing; it turns out that, despite the slightly negative tone of some of the remarks in the previous section, there's really quite a lot of good material to cover. What's more, the material *builds*. Thus, while the first few chapters might seem to be going rather slowly, I think you'll find the pace picks up later on. Part of the point is the number of terms and concepts that need to be introduced; the ideas aren't really difficult, but they can seem a little overwhelming, at least until you're comfortable with the terminology. For that reason, at least in certain key parts of the book, I'll be presenting the material twice—first from an informal perspective, and then again from a more formal one. (As Bertrand Russell once memorably said: *Writing can be either readable or precise, but not at the same time.* I'm trying to have my cake and eat it too.)

---

[12]The quote—which I've edited somewhat here (the italics are mine)—is taken from Codd's paper "Extending the Database Relational Model to Capture More Meaning," *ACM Transactions on Database Systems 4*, No. 4 (1979). E. F. ("Ted") Codd was, of course, the inventor of the relational model. What's more, he was also the person who first defined the concept of normalization in general, as well as the first three normal forms (1NF, 2NF, 3NF) in particular.

And talking of Bertrand Russell, it seems appropriate to close this chapter with another wonderful quote from his writings:[13]

> I have been accused of a habit of changing my opinions ... I am not myself in any degree ashamed of [that habit]. What physicist who was already active in 1900 would dream of boasting that his opinions had not changed during the last half century? ... The kind of philosophy that I value and have endeavoured to pursue is scientific, in the sense that there is some definite knowledge to be obtained and that new discoveries can make the admission of former error inevitable to any candid mind. For what I have said, whether early or late, I do not claim the kind of truth which theologians claim for their creeds. I claim only, at best, that the opinion expressed was a sensible one to hold at the time ... I should be much surprised if subsequent research did not show that it needed to be modified. [Such opinions were not] intended as pontifical pronouncements, but only as the best I could do at the time towards the promotion of clear and accurate thinking. Clarity, above all, has been my aim.

I've quoted this extract elsewhere—in the preface to my book *An Introduction to Database Systems* (8th edition, Addison-Wesley, 2004) in particular. The reason I mention this latter book is that it includes among other things a tutorial treatment of some of the material covered in more depth in the present book. But the world has moved on; my own understanding of the theory is, I hope, quite a lot better than it was when I wrote that earlier book, and there are aspects of the treatment in that book that I would frankly now like to revise. One problem with that earlier treatment was that I attempted to make the material more palatable by adopting the fiction that every relvar has just one key, which could then harmlessly be regarded as the primary key. But a consequence of that simplifying assumption was that several of the definitions I gave (e.g., of 2NF and 3NF) were less than fully accurate. This state of affairs has led to a certain amount of confusion in the community—partly my fault, I freely admit, but partly also the fault of people who took the definitions out of context.

---

[13]The quote is from the preface to *The Bertrand Russell Dictionary of Mind, Matter and Morals* (ed., Lester E. Denonn; Citadel Press, 1993). I've edited it just slightly here.

Exercises

The purpose of these exercises is to give some idea of the scope of the chapters to come, and also perhaps to test the extent of your existing knowledge. They can't be answered from material in the present chapter alone.

1.1 Is it true that the relational model doesn't require relvars to be in any particular normal form?

1.2 Should data redundancy always be eliminated? Can it be?

1.3 What's the difference between 3NF and BCNF?

1.4 Is it true that every "all key" relvar is in BCNF?

1.5 Is it true that every binary relvar is in 4NF?

1.6 Is it true that every "all key" relvar is in 5NF?

1.7 Is it true that every binary relvar is in 5NF?

1.8 Is it true that if a relvar is in BCNF but not 5NF, then it must be all key?

1.9 Is it true that if a relvar has just one key and just one other attribute, then it's in 5NF?

1.10 Can you give a precise definition of 5NF?

1.11 Is it true that if a relvar is in 5NF, then it's redundancy free?

1.12 What *precisely* is denormalization?

1.13 What's Heath's Theorem, and why is it important?

1.14 What's *The Principle of Orthogonal Design?*

1.15 What makes some JDs irreducible and others not?

1.16 What's dependency preservation, and why is it important?

1.17 What's the chase?

1.18 How many normal forms can you name?

Answers

Note: All mistakes in this and other "Answers" sections in this book are deliberate *<joke>*.

1.1   Yes, it is. Good design benefits the user, and to some extent the DBMS as well, but the relational model as such doesn't care how the database happens to be designed, just so long as the objects it has to deal with are indeed relations and not something else (which, sadly, they often are, in SQL[14]).

1.2   See Chapter 17.

1.3   See Chapters 4 and 5.

1.4   Yes (see Chapters 4 and 5).

1.5   No. (Actually, it's not even true that every binary relvar is in 2NF. See Exercise 4.6.)

1.6   No (see Chapters 9 and 10).

1.7   No a fortiori, given the answer to Exercise 1.5.

1.8   No (see Chapter 13).

1.9   No (see Chapter 13).

1.10   See Chapter 10.

1.11   No (see Chapters 9 and 17).

1.12   See Chapter 8.

1.13   See Chapter 5.

1.14   See Chapter 16.

---

[14]Actually, "the objects the DBMS has to deal with" are *never* relations in SQL!—except in the very special case in which the object in question is an SQL table with (a) just one column (and that column is properly named), (b) no duplicate rows, and (c) no nulls. Moreover, to comply with the prescriptions of the relational model, they should also (d) contain no pointers (see the answer to Exercise 2.2h in Chapter 2).

1.15   See Chapter 11.

1.16   See Chapter 7.

1.17   See Chapter 11.

1.18   See Chapter 15.

CHAPTER 2

Prerequisites

The world is everything that is the case.

—Ludwig Wittgenstein: *Tractatus Logico-Philosophicus* (1921)

You're supposed to be a database professional, by which I mean someone who (a) is a database practitioner and (b) has a reasonable degree of familiarity with relational theory. Please note that—I'm sorry to have to say this, but it's true—a knowledge of SQL, no matter how deep, is *not* sufficient to satisfy part (b) of this requirement. As I said in *SQL and Relational Theory*:

> I'm sure you know something about SQL; but—and I apologize
> for the possibly offensive tone here—if your knowledge of the
> relational model derives only from your knowledge of SQL, then
> I'm afraid you won't know the relational model as well as you
> should, and you'll probably know some things that ain't so.
> I can't say it too strongly: *SQL and the relational model aren't the
> same thing.*

The purpose of this chapter, then, is to tell you some things that I hope you already know. If you do, then the chapter will serve as a refresher; if you don't, then I hope it'll serve as an adequate tutorial. More specifically, what I want to do is spell out in some detail certain fundamental aspects of relational theory that I'll be relying on heavily in the pages ahead. The aspects in question are ones that, in my experience, database practitioners often aren't aware of (at least, not explicitly). Of course, there are other aspects of relational theory I'll be relying on as well, but I'll elaborate on those, if I think it necessary, when I come to make use of them.

© C. J. Date 2019
C. J. Date, *Database Design and Relational Theory*, https://doi.org/10.1007/978-1-4842-5540-7_2

Overview

Let me begin by giving a quick summary, mainly just for purposes of subsequent reference, of those "fundamental aspects of relational theory" just mentioned:

- Any given database consists of a set of *relation variables* (relvars for short).

- The value of any given relvar at any given time is a *relation value* (relation for short).

- Every relvar represents a certain *predicate* (the "relvar predicate").

- Within any given relvar, every tuple represents a certain *proposition*.

- Relvar *R* at time *T* contains all and only those tuples that represent instantiations of the predicate corresponding to relvar *R* that evaluate to TRUE at time *T*.

The next two sections (which are heavily based on material from *SQL and Relational Theory*) elaborate on these ideas.

Relations and Relvars

Take another look at Figure 1-1, the suppliers-and-parts database, in Chapter 1. That figure shows three relations: namely, the relations that happen to exist in the database at some particular time. But if we were to look at the same database at some different time, we would probably see three different relations appearing in their place. In other words, S, P, and SP are really variables—relation variables, to be precise—and just like variables in general, they have different values at different times. And since they're relation variables specifically, their values at any given time are, of course, relation values.

As a basis for examining these ideas further, consider Figure 2-1. That figure shows (a) on the left, a very much reduced version of the shipments relation from Figure 1-1; (b) on the right, the relation that results after a certain update has been performed. Using the terminology of the previous paragraph, we can say that (a) on the left of the figure we see the relation value that's the value of relation variable SP at some particular time *T1*; (b) on the right, we see the relation value that's the value of that same relation variable at some presumably later time *T2*, after an additional tuple has been inserted.

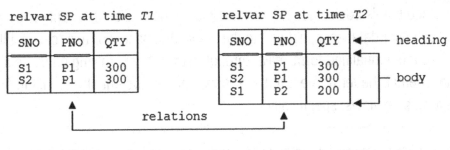

Predicate: *Supplier SNO supplies part PNO in quantity QTY*
Propositions: *Supplier S1 supplies part P1 in quantity 300*
                Supplier S2 supplies part P1 in quantity 300
                Supplier S1 supplies part P2 in quantity 200

Figure 2-1. *Relation values and variables—an example*

So there's an obvious logical difference between relation values and relation variables. The trouble is, the database community has historically used the same term, *relation*, to stand for both concepts, and that practice has certainly led to confusion (not least in contexts that are the subject of the present book, such as further normalization). In this book, therefore, I'll distinguish very carefully between the two from this point forward—I'll talk in terms of relation values when I mean relation values and relation variables when I mean relation variables. However, I'll also abbreviate *relation value*, most of the time, to just *relation* (exactly as we abbreviate *integer value* most of the time to just *integer*). And I'll abbreviate *relation variable* most of the time to ***relvar***; for example, I'll say the suppliers-and-parts database contains three *relvars* (more precisely, three *base* relvars; views are relvars too, but I have little to say about views as such in this book).

Actually, there's one thing I do want to say about views. *The Principle of Interchangeability* (of views and base relvars) says, in effect, that—at least as far as the user is concerned—views are supposed to look and feel just like base relvars. (I don't mean views that are defined as mere shorthands, I mean views that are intended to insulate the user from the "real" database in some way. See Chapter 17 for an elaboration of this point.) In general, in fact, the user interacts not with a database that contains base relvars only (the "real" database), but rather with what might be called a *user* database that contains some mixture of base relvars and views. But that user database is supposed to look and feel just like a real database as far as the user is concerned; thus, all of the design principles to be discussed in this book, such as the principles of normalization, apply equally well to such user databases, not just to the "real" database. For this reason, I'll feel free to use the unqualified term *relvar* throughout this book, relying on context to indicate whether the term refers to base relvars and views equally, or just to base relvars (or just to views) specifically.

Let's get back to Figure 2-1. As that figure suggests, relations have two parts, a *heading* and a *body*. Basically, the heading is a set of attributes, and the body is a set of tuples that conform to that heading. For example, the two relations shown in Figure 2-1 both have a heading consisting of three attributes; also, the relation on the left of that figure has a body consisting of two tuples and the one on the right has a body consisting of three. Note, therefore, that a relation doesn't really contain tuples, at least not directly—it contains a body, and that body in turn contains the tuples. In practice, however, we do usually talk as if relations contained tuples directly, for simplicity. Points arising:

- The terminology of headings and bodies extends in the obvious way to relvars too. Of course, the heading of a relvar (like that of a relation) never changes—it's identical to the heading of all possible relations that might ever be assigned to the relvar in question. By contrast, the body does change; to be specific, it changes as updates are performed on the relvar in question.

- I've said a heading is a set of attributes. As far as the present book is concerned, however, it's simpler to think of a heading as just a set of attribute *names*—an oversimplification, certainly, but not one that has any serious negative impact on the matters to be discussed.

- Actually it would be more correct to think of a heading as a set of *attribute-name / type-name pairs* (while retaining the requirement that the attribute names in question must all be distinct, of course). For example, I'm going to assume in examples throughout this book that attributes SNO and PNO are each of type CHAR (character strings of arbitrary length) and attribute QTY is of type INTEGER (integers).[1] And when I talk about tuples conforming to some heading, I mean each attribute value within the tuple in question must be a value of the pertinent type. For example, in order for a tuple to conform to the heading of relvar SP, it must have attributes SNO, PNO, and QTY (and no others), and the values of those attributes must be of types CHAR, CHAR, and INTEGER, respectively.

All of that being said, I must now say too that types are mostly not very important for the purposes of relational design theory. That's why I'll feel free from this point forward to simplify my definition of what a heading is. What's more, I'll also feel free, in most of my sample relations and relvars (and relvar definitions), to show the attribute names only and not bother about or even mention the corresponding types.

- The number of attributes in a given heading is the *degree* (sometimes the *arity*) of that heading. It's also the degree of any relation or relvar having that heading.

  Note: The term *degree* is also used in connection with both tuples and keys (and foreign keys). For example, the tuples of relvar SP are all, like that relvar itself, of degree three; the sole key of that relvar, {SNO,PNO}, is of degree two; and the two foreign keys in that relvar, {SNO} and {PNO}, are each of degree one.

- The number of tuples in a given body is the *cardinality* of that body. It's also the cardinality of any relation or relvar having that body.[2]

- The degree (of a heading or relation or whatever) can be any nonnegative integer. Degree 1 is said to be *unary*; degree 2, *binary*; degree 3, *ternary*; and so on. More generally, degree n is said to be n-ary.

---

[1] It might be more appropriate to define QTY to be of type NONNEGATIVE_INTEGER (with the obvious semantics), but few DBMSs if any currently support such a type. Of course, we could introduce it as a user defined type, but I don't want to get into the complications of user defined types in this book.

[2] I say "any" relation having that body, but actually two distinct relations can have the same body if and only if the body in question is empty. If it isn't, then there's exactly one relation that has the body in question (see the formal definition of *relation* in Chapter 5).

Predicates and Propositions

Again consider the shipments relvar SP. Like all relvars, that relvar is supposed to represent some portion of the real world. In fact, I can be more precise: The heading of that relvar represents a certain *predicate*, meaning it's a kind of generic statement about some portion of the real world (it's generic because it's *parameterized*, as I'll explain in just a moment). The predicate in question (i.e., the one for relvar SP) is quite simple:

> *Supplier SNO supplies part PNO in quantity QTY.*

This predicate is the *intended interpretation*—in other words, the *meaning*—for, or of, relvar SP.

Perhaps I should say a little more about the way I use the term *predicate* in this book. First of all, you're probably familiar with the term already, since SQL uses it extensively to refer to boolean or truth valued expressions (it talks about comparison predicates, IN predicates, EXISTS predicates, and so on). However, while this usage on SQL's part isn't exactly incorrect, it does usurp a very general term—one that's extremely important in database contexts—and give it a rather specialized meaning, which is why I prefer not to follow that usage myself.

Second, I should explain in the interest of accuracy that a predicate isn't really a statement as such; rather, it's the assertion made by that statement. For example, the predicate for relvar SP is what it is, regardless of whether it's expressed in English or Spanish or whatever. For simplicity, however, I'll assume in what follows that a predicate is indeed just a statement per se, typically but not necessarily expressed in some natural language such as English.

Finally, I've now explained what I mean by the term, but you should be aware that—the previous paragraph notwithstanding—there seems to be little consensus, even among logicians, as to *exactly* what a predicate is. In particular, some writers regard a predicate as a purely formal construct that has no meaning in itself, and regard what I've called the intended interpretation as something distinct from the predicate as such. I don't want to get into arguments about such matters here; for further discussion, I refer you to the paper "What's a Predicate?" in *Database Explorations: Essays on The Third Manifesto and Related Topics,* by C. J. Date and Hugh Darwen (Trafford, 2010).

You can think of a predicate, a trifle loosely, as *a truth valued function.* Like all functions, it has a set of parameters; it returns a result when it's invoked; and (because it's truth valued) that result is either TRUE or FALSE. In the case of the predicate for relvar SP, for example, the parameters are SNO, PNO, and QTY (corresponding of course to the attributes of the relvar), and they stand for values of the applicable types (CHAR, CHAR, and INTEGER, respectively, in this simple example). And when we invoke the function—when we *instantiate the predicate,* as the logicians say—we substitute arguments for the parameters. Suppose we substitute the arguments S1, P1, and 300, respectively. We obtain the following statement:

Supplier S1 supplies part P1 in quantity 300.

This statement is in fact a *proposition,* which in logic is something that evaluates to either TRUE or FALSE, unconditionally. Here are a couple of examples:

1.   Edward Abbey wrote *The Monkey Wrench Gang.*

2.   William Shakespeare wrote *The Monkey Wrench Gang.*

The first of these is true and the second false. Don't fall into the common trap of thinking that propositions must always be true! However, the ones I'm talking about at the moment *are* supposed to be true ones, as I now explain:

- First of all, as I've already said, every relvar has an associated predicate, called the *relvar predicate* for the relvar in question. (So *Supplier SNO supplies part PNO in quantity QTY* is the relvar predicate for relvar SP.)

- Let relvar *R* have predicate *P.* Then every tuple *t* appearing in *R* at some given time *T* can be regarded as representing a certain proposition *p*, derived by invoking (or *instantiating*) *P* at that time *T* with the attribute values from *t* as arguments.

- And (*very important!*) we assume by convention that each proposition *p* obtained in this manner evaluates to TRUE.

Given the sample value shown for relvar SP on the left of Figure 2-1, for example, we assume the following propositions both evaluate to TRUE at time *T1*:

> *Supplier S1 supplies part P1 in quantity 300.*

> *Supplier S2 supplies part P1 in quantity 300.*

What's more, we go further: If at some given time T a certain tuple plausibly could appear in some relvar but doesn't, then we're entitled to assume that the corresponding proposition is false at that time T. For example, the tuple

```
( 'S1' , 'P2' , 200 )
```

(to adopt an obvious shorthand notation) is certainly a plausible SP tuple; but it doesn't appear in relvar SP at time *T1*—I'm referring to Figure 2-1 again—and so we're entitled to assume that *it's not the case that* the following proposition is true at time *T1*:

> *Supplier S1 supplies part P2 in quantity 200.*

(On the other hand, this proposition *is* true at time *T2*.)

To sum up: A given relvar R contains, at any given time, *all* and *only* the tuples that represent true propositions (true instantiations of the relvar predicate for R) at the time in question—or, at least, that's what we always assume in practice. In other words, we adopt in practice what's called *The Closed World Assumption*. And since that assumption is so crucial—it underlies just about everything we do when we use a database, even though it's seldom acknowledged explicitly—I'd like to spell it out here for the record:

> **Definition (*The Closed World Assumption*):** Let relvar R have predicate P. Then *The Closed World Assumption* (CWA) says (a) if tuple t appears in R at time T, then the instantiation p of P corresponding to t is assumed to be true at time T; conversely, (b) if tuple t plausibly could appear in R at time T but doesn't, then the instantiation p of P corresponding to t is assumed to be false at time T. In other words (a trifle loosely): Tuple t appears in relvar R at time T if and only if it "satisfies the predicate" for R at time T.

More on Suppliers and Parts

Now let's get back to the suppliers-and-parts database as such, with sample values as shown in Figure 1-1 in the previous chapter. Here now are definitions of the three relvars in that database, expressed in a language called **Tutorial D** (see further explanation following the definitions):

```
VAR S BASE RELATION
  { SNO CHAR , SNAME CHAR , STATUS INTEGER , CITY CHAR }
   KEY { SNO } ;

VAR P BASE RELATION
  { PNO CHAR , PNAME CHAR , COLOR CHAR , WEIGHT RATIONAL , CITY CHAR }
   KEY { PNO } ;

VAR SP BASE RELATION
  { SNO CHAR , PNO CHAR , QTY INTEGER }
   KEY { SNO , PNO }
   FOREIGN KEY { SNO } REFERENCES S
   FOREIGN KEY { PNO } REFERENCES P ;
```

As I said, these definitions are expressed in a language called **Tutorial D**. Now, I believe that language is pretty much self-explanatory; however, a comprehensive description can be found if needed in the book *Databases, Types, and the Relational Model: The Third Manifesto* (3rd edition), by C. J. Date and Hugh Darwen (Addison-Wesley, 2007).[3] *Note:* As its title suggests, that book also introduces and explains *The Third Manifesto*, a precise though somewhat formal definition of the relational model and a supporting type theory (including, incidentally, a comprehensive model of type inheritance).[4] In particular, it uses the name **D** as a generic name for any language that conforms to the principles laid down by *The Third Manifesto*. Any number of distinct languages could qualify as a valid **D**; sadly, however, SQL isn't one of them, which is

---

[3]Actually **Tutorial D** (note the boldface!) has been revised and extended somewhat since that book was published. A description of the revised version, which is the version I'll be using throughout the present book, can be found in *Database Explorations: Essays on The Third Manifesto and Related Topics*, by C. J. Date and Hugh Darwen (Trafford, 2010), as well as on the website www.thethirdmanifesto.com.

[4]See the website mentioned in the previous footnote, www.thethirdmanifesto.com, for further information.

why examples in this book are expressed for the most part in **Tutorial D** and not in SQL. (Of course, **Tutorial D** is a valid **D**; in fact, it was explicitly designed to be suitable as a vehicle for illustrating and teaching the ideas of *The Third Manifesto*.)

This is as good a point as any to mention that the terminology used in the present book is based on that of *The Third Manifesto* ("the *Manifesto*" for short). As a consequence, it does differ on occasion from that found in some of the design theory literature. For example, that literature typically doesn't talk about relation headings; instead, it uses the term *relation schema*.[5] Nor does it talk about relation variables (relvars); instead, what this book refers to as a (relation) value that's assigned to some relvar it calls an *instance* of the corresponding *schema*.

Back to the relvar definitions. As you can see, each of those definitions includes a KEY specification, which means that every relation that might ever be assigned to any of those relvars is required to satisfy the corresponding *key constraint*. (Recall from Chapter 1 that every relvar does have at least one key.) For example, every relation that might ever be assigned to relvar S is required to satisfy the constraint that no two distinct tuples in that relation have the same SNO value. What's more, I'm going to assume throughout this book, barring explicit statements to the contrary, that the following *functional dependency*[6] (FD) also holds in relvar S:

{ CITY } → { STATUS }

You can read this FD, informally, as *STATUS is functionally dependent on CITY*, or as *CITY functionally determines STATUS*, or more simply as just *CITY arrow STATUS*. What it means is that every relation that might ever be assigned to relvar S is required to satisfy the constraint that if two tuples in that relation have the same CITY value, then they

---

[5]I mustn't give the impression that headings and (relation) schemas are exactly the same thing. Rather, a schema is the combination of a heading together with certain *dependencies* (see the next footnote), including but not necessarily limited to functional and join dependencies as discussed in detail later in this book.

[6]Also known as functional dependence. The terms *dependence* and *dependency* are used more or less interchangeably in the literature. However, *dependence* seems slightly better for the concept in general and *dependency* seems slightly better for a specific instance of the concept (and when a plural is needed—as it is in connection with instances of the concept but not with the concept as such—*dependencies* seems to trip off the tongue a little better than *dependences* does).

must also have the same STATUS value.[7] Observe that the sample value of relvar S given in Figure 1-1 does indeed satisfy this constraint. *Note:* I'll have a great deal more to say about FDs later in Parts II and III of this book, but I'm sure you're already familiar with the basic idea anyway.

Now, just as KEY specifications are used to declare key constraints, so we need some kind of syntax in order to be able to declare FD constraints. **Tutorial D** provides no specific syntax for that purpose, however[8] (neither does SQL, come to that). It does allow them to be expressed in a somewhat roundabout fashion—for example:

```
CONSTRAINT XCT
    COUNT ( S { CITY } ) = COUNT ( S { CITY , STATUS } ) ;
```

Explanation: In **Tutorial D**, an expression of the form $rx\{A1,...,An\}$ denotes the projection on attributes $A1$, ..., An of the relation r that results from evaluation of the relational expression rx. If the current value of relvar S is the relation s, therefore, (a) the expression S{CITY} denotes the projection of s on CITY; (b) the expression S{CITY,STATUS} denotes the projection of s on CITY and STATUS; and (c) the constraint overall—which I've named, arbitrarily, XCT—requires the cardinalities, denoted by the two COUNT invocations, of those two projections to be equal. (If it's not obvious that requiring these two cardinalities to be equal is equivalent to requiring the desired FD constraint to hold, try interpreting constraint XCT as stated in terms of the sample data in Figure 1-1.)

---

[7]This example of what FDs mean also serves to show why such dependencies are called functional. To elaborate: A function in mathematics is a mapping from one set A to another set B, not necessarily distinct from A, with the property that each element in A maps to just one element in B (but any number of distinct elements in A can map to the same element in B). In the example, therefore, we could say there's a mapping from the set of CITY values in S to the set of STATUS values in S, and that mapping is indeed a mathematical function.

[8]One reason it doesn't is that if the design recommendations discussed in the present book are followed, there should rarely be a need to declare FDs explicitly anyway.

You might feel, not unreasonably, that those appeals to COUNT in the formulation of constraint XCT are somehow a little inelegant. If so, then here's an alternative formulation that avoids them:

```
CONSTRAINT XCT
    WITH ( CT := S { CITY , STATUS } ) :
    AND ( ( CT JOIN ( CT RENAME { STATUS AS X } ) , STATUS = X ) ;
```

Explanation: First, the WITH specification ("WITH (…):") serves merely to introduce a name, CT, that can be used later in the overall expression to avoid having to write out the expression it stands for, possibly several times over. Second, the **Tutorial D** RENAME operator is more or less self-explanatory (but is defined anyway, in the answer to Exercise 2.15). Third, the **Tutorial D** expression AND(*rx,bx*), where *rx* is a relational expression and *bx* is a boolean expression, returns TRUE if and only if the condition denoted by *bx* evaluates to TRUE for every tuple in the relation denoted by *rx*.

The foregoing state of affairs notwithstanding, I'll assume throughout this book that FDs can be stated (or "declared") using the simple arrow notation illustrated earlier. Analogous remarks apply to other kinds of dependencies also (in particular, to join dependencies and multivalued dependencies, which I'll be introducing in Chapters 9 and 12, respectively).

I'll close this chapter with a little teaser. Assuming the only constraints that apply to the suppliers-and-parts database are the foregoing FD constraint and the specified key (and foreign key) constraints, then we can say that relvars S, P, and SP are in second, fifth, and sixth normal form, respectively. To understand the significance of these observations, please read on!

Exercises

The purpose of these exercises is to test your knowledge of relational theory. Most of them can't be answered from material in the present chapter alone. However, everything mentioned in those exercises, and in the answers to them in the next section, is discussed in detail in *SQL and Relational Theory*.

2.1   What's *The Information Principle?*

2.2   Which of the following statements are true?

    a. Relations (and hence relvars) have no ordering to their tuples.

    b. Relations (and hence relvars) have no ordering to their attributes.

    c. Relations (and hence relvars) never have any unnamed attributes.

    d. Relations (and hence relvars) never have two or more attributes with the same name.

    e. Relations (and hence relvars) never contain duplicate tuples.

    f. Relations (and hence relvars) never contain nulls.

    g. Relations (and hence relvars) are always in 1NF.

    h. The types over which relational attributes are defined can be arbitrarily complex.

    i. Relations (and hence relvars) themselves have types.

2.3   Which of the following statements are true?

    a. Every subset of a heading is a heading.

    b. Every subset of a body is a body.

    c. Every subset of a tuple is a tuple.

2.4   The term *domain* is usually found in texts on relational theory, but it wasn't mentioned in the body of the chapter. What do you make of this fact?

2.5   Define the terms *proposition* and *predicate*. Give examples.

2.6   State the predicates for relvars S, P, and SP from the suppliers-and-parts database.

2.7   Let *DB* be any database you happen to be familiar with and let *R* be any relvar in *DB*. What's the predicate for *R*? *Note:* The point of this exercise is to get you to apply some of the ideas discussed in the body of this chapter to your own data, in an attempt to get you thinking about data in general in such terms. Obviously the exercise has no unique right answer.

2.8   Explain *The Closed World Assumption* in your own terms. Could there be such a thing as *The Open World Assumption*?

2.9   Give definitions, as precise as you can make them, of the terms *tuple* and *relation.*

2.10 State as precisely as you can what it means for (a) two tuples to be equal; (b) two relations to be equal.

2.11 A tuple is a set (a set of components); so do you think it might make sense to define versions of the usual set operators (union, intersection, etc.) that apply to tuples?

2.12 To repeat, a tuple is a set of components. But the empty set is a legitimate set; thus, we could define an *empty tuple* to be a tuple where the pertinent set of components is empty. What are the implications? Can you think of any uses for such a tuple?

2.13 A key is a set of attributes and the empty set is a legitimate set; thus, we could define an *empty key* to be a key where the pertinent set of attributes is empty. What are the implications? Can you think of any uses for such a key?

2.14 A predicate has a set of parameters and the empty set is a legitimate set; thus, a predicate could have an empty set of parameters. What are the implications?

2.15 The normalization discipline makes heavy use of the relational operators projection and join. Give definitions, as precise as you can make them, of these two operators. Also, have a go at defining the attribute renaming operator (RENAME in **Tutorial D**).

2.16 The operators of the relational algebra form a closed system. What do you understand by this remark?

Answers

2.1   *The Information Principle* is a fundamental principle that underpins the entire relational model. It can be stated as follows:

Definition (*The Information Principle*): The only kind of variable allowed in a relational database is the relation variable or relvar. Equivalently, the entire information content of the database at any given time is represented in one and only one way—namely, as values in attribute positions in tuples in relations.

Note that SQL tables (at least, SQL tables in the database) that involve left to right column ordering or contain duplicate rows or nulls all violate *The Information Principle* (see the answer to the next exercise). Interestingly, however, SQL tables with anonymous columns or columns with nonunique names apparently don't violate the principle. The reason is that the principle as stated applies explicitly to relvars or relations *in the database*. And while SQL tables in general can have anonymous columns or columns with nonunique names, such tables can't be part of the database. This state of affairs suggests rather strongly that *The Information Principle* could do with a little tightening up.

2.2   True. b. True. c. True. d. True. e. True. f. True. g. True. h. False. However, it's "almost" true; there are two small exceptions, both of which I'll simplify just slightly for present purposes. The first is that if relation *r* is of type *T*, then no attribute of *r* can itself be of type *T*. The second is that no relation in the database can have an attribute of any pointer type.[9] i. True.

Subsidiary exercise: Would any of the foregoing answers change if the original statements were framed in terms of SQL tables instead of relations and relvars?

---

[9]The first exception here is a logical necessity. The second isn't but is, rather, a deliberate limitation imposed by the relational model.

Answer: Yes, they would all change except for a. and h. In the case of h., moreover, the answer ought really to change too, from "False" to "False, but even more so." One reason for this state of affairs—not the only one—is that SQL has no proper notion of table type, and SQL columns thus can't possibly be of such a type a fortiori.

2.3   True. b. True. c. True. *Note:* Let me state for the record here that throughout this book, in accordance with standard mathematical practice, I take expressions of the form "*B* is a subset of *A*" (in symbols, "$B \subseteq A$") to include the possibility that *B* and *A* might be equal. Thus, e.g., every heading is a subset of itself, and so is every body, and so is every tuple. When I want to exclude such a possibility, I'll talk explicitly in terms of *proper* subsets (in symbols, "$B \subset A$"). For example, the body of our usual suppliers relation is certainly a subset of itself, but not a proper subset of itself (*no* set is a proper subset of itself). What's more, the foregoing remarks apply equally to supersets, mutatis mutandis; for example, the body of our usual suppliers relation is a superset of itself, but not a proper superset of itself. *More terminology:* A set is said to *include* its subsets. By the way, don't confuse inclusion with *containment*—a set *includes* its subsets but *contains* its elements.

2.4   The reason the term wasn't mentioned in the body of the chapter is that it's just a synonym for *type*. (Early relational writings, my own included, tended to use it, but more recent ones use *type* instead, since it's shorter and has a more extensive pedigree anyway, at least in the computing world.) Thus, a domain is a named, finite set of values—all possible values of some specific kind: for example, all possible integers, or all possible character strings, or all possible triangles, or all possible XML documents, or all possible relations with a specific heading (etc., etc.). By the way, don't confuse domains as understood in the relational world with the construct of the same name in SQL, which (as explained in *SQL and Relational Theory*) can be regarded at best as a very weak kind of type.

2.5   See the body of the chapter.

2.6   Relvar S: *Supplier SNO is named SNAME and is located in city CITY, which has status STATUS.* Relvar P: *Part PNO is named PNAME, has color COLOR and weight WEIGHT, and is stored in city CITY.* Relvar SP: *Supplier SNO supplies part PNO in quantity QTY.*

2.7   *No answer provided.*

2.8   *The Closed World Assumption* says, loosely, that everything stated or implied by the database is true and everything else is false.[10] And *The Open World Assumption*—yes, there is such a thing— says that everything stated or implied by the database is true and everything else is unknown. What are the implications? Well, first let's agree to abbreviate *Closed World Assumption* and *Open World Assumption* to CWA and OWA, respectively. Now consider the query "Is supplier S6 in Rome?" (meaning, more precisely, "Is there a tuple for supplier S6 in relvar S with CITY value equal to Rome?"). **Tutorial D** formulation:

```
( S WHERE SNO = 'S6' AND CITY = 'Rome' ) { }
```

As explained in *SQL and Relational Theory*, this expression evaluates to either TABLE_DEE or TABLE_DUM. TABLE_DEE and TABLE_DUM are the only relations of degree zero; TABLE_DEE contains just one tuple (the empty tuple, in fact), and TABLE_DUM contains no tuples at all. Under the CWA, moreover, if the result is TABLE_DEE, it means the answer is *yes*, it's indeed the case that supplier S6 exists and is in Rome; if the result is TABLE_DUM, it means the answer is *no*, it's not the case that supplier S6

---

[10]To illustrate what I mean by "stated or implied" here, consider the shipment tuple (S1, P1,300) shown in Figure 1-1. (Re the lack of quotes around S1 and P1 here, see footnote 12 later in this chapter.) That tuple *states* the proposition "Supplier S1 supplies part P1 in quantity 300." However, it also *implies* several further propositions—for example, the propositions "Supplier S1 supplies some part in quantity 300"; "Supplier S1 supplies some part in some quantity"; "Some supplier supplies some part in quantity 300"; and even "Some supplier supplies some part in some quantity." (To pursue the point a moment longer, in fact that tuple (S1, P1,300) implies exactly seven such "further propositions." Why exactly seven, do you think?)

exists and is in Rome. Under the OWA, by contrast, TABLE_DEE still means *yes*, but TABLE_DUM means it's *unknown* whether supplier S6 exists and is in Rome.

Now consider the query "If supplier S6 exists, is that supplier in Rome?" (note the logical difference between this query and the one discussed above). Observe that the answer to this query has to be *no* if relvar S shows supplier S6 as existing but in some city other than Rome, regardless of whether we're talking about the CWA or the OWA.[11] So here's the **Tutorial D** formulation:

```
TABLE_DEE MINUS ( ( S WHERE SNO = 'S6' AND
                    CITY ≠ 'Rome' ) { } )
```

Note carefully, therefore, that if this expression evaluates to TABLE_DUM, that TABLE_DUM has to mean *no*, *even under the OWA*. Thus, the OWA suffers from an inherent ambiguity: Sometimes TABLE_DUM has to mean *unknown* and sometimes it has to mean *no*—and of course we can't say (in general) which interpretation applies when.

Just to beat the point to death: TABLE_DEE and TABLE_DUM simply do mean *yes* and *no*, respectively, in the relational world, and there's no "third relation" of degree zero available to represent the "third truth value" that the OWA fundamentally requires. Thus, the OWA and the relational model are fundamentally incompatible with one another.

2.9   Precise definitions are given in Chapter 5.

2.10   Two values of any kind are equal if and only if they're the very same value (meaning they must be of the same type, a fortiori). So two tuples are equal if and only if they're the very same tuple, and

---

[11]By contrast, the answer has to be *yes* if relvar S has no tuple for supplier S6 (in logic, "if *p* then *q*" is true if *p* is false—again, regardless of whether we're talking about the CWA or the OWA).

two relations are equal if and only if they're the very same relation. But we can be more specific and spell out the details, thus:

a. Two tuples t and t' are equal if and only if they have the same attributes $A1, ..., An$ and for all i ($i = 1, ..., n$), the value of Ai in t is equal to the value of Ai in t'.

b. Two relations r and r' are equal if and only if they have the same heading and the same body (i.e., their headings are equal and their bodies are equal). Note in particular, therefore, that two "empty relations" (i.e., relations without any tuples, or equivalently relations with empty bodies) are equal if and only if their headings are equal.

2.11 Yes! However, we would of course want such operators always to produce a valid tuple as a result (i.e., we would want *closure* for such operations, just as we have closure for relational operations—see the answer to Exercise 2.16 below). For tuple union, for example, we would want the input tuples to be such that attributes with the same name have the same value (and are therefore of the same type, a fortiori). By way of example, let $t1$ and $t2$ be a supplier tuple and a shipment tuple, respectively, and let $t1$ and $t2$ have the same SNO value. Then the union of $t1$ and $t2$, UNION{$t1,t2$}, is—to use **Tutorial D** notation—a tuple of type TUPLE {SNO CHAR, SNAME CHAR, STATUS INTEGER, CITY CHAR, PNO CHAR, QTY INTEGER}, with attribute values as in $t1$ or $t2$ or both (as applicable). E.g., if $t1$ is (S1,Smith, 20,London) and $t2$ is (S1,P1,300)—to use the shorthand notation for tuples introduced in the section "Predicates and Propositions" in the body of the chapter[12]—then their union is the tuple (S1,Smith,20,London,P1,300). *Note:* This operation might equally well be called *tuple join* instead of tuple union.

---

[12]Actually it's a simplified form of that shorthand, because I haven't even bothered to show the single quotes that really ought to enclose character string values such as 'S1' and 'London'. Please note that I'll be making heavy use of this simplified shorthand in the pages ahead, at least in regular text.

CHAPTER 2 PREREQUISITES

By the way, it's not just the usual set operators that might be adapted to apply to tuples—the same goes for certain of the well known relational operators, too (as in fact I've just suggested with respect to join in particular). One important example is the tuple projection operator, which is a straightforward adaptation of the relational projection operator. For example, let *t* be a supplier tuple; then the projection *t*{SNO,CITY} of *t* on attributes {SNO,CITY} is that subtuple of *t* that contains just the SNO and CITY components from *t*. (Of course, a subtuple is itself a tuple in its own right.) Likewise, *t*{CITY} is that subtuple of *t* that contains just the CITY component from *t*, and *t*{ } is that subtuple of *t* that contains no components at all (in other words, it's the 0-tuple— see the answer to Exercise 2.12 below). In fact, it's worth noting explicitly that *every* tuple has a projection on the empty set of attributes whose value is, precisely, the 0-tuple.

2.12 The empty tuple (note that there's exactly one such; equivalently, all empty tuples are equal to one another) is the same thing as the 0-tuple, mentioned in the answer to the previous exercise. As for uses for such a tuple, I'll just say that, conceptually at least, the fact that such a tuple does exist is crucially important in numerous ways. In particular, the empty tuple is the only tuple in the special relation TABLE_DEE, already mentioned in the answer to Exercise 2.8.

2.13 To say relvar *R* has an empty key is to say *R* can never contain more than one tuple. Why? Because every tuple has the same value for the empty set of attributes—namely, the empty tuple (see the answers to the previous two exercises); thus, if *R* had an empty key, and if *R* were to contain two or more tuples, we would have a key uniqueness violation on our hands. And, yes, constraining *R* never to contain more than one tuple could certainly be useful. I'll leave finding an example of such a situation as a subsidiary exercise.

2.14 A predicate with an empty set of parameters is a proposition. In other words, a proposition is a degenerate predicate; all propositions are predicates, but "most" predicates aren't propositions.

2.15   Definitions of projection and join are given in Chapter 5, but here's a definition of RENAME:

> **Definition (attribute renaming):** Let r be a relation, let A be an attribute of r, and let r not have an attribute named B. Then the renaming r RENAME $\{A$ AS $B\}$ is a relation r' with (a) heading identical to that of r except that attribute A in that heading is renamed B and (b) body identical to that of r except that all references to A in that body (more precisely, in tuples in that body) are replaced by references to B.

> *Note:* **Tutorial D** additionally supports a form of RENAME that allows two or more separate attribute renamings to be carried out in parallel ("multiple RENAME"). Examples are given in Chapter 16.

2.16   The relational algebra consists of operators that (speaking *very* loosely) allow us to derive "new" relations from "old" ones. Each such operator takes one or more relations as input and produces another relation as output (for example, the difference operator takes two relations as input and "subtracts" one from the other to derive another relation as output). And it's because the output is the same kind of thing as the input (or inputs) that the algebra is said to be a closed system. In particular. it's that closure property that (among other things) lets us write nested relational expressions—since the output from every operation is the same kind of thing as the input, the output from one operation can become input to another. For example, we can take the difference between relations *r1* and *r2* (in that order), feed the result as input to a union with some relation *r3*, feed *that* result as input to a projection or restriction, and so on.

PART II

Functional Dependencies, Boyce/Codd Normal Form, and Related Matters

Although normal forms as such aren't the whole of design theory, it's undeniable that they're a very large part of that theory, and they form the principal topic of Parts II–IV of this book. The present part, Part II, takes the story as far as Boyce/Codd normal form (BCNF), which is "the" normal form with respect to functional dependencies (FDs).

CHAPTER 3

Normalization: Some Generalities

Normal: See abnormal.

—from an early IBM PL/I reference manual (1960s)

In this chapter, I want to clarify certain general aspects of further normalization before I start getting into specifics (which I'll do in the next chapter). I'll begin by taking a closer look at the sample value of relvar S from Figure 1-1 (repeated for convenience as Figure 3-1 below):

S

SNO	SNAME	STATUS	CITY
S1	Smith	20	London
S2	Jones	30	Paris
S3	Blake	30	Paris
S4	Clark	20	London
S5	Adams	30	Athens

Figure 3-1. *The suppliers relvar—sample value*

Recall now that the functional dependency (FD)

$\{ CITY \} \rightarrow \{ STATUS \}$

© C. J. Date 2019
C. J. Date, *Database Design and Relational Theory*, https://doi.org/10.1007/978-1-4842-5540-7_3

holds in relvar S (I've included an arrow in the figure to suggest this fact). Because that FD holds in that relvar,[1] it turns out that the relvar is in second normal form (2NF) but not in third (3NF). As a consequence, it suffers from redundancy; to be specific, the fact that a given city has a given status appears many times, in general. And the discipline of *further normalization*—which, please note, from this point forward I'll abbreviate most of the time to just *normalization*, unqualified—would therefore suggest that we decompose the relvar into two relvars SNC and CT of lesser degree, as indicated in Figure 3-2 (which shows, of course, values for those relvars corresponding to the sample value shown for relvar S in Figure 3-1).

SNC

SNO	SNAME	CITY
S1	Smith	London
S2	Jones	Paris
S3	Blake	Paris
S4	Clark	London
S5	Adams	Athens

CT

CITY	STATUS
Athens	30
London	20
Paris	30

Figure 3-2. *Relvars SNC and CT—sample values*

Points arising from this example:

- First, the decomposition, or normalization, certainly eliminates the redundancy—the fact that a given city has a given status now appears exactly once.

- Second, the decomposition process is basically a process of *taking projections*—the relations shown in Figure 3-2 are each projections of the relation shown in Figure 3-1. In fact, we can write a couple of equations:[2]

SNC = S { SNO , SNAME , CITY }

CT   = S { CITY , STATUS }

---

[1]And because no others do, apart from ones implied by the sole key {SNO}. See Chapter 4.

[2]Recall from Chapter 2 that the **Tutorial D** syntax of the form $rx\{A1,...,An\}$ denotes the projection on attributes $A1, ..., An$ of the relation r that results from evaluating the relational expression rx. *Note:* **Tutorial D** also supports syntax of the form $rx\{ALL\ BUT\ B1,...,Bm\}$, which denotes the projection of the relation r that results from evaluation of the relational expression rx on all of its attributes except for $B1, ..., Bm$. For example, the projection corresponding to SNC in the example could alternatively be expressed thus: S {ALL BUT STATUS}.

Note: Other kinds of decomposition are also possible, but I'll assume until further notice that the term *decomposition*, unqualified, means decomposition via projection specifically.

- Third, the decomposition process is *nonloss* (also called *lossless*)— no information is lost in the process, because the relation shown in Figure 3-1 can be reconstructed by taking the *join* of the relations shown in Figure 3-2:

```
S  =  SNC JOIN CT
```

(**Tutorial D** syntax again). Thus, we can say the relation in Figure 3-1 and the pair of relations in Figure 3-2 are *information equivalent*—or, to state the matter more precisely, for any query that can be performed against the relation of Figure 3-1, there's a corresponding query that can be performed against the relations of Figure 3-2 (and vice versa) that produces the same result. Clearly, such "losslessness" of decompositions is an important property; whatever we do by way of normalization, we certainly mustn't lose any information when we do it.

- It follows from the foregoing that just as projection is the decomposition operator (with respect to normalization as conventionally understood), so join is the corresponding *re*composition operator.

Normalization Serves Two Purposes

So far, so good; this is all very familiar stuff. But now I want to point out that if you've been paying careful attention, you might reasonably accuse me of practicing a tiny (?) deception in the foregoing ... To be specific, I've considered what it means for a decomposition of *relations* to be nonloss; but normalization, which is what we're supposed to be talking about, isn't a matter of decomposing relations, it's a matter of decomposing *relvars*. (After all, database design by definition is all about choosing what relvars, not what relations, should exist in the database.)

Suppose we do decide to perform the suggested decomposition of relvar S into relvars SNC and CT. Observe that now I really am talking about relvars and not relations; for definiteness, however, let's assume the relvars in question have the sample values shown in Figures 3-1 and 3-2, respectively. For definiteness again, let's focus on relvar CT specifically. Well, that relvar is indeed a relvar—I mean, it's a variable—and so we can update it. For example (using the shorthand notation for tuples introduced in Chapter 2), we might insert the tuple

('Rome' , 10)

But after that update, relvar CT contains a tuple that had no counterpart in relvar S (it doesn't have a counterpart in relvar SNC either, come to that). Now, such a possibility is often used—indeed, Codd used it himself in his very first papers on normalization (see Appendix D)—as an argument in favor of doing the decomposition in the first place: The resulting two-relvar design is capable of representing certain information that the original one-relvar design isn't. (In the case at hand, it can represent status information for cities that currently have no supplier located in them.) But that same fact also means that the two designs aren't really information equivalent after all, and moreover that relvar CT isn't exactly a "projection" of relvar S after all[3]—it contains a tuple that isn't a projection of, or otherwise derived from, any tuple in relvar S.[4] Or rather (and perhaps more to the point), CT isn't a projection of the join of SNC and CT, either, and so that join "loses information," in a sense; to be specific, it loses the information that the status for Rome is 10.[5]

A similar situation arises if we delete the tuple

('S5' , 'Adams' , 'Athens')

---

[3]See later in this section for an explanation of why I place the term "projection" in quotation marks here.

[4]Regarding the idea that it might make sense to talk about projections of tuples, see the answer to Exercise 2.11 in Chapter 2.

[5]Joins such as that of SNC and CT are sometimes called *lossy joins* for this very reason. However, this term is probably best avoided, because it could also be used to refer to joins such as the join of the projections of S on{SNO,SNAME,STATUS} and {CITY,STATUS}, which lose information for a different reason. See the discussion of this latter example in the section "Heath's Theorem" in Chapter 5; see also Exercise 3.2.

from relvar SNC. After that update, we could say, a trifle loosely,[6] that relvar S contains a tuple that has no counterpart in relvar SNC (though it does have one in relvar CT). So again the two designs aren't really information equivalent; and this time relvar S isn't exactly a "join" of relvars SNC and CT, since it contains a tuple that doesn't correspond to any tuple in relvar SNC.

The two designs are thus not information equivalent after all. But didn't I say earlier that "losslessness" of decompositions is an important property? Don't we generally assume that if Design *B* is produced by normalizing Design *A*, then Design *B* and Design *A* are supposed to be information equivalent? What exactly is going on here?

In order to answer these questions, it's helpful to look at the relvar predicates. The predicate for SNC is:

Supplier SNO is named SNAME and is located in city CITY.

And the predicate for CT is:

City CITY has status STATUS.

Now suppose it's possible for a city to have a status even if no supplier is located in that city; in other words, suppose it's possible for relvar CT to contain a tuple such as (Rome,10) that has no counterpart in relvar SNC.[7] *Then the design consisting of just relvar S is simply wrong.* That is, if it's possible for a true instantiation to exist of the predicate *City CITY has status STATUS* without there existing—at the same time and with the same CITY value—a true instantiation of the predicate *Supplier SNO is named SNAME and is located in city CITY,* then a design consisting just of relvar S doesn't faithfully reflect the state of affairs in the real world (because that design is incapable of representing the status for a city in which no supplier is located).

Similarly, suppose it's possible for a supplier to be located in a city even if that city has no status; in other words, suppose it's possible for relvar SNC to contain a tuple, say (S6,Lopez,Madrid), that has no counterpart in relvar CT. Then, again, the design consisting just of relvar S is simply incorrect, because it requires every city in which a supplier is located to have some status.

---

[6]In effect, by pretending that relvars S, SNC, and CT all coexist—living alongside one another, as it were.

[7]Note that I write (Rome,10) here instead of ('Rome',10), omitting the single quotes that ought really to enclose character string values. See footnote 12 in Chapter 2.

Here's another way to look at the foregoing argument. Suppose the design consisting just of relvar S did faithfully reflect the state of affairs in the real world after all. Then relvars SNC and CT would be subject to the following integrity constraint ("Every city in SNC appears in CT and vice versa"):

```
CONSTRAINT ... SNC { CITY } = CT { CITY } ;
```

But this constraint—which is an example of what later I'm going to be calling an *equality dependency* or EQD—manifestly isn't satisfied in the example under discussion. *Note:* For simplicity, I haven't bothered to give this constraint a name, as you can see. Indeed, I'll omit such names from all of my examples in this book from this point forward, except where there's some compelling reason to do otherwise.

To sum up, we see that normalization can be (and is) used to address two rather different problems:

1. It can be used to fix a logically incorrect design, as in the example discussed earlier in this section. *Exercise:* Do issues analogous to those raised in that example apply to the STP example from the section "The Place of Design Theory" in Chapter 1? (*Answer:* Yes, they do.)

2. It can be used to reduce redundancy in an otherwise logically correct design. (Obviously a design doesn't have to be logically incorrect in the foregoing sense in order to display redundancy.)

Much confusion arises in practice because these two cases are often not clearly distinguished. Indeed, most of the literature focuses on Case 2—and for definiteness I'll assume Case 2 myself in what follows, where it makes any difference—but please don't lose sight of Case 1, which in practice is at least as important, if not more so.

Further, I should point out that, strictly speaking, the terminology of projections and joins applies only to Case 2. That's because in Case 1, as we've seen, the "new" relvars aren't necessarily projections of the "old" one, nor is the "old" one necessarily the join of the "new" ones (if you see what I mean). In fact, what does it mean to talk about projections and joins of relvars (as opposed to relations) anyway? Well, as I've written elsewhere, more or less:[8]

---

[8]E.g., in *The **New** Relational Database Dictionary* (O'Reilly, 2016).

By definition, the operators projection, join, and so on apply to
relation values specifically. In particular, of course, they apply to the
values that happen to be the current values of relvars. It thus clearly
makes sense to talk about, e.g., the projection of relvar S on attributes
{CITY,STATUS}, meaning the relation that results from taking the
projection on those attributes of the relation that's the current
value of that relvar S. In some contexts, however (normalization,
for example), it turns out to be convenient to use expressions
like "the projection of relvar S on attributes {CITY,STATUS}" in a
slightly different sense. To be specific, we might say, loosely but very
conveniently, that some *relvar*, CT, is the projection of relvar S on
attributes {CITY,STATUS}—meaning, more precisely, that the value
of relvar CT at all times is equal to the projection on those attributes
of the value of relvar S at the time in question. In a sense, therefore,
we can talk in terms of projections of relvars per se, rather than
just in terms of projections of current values of relvars. Analogous
remarks apply to all of the relational operations.

In other words, we do still use the projection / join terminology, even in Case 1. Such
talk is somewhat inappropriate—not to say sloppy—but it is at least succinct. But it would
really be more accurate to say, not that decomposition is a process of taking projections
as such, but rather that it's a process that's *reminiscent of*, but not quite the same as, what
we do when we take projections (and similarly for recomposition and join).

Update Anomalies

The concept of *update anomalies* is frequently mentioned in connection with
normalization. Now, it should be clear that redundancy of any kind can always lead
to anomalies—because redundancy means, loosely, that some piece of information
is represented twice, and so there's always the possibility that the two representations
don't agree (i.e., if one is updated and the other isn't). More specifically, let's consider
the case of relvar S, where the following FD holds:

```
{ CITY } → { STATUS }
```

The redundancy, as such, that this FD gives rise to—viz., the repeated, or duplicated,
representation of the fact that a given city has a given status—has already been

discussed. It leads to anomalies like the following (these examples assume the sample value shown for relvar S in Figure 3-1):

- **Insertion anomaly:** We can't insert the fact that the status for Rome is 10 until there's a supplier in Rome.

- **Deletion anomaly:** If we delete the only supplier in Athens, we lose the fact that the status for Athens is 30.

- **Modification anomaly:** We can't change ("modify") the city for a given supplier without changing ("modifying") the status for that supplier as well (in general). And we can't modify the status for a given supplier without making the same modification for all suppliers in the pertinent city.

Replacing relvar S by the two "projection" relvars SNC and CT solves these problems (how, exactly?). Moreover, let me state for the record that relvar S is (as previously noted) in second normal form and not in third, while relvars SNC and CT are both in third normal form, and in fact in BCNF as well. In general, BCNF is the solution to the problems caused by the kinds of anomalies mentioned above.

The Normal Form Hierarchy

As you know, there are many different normal forms. Figure 3-3 below is our first take on what I'll call the normal form hierarchy (but please note immediately that I'll be expanding that hierarchy in later chapters—in Chapters 13-15, to be specific).

1NF
2NF
3NF
BCNF

4NF
5NF

BCNF and 5NF are the important ones
(at least until further notice)

Figure 3-3. *The normal form hierarchy (I)*

Points arising:

- First of all, you might think the hierarchy is upside down, since it shows the highest normal form at the bottom and the lowest at the top. I don't want to argue the point; let me just say that showing it the way I've done in the figure fits better (in my view) with the fact that, e.g., all 2NF relvars are in 1NF but some 1NF relvars aren't in 2NF.

- There are many different normal forms: first, second, third, and so on. The figure shows six of them, but as you can see they aren't labeled first, ..., sixth (not quite)—there's an interloper, BCNF, between third and fourth. I'll explain the reason for this terminological oddity in Chapter 4; for now, let me just say that the name BCNF is short for *Boyce/Codd normal form*. Despite the BCNF exception, however, it's convenient to use the term *nth normal form* to refer generically to the different levels of normalization, and I'll adopt that usage from time to time in what follows.

- The figure also shows a deliberate gap between BCNF and 4NF. However, that gap isn't meant to suggest there might be some "missing" normal forms at that point (in fact there aren't); rather, it reflects the fact that there's a kind of conceptual jump, or shift, in the hierarchy between the first four normal forms and the last two. See Part III of this book for further explanation.

- All of the normal forms apart from the first (1NF) are defined in terms of certain *dependencies*—in this context, just another term for integrity constraints. The principal kinds of dependencies from a normalization perspective are *functional* dependencies (FDs) and *join* dependencies (JDs).

- BCNF and 5NF are highlighted (set in boldface) in the figure to indicate their relative importance, compared to the other normal forms shown. BCNF is defined in terms of functional dependencies, and 5NF is defined in terms of join dependencies. Indeed, as we'll see in subsequent chapters , BCNF is really "the" normal form so far as functional dependencies (FDs) are concerned, and 5NF is really "the" normal form so far as join dependencies (JDs) are concerned.

- Generally speaking, the higher the level of normalization the better, from a design point of view—because the higher the level of normalization, the fewer the redundancies that can occur, and the fewer the update anomalies that can therefore occur as well.

- It's possible for a relvar to be in nth normal form and not in $(n+1)$st.

- By contrast, if relvar R is in $(n+1)$st normal form, then it's certainly in nth. In other words, fifth normal form (5NF) implies fourth normal form (4NF), and so on. It follows that to say that, e.g., relvar R is in BCNF doesn't preclude the possibility that R is in 5NF as well. In practice, however, it's common for statements to the effect that relvar R is in, say, BCNF to be taken to mean that R is in BCNF *and not in any higher normal form*. Please note carefully, therefore, that I do *not* follow that usage in this book.

- If relvar R is in nth normal form and not in $(n+1)$st, then it can always be decomposed via projection, in a nonloss way, such that (a) the projections are, typically, in $(n+1)$st normal form and (b) R is equal to the join of those projections.

- Finally, it follows from the previous point that any given relvar R can always be decomposed into 5NF projections in particular. In other words, 5NF is always achievable.

A note on the concept of redundancy: In Chapter 1 I said design theory is largely—not exclusively—about reducing redundancy, and I've referred to redundancy repeatedly in the present chapter; in particular, I've said the higher the level of normalization, the more redundancy is prevented. But coming up with a precise definition of what redundancy really is seems to be quite difficult!—so much so, in fact, that I don't think it would be appropriate, at this early point in the book, even to try to define it, and so I won't. In other words, I'm just going to assume until further notice that we can at least recognize it (redundancy, that is) when we see it—though, actually, even that's a pretty big assumption. Chapter 17 examines the concept in depth.

Normalization and Constraints

There's another issue that arises in connection with normalization, one that's often overlooked. Again consider the example of decomposing relvar S into its projections SNC and CT—SNC on {SNO,SNAME,CITY} and CT on {CITY,STATUS}. Then there are three cases to consider:

1. Suppose the original design, consisting of just relvar S, was at least logically correct (i.e., it merely suffered from redundancy). As I pointed out in the section "Normalization Serves Two Purposes," then, there's a certain constraint (an "equality dependency") that holds between the two projections:

   ```
   CONSTRAINT ... SNC { CITY } = CT { CITY } ;
   ```

   ("every city in SNC appears in CT and vice versa").

2. Alternatively, suppose it's possible for one of SNC and CT to contain a tuple that has no counterpart in the other, while the converse is not possible. To fix our ideas, suppose again that it's possible for CT to contain a tuple such as (Rome,10) that has no counterpart in SNC, while SNC can never contain a tuple that has no counterpart in CT. Then a *foreign key constraint* holds between the two projections (from SNC to CT, in the specific example just mentioned):[9]

   ```
   FOREIGN KEY { CITY } REFERENCES CT
   ```

3. The third possibility, perhaps less likely than the first two, is that CT and SNC might both be allowed to contain tuples with no counterpart in the other. For example, it might be that CT contains the tuple (Rome,10) but no supplier is located in Rome, while SNC contains the tuple (S6,Lopez, Madrid) but Madrid has no status. In this case, clearly there's no constraint involving cities that holds between the two relvars at all (at least, let's assume not for the sake of the example).

---

[9]In fact such foreign key constraints held in Case 1 also, but were subsumed by the EQD that also held in that case.

Now, simplifying somewhat, I've said that a relvar R in nth normal form can always be nonloss decomposed into projections in $(n+1)$st normal form. As the foregoing discussion indicates, however, *such decomposition usually means there's at least one new constraint that now needs to be maintained*. What makes matters worse is that the constraint in question is a *multirelvar* constraint (i.e., it spans two relvars, and in some cases possibly more than two). So there's a tradeoff: Do we want the benefits of decomposition, or do we want to avoid that multirelvar constraint?[10]

It might be argued, at least in the SNC and CT example, that the decomposition also means there's now a constraint that *doesn't* have to be maintained: viz., the FD {CITY} → {STATUS}. But this argument isn't entirely valid—all the decomposition does, in this respect, is move that constraint from one relvar to another (actually from relvar S to relvar CT, where it's maintained as a side effect of maintaining the constraint that {CITY} is a key).

Now, in the simple example under discussion, the benefits of doing the decomposition almost certainly outweigh the benefits of not doing so. But such is not always the case; indeed, the question of whether or not to decompose, in more complicated situations, can be a fairly vexing one. In what follows, in order to avoid a lot of repetitive text, I'll generally assume we do always want to do the decomposition— but please don't forget there can sometimes be persuasive arguments for not doing so, especially in examples more complex than the one at hand, such as are discussed in Parts III and IV of this book.

Equality Dependencies

Again consider the example of decomposing relvar S into its projections SNC and CT on {SNO,SNAME,CITY} and {CITY,STATUS}, respectively. Assume the case in which the following constraint holds between the two projections:

```
CONSTRAINT ... SNC { CITY } = CT { CITY } ;
```

---

[10]Of course, maintaining that constraint, if it has to be done, should be done by the system and not the user—but the constraint will at least have to be declared, and users will have to be aware of it.

("every city in SNC appears in CT and vice versa"). As mentioned in the previous section, this constraint is an example of what's called an *equality dependency*. I'll define that concept precisely in just a moment. First, however, I want to introduce a convention that I'll be using from this point forward for simplifying the notation for projection slightly.[11] Let relational expression rx evaluate to relation r; let relation r have heading H; let X be a subset of H; and let $A1, ..., An$ be all of the attributes of X (i.e., $X = \{A1, ..., An\}$). Then we allow the projection expression $rx\{A1,...,An\}$ to be abbreviated—a trifle illogically—to just $rx\{X\}$.

Now I can define the EQD concept:

> **Definition (equality dependency):** Loosely, a constraint that requires two specified relations to be equal. More precisely, let $R1$ and $R2$ be relvars with headings $H1$ and $H2$, respectively. Also, let $X1$ and $X2$ be subsets of $H1$ and $H2$, respectively, such that there exists a possibly empty set of attribute renamings such that the result, R, of applying those renamings to the projection $R1$ on the attributes of $X1$ has heading $X2$. Then an equality dependency (EQD) between $R1$ and $R2$ is a statement to the effect that R and the projection of $R2$ on the attributes of $X2$ must be equal—i.e., $R = R2\{X2\}$.

In fact, equality dependencies are an important special case of a more general phenomenon known as *inclusion* dependencies:

> **Definition (inclusion dependency):** Loosely, a constraint that requires one specified relation to be included in another. More precisely, let $R1$ and $R2$ be relvars with headings $H1$ and $H2$, respectively. Also, let $X1$ and $X2$ be subsets of $H1$ and $H2$, respectively, such that there exists a possibly empty set of attribute renamings such that the result, R, of applying those renamings to the projection $R1$ on the attributes of $X1\}$ has heading $X2$. Then an inclusion dependency (IND) from $R1$ to $R2$ is a statement to the effect that R must be included in (i.e., be a subset of) the projection of $R2$ on the attributes of $X2$—in symbols, $R \subseteq R2\{X2\}$.

---

[11]I.e., in definitions and the like, not in concrete **Tutorial D** syntax. *Note:* Later I'll be using the same kind of simplification for tuple projection as well as regular relational projection (see Chapter 5).

Points arising from this latter definition:

- A foreign key constraint is a special case of an IND. In the suppliers-and-parts database, for example, {SNO} in relvar SP is a foreign key, referencing the key {SNO} in relvar S; thus, there's an IND from SP to S—the projection of SP on {SNO} is included in the projection of S on {SNO} (in symbols, SP{SNO} ⊆ S{SNO}). But note that (to use the notation of the foregoing definition) INDs in general, unlike foreign key constraints in particular, don't require $X2$ to be a key[12] for $R2$.

- As already noted, an EQD is a special case of an IND, too. To be more specific, the EQD "$A = B$" is equivalent to the pair of INDs "A is included in B" and "B is included in A" (in symbols, $A \subseteq B$ and $B \subseteq A$). In other words, an EQD is an IND that goes both ways, as it were.

Now, we're going to be seeing lots of examples of EQDs in particular, as opposed to INDs in general, in the pages ahead. In fact this state of affairs should be obvious: Nonloss decomposing a relvar into projections usually leads to INDs at least and often to EQDs, as we already know. However, it's EQDs that don't arise as a result of nonloss decomposition that are the interesting ones, in a way. The reason is that the existence of such an EQD often turns out to be a mark of redundancy—because if (as I put it earlier) some piece of information is represented twice, an EQD might be what's needed to keep the two representations in agreement.

If you've never heard of EQDs before, you might be wondering why not, given their conceptual importance. Certainly they don't seem to have received very much attention in the literature. In my opinion, the most likely reason for this unfortunate state of affairs is the SQL language ... As you'll know if you've ever tried the exercise, EQDs are extremely awkward to formulate in SQL, because SQL has no direct way of expressing relational comparisons.[13] A striking example in support of this contention can be found in the discussion of Example 12 in Chapter 17 of this book.

---

[12]Or even a superkey (see Chapter 4).

[13]By *SQL* here, I mean SQL as defined by the SQL standard. The situation is even worse in mainstream implementations, where most EQDs can't be formulated at all, owing to the fact that the implementations in question don't allow subqueries in constraint formulations.

Concluding Remarks

I'd like to close this chapter by addressing a question I haven't discussed in this book at all so far. It's a matter of terminology. To be specific, why are 1NF, 2NF, and the rest called normal forms, anyway? Come to that, why is normalization called normalization?

The answers to these questions derive from mathematics, though the ideas involved spill over into several related disciplines, including the computing discipline in particular. In mathematics, we often find ourselves having to deal with some large, possibly even infinite, set of objects of some kind: for example, the set of all matrices, or the set of all rational numbers, or—coming a little closer to home—the set of all relations. In such a situation, it's desirable to find a set of *canonical forms* for the objects in question.[14] Here's a definition:

> **Definition (canonical form):** Given a set *s1*, together with a defined notion of equivalence among elements of that set, subset *s2* of *s1* is a set of canonical forms for *s1* if and only if every element *x1* of *s1* is equivalent to just one element *x2* of *s2* under that notion of equivalence (and that element *x2* is the canonical form for the element *x1*).[15] Various "interesting" properties that apply to *x1* also apply to *x2*; thus, we can study just the small set *s2*, not the large set *s1*, in order to prove a variety of "interesting" theorems or results.

As a trivial illustration of this notion, let *s1* be the (infinite) set of nonnegative integers {0,1,2,...}, and let two such integers be equivalent if and only if they leave the same remainder on division by five. Then we can define *s2* to be the set {0,1,2,3,4}. As for an "interesting" theorem that applies in this example, let *x1*, *y1*, and *z1* be any three elements of *s1* (i.e., any three nonnegative integers), and let their canonical forms in *s2* be *x2*, *y2*, and *z2*, respectively; then the product $y1 \times z1$ is equivalent to *x1* if and only if the product $y2 \times z2$ is equivalent to *x2*.

Now, *normal form* is just another term for canonical form. So when we talk about normal forms in the database context, we're talking about a canonical representation for data. To spell the point out: Any given collection of data can be represented relationally

---

[14]Floating point numbers provide an obvious example in computing.

[15]It's reasonable to require also that every element *x2* of *s2* be equivalent to at least one element *x1* of *s1*.

in many different ways, as we know. Of course, all of those ways are—in fact, must be—information equivalent; that is, information equivalence is the "defined notion of equivalence" we appeal to in this particular context. However, some of those ways (i.e., of representing the given information) are preferred over others for various reasons. And those preferred ways are, of course, the relational normal forms that are the subject of much of this book.

As for the term *normalization*, it simply refers to the general process of mapping some given object into its canonical equivalent. In the database context in particular, therefore, it's used (as we know) to refer to the process of mapping some given relvar into a collection of relvars that (a) when considered together, are information equivalent to the original relvar, but (b) are each individually in some preferred normal form.

To the foregoing I should perhaps add the following. As far as I know, Codd himself never mentioned, in his early writings on the subject, his reasons for introducing the terminology of normal forms or normalization. But many years afterward, he did go on record with his own, possibly tongue in cheek, explanation:[16]

> ***Interviewer:*** Where did "normalization" come from?
>
> ***Codd:*** It seemed to me essential that some discipline be introduced into database design. I called it normalization because then President Nixon was talking a lot about normalizing relations with China. I figured that if he could normalize relations, so could I.

Exercises

3.1   Consider the STP example from the section "The Place of Design Theory" in Chapter 1. Give examples of the update anomalies that can arise with that design. Also give an appropriate decomposition, and show how that decomposition avoids those anomalies.

---

[16]In "A Fireside Chat: Interview with Dr. Edgar F. Codd" (*DBMS Magazine 6*, No. 13, December 1993).

3.2 Nonloss decomposition is based on the idea that a relation can be decomposed into projections in such a way that the original relation can be recovered by joining those projections back together again. In fact, if projections *r1* and *r2* of relation *r* are such that every attribute of *r* is retained in at least one of *r1* and *r2*, then joining *r1* and *r2* will always produce every tuple of *r* (as well as others, possibly). Prove this assertion.

Note: It follows from the foregoing that the problem with a decomposition that's not nonloss isn't that the join loses tuples— rather, it's that it produces additional, or "spurious," ones. Since we have no way in general of knowing which if any of the tuples in the join are spurious and which are genuine, the decomposition has lost information.

3.3 "Normalization serves two purposes." Explain this remark in your own words. Do you think the point is widely understood?

3.4 Explain the following in your own words: (a) equality dependency; (b) inclusion dependency; (c) foreign key constraint; (d) canonical form.

Answers

3.1 With reference to the sample value shown for relvar STP in Chapter 1 (Figure 1-2), we can't insert the fact that supplier S5 has status 30 until supplier S5 supplies some part; we can't delete the shipment for supplier S3 without losing the fact that supplier S3 has status 30; and we can't modify the status in one tuple for a given supplier, say supplier S1, without modifying it in all of them. The obvious decomposition is into relvars with headings {SNO,STATUS} and {SNO,PNO,QTY}; it's also obvious that this decomposition avoids the anomalies.

Note: It's worth pointing out that the insertion and deletion anomalies in this example are caused by the fact that the design is logically incorrect, whereas the modification anomaly is caused by the fact that it displays redundancy (see Exercise 3.3).

3.2   Let the heading of *r* be partitioned into sets of attributes *X*, *Y*, and *Z*, and let the projections *r1* and *r2* be on {*X*,*Y*} and {*Y*,*Z*}, respectively. (Note that *X*, *Y*, and *Z* are disjoint by definition.) Now let (x,y,z) be a tuple of *r*;[17] then (x,y) and (y,z) are tuples of *r1* and *r2*, respectively, and so (x,y,z) is a tuple in the join of *r1* and *r2*. *Subsidiary exercise:* What happens to the foregoing proof if the set *Y* is empty?

3.3   The two purposes (correcting an incorrect design and reducing redundancy) are explained in the body of the chapter. As for whether you think the point is widely understood: Well, only you can answer this question, but speaking for myself I have to say I don't think it is.

3.4   See the body of the chapter.

---

[17]Of course, *x*, *y*, and *z* here are to be understood as values of *X*, *Y*, and *Z*, respectively.

CHAPTER 4

FDs and BCNF (Informal)

It is downright sinful to teach the abstract before the concrete.

—Z. A. Melzak: *Companion to Concrete Mathematics* (1973)

As noted in the previous chapter, Boyce/Codd normal form (BCNF for short) is defined in terms of functional dependencies (FDs); indeed, it's really *the* normal form with respect to functional dependencies, just as—to get ahead of ourselves for a moment— 5NF is really *the* normal form with respect to join dependencies (JDs). The overall purpose of the present chapter is to explain BCNF and FDs in detail; as the chapter title indicates, however, the various explanations and associated definitions are all intentionally a little informal at this stage. (Informal, but not inaccurate; I won't tell any deliberate lies.) A more formal treatment of the material appears in the next chapter.

First Normal Form

Let relation *r* have attributes $A1, ..., An$, of types $T1, ..., Tn$, respectively. By definition, then, if tuple *t* appears in relation *r*, the value of attribute Ai in *t* is, and of course must be, of type Ti ($i = 1, ..., n$). For example, if *r* is the relation that's the current value of the shipments relvar SP (see Figure 1-1 in Chapter 1), then every tuple in *r* has an SNO value that's of type CHAR, a PNO value that's also of type CHAR, and a QTY value that's of type INTEGER.

Now, another way of saying what the first two sentences of the previous paragraph say is simply that relation *r* is in *first normal form* (1NF). Thus, *every* relation is in 1NF!— because a "relation" *r* for which those two sentences fail to hold simply isn't a relation

65

© C. J. Date 2019
C. J. Date, *Database Design and Relational Theory*, https://doi.org/10.1007/978-1-4842-5540-7_4

in the first place. My apologies for the repetition, therefore, but here for the record is a precise definition:[1]

> **Definition (first normal form):** Let relation *r* have attributes
> *A1*, ..., *An*, of types *T1*, ..., *Tn*, respectively. Then *r* is in first normal
> form (1NF) if and only if, for all tuples *t* appearing in *r*, the value of
> attribute *Ai* in *t* is of type *Ti* ($i = 1, ..., n$).

To say it in different words, 1NF just means that each tuple in the relation in question contains exactly one value, of the appropriate type, for each attribute. *Observe in particular, therefore, that 1NF places absolutely no limitation on what those attribute types are allowed to be.*[2] They can even be relation types! That is, relations with relation valued attributes—RVAs for short—are legal (you might be surprised to hear this, but it's true). An example is given in Figure 4-1 below.

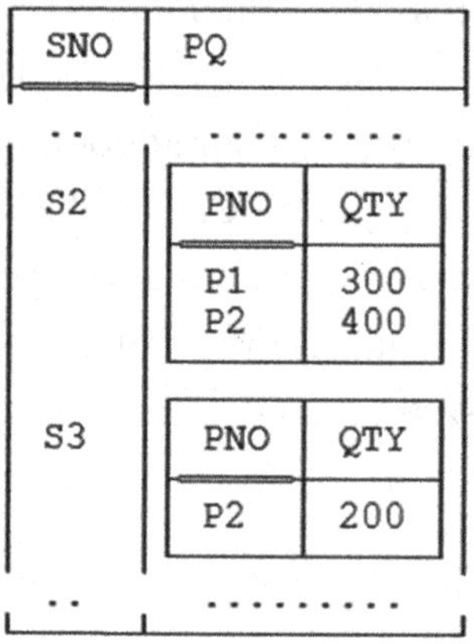

Figure 4-1. *A relation with a relation valued attribute*

---

[1]One reviewer accused me of rewriting history with this definition. Guilty as charged, perhaps, but I do have my reasons; to be specific, earlier "definitions" of the concept were all, in my opinion, either too vague to be useful or flat out wrong. See *SQL and Relational Theory* for further discussion, also Exercise 4.16 at the end of the chapter.

[2]This sentence is 100% correct as stated. However, I don't want to mislead you; the fact is, there *are* some exceptions—exceptions, that is, to the statement that relational attributes can be of any type whatsoever—but those exceptions have nothing to do with 1NF as such. (The exceptions in question were given in the answer to Exercise 2.2 in Chapter 2, but I repeat them here for convenience. First, if relation *r* is of type *T*, then no attribute of *r* can itself be of type *T* (think about it!). Second, no relation in the database can have an attribute of any pointer type.)

I'll have more to say about RVAs in just a moment, but first I need to get a couple of small points out of the way. To start with, I need to define what it means for a relation to be *normalized*:

> **Definition (normalized):** Relation *r* is normalized if and only if it's in 1NF.

In other words, *normalized* and *first normal form* mean exactly the same thing—all normalized relations are in 1NF, all 1NF relations are normalized. The reason for this slightly strange state of affairs is that *normalized* was the original (historical) term; the term *1NF* wasn't introduced until people started talking about 2NF and higher levels of normalization, when a term was needed to describe relations[3] that weren't in one of those higher normal forms. Of course, it's common nowadays for the term *normalized* to be used to mean some higher normal form (often 3NF specifically, or perhaps BCNF); indeed, I've been known to use it that way myself, though I generally try not to—because strictly speaking such usage is sloppy and incorrect, and it's probably better avoided unless there's no chance of confusion.

Turning to the second of my "small points": Observe now that all of the discussions in this section so far (the definitions in particular) have been framed in terms of relations, not relvars. But since every relation that can ever be assigned to a relvar is in 1NF by definition, no harm is done if we extend the 1NF concept in the obvious way to apply to relvars as well—and it's desirable to do so, because (as we'll see) all of the other normal forms are defined to apply to relvars, not relations. In fact, it could be argued that the reason 1NF *is* defined in terms of relations and not relvars has to do with the fact that it was, regrettably, many years before that distinction (I mean the distinction between relations and relvars) was properly drawn, anyway.

Back to RVAs. I've said, in effect, that relvars with RVAs are legal—but now I need to add that from a design point of view, at least, such relvars are usually (not always) contraindicated. Now, this fact doesn't mean you should avoid RVAs entirely (in particular, there's no problem if some attribute of some query result happens to be relation valued)—it just means we don't usually want RVAs "designed into the database,"

---

[3]Or relvars, rather (see my second "small point" in just a moment).

as it were. I don't want to get into a lot of detail on this issue in this book; let me just say that relvars with RVAs tend to look very much like the hierarchic structures found in older, nonrelational systems like IMS,[4] and all of the old problems that used to arise with hierarchies therefore raise their ugly head once again. Here for reference is a list of some of those problems:

- The fundamental point is that hierarchies are asymmetric. Thus, while they might make some tasks easier, they certainly make others more difficult.

- As a specific illustration of the previous point, queries in particular are asymmetric, as well as being more complicated than their symmetric counterparts. For example, consider what's involved in formulating the queries "Get part numbers for parts supplied by supplier S2" and "Get supplier numbers for suppliers who supply part P2" against the relation of Figure 4-1. The natural language versions of these queries are symmetric with respect to each other, but their formulations in SQL[5]—or **Tutorial D**, or any other formal language, come to that—most certainly aren't (see Exercise 4.14).

- Similar remarks apply to security and integrity constraints.

- Similar remarks apply to updates, perhaps with even more force.

- There's no guidance, in general, as to how to choose the "best" hierarchy. In the case of suppliers and parts, for example, should we make parts subordinate to suppliers—which is effectively what the design illustrated in Figure 4-1 does—or suppliers subordinate to parts?

- Even "natural" hierarchies like organization charts and bill of materials structures are still best represented, usually, by nonhierarchic designs.

---

[4]And, perhaps more to the point, newer ones like XML (see Exercise 4.12).

[5]I note in passing that SQL does support something a little bit like RVAs, in the form of columns whose type is *RT* MULTISET, where *RT* is some specified "row type."

Violating First Normal Form

By now you might be wondering, if all relvars are in 1NF by definition, what it could possibly mean for something *not* to be in 1NF. Perhaps surprisingly, this question does have a sensible answer. The point is, today's commercial DBMSs don't properly support relvars (or relations) at all—instead, they support a construct that for convenience I'll call a *table*, though by that term I don't necessarily mean to limit myself to the kinds of tables found in SQL systems specifically.[6] And tables, as opposed to relvars, might indeed not be in 1NF. To elaborate:

> **Definition (normalized table):** A table is in first normal form (1NF)—equivalently, such a table is normalized—if and only if it's a direct and faithful representation of some relvar.

So of course the question is: What does it mean for a table to be a direct and faithful representation of a relvar? The answer to this question involves five basic requirements, all of which are immediate consequences of the fact that the value of a relvar at any given time is (of course) always a relation specifically:

1. The table never contains any duplicate rows.

2. There's no left to right ordering to the columns.

3. There's no top to bottom ordering to the rows.

4. All columns are regular columns.

5. Every row and column intersection always contains exactly one value of the applicable type, and nothing else.

---

[6]As we've seen, the relational world in general very unfortunately uses the term *relation* to mean sometimes a relation value and sometimes a relation variable. In exactly the same kind of way, SQL in particular uses the term *table* to mean sometimes a table value and sometimes a table variable. Be aware, therefore, that in this section I use the term *table* to mean a table variable specifically, not a table value.

Requirements 1-3 are self-explanatory,[7] but the other two merit a little more explanation, perhaps. First, then, consider Requirement 4 ("All columns are regular columns"). In order to satisfy this requirement, the table in question must be such that both of the following are true:

a. Every column has a proper name (i.e., one that could be specified as a column name in a CREATE TABLE statement, in SQL terms), and that name is unique among the column names that apply to the table in question.

b. No row is allowed to contain anything extra, over and above values of those columns just mentioned. Thus, there are no "hidden" columns that can be accessed only by special operators instead of by regular column references (where a "regular column reference" is basically just a column name), and there are no columns that cause invocations of regular operators on rows to have irregular effects. In particular, therefore, there are no *identifiers* other than regular relational key values (no hidden "row IDs" or "object IDs," as are unfortunately found in some SQL products today), and there are no hidden *timestamps* as are found in certain "temporal database" proposals in the literature.

As for Requirement 5: Observe first of all that this requirement means that nulls are prohibited (since nulls, whatever else they might be, certainly aren't values). More generally, however, the requirement is intended to address the issue of *data value atomicity*. That's the one thing that "everybody knows" about relations in the relational model—namely, that attribute values within such relations are supposed to be atomic (right?). So what exactly does *atomic* mean in this context? Well, in his famous 1970 paper,[8] Codd merely said it meant "nondecomposable." And in later writings he went on to say that *nondecomposable* in turn meant "nondecomposable by the DBMS," which I take to mean there's no way the user can ask the DBMS to perform some such

---

[7]Though I note I passing that Requirement 2 in particular effectively means that SQL tables are *never* normalized—except, possibly, in the case of such a table with just one column (see footnote 14 in Chapter 1). However, the disciplines recommended in *SQL and Relational Theory* allow us among other things to treat such tables as if they were normalized after all (most of the time but, sadly, not *all* of the time).

[8]E. F. Codd: "A Relational Model of Data for Large Shared Data Banks," *Communications of the ACM 13*, No. 6 (June 1970).

decomposition, either explicitly or implicitly, on his or her behalf. All right, so let's consider a few examples:

- *Character strings:* Are character strings nondecomposable in the foregoing sense? Clearly not—think of SQL's SUBSTRING, LIKE, and concatenate operators, for example, all of which clearly rely on the fact that character strings in general have some internal structure and are thus decomposable into smaller pieces. Yet surely no one would argue that character strings shouldn't be allowed in relations.

- *Fixed point numbers:* Can be decomposed into integer and fractional parts.

- *Integers:* Can be decomposed into their prime factors. (Of course, I realize this isn't the kind of decomposability we usually consider in this context; I'm just trying to show that the notion of decomposability is itself open to a variety of interpretations.)

- *Dates and times:* Can be decomposed into year / month / day and hour / minute / second components, respectively.

- *Relational expressions:* Consider, e.g., view definitions in the catalog. Such expressions are certainly "decomposable"—decomposable by the DBMS, in fact—because if they weren't, there'd be no point in keeping them in the catalog in the first place.

The bottom line from all of these examples, and many others like them, is that if relation *r* has an attribute *A*, then the values of *A* within *r* can be *anything whatsoever*, just so long as they're values of the type *T* that's the type defined for that attribute *A*. And that type *T* in turn can be any type whatsoever![9] It can even be a relation type (whence the possibility of relation valued attributes, discussed a few pages back).

The 1NF "atomicity" requirement is sometimes stated in the form "no repeating groups." Indeed, I've stated it in that form myself in numerous earlier writings—in the previous edition of the present book in particular, where I attempted (but failed, I think) to give a precise definition of what a repeating group might be. On further reflection, I've come to the conclusion that it's better not to try to think about repeating groups at all in this context, but rather to focus on (and then, as I've just done, to debunk!) the

---

[9]Except as noted in footnote 2.

notion of atomicity instead. In other words, I now think the injunction against repeating groups is and always was essentially meaningless—and I hereby apologize to anyone who might have been misled by my earlier efforts in this regard.

In conclusion, if any of the five requirements are violated, the table in question doesn't "directly and faithfully" represent a relvar, *and all bets are off*. In particular, relational operators such as join are no longer guaranteed to work as expected (as you'll already know if—as I assume—you're familiar with SQL). The relational model deals with *relation* values and variables, and relation values and variables *only*.

Functional Dependencies

So much for 1NF; now I can move on and begin to discuss some of the higher normal forms. Now, I've already said that Boyce/Codd normal form (BCNF) is defined in terms of functional dependencies (FDs), and of course the same is true of second normal form (2NF) and third normal form (3NF) as well. So here's a definition:

> **Definition (functional dependency):** Let X and Y be subsets of the heading of relvar R; then the functional dependency (FD)
>
> $X \rightarrow Y$
>
> holds in R if and only if, whenever two tuples of R agree on X, they also agree on Y.[10] X and Y here are called the determinant and the dependant, respectively, and the FD overall can be read as "X functionally determines Y," or as "Y is functionally dependent on X," or more simply just as "X arrow Y."

Here are a couple of examples:

- The FD {CITY} → {STATUS} holds in relvar S, as we know from Chapter 2. Note the braces, by the way; X and Y in the definition are subsets of the heading of R, and are therefore sets (of attributes), even when, as in the example, they happen to be singleton sets. By the same token, X and Y values are tuples, even when, as in the example, they happen to be tuples of degree one.

---

[10]"Agree on," in contexts like the one at hand, is standard shorthand for "have the same value for."

- The FD {SNO} → {SNAME,STATUS} also holds in relvar S, because {SNO} is a key—in fact, the only key—for that relvar, and there are *always* "arrows out of keys" (see the section "Keys," immediately following this one). *Note:* In case it isn't obvious, I use the phrase "arrow out of X" to mean there exists some Y such that the FD $X \rightarrow Y$ holds in the pertinent relvar (where X and Y are subsets of the heading of that relvar).

Now here's a useful thing to remember: If the FD $X \rightarrow Y$ holds in relvar R, then the FD $X'' \rightarrow Y'$ also holds in relvar R for all supersets X'' of X and all subsets Y' of Y (just so long as X'' is still a subset of the heading, of course). In other words, we can always add attributes to the determinant or subtract them from the dependant, and what we get will still be an FD that holds in the relvar in question. For example, here's another FD that holds in relvar S:

```
{ SNO , CITY } → { STATUS }
```

(I started with the FD {SNO} → {SNAME,STATUS} and added CITY to the determinant and subtracted SNAME from the dependant.)

I also need to explain what it means for an FD to be *trivial*:

> **Definition (trivial FD):** The FD $X \rightarrow Y$ is trivial if and only if there's no way it can be violated.

For example, the following FDs all hold trivially in any relvar with attributes called STATUS and CITY:[11]

```
{ CITY , STATUS } → { CITY }
{ CITY , STATUS } → { STATUS }
{ CITY }          → { CITY }
{ CITY }          → { }
```

To elaborate briefly (but considering just the first of these examples, for simplicity): If two tuples have the same value for CITY and STATUS, they certainly have the same value for CITY. In fact, it's easy to see that the FD $X \rightarrow Y$ is trivial if and only if Y is a subset of X (in symbols, $Y \subseteq X$). Now, when we're doing database design, we don't usually bother with trivial FDs because they're, well, trivial; but when we're trying to be formal and precise about these matters—in particular, when we're trying to develop a *theory* of design—then we need to take all FDs into account, trivial ones as well as nontrivial.

---

[11]In connection with the last of these examples in particular, see Exercise 4.10 at the end of the chapter.

Keys Revisited

I discussed the concept of keys in general terms in Chapter 1, but it's time to get a little more precise about the matter and to introduce some more terminology. First, here for the record is a precise definition of the term *candidate key*—which, as noted in Chapter 1, I abbreviate to just *key* throughout most of this book:

> **Definition (candidate key, key):** Let *K* be a subset of the heading of relvar *R*. Then *K* is a candidate key (or just a key for short) for *R* if and only if it possesses both of the following properties:
>
> 1. *Uniqueness:* No legitimate value for *R* contains two distinct tuples with the same value for *K*.
>
> 2. *Irreducibility:* No proper subset of *K* has the uniqueness property.

This is the first definition we've encountered that involves some kind of irreducibility, but we'll meet several more in the pages ahead—irreducibility of one kind or another is ubiquitous, and important, throughout the field of design theory in general, as we'll see. Regarding key irreducibility in particular, one reason (not the only one) why it's important is that if we were to specify a "key" that wasn't irreducible, the DBMS wouldn't be able to enforce the proper uniqueness constraint. For example, suppose we told the DBMS (lying!) that {SNO,CITY} was a key, and in fact the only key, for relvar S. Then the DBMS couldn't enforce the constraint that supplier numbers are "globally" unique; instead, it could enforce only the weaker constraint that supplier numbers are "locally" unique, in the sense that they're unique within the pertinent city.

I'm not going to discuss the foregoing definition any further here, since the concept is so familiar[12]—but observe how the next few definitions depend on it:

> **Definition (key attribute):** Attribute *A* of relvar *R* is a key attribute for *R* if and only if it's part of at least one key of *R*.

---

[12]Do note, however, that there's no suggestion that relvars have just one key. *Au contraire*, in fact: A relvar can have any number of distinct keys, subject only to a limit that's a logical consequence of the degree of the relvar in question (see Exercise 4.9 at the end of the chapter).

Definition (nonkey attribute): Attribute *A* of relvar *R* is a nonkey attribute for *R* if and only if it's not part of any key of *R*.[13]

For example, in relvar SP, SNO and PNO are key attributes and QTY is a nonkey attribute.

Definition ("all key" relvar): A relvar is "all key" if and only if the entire heading is a key (in which case it's the only key, necessarily)—equivalently, if and only if no proper subset of the entire heading is a key.

Note: If a relvar is "all key," then it certainly has no nonkey attributes, but the converse is false—a relvar can be such that all of its attributes are key attributes and yet not be "all key" (right?).

Definition (superkey): Let *SK* be a subset of the heading of relvar *R*. Then *SK* is a superkey for *R* if and only if it possesses the following property:

1. *Uniqueness:* No legitimate value for *R* contains two distinct tuples with the same value for *SK*.

More succinctly, a superkey for *R* is a subset of the heading of *R* that's unique but not necessarily irreducible. In other words, we might say, loosely, that a superkey is a superset of a key ("loosely," because of course the superset in question must still be a subset of the pertinent heading). Observe, therefore, that all keys are superkeys, but "most" superkeys aren't keys. *Note:* A superkey that isn't a key is sometimes said to be a *proper* superkey.

It's convenient to define the notion of a *subkey* also:

Definition (subkey): Let *SK* be a subset of the heading of relvar *R*. Then *SK* is a subkey for *R* if and only if it's a subset of at least one key of *R*.

Note: A subkey that isn't a key is sometimes said to be a *proper* subkey.

---

[13]As a historical note, I remark that key and nonkey attributes were called prime and nonprime attributes, respectively, in Codd's original normalization papers (see Appendix D).

By way of example, consider relvar SP, which has just one key, viz., {SNO,PNO}. That relvar has:

a.   Two superkeys:

```
{ SNO , PNO }
{ SNO , PNO , QTY }
```

Note that the heading is always a superkey for any relvar R.

b.   Four subkeys:

```
{ SNO , PNO }
{ SNO }
{ PNO }
{ }
```

Note that the empty set of attributes is always a subkey for any relvar R.

To close this section, note that if H and SK are the heading and a superkey, respectively, for relvar R, then the FD $SK \rightarrow H$ holds in R, necessarily. (Equivalently, the FD $SK \rightarrow Y$ holds in R for all subsets Y of H.) The reason is that if two tuples of R have the same value for SK, then they must in fact be the very same tuple, in which case they obviously must have the same value for Y. Of course, all of these remarks apply in the important special case in which SK is not just a superkey but a key; as I put it earlier (very loosely, of course), there are always arrows out of keys. In fact, we can now make a more general statement: There are always arrows out of superkeys.

Second Normal Form

There's one more concept I need to introduce, viz., *FD irreducibility* (another kind of irreducibility, observe), before I can get on to the definitions of 2NF, 3NF, and BCNF as such:

> **Definition (irreducible FD):** The FD $X \rightarrow Y$ is irreducible with respect to relvar R (or just irreducible, if R is understood) if and only if it holds in R and $X' \rightarrow Y$ doesn't hold in R for any proper subset X' of X.

For example, the FD {SNO,PNO} → {QTY} is irreducible with respect to relvar SP. *Note:* This kind of irreducibility is sometimes referred to more explicitly as *left irreducibility* (since it's really the left side of the FD that we're talking about), but I've chosen to elide that "left" here for simplicity.

Now—at last, you might be forgiven for thinking—I can define 2NF:

> **Definition (second normal form):** Relvar *R* is in second normal form (2NF) if and only if, for every key *K* of *R* and every nonkey attribute *A* of *R*, the FD *K* → {*A*} (which holds in *R*, necessarily) is irreducible.

Note: The following ("preferred") definition is logically equivalent to the one just given—see Exercise 4.4 at the end of the chapter—but can sometimes be more useful:

> **Definition (second normal form, preferred):** Relvar *R* is in second normal form (2NF) if and only if, for every nontrivial FD *X* → *Y* that holds in *R*, at least one of the following is true:
>
> a. *X* is a superkey.
>
> b. *Y* is a subkey.
>
> c. *X* is not a subkey.

Points arising:

- First of all, please understand that it would be very unusual to regard 2NF as the ultimate goal of the design process. In fact, both 2NF and 3NF are mainly of historical interest; they're both regarded at best as stepping stones on the way to BCNF, which is of much more pragmatic (as well as theoretical) interest.

- Definitions of 2NF in the literature often take the form "*R* is in 2NF if and only if it's in 1NF and … ." However, such definitions are usually based on a mistaken understanding of what 1NF is. As we've seen, *all* relvars are in 1NF, and the words "it's in 1NF and" therefore add nothing.

Let's look at an example. Actually, it's usually more instructive with the normal forms to look at a counterexample rather than an example per se. Consider, therefore, a revised version of relvar SP—let's call it SCP—that has an additional attribute CITY, representing the city of the applicable supplier. Here are some sample tuples:

SCP

SNO	CITY	PNO	QTY
S1	London	P1	300
S1	London	P2	200
S1	London	P3	400
..	......	..	...
S2	Paris	P1	300
S2	Paris	P2	400
..	......	..	...

This relvar clearly suffers from redundancy: Every tuple for supplier S1 tells us S1 is in London, every tuple for supplier S2 tells us S2 is in Paris, and so on. And (appealing to the first of the foregoing definitions of 2NF) the relvar isn't in second normal form—its sole key is {SNO,PNO}, and the FD {SNO,PNO} → {CITY} therefore certainly holds, but that FD isn't irreducible; to be specific, we can drop PNO from the determinant and what remains, {SNO} → {CITY}, is still an FD that holds in the relvar. Equivalently, we can say the FD {SNO} → {CITY} holds and is nontrivial; moreover, (a) {SNO} isn't a superkey, (b) {CITY} isn't a subkey, and (c) {SNO} *is* a subkey, and so again (appealing now to the second, "preferred" definition of 2NF) the relvar isn't in second normal form.

Third Normal Form

This time I'll just start with my preferred definition:

> **Definition (third normal form, preferred):** Relvar R is in third normal form (3NF) if and only if, for every nontrivial FD $X \to Y$ that holds in R, at least one of the following is true:
>
> a. X is a superkey.
>
> b. Y is a subkey.

Points arising:

- To repeat something I said in the previous section (and contrary to popular opinion, perhaps), 3NF is mainly of historical interest—it should be regarded at best as no more than a stepping stone on the way to BCNF. *Note:* The reason I say *contrary to popular opinion* here is that many of the "definitions" of 3NF commonly found (at least in the popular literature) are actually definitions of BCNF—and BCNF, as I've already indicated, *is* important. *Caveat lector.*

- Definitions of 3NF in the literature often take the form "*R* is in 3NF if and only if it's in 2NF and ... ." I prefer a definition that makes no mention of 2NF. Note, however, that my definition of 3NF can in fact be derived from my preferred definition for 2NF by dropping condition (c) ("*X* is not a subkey"). It follows that 3NF implies 2NF— that is, if a relvar is in 3NF, then it's certainly in 2NF.

We've already seen an example of a relvar that's in 2NF but not 3NF: namely, the suppliers relvar S (see Figure 3-1 in Chapter 3). To elaborate: The nontrivial FD {CITY} → {STATUS} holds in that relvar, as we know; moreover, {CITY} isn't a superkey and {STATUS} isn't a subkey, and so the relvar isn't in 3NF. (It's certainly in 2NF, however. *Exercise:* Check this claim!)

Boyce/Codd Normal Form

As I said earlier, Boyce/Codd normal form (BCNF) is *the* normal form with respect to FDs—but now I can define it precisely:

> **Definition (Boyce/Codd normal form):** Relvar *R* is in Boyce/Codd normal form (BCNF) if and only if, for every nontrivial FD $X \rightarrow Y$ that holds in *R*, the following is true:
>
> a. *X* is a superkey.

Points arising:

- It follows from the definition that the only FDs that hold in a BCNF relvar are either trivial ones (we can't get rid of those, obviously) or arrows out of superkeys (we can't get rid of those, either). Or as some people like to say: *Every fact is a fact about the key, the whole key, and nothing but the key*—though I must immediately add that this informal characterization, intuitively attractive though it is, isn't really accurate, because it assumes among other things that there's just one key.

- The definition makes no reference to 2NF or 3NF. Note, however, that the definition can be derived from the 3NF definition by dropping condition (b) ("*Y* is a subkey"). It follows that BCNF implies 3NF—that is, if a relvar is in BCNF, then it's certainly in 3NF.

By way of an example of a relvar that's in 3NF but not BCNF, consider a revised version of the shipments relvar—let's call it SNP—that has an additional attribute SNAME, representing the name of the pertinent supplier. Suppose also that supplier names are necessarily unique (i.e., no two suppliers ever have the same name at the same time). Here are some sample tuples:

SNP

SNO	SNAME	PNO	QTY
S1	Smith	P1	300
S1	Smith	P2	200
S1	Smith	P3	400
..	.....	..	...
S2	Jones	P1	300
S2	Jones	P2	400
..	.....	..	...

Once again we observe some redundancy: Every tuple for supplier S1 tells us S1 is named Smith, every tuple for supplier S2 tells us S2 is named Jones, and so on; likewise, every tuple for Smith tells us Smith's supplier number is S1, every tuple for Jones tells us Jones's supplier number is S2, and so on. And the relvar isn't in BCNF. First of all, it has two keys, {SNO,PNO} and {SNAME,PNO}.[14] Second, every subset of the heading—the subset {QTY} in particular—is (of course) functionally dependent on both of those keys. Third, however, the FDs {SNO} → {SNAME} and {SNAME} → {SNO} also hold; these FDs are certainly not trivial, nor are they arrows out of superkeys, and so the relvar isn't in BCNF (though it is in 3NF).

---

[14]That's why I didn't show any double underlining when I showed the sample tuples—there are two candidate keys, and there doesn't seem to be any good reason to make either of them primary and thus somehow "more equal than the other."

Finally, as I'm sure you know, the normalization discipline says: If relvar *R* isn't in BCNF, then decompose it into projections that are. In the case of relvar SNP, either of the following decompositions will meet this objective:

- Projecting on {SNO,SNAME} and {SNO,PNO,QTY}

- Projecting on {SNO,SNAME} and {SNAME,PNO,QTY}

I can now explain why BCNF is the odd one out, as it were, in not simply being called "*n*th normal form" for some *n*. To quote from the paper in which Codd first described this new normal form:[15]

> More recently, Boyce and Codd developed the following definition: A [relvar] R is in third normal form if it is in first normal form and, for every attribute collection C of R, if any attribute not in C is functionally dependent on C, then all attributes in R are functionally dependent on C [*in other words, C is a superkey*].

So Codd was giving here what he regarded as a "new and improved" definition of *third* normal form. But the trouble was, the new definition was (and is) strictly stronger than the old one; that is, any relvar that's in 3NF by the new definition is certainly in 3NF by the old one, but the converse isn't true—a relvar can be in 3NF by the old definition and not in 3NF by the new one (relvar SNP, discussed above, is a case in point). So what that "new and improved" definition really defined was a new and stronger normal form, which therefore needed a distinct name of its own. However, by the time this point was adequately recognized, Fagin had already defined what he called fourth normal form, so *that* name wasn't available.[16] Hence the anomalous name *Boyce/Codd normal form*.

---

[15]E. F. Codd: "Recent Investigations into Relational Data Base Systems," Proc. IFIP Congress, Stockholm, Sweden (1974).

[16]Actually, when Raymond Boyce first came up with what became BCNF, he did call it fourth! The paper in which he first described the concept, *IBM Technical Disclosure Bulletin 16*, No. 1 (June 1973), had as its title "Fourth Normal Form and its Associated Decomposition Algorithm." Since that paper predated Fagin's paper on 4NF by several years (see Appendix D), Boyce's original name could perfectly well have been used at the time. It was Codd who insisted on calling the new normal form "third"—describing Boyce's definition as merely an improved version of one that already existed—and who thereby gave rise to a confusion (admittedly minor, but all logical differences are big differences) that continues to this day.

Exercises

4.1   How many FDs hold in relvar SP? Which ones are trivial? Which are irreducible?

4.2   Is it true that the FD concept relies on the notion of tuple equality?

4.3   Give examples from your own work environment of (a) a relvar not in 2NF; (b) a relvar in 3NF but not 2NF; (c) a relvar in BCNF but not 3NF.

4.4   Prove that the two definitions of 2NF given in the body of the chapter are logically equivalent.

4.5   Is it true that if a relvar isn't in 2NF, then it must have a composite key?

4.6   Is it true that every binary relvar is in BCNF?

4.7   (*Same as Exercise 1.4.*) Is it true that every "all key" relvar is in BCNF?

4.8   Write **Tutorial D** CONSTRAINT statements to express the fact that the pair of FDs {SNO} → {SNAME} and {SNAME} → {SNO} hold in relvar SNP (see the section "Boyce/Codd Normal Form").

   Note: This is the first exercise in any chapter that asks you to give an answer in **Tutorial D**. Of course, I realize you might not be completely conversant with that language; in all such exercises, therefore—for example, in Exercises 4.14 and 4.15 below—please just do the best you can. I do think it's worth your while at least to attempt the exercises in question.

4.9   Let R be a relvar of degree n. What's the maximum number of FDs that can possibly hold in R (trivial ones as well as nontrivial)? What's the maximum number of keys it can have?

4.10   Given that X and Y in the FD $X \to Y$ are both sets of attributes, what happens if either of those sets is empty?

4.11   Can you think of a situation in which it really would be reasonable to have a base relvar with an RVA?

4.12   There's been a lot of discussion in the industry in recent years of the possibility of *XML databases*. But XML documents are inherently hierarchic in nature; so do you think the criticisms of hierarchies in the body of the chapter apply to XML databases? (Well, yes, they do, as I indicated in footnote 4 earlier in the chapter. So what do you conclude?)

4.13   In Chapter 1 I said I'd be indicating primary key attributes, in tabular pictures of relations, by double underlining. At that point, however, I hadn't properly discussed the difference between relations and relvars, and now we know that keys in general apply to relvars, not relations. Yet we've seen several tabular pictures since then that represent relations as such (I mean, relations that aren't just a sample value for some relvar)—see, e.g., Figure 4-1 for three examples[17]—and I've certainly been using the double underlining convention in those pictures. So what can we say about that convention now?

4.14   Give **Tutorial D** formulations of the following queries against the relation shown in Figure 4-1:

a.   Get part numbers for parts supplied by supplier S2.

b.   Get supplier numbers for suppliers who supply part P2.

4.15   Suppose we need to update the database to show that supplier S2 supplies part P5 in a quantity of 500. Give **Tutorial D** formulations of the required update against (a) the non RVA design of Figure 1-1, (b) the RVA design of Figure 4-1.

4.16   Given the RVA design illustrated in Figure 4-1, state as precisely as you can the corresponding relvar predicate.

---

[17]Yes, I do mean three.

4.17   Here are some definitions of 1NF from the technical literature. In view of the discussion of such matters in the body of the present chapter, do you have any comments on them?

- **First normal form** (1NF) ... states that the domain of an attribute must include only *atomic* (simple, indivisible) *values* and that the value of any attribute in a tuple must be a *single value* from the domain of that attribute ... 1NF disallows having a set of values, a tuple of values, or a combination of both as an attribute value for a *single tuple* ... 1NF disallows "relations within relations" or "relations as attribute values within tuples" ... the only attribute values permitted by 1NF are single **atomic** (or **indivisible**) values (Ramez Elmasri and Shamkant B. Navathe, *Fundamentals of Database Systems*, 4th edition, Addison-Wesley, 2004)

- A relation is in **first normal form** if every field contains only atomic values, that is, no lists or sets (Raghu Ramakrishnan and Johannes Gehrke, *Database Management Systems*, 3rd edition, McGraw-Hill, 2003)

- *First normal form* is simply the condition that every component of every tuple is an atomic value (Hector Garcia-Molina, Jeffrey D. Ullman, and Jennifer Widom, *Database Systems: The Complete Book*, Prentice Hall, 2002)

- A domain is **atomic** if elements of the domain are considered to be indivisible units ... we say that a relation schema R is in **first normal form** (1NF) if the domains of all attributes of R are atomic (Abraham Silberschatz, Henry F. Korth, and S. Sudarshan, *Database System Concepts*, 4th edition, McGraw-Hill, 2002)

- A relation is said to be in **first normal form** (abbreviated 1NF) if and only if it satisfies the condition that it contains scalar values only (C. J. Date, *An Introduction to Database Systems*, 6th edition, Addison-Wesley, 1995)

Answers

4.1   The complete set of FDs—what's known, formally, as the *closure* (see Chapter 7), though it has nothing to do with the closure property of the relational algebra—for relvar SP contains a total of 31 distinct FDs, as follows:

```
{ SNO , PNO , QTY } → { SNO , PNO , QTY }
{ SNO , PNO , QTY } → { SNO , PNO }
{ SNO , PNO , QTY } → { SNO , QTY }
{ SNO , PNO , QTY } → { PNO , QTY }
{ SNO , PNO , QTY } → { SNO }
{ SNO , PNO , QTY } → { PNO }
{ SNO , PNO , QTY } → { QTY }
{ SNO , PNO , QTY } → { }

{ SNO , PNO }       → { SNO , PNO , QTY }
{ SNO , PNO }       → { SNO , PNO }
{ SNO , PNO }       → { SNO , QTY }
{ SNO , PNO }       → { PNO , QTY }
{ SNO , PNO }       → { SNO }
{ SNO , PNO }       → { PNO }
{ SNO , PNO }       → { QTY }
{ SNO , PNO }       → { }

{ SNO , QTY }       → { SNO , QTY }
{ SNO , QTY }       → { SNO }
{ SNO , QTY }       → { QTY }
{ SNO , QTY }       → { }

{ PNO , QTY }       → { PNO , QTY }
{ PNO , QTY }       → { PNO }
{ PNO , QTY }       → { QTY }
{ PNO , QTY }       → { }

{ SNO }             → { SNO }
{ SNO }             → { }
```

```
{ PNO }                    → { PNO }
{ PNO }                    → { }

{ QTY }                    → { QTY }
{ QTY }                    → { }

{ }                        → { }
```

Of these, the only ones that aren't trivial are the following four:

```
{ SNO , PNO } → { SNO , PNO , QTY }
{ SNO , PNO } → { SNO , QTY }
{ SNO , PNO } → { PNO , QTY }
{ SNO , PNO } → { QTY }
```

And the only ones that are irreducible are the following eleven:

```
{ SNO , PNO } → { SNO , PNO , QTY }
{ SNO , PNO } → { SNO , PNO }
{ SNO , PNO } → { SNO , QTY }
{ SNO , PNO } → { PNO , QTY }
{ SNO , PNO } → { QTY }

{ SNO , QTY } → { SNO , QTY }

{ PNO , QTY } → { PNO , QTY }

{ SNO }          → { SNO }

{ PNO }          → { PNO }

{ QTY }          → { QTY }

{ }              → { }
```

4.2   Yes, it is ("whenever two tuples agree on X, they also agree on Y"
      implies an equality comparison between the projections of the
      tuples in question on the attributes of X and Y, respectively, and
      those two projections in turn are themselves tuples). *Note:* See the
      answer to Exercise 2.10 in Chapter 2 regarding the notion of tuple
      equality in general.

4.3   *No answer provided.*

4.4   First of all, here again are the two definitions, numbered for purposes of subsequent reference:

1. Relvar R is in 2NF if and only if, for every key K of R and every nonkey attribute A of R, the FD $K \rightarrow \{A\}$ is irreducible.

2. Relvar R is in 2NF if and only if, for every nontrivial FD $X \rightarrow Y$ that holds in R, at least one of the following is true: (a) X is a superkey; (b) Y is a subkey; (c) X is not a subkey.

Let R not be in 2NF by Definition 1. Then there exists an FD— nontrivial by definition—$K \rightarrow \{A\}$, where K is a key of R and A is a nonkey attribute of R, that holds in R and is reducible. Since it's reducible, the (also nontrivial) FD $X \rightarrow \{A\}$ holds in R for some proper subkey X ($X \subset K$). Thus, denoting $\{A\}$ by Y, we have a nontrivial FD $X \rightarrow Y$ that holds in R such that X isn't a superkey, Y isn't a subkey, and X is a subkey. So R isn't in 2NF by Definition 2. So, loosely, Definition 2 implies Definition 1.[18]

Now let R not be in 2NF by Definition 2. Then there exists a nontrivial FD $X \rightarrow Y$ (F, say) that holds in R, such that X isn't a superkey, Y isn't a subkey, and X is a subkey. But if X is a subkey and not a superkey, it must be a *proper* subkey of some key K. Now there are two cases to consider:

a. Y contains a nonkey attribute A. In this case $K \rightarrow \{A\}$ holds in R but is reducible, and so R isn't in 2NF by Definition 1; so, again loosely, Definition 1 implies Definition 2.

b.   No such F exists such that Y contains a nonkey attribute A. But then, for every F, every attribute A contained in Y is such that $\{A\}$ is a subkey. Hence R is in *3NF* (and therefore certainly in 2NF): Contradiction.

It follows that Definitions 1 and 2 are equivalent.

---

[18]You might think this is the wrong way round, but it isn't. What I've shown is that *not 2NF by Definition 1* implies *not 2NF by Definition 2*. Given that "p implies q" is equivalent to "(not p) or q," therefore, it follows that what I've shown is that *2NF by Definition 2* implies *2NF by Definition 1*, or (loosely) *Definition 2 implies Definition 1* as stated. Apologies if you find this confusing!

4.5   Consider the following (invalid!) argument.

> Let relvar R not be in 2NF. Then there must be some key K of R and some nonkey attribute A of R such that the FD $K \rightarrow \{A\}$ (which holds in R, necessarily) is reducible—meaning some attribute can be dropped from K, yielding K' say, such that the FD $K' \rightarrow \{A\}$ still holds. Hence K must be composite.

> This argument appears to show that the answer to the exercise must be *yes*—i.e., if a relvar isn't in 2NF, it must have a composite key. But the argument is incorrect! Here's a counterexample. Let USA be a binary relvar with attributes COUNTRY and STATE; the predicate is *STATE is part of COUNTRY*, but COUNTRY is the United States in every tuple. Now, {STATE} is the sole key for this relvar, and the FD {STATE} $\rightarrow$ {COUNTRY} thus certainly holds. However, the FD { } $\rightarrow$ {COUNTRY} clearly holds as well (see the answer to Exercise 4.10 below); the FD {STATE} $\rightarrow$ {COUNTRY} is thus reducible, and so the relvar isn't in 2NF, and yet the key {STATE} isn't composite.

4.6   No! By way of a counterexample, consider relvar USA from the answer to the previous exercise. That relvar is subject to the FD { } $\rightarrow$ {COUNTRY}, which is neither trivial nor an arrow out of a superkey, and so the relvar isn't in BCNF. (In fact, of course, it isn't even in 2NF, as we saw in the answer to the previous exercise.) It follows that the relvar can be nonloss decomposed into its two unary projections on {COUNTRY} and {STATE}, respectively. (Note that the corresponding join, needed to reconstruct the original relvar, in fact reduces to a cartesian product.)

4.7   Yes, it is. If no nontrivial FDs hold at all—which is certainly the case for an "all key" relvar—then there's certainly no nontrivial FD that holds for which the determinant isn't a superkey, and so the relvar is in BCNF.

4.8   CONSTRAINT ...
        COUNT (SNP { SNO , SNAME }) = COUNT (SNP { SNO }) ;
      CONSTRAINT ...
        COUNT (SNP { SNO , SNAME }) = COUNT (SNP { SNAME }) ;

Note: This trick for specifying that an FD holds (i.e., by stating that two projections have the same cardinality) certainly does the job. As noted in Chapter 2, however, it's hardly very elegant, and for that reason I showed an alternative approach to formulating such constraints, using AND, JOIN, and RENAME, in that chapter. Here are revised formulations of the two constraints just shown that make use of that alternative approach:

```
CONSTRAINT ...
    WITH ( SS := S { SNO , SNAME } ) :
    AND ( ( SS JOIN ( SS RENAME { SNAME AS X } ) , SNAME = X ) ;

CONSTRAINT
    WITH ( SS := S { SNO , SNAME } ) :
    AND ( ( SS JOIN ( SS RENAME { SNO AS X } ) , SNO = X ) ;
```

Alternatively, Hugh Darwen and I have proposed[19] that **Tutorial D** should support another form of CONSTRAINT statement in which the usual boolean expression is replaced by a relational expression accompanied by one or more key specifications. Under this proposal, the foregoing constraints could be expressed as a single constraint, thus:

```
CONSTRAINT ... SNP { SNO , SNAME }
                  KEY { SNO }
                  KEY { SNAME } ;
```

Explanation: Think of the relational expression—SNP {SNO,SNAME}, in the example—as defining some temporary relvar (perhaps a view); then the key specifications—KEY {SNO} and KEY {SNAME}, in the example—indicates that the specified attributes would constitute keys for that relvar.[20]

---

[19]In our book *Database Explorations: Essays on The Third Manifesto and Related Topics* (Trafford, 2010) and elsewhere.

[20]Actually there's no need for the projection in the example—CONSTRAINT SNP KEY {SNO} KEY {SNAME} would suffice.

As an aside, I note that Darwen and I have also proposed allowing foreign key constraints to be specified for expressions in the same kind of way.

4.9   Let the FD $X \rightarrow Y$ hold in R. By definition, X and Y are subsets of the heading of R. Given that a set of n elements has 2^n possible subsets, it follows that each of X and Y has 2^n possible values, and hence an upper limit on the number of possible FDs that might hold in R is 2^{2n}. For example, if R is of degree five, the upper limit on the number of FDs that might hold is 1,024 (of which 243 are trivial). *Subsidiary exercises:*

a.   Where did that figure of 243 come from?

Answer: I'll let you figure this one out for yourself!

b.   Suppose those 1,024 FDs do all in fact hold. What can we conclude about R in that case?

Answer: It must have cardinality less than two. The reason is that one FD that holds in such a case is $\{ \} \rightarrow H$, where H is the heading; it follows that $\{ \}$ is a key, and so R is constrained to contain at most one tuple, as explained in the answer to the next exercise below.

As for how many keys R can have: Let m be the smallest integer greater than or equal to $n/2$. R will have the maximum possible number of keys if either (a) every distinct set of m attributes is a key or (b) m is odd and every distinct set of $(m - 1)$ attributes is a key. Either way, it follows that the maximum number of keys is $n! / (m! \times (n - m)!)$.[21] For example, a relvar of degree five can have at most ten, and one of degree three can have at most three, distinct keys. (An example of this latter case can be found in Appendix C.)

4.10   Let the specified FD $X \rightarrow Y$ hold in relvar R. Now, *every* tuple (regardless of whether it's a tuple of R) has the same value—namely, the 0-tuple—for the projection of that tuple over the

---

[21]The symbol r! is pronounced "r factorial" (sometimes "r bang") and denotes the product $r \times (r\text{-}1) \times \dots \times 2 \times 1$.

empty set of attributes (see the answer to Exercise 2.12 in Chapter 2). If Y is empty, therefore, the FD $X \rightarrow Y$ holds for all possible sets X of attributes of R; in fact, it's a trivial FD (and so it isn't very interesting), because the empty set is a subset of every set and so Y is definitely a subset of X in this case. On the other hand, if X is empty, the FD $X \rightarrow Y$ means that, at any given time, all tuples of R have the same value for Y (since they certainly all have the same value for X). What's more, if Y in turn is the entire heading of R–in other words, if X is a superkey—then R is constrained to contain at most one tuple (for otherwise R would suffer from a superkey uniqueness violation). *Note:* In this latter case, X isn't just a superkey but in fact a key, since it's certainly irreducible. What's more, it's the *only* key, because every other subset of the heading includes it as a proper subset.

4.11   Consider a relvar (FDR, say) in the database catalog whose purpose is to record the FDs that hold in various relvars in the database. Given that an FD is an expression of the form $X \rightarrow Y$ where X and Y are sets of attribute names, a reasonable design for that relvar FDR is one with attributes R (relvar name), X (determinant), and Y (dependant), and predicate (deliberately stated here somewhat loosely) *The FD $X \rightarrow Y$ holds in relvar R.* For any given relvar R in the database, therefore, the corresponding tuple in relvar FDR has X and Y values that are each relations of degree one, the tuples of which contain names of attributes of relvar R (and so X and Y are RVAs).

For another example, involving a "user relvar" instead of a relvar in the catalog, you might like to think about the following problem:

I decided to throw a party, so I drew up a list of people I wanted to invite and made some preliminary soundings. The response was good, but several people made their acceptance conditional on the acceptance of certain other invitees. For example, Bob and Cal both said they would come if and only if Amy came; Fay said she would come if and only if Don and Eve both came; Guy said he would come anyway; Hal said he would come if and only if Bob and Amy both came; and so on. Design a database to show whose acceptance is based on whose. (*With acknowledgments to Hugh Darwen.*)

It seems to me that a reasonable design here would involve a relvar with two attributes X and Y, both relation valued, and predicate (again deliberately stated somewhat loosely) *The set of people X will attend if and only if the set of people Y will attend.*

Subsidiary exercise: Can you think of any refinements you might want to make to this design? *Hint:* Is it true that Bob will attend if and only if Bob will attend?

4.12   Well, I don't know what you conclude, but I know what I do. One thing I conclude is that we should always be on our guard against getting seduced by the latest fad. (I could say quite a lot more regarding this latter, but I don't think this book is the right place for it.)

4.13   There are two cases to consider:

    a.   The relation depicted is a sample value for some relvar R.

    b.   The relation depicted is a sample value for some relational expression *rx*, where *rx* is something other than a simple relvar reference (where a relvar reference is basically just the pertinent relvar name).

In Case a., double underlining simply indicates that a primary key *PK* has been declared for R[22] and the pertinent attribute is part of *PK*. In Case b., you can think of *rx* as the defining expression for some temporary relvar *R* (think of it as a view defining expression and *R* as the corresponding view, if you like); then double underlining indicates that a primary key *PK* could in principle be declared for *R* and the pertinent attribute is part of *PK*.

---

[22]Well, that's not quite the situation as far as this book is concerned, because in this book I almost never declare primary keys as such (in fact **Tutorial D** provides no way of doing so)—but I think you see what I mean.

4.14   I assume for the sake of this exercise and the next that the relation shown in Figure 4-1 is a sample value for a relvar SPQ. Here then are **Tutorial D** formulations (not the only ones possible) for the two queries:

a.   ((SPQ WHERE SNO = 'S2') UNGROUP (PQ)) { PNO }

b.   ((SPQ UNGROUP (PQ)) WHERE PNO = 'P2') { SNO }

Observe that the first of these expressions involves a restriction followed by an ungrouping, while the second involves an ungrouping followed by a restriction (there's the asymmetry).

Note: The UNGROUP operator wasn't discussed in the body of the chapter, but its semantics should be obvious from the examples. Basically, it's used to map a relation with an RVA to one without such an attribute. (There's a GROUP operator too, for "going the other way"—that is, mapping a relation without an RVA to one with one.) For further explanation, see *SQL and Relational Theory*.

4.15   Here I think it might be helpful first to give part of the **Tutorial D** grammar for *<relation assign>*, which is the fundamental relational update operator in **Tutorial D**. (Please note that the grammar is slightly simplified for present purposes, though. As for the names of the various syntactic categories, they're meant to be intuitively self-explanatory.)

```
<relation assign>
    ::=    <relvar name> := <relation exp>
        | <insert> | <delete> | <update>

<insert>
    ::=    INSERT <relvar name> <relation exp>

<delete>
    ::=    DELETE <relvar name> <relation exp>
        | DELETE <relvar name> [ WHERE <boolean exp> ]
```

```
<update>
    ::=   UPDATE <relvar name> [ WHERE <boolean exp> ] :
                                    { <attribute assign commalist> }
```

And an *<attribute assign>*, if the attribute in question happens
to be relation valued, is basically just a *<relation assign>* (except
that the pertinent *<attribute name>* appears in place of the target
<relvar name> in that *<relation assign>*), and that's where we came
in. Here then are **Tutorial D** statements for the required updates:

a. `INSERT SP RELATION { TUPLE { 'S2' , 'P5' , 500 } } ;`

b. `UPDATE SPQ WHERE SNO = 'S2' :`
    `{ INSERT PQ RELATION { TUPLE { PNO 'P5' , QTY 500 } } } ;`

4.16 Supplier SNO supplies part PNO in quantity QTY if and only if
      (PNO,QTY) is a tuple in PQ.

4.17 One obvious comment is that I was just as confused as everybody
      else, back in 1995! Though I did inadvertently (?) conceal my
      confusion by using the comparatively respectable term *scalar*
      from the programming languages world in place of that rather
      suspect term *atomic*. However, I've come to realize that *scalar* is
      really no more formal or precise than *atomic* is, in this context.
      The fact is, neither term has any absolute meaning—it simply
      depends on what we want to do with the data. For example,
      sometimes we want to deal with an entire set of part numbers as
      a single thing; at other times, we want to deal with individual part
      numbers within that set—but then we're descending to a lower
      level of detail (in other words, to a lower level of abstraction). The
      following analogy might help clarify this point. In physics—which
      after all is where the "atomicity" terminology comes from—the
      situation is precisely parallel: Sometimes we want to think about
      individual physical atoms as indivisible objects; at other times,
      we want to think about the protons, neutrons, and electrons that
      go to make up those atoms. And of course those protons and
      neutrons aren't really indivisible, either—they contain a variety of
      "subsubatomic" particles called *quarks*. And so on, possibly (?).

One last point: An attempt *might* be made to rescue the notion of absolute atomicity, as follows. Let's agree to say a value is *not* atomic if and only if operators exist to "take the value apart," as it were. (I think this idea, or something very like it, was probably what was in Codd's mind when he said that *nondecomposable* meant, specifically, "nondecomposable by the DBMS.") Thus, a character string isn't atomic because it can be taken apart by means of the SUBSTRING operator; a set isn't atomic because it can be taken apart by means of operators that extract either elements or subsets from the set; and so on. By contrast, a fixed point number is atomic, if there are no operators to extract its integer and fractional parts (say). But even if we were to accept this argument, it seems to me we would then also have to accept the argument that the very same value might be atomic today and composite tomorrow! Such would be the case for a fixed point number, for example, if there were originally no operators to extract its integer and fractional parts but such operators were subsequently introduced. And it further seems to me that if the notion of atomicity is time dependent in this way, then (as previously claimed) it really doesn't have any absolute meaning.

CHAPTER 5

FDs and BCNF (Formal)

What's formal is normal
What's not so is not
And if normal is formal,
Informal is what?

—Anon: *Where Bugs Go*

Now I want to step back, take a deep breath as it were, and consider FDs and BCNF all over again—but this time I want to do it properly (with apologies for the small amount of repetition involved). As you'll quickly see, the treatment in this chapter is rather more abstract than that in the previous one; it shouldn't be too difficult to follow, if you're fully comfortable with the material of that previous chapter, but it'll certainly be more formal. For that reason, *I don't want you to look at this chapter at all until you've absorbed everything in the previous one.* (Of course, that shouldn't be hard to do, since most of what was in that chapter was surely familiar to you anyway.)

One general point up front: Since BCNF is *the* normal form with respect to FDs, I won't have anything to say in this chapter regarding 2NF or 3NF (or indeed 1NF). As I've more or less said already, 2NF and 3NF just aren't all that interesting in themselves any more.

Preliminary Definitions

In this section I simply give definitions, with little by way of further elaboration, of a few familiar but absolutely fundamental concepts—definitions that are rather more precise than the ones typically found in the literature (as well as being more precise, in some

© C. J. Date 2019
C. J. Date, *Database Design and Relational Theory*, https://doi.org/10.1007/978-1-4842-5540-7_5

cases, than the ones given earlier in this book). Production of examples to illustrate the definitions is left as an exercise.

>**Definition (heading):** A heading H is a set of attribute names.

I remind you that the foregoing definition is deliberately not quite the same as the one I gave in Chapter 2, q.v. In fact it's simpler than that previous definition,[1] and so therefore are certain of the definitions to come.

>**Definition (tuple):** A tuple with heading H is a set of ordered pairs <A,v> (one such pair for each attribute name A appearing in H), where v is a value. The phrase *tuple with heading H* can be abbreviated to just *tuple*, if H is either understood or irrelevant for the purpose at hand.

>**Definition (tuple projection):** Let t be a tuple with heading H and let X be a subset of H. Then the (tuple) projection $t\{X\}$ of t on the attributes of X is a tuple with heading X—namely, that subset of t containing just those <A,v> pairs such that A appears in X.[2]

The foregoing definition defines a version of the usual relational projection operator that applies to individual tuples (see Exercise 2.11 in Chapter 2). I'll be appealing to this definition many times in the pages ahead. Note that, just as every projection of a relation is itself a relation, so every projection of a tuple is itself a tuple.

>**Definition (relation):** A relation r is an ordered pair <H,h>, where h is a set of tuples (the body of r) all having heading H. H is the heading of r and the attributes of H are the attributes of r. The tuples of h are the tuples of r.

>**Definition (projection):** Let r be the relation <H,h> and let X be a subset of H. Then the projection $r\{X\}$ of r on the attributes of X is the relation <X,x>, where x is the set of all tuples $t\{X\}$ such that t is a tuple of h.

---

[1]In particular because it ignores attribute types. In fact I'm going to ignore attribute types throughout the rest of this chapter (except in the definition of join), and indeed throughout most of the rest of this book.

[2]Refer to the section "Equality Dependencies" in Chapter 3 for an explanation of the shorthand notation I'm using here.

Definition (join): Let relations $r1, ..., rn$ ($n \geq 0$) be joinable—i.e., let them be such that attributes with the same name are of the same type. Then the join of $r1, ..., rn$, JOIN $\{r1,...,rn\}$, is a relation with (a) heading the union of the headings of $r1, ..., rn$ and (b) body the set of all tuples t such that t is the union of a tuple from $r1, ...,$ and a tuple from rn.

Points arising:

- The kind of join just defined is what's sometimes called, more explicitly, the *natural* join.

- Note carefully that join as defined here is an n-adic operator, not a dyadic operator merely—$n = 2$ is just a common special case. (As for $n < 2$, see Exercise 5.1 at the end of the chapter.) Precisely because of this fact, **Tutorial D** uses the prefix syntactic style mentioned in the definition—

```
JOIN { r1 , ..., rn }
```

—though in the special case of $n = 2$, it supports an infix style as well:

```
r1 JOIN r2
```

In this book, however, I'll favor the prefix style from this point forward.

- Note too that in the special case in which no two of the operand relations $r1, ..., rn$ have any attribute names in common, join reduces to cartesian product.

One final definition to close this section:

Definition (relation variable, relvar): A relation variable or relvar with heading H is a variable R such that a value r can be assigned to that variable only if that value r is a relation with heading H. The attributes of H are the attributes of R. Also, if relation r is assigned to relvar R, then the body and tuples of r are the body and tuples of R, respectively, under that assignment.

Note: The foregoing definition says that relation *r* can be assigned to relvar *R only if* it has the same heading as *R*. More precisely, relation *r* can be assigned to relvar *R if and only if* (a) it has the same heading as *R and* (b) it satisfies all of the constraints that apply to *R*, where the phrase "all of the constraints that apply to *R*" includes the functional dependencies that hold in *R*—see the section immediately following—but isn't limited to functional dependencies alone.

Functional Dependencies Revisited

Now I'm in a position to deal properly with the concept of functional dependence. Again I'll be presenting precise definitions—but in this section (as compared to the previous one) I'll have rather more to say about those definitions and some of their implications.

> **Definition (functional dependency):** Let *H* be a heading; then a functional dependency (FD) with respect to *H* is an expression of the form $X \rightarrow Y$, where *X* (the determinant) and *Y* (the dependant) are both subsets of *H*. The phrase *FD with respect to H* can be abbreviated to just *FD*, if *H* is understood.

Here are a couple of examples:

```
{ CITY }  →  { STATUS }
{ CITY }  →  { SNO }
```

Note carefully that—contrary to popular opinion, perhaps—FDs are formally defined with respect to some *heading*, not with respect to some relation or some relvar. The two FDs just shown, for example, are defined with respect to any heading that contains attributes called CITY, STATUS, and SNO (and others as well, possibly). Note too that from a formal point of view, an FD is just an *expression*: an expression that, when interpreted with respect to some specific relation, becomes a *proposition* that (by definition) evaluates to either TRUE or FALSE. For example, if the two FDs shown above are interpreted with respect to the relation that's the current value of relvar S (see Figure 1-1 in Chapter 1), then the first evaluates to TRUE and the second to FALSE. Of course, it's common informally to define such an expression to be an FD, in some specific context, only if it evaluates to TRUE in that context; however, such a definition leaves no way of saying a given relation fails to satisfy, or in other words violates, some given FD. Why? Because, by that informal definition, an FD that isn't satisfied wouldn't be an FD in the first place! For example, we wouldn't be able to say the relation that's the current value of relvar S violates the second of the FDs shown above.

I really can't stress the foregoing point strongly enough. For most people, it represents a shift in thinking; however, it's a shift that has to be made if you're ever to understand what design theory is all about. The point is this: Most writings on FDs— including the early research papers that first introduced the concept—don't actually define the concept of an FD, as such, at all! Instead, they say something along the lines of "*Y* is functionally dependent on *X* in relation *r* if and only if, whenever two tuples of *r* agree on *X*, they also agree on *Y*." Which is perfectly true, of course—but it's not a definition of an FD; instead, it's a definition of what it means for an FD to be *satisfied*. But if we want to develop a theory of FDs as such, then we clearly need to be able to talk about FDs as objects in their own right, divorced from the context of some particular relation or some particular relvar. More specifically, we need to divorce the idea of an FD as such from the idea that it might have some interpretation, or meaning, in some context. In fact, design theory can be regarded as a small piece of logic, and logic isn't about meaning at all—it's about formal manipulations.

To get back to the definitions:

> **Definition (satisfying or violating an FD):** Let relation *r* have heading *H* and let $X \to Y$ be an FD, *F* say, with respect to *H*. If all pairs of tuples *t1* and *t2* of *r* are such that whenever $t1\{X\} = t2\{X\}$, then $t1\{Y\} = t2\{Y\}$, then *r* satisfies *F*; otherwise *r* violates *F*.

Observe that it's relations, not relvars, that satisfy or violate some given FD. For example, the relation that's the current value of relvar S (see Figure 3-1) satisfies both of these FDs—

```
{ CITY }  → { STATUS }
{ SNAME } → { CITY }
```

—and violates this one:

```
{ CITY } → { SNO }
```

> **Definition (FD holding):** The FD *F* holds in relvar *R* (equivalently, relvar *R* is subject to the FD *F*) if and only if every relation that can be assigned to relvar *R* satisfies *F*. The FDs that hold in relvar *R* are the FDs of *R*.

Important: Please note the terminological distinction I'm drawing here—FDs are *satisfied* (or violated) by relations, but *hold* (or don't hold) in relvars. Please note too that I'll adhere to this distinction throughout this book. By way of example, the following FD holds in relvar S—

```
{ CITY } → { STATUS }
```

—and these two don't:

```
{ SNAME } → { CITY }
{ CITY }  → { SNO }
```

(Contrast the examples following the previous definition.) So now, at last, we know precisely what it means for a given relvar to be subject to a given FD.

Boyce/Codd Normal Form Revisited

With a proper understanding of FDs under our belt, as it were, I can now go on to tackle the question of what it means for a relvar to be in BCNF. Again I proceed by means of a series of precise definitions.

> **Definition (trivial FD):** Let $X \to Y$ be an FD, F say, with respect to heading H. Then F is trivial if and only if it's satisfied by every relation with heading H.

Now, in Chapter 4 I defined a trivial FD to be one that can't possibly be violated. There's nothing wrong with that definition, of course; however, the one just given is preferable because it explicitly mentions the pertinent heading. I also said in Chapter 4 that it's easy to see that the FD $X \to Y$ is trivial if and only if Y is a subset of X. Well, that's true too; but I can now say that this latter fact isn't really a definition but rather a *theorem*, easily proved from the definition as such. (On the other hand, the definition as such isn't very helpful in determining whether a given FD is trivial, whereas the theorem is. For that reason, we might regard the theorem as an *operational* definition, inasmuch as it provides an effective test that can easily be applied in practice.) Let me state the theorem explicitly for the record:

> **Theorem:** Let $X \to Y$ be an FD, F say. Then F is trivial if and only if the dependant Y is a subset of the determinant X (in symbols, $Y \subseteq X$).

Distinctions like the one I'm drawing here are sometimes characterized as *semantic vs. syntactic* distinctions. To spell the point out: The original definition—*F* is trivial if and only if it's satisfied by every relation with the pertinent heading—is semantic, because it defines what the concept means; by contrast, the theorem, or what I've called the "operational" definition—*F* is trivial if and only if *Y* is a subset of *X*—is syntactic, because it provides a check that can be performed in a purely syntactic way. We'll be meeting this distinction between semantic and syntactic notions again (fairly frequently, in fact) in the pages ahead. Indeed, one case in point arises almost immediately in connection with the notion of FD irreducibility (see below).

To continue with the definitions:

> **Definition (superkey):** A superkey of relvar *R* is a subset *SK* of the heading *H* of *R* such that the FD *SK* → *H* holds in *R* ("is an FD of *R*"). That FD is a superkey constraint on *R*.

For example, {SNO}, {SNO,CITY}, and {SNO,CITY,STATUS} are all superkeys for relvar S.

> **Definition (irreducible FD):** The FD *X* → *Y* is irreducible with respect to relvar *R* (or just irreducible, if *R* is understood) if and only if it holds in *R* and *X'* → *Y* doesn't hold in *R* for any proper subset *X'* of *X*.

For example, the FD {CITY} → {STATUS} is irreducible with respect to relvar S. By contrast, the FD {CITY,SNO} → {STATUS}, though certainly an FD of S, is *reducible* with respect to S. Observe that while FDs as such are defined with respect to some *heading*, FD irreducibility is defined with respect to some *relvar*. In other words, FDs as such are just a syntactic notion (an FD is just an expression that takes a certain syntactic form), while FD irreducibility is a matter of semantics (it has to do with what the pertinent FD means in connection with the pertinent relvar). *Note:* I don't assume in what follows that the FDs we're talking about are irreducible ones only, though in practice we typically do.

> **Definition (key):** A key of relvar *R* is a subset *K* of the heading *H* of *R* such that the FD *K* → *H* is an irreducible FD of *R*. That FD is a key constraint on *R*.

Note the appeal to FD irreducibility in the foregoing definition.

> **Definition (FD implied by keys):** Let relvar R have heading H and let $X \to Y$ be an FD, F say, with respect to H. Then F is implied by the keys of R if and only if every relation r that satisfies R's key constraints also satisfies F.

This definition requires some elaboration. First of all, if some relation satisfies some key constraint, then of course it satisfies the pertinent uniqueness requirement; and if it satisfies the uniqueness requirement for the set of attributes that constitute some key, it certainly also satisfies the uniqueness requirement for every superset of that set of attributes (just so long as that superset is a subset of the pertinent heading, of course)—in other words, for every corresponding superkey. Thus, the phrase "satisfies R's key constraints" in the definition could be replaced by the phrase "satisfies R's superkey constraints" without making any significant difference. Likewise, the concept "implied by keys" could just as well be "implied by superkeys," again without making any significant difference.

Second, what happens if the FD F mentioned in the definition is trivial? Well, in that case, by definition, F is satisfied by every relation r with heading H, and so F is certainly satisfied by every relation r that satisfies R's key constraints, a fortiori. So trivial FDs are always "implied by keys," trivially.

Third, then, suppose F is nontrivial. Then it's easy to prove the following theorem:

> **Theorem:** Let F be an FD that holds in relvar R. Then F is implied by the keys of R if and only if it's a superkey constraint on R.

In other words, it's like that business with trivial FDs: The formal definition as such isn't much help in determining whether a given FD is implied by keys, but the theorem is. For that reason, we can regard the theorem as an *operational* definition, since it provides an effective test that can easily be applied in practice.

And now, at last, I can define BCNF:

> **Definition (Boyce/Codd normal form):** Relvar R is in Boyce/Codd normal form (BCNF) if and only if every FD of R is implied by the keys of R.

However, given the various definitions and theorems already discussed in this section, we can see that the following operational or "syntactic" definition (or theorem) is valid too:

> **Definition (Boyce/Codd normal form):** Relvar R is in Boyce/Codd normal form (BCNF) if and only for every nontrivial FD $X \to Y$ that holds in R, X is a superkey for R.

As I put it in Chapter 4, it follows from this definition that the only FDs that hold in a BCNF relvar are either trivial ones (we can't get rid of those, obviously) or arrows out of superkeys (we can't get rid of those, either). Though now I'd like to add that when I talk about "getting rid of" some FD, I fear I'm being—I hope uncharacteristically—a little sloppy ... For example, consider relvar S. That relvar is subject to the FD {CITY} $\to$ {STATUS}, among others; as explained in Chapter 3, therefore, the recommendation is to decompose the relvar into its projections SNC, on {SNO,SNAME,CITY}, and CT, on {CITY,STATUS}. But if we do, then the FD {SNO} $\to$ {STATUS}, which also holds in relvar S, "disappears," in a sense; thus we have indeed "gotten rid of it," in a sense. But what does it mean to say the FD has disappeared? The answer is: It's been replaced by a multirelvar constraint (that is, a constraint that spans two or more relvars). So the constraint certainly still exists—it just isn't an FD any more.[3] Similar remarks apply throughout this book whenever I talk of "getting rid of" dependencies of any kind, be they FDs or otherwise.

Heath's Theorem

Consider relvar S once again, with its FD {CITY} $\to$ {STATUS}. Suppose we decompose that relvar, not as in Chapter 3 into relvars SNC and CT, but instead into relvars *SNT* and CT—where CT is the same as before, but SNT has heading {SNO,SNAME,STATUS} instead of {SNO,SNAME,CITY}. Sample values for SNT and CT corresponding to the value shown for S in Figure 3-1 are shown in Figure 5-1:

---

[3]Well ... it *is* an FD, but one that holds in the join of two relvars (viz., SNC and CT), rather than in an individual relvar as such. Note, however, that enforcing the key constraints on those two relvars will enforce that multirelvar constraint "automatically"; that is, the multirelvar constraint in question is implied by—equivalently, is a logical consequence of—certain explicitly declared constraints (actually key constraints, in the case at hand).

SNT

SNO	SNAME	STATUS
S1	Smith	20
S2	Jones	30
S3	Blake	30
S4	Clark	20
S5	Adams	30

CT

CITY	STATUS
Athens	30
London	20
Paris	30

Figure 5-1. *Relvars SNT and CT—sample values*

Given this decomposition, I hope you can see that:

- Relvars SNT and CT are both in BCNF (the keys are {SNO} and {CITY}, respectively, and the only nontrivial FDs that hold in those relvars are "arrows out of superkeys").

- Unlike the decomposition in Chapter 3, however, this decomposition is not nonloss but *lossy*. For example, we can't tell from Figure 5-1 whether supplier S2 is in Paris or Athens—note what happens if we join the two projections together[4]—and so we've lost information.

Let's take a slightly closer look at this example. First of all, here are the predicates for relvars SNT and CT:

- SNC: *Supplier SNO is named SNAME and has status STATUS.*

- CT: *City CITY has status STATUS.*

So the predicate for the join of those two relvars is:

> *Supplier SNO is named SNAME and has status STATUS* **and** *city CITY has status STATUS.*

Now recall the predicate for relvar S (see the answer to Exercise 2.6 in Chapter 2):

> *Supplier SNO is named SNAME and is located in city CITY,* **which** *has status STATUS.*

---

[4]See the remarks on *lossy joins* in footnote 5 in Chapter 3 (in the section "Normalization Serves Two Purposes"); see also the answer to Exercise 3.2 in that same chapter.

This latter predicate is clearly not the same as the predicate for the join. To be more precise, if some given tuple *t* satisfies it, then that tuple *t* also satisfies the predicate for the join, but the converse is false. That's why the join "loses information" or "is lossy"—just because some tuple appears in the join, we can't assume it also appears in the original relvar S.

So what exactly is it that makes some decompositions nonloss and others lossy? This is the question that lies at the heart of normalization theory. It can be stated formally thus:

> **Let r be a relation and let r1, ..., rn be projections of r. What conditions must be satisfied in order for r to be equal to the join of those projections?**

(By the way, note the tacit assumption here that—as noted earlier—join is an *n*-adic operator.)

An important, albeit partial, answer to this question was provided by Ian Heath in 1971[5] when he proved the following theorem:

> **Heath's Theorem** (*for relations*): Let relation *r* have heading *H* and let *X*, *Y*, and *Z* be such that their union is equal to *H* (so *X*, *Y*, and *Z* are all subsets of *H*). Let *XY* denote the union of *X* and *Y*, and similarly for *XZ*. If *r* satisfies the FD $X \rightarrow Y$, then *r* is equal to the join of its projections on *XY* and *XZ*.

By way of example, consider the suppliers relation once again (i.e., the current value of relvar S as shown in Figure 3-1). That relation satisfies the FD {CITY} → {STATUS}. Thus, taking *X* as {CITY}, *Y* as {STATUS}, and *Z* as {SNO,SNAME}, Heath's Theorem tells us that the decomposition of that relation into its projections on the sets of attributes {CITY,STATUS} and {CITY,SNO,SNAME}[6] is nonloss—as indeed we already know.

Now, it's important to understand that (to repeat) Heath's answer to the original question was only partial. I'll explain what this means in terms of the foregoing example. Basically, the theorem does tell us the decomposition into projections SNC and CT (see Figure 3-2 in Chapter 3) is nonloss; however, it doesn't tell us the one into SNT and CT (see Figure 5-1) is lossy. In other words, if we decompose on the basis of an FD,

---

[5]In his paper "Unacceptable File Operations in a Relational Database," Proc. 1971 ACM SIGFIDET Workshop on Data Description, Access, and Control, San Diego, Calif. (November 11th-12th, 1971).

[6]Or, as we would "more naturally" tend to write them, interchanging the two sets of attributes and specifying the individual attributes in a "more natural" order, on {SNO,SNAME,CITY} and {CITY,STATUS}.

as we did in the example of Figure 3-2, then Heath's Theorem says the decomposition will be nonloss; but if we decompose on some other basis, as we did in the example of Figure 5-1, then the theorem has nothing to say on the matter. Thus, the theorem gives a sufficient condition, but not a necessary one, for a given (binary) decomposition to be nonloss. It follows that it might be possible to decompose relation r in a nonloss way into its projections on XY and XZ even if it doesn't satisfy the FD $X \rightarrow Y$. *Note:* I'll be describing a stronger form of Heath's Theorem, one that gives both necessary and sufficient conditions for a given decomposition to be nonloss, later in this book (see Chapter 12).

As an aside, I remark that in the paper in which he proved his theorem, Heath also gave a definition of what he called "third" normal form that was in fact a definition of BCNF. Since that definition preceded Boyce and Codd's definition by some three years, it seems to me that BCNF ought by rights to be called *Heath* normal form. But it isn't.

Now, in Chapter 3, in the section "Normalization Serves Two Purposes," I said something like the following:

> If you've been paying careful attention, you might reasonably accuse me of practicing a tiny deception in the foregoing discussion. To be specific, I've considered what it means for a decomposition of *relations* to be nonloss; but normalization, which is what we're supposed to be talking about, isn't a matter of decomposing relations, it's a matter of decomposing *relvars*.

Well, these remarks apply here too! So let's get back to relvars ... Consider relvar S once again. Suppose we do decide to perform the recommended decomposition into the "projection" relvars SNC and CT; moreover, suppose we want that decomposition to be nonloss, as indeed we surely do. In other words, what we want is for the decomposition to be such that, *at all times*, the current value of relvar S is equal to the join of the current values of SNC and CT.[7] That is, we want relvar S to be subject to the following integrity constraint, YCT (actually it's an equality dependency—see Chapter 3):

```
CONSTRAINT YCT
    S = JOIN { S { SNO , SNAME , CITY } , S { CITY , STATUS } } ;
```

_____

[7] Here I'm adopting once again the convenient fiction that relvars S, SNC, and CT all coexist (living alongside one another, as it were).

Now, recall from Chapter 2 that relvar S is certainly subject to the constraint that I there called XCT:

```
CONSTRAINT XCT
   COUNT ( S { CITY } ) = COUNT ( S { CITY , STATUS } ) ;
```

Just to remind you, this latter constraint merely says the FD {CITY} → {STATUS} holds in S. Appealing to Heath's Theorem, therefore, we see that every possible value of relvar S, since it necessarily satisfies constraint XCT, necessarily satisfies constraint YCT as well. And it follows that constraint XCT *implies* constraint YCT (meaning, to spell the point out, that if relvar S is subject to XCT—which it is—then it's necessarily subject to YCT as well). So constraint YCT does hold, and the decomposition of relvar S into relvars SNC and CT is indeed nonloss, as required. It follows that we can take Heath's Theorem as applying to relvars after all, not just to relations. So let's restate it accordingly:

> **Heath's Theorem** (*for relvars*): Let relvar R have heading H and let X, Y, and Z be such that their union is equal to H (so X, Y, and Z are all subsets of H). Let XY denote the union of X and Y, and similarly for XZ. If R is subject to the FD X → Y, then R can be nonloss decomposed into its projections on XY and XZ.

There's one further point I want to make on the general topic of nonloss decomposition (to BCNF or otherwise). Once again consider relvar S, with its FD {CITY} → {STATUS}. By Heath's Theorem, that relvar can be nonloss decomposed into its projections on {SNO,SNAME,CITY} and {CITY,STATUS}. However, it can clearly also be nonloss decomposed into those two projections *together with* (say) the projection on {SNAME,STATUS}; that is, if we join all three of those projections together, we get back to where we started. (Check this claim for yourself, using our usual sample value for relvar S, if it isn't immediately obvious.) However, that third projection clearly isn't needed in the process of reconstructing the original relvar. Now, when we're doing database design, for obvious reasons we usually consider only decompositions for which every projection *is* needed in the reconstruction process—but in this book I'm discussing decompositions in general, and I won't limit myself to those in which every projection is needed for reconstruction (barring explicit statements to the contrary, of course).

Exercises

5.1   The version of join defined in the body of the chapter is an *n*-adic operator for arbitrary $n \geq 0$, not just a dyadic one ($n = 2$). So what happens if $n = 1$? Or $n = 0$?

5.2   Define as precisely as you can what it means for a relvar to be subject to a functional dependency.

5.3   Consider the following FDs:

    a. { CITY } → { STATUS }

    b. { SNO , CITY } → { STATUS }

    c. { SNO } → { SNO }

    d. { SNO , CITY } → { SNO }

    e. { SNO } → { SNO , CITY }

    f. { SNAME , SNO } → { STATUS , CITY }

    g. { SNO } → { STATUS }

    h. { SNAME } → { STATUS , SNO }

Which of these FDs are trivial? Which ones are satisfied by the current value of relvar S as given in Figure 3-1? Which hold in relvar S? Which are irreducible with respect to relvar S?

5.4   Prove Heath's Theorem (original version). Prove also that the converse of that theorem isn't valid. *Note:* In this connection, see also Exercise 11.3 in Chapter 11.

5.5   What exactly does it mean to say an FD is implied by a superkey? Or a key?

5.6   Here's a predicate:

On day D during period P, student S is attending lesson L, which is being taught by teacher T in classroom C, where D is a day of the week (Monday-Friday) and P is a period (1-8) within the day. Lessons are one period in duration and have a lesson identifier L that's unique with respect to all lessons taught in the week.

Design a set of BCNF relvars for this database. What are the keys?

5.7   Design a database for the following. The entities to be represented are employees and programmers. Every programmer is an employee, but not every employee is a programmer. Employees have an employee number, name, and salary. Programmers have a (single) programming language skill. What difference would it make to your design if programmers could have two or more such skills?

5.8   The definition of *key* given in the body of the chapter is somewhat different in form from the definition given in Chapter 4. Are those definitions logically equivalent?

Answers

5.1   The join of a single relation, JOIN{*r*}, is just *r*; the join of no relations at all, JOIN{ }, is TABLE_DEE (the only relation of degree zero and cardinality one). For further explanation, see *SQL and Relational Theory*.

5.2   See the body of the chapter.

5.3   FDs c. and d. (only) are trivial. All eight FDs a. – h. are satisfied by the current value of relvar S. All but h. hold in relvar S. FDs a., c., e., and g. are irreducible with respect to relvar S; FDs b., d., and f. are reducible. (As for h., the question of irreducibility doesn't arise, since that FD doesn't hold in the relvar. Check the definition of FD irreducibility if you don't immediately grasp this point.)

5.4   The original version of Heath's Theorem says that if (a) relation *r* has heading *H*, (b) *X*, *Y*, and *Z* are subsets of *H* whose union is equal to *H*, and (c) *r* satisfies the FD $X \to Y$, then (d) *r* is equal to the join of its projections on *XY* and *XZ* (where *XY* denotes the union of *X* and *Y*, and similarly for *XZ*). In what follows, I show a proof of this theorem in excruciating detail. *Note:* The proof makes much use of expressions of the form "$t \in r$." This expression can be read as "tuple *t* appears in relation *r*."

First consider the simplest possible case, in which X, Y, and Z are singleton sets (i.e., contain just one attribute each). Let the attributes in question be A, B, and C, respectively. Now, we know from the answer to Exercise 3.2 in Chapter 3 that no tuple of r is lost by taking the projections $r1$ of r on XY (i.e., on $\{A,B\}$) and $r2$ of r on XZ (i.e., on $\{A,C\}$), respectively, and then joining $r1$ and $r2$ back together again. I now show that, conversely, every tuple of the join is indeed a tuple of r (in other words, the join doesn't generate any "spurious" tuples). Let $(a,b,c) \in$ JOIN $\{r1,r2\}$. In order to generate such a tuple in the join, we must have $(a,b) \in r1$ and $(a,c) \in r2$. Hence there must exist tuples $(a,b,c') \in r$ and $(a,b',c) \in r$ for some b' and some c'. But r satisfies $\{A\} \to \{B\}$; hence $b = b'$, and so $(a,b,c) \in r$.

The next simplest case is the one in which X, Y, and Z aren't necessarily singleton sets but are pairwise disjoint. In this case, we can effectively regard the attributes constituting X as a single attribute (and similarly for Y and Z), and the argument of the previous paragraph then applies directly.

We now need to consider what happens if X, Y, and Z aren't pairwise disjoint. There are three cases to consider: X and Y not disjoint, X and Z not disjoint, and Y and Z not disjoint.

First, then, let X and Y not be disjoint, but let X and Z be disjoint and let Y and Z be disjoint (hence $Z = H - XY$). Recall now that if $X \to Y$ is satisfied, then so is $X \to Y'$ for all subsets Y' of Y. Hence the FD $X \to Y - X$ is satisfied. But X and $Y - X$ are disjoint; by the previous result, therefore, r is equal to the join of its projections on (a) the union of X and $Y - X$ and (b) XZ. But (again) X and $Y - X$ are disjoint, so their union is equal to XY. So the theorem applies in this case also, and we can (and I will) assume without loss of generality in the remainder of the proof that X and Y are disjoint.

Now let X and Z not be disjoint, but let Y and Z be disjoint. By the previous result, then, r is equal to the join of its projections on (a) XY and (b) the union of X and $Z - X$. But the union of X and $Z - X$ is equal to XZ. So the theorem applies in this case also, and we can (and I will) assume without loss of generality in the remainder of the proof that X and Z are disjoint.

Now let Y and Z not be disjoint. Let $W = Z - Y$. Since r satisfies the FD $X \to Y$, then, it also satisfies the FD $X \to Y - W$, and $Y - W$ and Z are disjoint. By the previous result, therefore, r is equal to the join of its projections on (a) the union of X and $Y - W$ and (b) XZ. I now appeal to a lemma, easily proved (see below), to the effect that if (a) $r1$ and $r2$ are projections of r such that JOIN$\{r1,r2\} = r$, (b) H' is a subset of H but a superset of the heading of $r1$, and (c) r' is the projection of r on H', then (d) JOIN$\{r',r2\} = r$; in other words, loosely, $r1$ can be extended with arbitrary attributes of $r2$ without altering the result of the join. From this lemma, it follows immediately that r is equal to the join of its projections on XY and XZ; so the theorem applies in this case also.

Conclusion: Heath's Theorem is valid in all possible cases.

Lemma: Let r have heading H and let H be partitioned into A, B, C, and D, and assume for simplicity that none of these four subsets is empty. (Extending the proof to cover the case where that assumption fails to hold is left as a subsidiary exercise.) Without loss of generality, we can treat A, B, C, and D as if they were individual attributes. So let $r1 = R\{A,B\}$ and $r2 = r\{B,C,D\}$, and let $(a,b) \in r1$ and $(b,c,d) \in r2$. Since $r = $ JOIN$\{r1,r2\}$, it follows that $(a,b,c,d) \in r$; hence $(a,b,c) \in r\{A,B,C\}$ and $(b,c,d) \in r\{B,C,D\}$; hence $(a,b,c,d) \in$ JOIN$\{r\{A,B,C\},r\{B,C,D\}\}$. The desired result follows—$r\{B,C,D\}$ is $r2$, and $r\{A,B,C\}$ can be taken as r', with $H' = \{A,B,C\}$.

The converse of Heath's Theorem would say that if relation r is equal to the join of its projections on XY and XZ, then r satisfies the FD $X \to Y$. This converse is false. To show this is so, it's sufficient to exhibit a counterexample. So consider a relvar CTX, with attributes CNO (course), TNO (teacher), and XNO (textbook), and predicate *Course CNO can be taught by teacher TNO and uses textbook XNO*. Here's a sample value for this relvar:

CNO	TNO	XNO
C1	T1	X1
C1	T1	X2
C1	T2	X1
C1	T2	X2

This sample value is equal to the join of its projections on {CNO,TNO} and {CNO,XNO}, but it clearly fails to satisfy the FD {CNO} → {TNO} (or the FD {CNO → {XNO}, come to that). *Note:* I'll have more to say about this particular example in Chapter 12.

5.5   See the body of the chapter.

5.6   Suppose we start with a relvar with attributes D, P, S, L, T, and C corresponding to parameters of the predicate in the obvious way. Then the following nontrivial FDs hold in that relvar:

```
{ L }           → { D , P , C , T }
{ D , P , C } → { L , T }
{ D , P , T } → { L , C }
{ D , P , S } → { L , C , T }
```

A possible set of BCNF relvars (in outline) is:[8]

```
SCHEDULE { L , D , P , C , T }
        KEY { L }
        KEY { D , P , C }
        KEY { D , P , T }

STUDYING { S , L }
        KEY { S , L }
```

Note that the FD {D,P,S} → {L,C,T} is "lost" in this decomposition (see Chapter 6).

5.7   The simplest design (in outline) is:

```
EMP  { ENO , ENAME , SALARY }
     KEY { ENO }

PGMR { ENO , LANG }
     KEY { ENO }
     FOREIGN KEY { ENO } REFERENCES EMP
```

---

[8]*Subsidiary exercise:* What are the predicates for these relvars?

Every employee has a tuple in EMP (and EMP has no other tuples). Employees who happen to be programmers additionally have a tuple in PGMR (and PGMR has no other tuples). Note that the join of EMP and PGMR gives full information—employee number, name, salary, and language skill—for programmers (only).

The only significant difference if programmers could have two or more language skills is that relvar PGMR would be "all key" (i.e., its sole key would be {ENO,LANG}), thus:

```
PGMR { ENO , LANG }
      KEY { ENO , LANG }
      FOREIGN KEY { ENO } REFERENCES EMP
```

5.8   Yes, they are (of course!).

CHAPTER 6

Preserving FDs

Nature does require
Her times of preservation

—William Shakespeare: *Henry VIII* (1613)

Once again consider our usual suppliers relvar S. Since {SNO} is a key, that relvar is certainly subject to the FD {SNO} → {STATUS}. Thus, taking X as {SNO}, Y as {STATUS}, and Z as {SNAME,CITY}, Heath's Theorem tells us we can decompose that relvar into relvars SNC and ST, where SNC has heading {SNO,SNAME,CITY} and ST has heading {SNO,STATUS}. Sample values for SNC and ST corresponding to the value shown for S in Figure 3-1 are shown in Figure 6-1:

SNC

SNO	SNAME	CITY
S1	Smith	London
S2	Jones	Paris
S3	Blake	Paris
S4	Clark	London
S5	Adams	Athens

ST

SNO	STATUS
S1	20
S2	30
S3	30
S4	20
S5	30

Figure 6-1. *Relvars SNC and ST—sample values*

In this decomposition:

- Relvars SNC and ST are both in BCNF—{SNO} is the key for both, and the only nontrivial FDs that hold in those relvars are "arrows out of superkeys."

- What's more, the decomposition is certainly nonloss (as is in fact guaranteed by Heath's Theorem)—if we join SNC and ST together, we get back to S.

117

© C. J. Date 2019
C. J. Date, *Database Design and Relational Theory*, https://doi.org/10.1007/978-1-4842-5540-7_6

- However, *the FD {CITY} → {STATUS} has been lost*—by which I mean, of course, that it's been replaced by a certain multirelvar constraint, as explained in the previous chapter.[1] The multirelvar constraint in question can be stated as follows:

```
CONSTRAINT ... WITH ( SNCT := JOIN { SNC , ST } ) :
                  COUNT ( SNCT { CITY } ) =
                  COUNT ( SNCT { CITY , STATUS } ) ;
```

Explanation: What this constraint says is that if we join SNC and ST, we get a result—call it SNCT—in which the number of distinct cities is equal to the number of distinct city / status pairs. And the fact that this latter property holds is equivalent to saying that the FD {CITY} → {STATUS} holds in that join, and hence in the original relvar S also (since the decomposition was nonloss, meaning S and that join SNCT are logically identical).

So we've "lost" an FD. What are the implications? Well, certainly the multirelvar constraint that replaces it is harder to state, as we've just seen. More to the point, perhaps, it's harder to enforce: harder, that is, than it would have been with the preferred decomposition into projections SNC and CT, as illustrated in Figure 3-2 in Chapter 3.[2] For example, suppose we update relvar SNC to change the city for supplier S1 from London to Athens; then we must also update relvar ST to change the status for supplier S1 from 20 to 30—because if we don't, then joining SNC and ST back together will produce a result that isn't a legitimate value for relvar S. (By contrast, if we update relvar SNC to change the city for supplier S2 from Paris to Athens, then we *don't* have to update relvar ST as well—but we still have to inspect relvar ST in order to determine that fact.)

---

[1]To say an FD is "lost" in such circumstances is usual but is also (as explained at the end of the section "Boyce/Codd Normal Form Revisited" in the previous chapter) a trifle inappropriate—to repeat, what's really happening here is that the FD in question has been replaced by another constraint. However, the present situation differs from that described in the previous chapter in that the new constraint isn't enforced automatically as a logical consequence of enforcing certain other constraints. That's the point.

[2]There might be performance penalties, too. Now, I shouldn't really mention this fact; as I said in Chapter 1, I never want performance considerations to be the driving force behind my logical design. But in the case at hand, performance is just an additional point that happens to reinforce my main argument.

It might be possible, given a well architected DBMS, to get the system to do that necessary inspection of relvar ST "automatically," instead of the user having to do it. It might even be possible to get the system to perform any necessary additional updates "automatically," too. Even in such a system, however, it's still the case that the constraint is harder to enforce (i.e., more work still has to be done, even if it's done by the system and not the user). In any case, such possibilities are just a pipedream at the time of writing—today's commercial products mostly don't even allow multirelvar constraints to be stated, in general, let alone enforce them; the foregoing possibilities are out of reach today, and dealing with (and in particular enforcing) such constraints is thus the user's responsibility.

So the message is: Try to choose a decomposition that preserves FDs instead of one that loses them. (In the case at hand, replacing the projection on {SNO,STATUS} by that on {CITY,STATUS} solves the problem.) Loosely speaking, in other words, if the FD $X \rightarrow Y$ holds in the original relvar, try not to choose a decomposition in which X winds up in one relvar and Y in another. *Note:* Of course, I'm assuming here that the decomposition isn't being done on the basis of that FD $X \rightarrow Y$ itself—because if it is, we'll effectively wind up with two X's, one of which will be in the same relvar as Y (necessarily so) and the other won't. I'm also assuming, tacitly, that $X \rightarrow Y$ is part of what's called an *irreducible cover* for the total set of FDs that hold in the original relvar. I'll be discussing irreducible covers later in this chapter.

An Unfortunate Conflict

The basic idea of FD preservation is fairly straightforward; unfortunately, however, there are complications, and it turns out that there's quite a bit more that needs to be said on the subject. By way of a gentle introduction to some of those complications, I'll present what some might regard as a pathological example. We're given a relvar SJT with attributes S (student), J (subject), and T (teacher), and predicate *Student S is taught subject J by teacher T.* The following business rules apply:[3]

- For each subject, each student of that subject is taught by only one teacher.

- Each teacher teaches only one subject.

- Each student studies several subjects, and hence is taught by several teachers (in general).

- Each subject is studied by several students (in general).

- Each subject is taught by several teachers (in general).

- Distinct students of the same subject might or might not be taught that subject by the same teacher.

A sample value for this relvar that conforms to these rules is shown in Figure 6-2:

S	J	T
Smith	Math	Prof. White
Smith	Physics	Prof. Green
Jones	Math	Prof. White
Jones	Physics	Prof. Brown

Figure 6-2. *Sample value for relvar SJT*

What are the FDs for relvar SJT? From the first business rule, we have $\{S,J\} \rightarrow \{T\}$. From the second, we have $\{T\} \rightarrow \{J\}$. A careful analysis of the remaining rules shows that no other FDs hold other than ones that are either trivial or reducible (or both). Thus, the only nontrivial, irreducible FDs that hold are these two:

```
{ S , J } → { T }
{ T }     → { J }
```

---

[3]This is the first time we've encountered the term *business rule* in this book, but we'll see many more examples of its use in later chapters. Basically, a business rule is a statement, usually expressed (as here) somewhat informally in natural language, that's supposed to capture some aspect of what the data in the database means and/or how it's constrained. There's no consensus on any more precise definition of the term, though most writers would at least agree that relvar predicates are an important special case. See Appendix A for further discussion.

So what are the keys? Well, {S,J} is a key, since the entire heading is clearly functionally dependent on {S,J} and not on any proper subset of {S,J}. Also, {S,T} is a key, because:

a. It's certainly the case, given that the FD {T} → {J} holds, that the entire heading is functionally dependent on {S,T}.

b. It's also the case, given that the FDs {S} → {J} and {T} → {S} do *not* hold, that the entire heading isn't functionally dependent on any proper subset of {S,T}.

So there are two keys, {S,J} and {S,T}.[4] Perhaps more to the point, {T} is *not* a key, and so relvar SJT is subject to an FD that's not "an arrow out of a key" (i.e., it's not implied by keys, to state the matter a trifle more formally). As a consequence, the relvar isn't in BCNF, though it is in 3NF. (*Exercise:* Check this claim.) And it suffers from redundancy; for example, given the sample value shown in Figure 6-2, the fact that Professor White teaches Math appears twice. As you would expect, therefore, it also suffers from update anomalies; for example, with respect to Figure 6-2 again, we can't delete the fact that Jones is studying Physics without losing the information that Professor Brown teaches Physics.

Now, we can get over these problems by decomposing the relvar appropriately. Applying Heath's Theorem to the FD {T} → {J} (take *X*, *Y*, and *Z* to be {T}, {J}, and {S}, respectively), we obtain the following nonloss decomposition:

```
TJ { T , J }
   KEY { T }

TS { T , S }
   KEY { T , S }
```

I'll leave it as another exercise for you (a) to show the values of these two relvars corresponding to the value of SJT shown in Figure 6-2, (b) to show that these relvars are in BCNF, and (c) to check that the decomposition does in fact avoid the redundancy and update anomalies mentioned above. Observe in particular that the FD {T} → {J} becomes a key constraint in this decomposition; in the original design, by contrast, it wasn't, and so it had to be stated and enforced separately (over and above the key constraints, I mean).

---

[4]Which overlap, as you can see. By the way, as with relvar SNP in Chapter 4, I've chosen not to make either of those keys primary, which is why there's no double underlining in Figure 6-2.

So far, so good. But there's another problem. The fact is, although the decomposition into TJ and TS does indeed solve certain problems, it unfortunately introduces others. To be specific, the FD

$$\{\ S\ ,\ J\ \}\ \rightarrow\ \{\ T\ \}$$

is lost (certainly it isn't implied by the FD $\{T\} \rightarrow \{J\}$, which is the only nontrivial FD to hold in the result of the decomposition). As a consequence, relvars TJ and TS can't be independently updated. For example, an attempt to insert the tuple

```
( Smith , Prof. Brown )
```

into TS must be rejected, because Professor Brown teaches Physics and Smith is already being taught Physics by Professor Green; yet this fact can't be detected without inspecting TJ.

To sum up, what the example shows is as follows: There are two objectives we typically aim for in nonloss decomposition, BCNF projections and FD preservation, and, sadly, these objectives can be in conflict with one another. In other words, it isn't always possible to achieve both.

Now, at this point in an earlier draft of this chapter, I wrote the following:

> So which objective do we give up on? Well, I'd tell you if I could, but I can't. What the SJT example demonstrates is that the theory of normalization, important though it is, isn't enough as it stands; I mean, there are questions it doesn't answer. So the message is: *We need more science!* Normalization theory is certainly scientific, but it doesn't solve all design problems.

At the prompting of one of my reviewers, however, I've come to the conclusion that the foregoing paragraph is probably overstated. It's not so much more science we need here, it's better implementations! That is, the main argument for tolerating a less than properly normalized design, in cases like the one at hand, is the fact that today's DBMSs make it quite awkward to deal with multirelvar constraints like the "lost" FD in the example. So let me set a stake in the ground and state for the record that dependency preservation is probably the objective to give up on, in those cases in which there's a conflict.[5]

---

[5]In the case at hand, of course, we *must* decompose the relvar as indicated if we want to be able to record the fact that (say) Professor Black teaches physics even though Professor Black has no students at the moment.

Another Example

I suggested at the beginning of the previous section that the SJT example might be considered pathological. Now, however, I'm going to claim it's not, not entirely; I'm going to give several more examples that (as far as I'm concerned) demonstrate that the issue of FD preservation arises more often than you might think.

Normalization as commonly perceived is a process of stepping from 1NF to 2NF to 3NF (etc.) in sequence. Let's agree to refer to that process as commonly perceived—i.e., stepping from 1NF to 2NF to 3NF (etc.) in sequence—as "the conventional normalization procedure." In this section and the next two, then, I want to present a series of examples to demonstrate that the conventional normalization procedure isn't necessarily a good idea if followed too blindly. My first example involves a relvar that looks like this:

RX1 { SNO , PNO , CITY , STATUS , QTY }

The name RX1 stands for "relvar example 1"; the predicate is *Supplier SNO is located in city CITY, which has status STATUS, and supplies part PNO in quantity QTY.* (I ignore supplier names for simplicity.) Let's assume, reasonably enough, that the following FDs hold in this relvar:

```
{ SNO }        → { CITY }
{ CITY }       → { STATUS }
{ SNO , PNO } → { QTY }
```

Now, it's intuitively obvious that the following FDs hold as well, implicitly:[6]

```
{ SNO }        → { STATUS }
{ SNO , PNO } → { CITY , STATUS }
```

In fact, the last of these FDs can be expanded to {SNO,PNO} → H, where H is the entire heading; in other words, {SNO,PNO} is a key for relvar RX1.

Recall now that a relvar R is in 2NF if and only if, for every key K and every nonkey attribute A, the FD $K \rightarrow \{A\}$ is irreducible. Clearly, then, RX1 isn't in 2NF, because the FD {SNO,PNO} → {CITY} is "an FD out of a key" of RX1 but isn't irreducible; to be specific, it isn't irreducible because the FD {SNO} → {CITY} also holds in that relvar. The conventional normalization procedure would thus recommend that we decompose the

---

[6]I'll have quite a lot more to say on the notion of FDs holding implicitly ("implicit FDs") in the next chapter, also in Chapter 11.

relvar by applying Heath's Theorem to that FD {SNO} → {CITY}. But if we do, then this is what we get:

```
RX1A { SNO , CITY }
    KEY { SNO }

RX1B { SNO , PNO , STATUS , QTY }
    KEY { SNO , PNO }
```

Observe now that the FD {CITY} → {STATUS} is lost in this decomposition. So one immediate lesson from this example is that the issue of FD preservation can be relevant to the step from 1NF to 2NF—not just to the step from 3NF to BCNF, which was the step illustrated by the SJT example in the previous section.

Relvar RX1A here is certainly in 2NF. By contrast, relvar RX1B isn't, because the FD {SNO,PNO} → {STATUS} is reducible. So we can apply Heath's Theorem again to decompose it into its projections on {SNO,STATUS} and {SNO,PNO,QTY}, both of which are in 2NF; however, the damage has already been done, as it were—the FD {CITY} → {STATUS} has already been lost.

How can we preserve the FD in this example? One answer is: By decomposing on the basis, not of the FD {SNO} → {CITY}, but rather of the FD {SNO} → {CITY,STATUS}. Note carefully, however, that this FD isn't one of the FDs originally listed explicitly, nor is it one of the ones I said were obviously implied by those explicit ones; it's thus unlikely to have been chosen as a basis for decomposition in the conventional normalization procedure. Nevertheless, suppose we do choose it and perform the corresponding decomposition. Here's the result:

```
RX1A' { SNO , CITY , STATUS }
    KEY { SNO }

RX1B' { SNO , PNO , QTY }
    KEY { SNO , PNO }
```

In this decomposition, STATUS appears in the relvar with key {SNO} and not the relvar with key {SNO,PNO}, and the FD {CITY} → {STATUS} is thereby preserved. *Note:* Of course, relvar RX1A' here is still not in 3NF, so we would probably want to decompose it further. Again, however, we need to be a little careful; to be specific, we need to decompose on the basis of the FD {CITY} → {STATUS}, not {SNO} → {STATUS}, or we'll lose an FD again. But {CITY} → {STATUS} is the FD the conventional normalization procedure would tell us to use, so there shouldn't be a problem here.

Now, an alternative to the foregoing would be to decompose the original relvar RX1 on the basis of the FD {CITY} → {STATUS}, yielding:

```
RX1A″ { CITY , STATUS }
      KEY { CITY }

RX1B″ { SNO , PNO , CITY , QTY }
      KEY { SNO , PNO }
```

This decomposition also preserves the FD {CITY} → {STATUS}. Note, however, that this FD isn't the one that caused the original 2NF violation in relvar RX1 (it isn't "an arrow out of a proper subkey"); again, therefore, it's quite unlikely in practice, if we're following the conventional normalization procedure, that we would have chosen it as a basis for decomposition at this stage. Note also that relvar RX1B″ here is still not in 3NF, so we would probably want to decompose it further. I'll leave the details of that further decomposition for you to think about.

… And Another

Let's look at another example. Suppose suppliers are partitioned into classes (C1, C2, etc.), so we have a relvar RX2 that looks like this (I'll ignore supplier names for simplicity, as I did in the RX1 example):

```
RX2 { SNO , CLASS , CITY , STATUS }
    KEY { SNO }
```

The predicate is *Supplier SNO is in class CLASS, is located in city CITY, and has status STATUS.* Suppose also that (a) each class has just one status and (b) each city has just one status as well, but that (c) classes and cities are otherwise quite independent of each other. Then the following FDs hold:

```
{ CLASS } → { STATUS }
{ CITY }  → { STATUS }
```

Note: I'm also assuming there's a business rule in effect that says that, for any given supplier, the city status is equal to the class status (that's why we're able to get away with just one STATUS attribute instead of two).[7]

Recall now that a relvar *R* is in 3NF if and only if, for every nontrivial FD $X \rightarrow Y$ that holds in *R*, either *X* is a superkey or *Y* is a subkey (or both). Clearly, then, RX2 isn't in 3NF, because in the FD {CITY} → {STATUS}, {CITY} isn't a superkey and {STATUS} isn't a subkey. The conventional normalization procedure would thus recommend that we decompose the relvar by applying Heath's Theorem to that FD {CITY} → {STATUS}. But if we do, this is what we get (two projection relvars both in 3NF):

```
RX2A { CITY , STATUS }
    KEY { CITY }

RX2B { SNO , CLASS , CITY }
    KEY { SNO }
```

Observe now that the FD {CLASS} → {STATUS} is lost in this decomposition. (Of course, if we had done the decomposition on the basis of that FD instead of the FD {CITY} → {STATUS}, then this latter FD would have been lost instead.) So now we see the issue of FD preservation can also be relevant to the step from 2NF to 3NF.

Now, we can preserve the FD in this example by decomposing on the basis of the FD {SNO} → {CLASS,CITY}—though once again this FD is unlikely to have been chosen as a basis for decomposition, since it wasn't stated explicitly.[8] Be that as it may, here's the result:

```
RX2A' { CLASS , CITY , STATUS }
    KEY { CLASS , CITY }

RX2B' { SNO , CLASS , CITY }
    KEY { SNO }
```

---

[7]So a more accurate version of the predicate would be: *Supplier SNO is in class CLASS (which has status STATUS) and is located in city CITY (which also has status STATUS).*

[8]Nor is it likely to have been, either, since {SNO} is a key (in fact the only key) for relvar RX2. At most we might expect to see two FDs stated separately, viz., {SNO} → {CLASS} and {SNO} → {CITY}—but even that's pretty unlikely.

In this decomposition, {CLASS,CITY} is a (composite) foreign key in RX2B′, referencing RX2A′. Relvar RX2B′ is in 3NF. However, relvar R2XA′ isn't even in 2NF, since the FD {CLASS,CITY} → {STATUS} is clearly reducible. So if we decide to keep that relvar, the FDs {CLASS} → {STATUS} and {CITY} → {STATUS} will have to be separately stated and enforced.[9] Alternatively, we could decompose the relvar into its projections on {CLASS,STATUS} and {CITY,STATUS}, in which case an appropriate multirelvar constraint will have to be separately stated and enforced. *Exercise:* What would that constraint look like?

... And Still Another

Consider now a revised version of the example from the previous section in which (a) suppliers are again partitioned into classes, but (b) each class now has just one city (where each city in turn has just one status, as before). So we have a relvar RX3 that looks like this (once again I ignore supplier names for simplicity):

```
RX3 { SNO , CLASS , CITY , STATUS }
```

In fact, of course, RX3 has the same heading as RX2 did, but the predicate is different: *Supplier SNO is in class CLASS, which has city CITY, which has status STATUS.* The following FDs hold among others:

```
{ SNO }   → { CLASS }
{ CLASS } → { CITY }
{ CITY }  → { STATUS }
```

Relvar RX3 isn't in 3NF, because in the FD {CLASS} → {CITY}, {CLASS} isn't a superkey and {CITY} isn't a subkey. (The same goes for {CITY} → {STATUS}, mutatis mutandis.) The conventional normalization procedure would thus recommend that we

---

[9]Note, moreover, that relvar RX2A′ isn't really even a correct design, since it prohibits tuples in which the specified class and city have different status values. To put it another way, the predicate for that relvar isn't just *Class CLASS and city CITY have status STATUS*—rather, it's something like this: *There exists some supplier s such that s has class CLASS and city CITY, both of which have status STATUS.*

decompose the relvar by applying Heath's Theorem to that FD {CLASS} → {CITY}. But if we do, this is what we get:

```
RX3A { CLASS , CITY }
    KEY { CLASS }

RX3B { SNO , CLASS , STATUS }
    KEY { SNO }
```

In this decomposition, RX3A is in 3NF but RX3B is only in 2NF—and as you can see, the FD {CITY} → {STATUS} is lost. In fact, it would have been better to decompose on the basis of that FD {CITY} → {STATUS}:

```
RX3A' { CITY , STATUS }
    KEY { CITY }

RX3B' { SNO , CLASS , CITY }
    KEY { SNO }
```

RX3A' is in 3NF while RX3B' is only in 2NF, but at least the FD {CITY} → {STATUS} has been preserved. What's more, we can now go on to decompose RX3B' on the basis of the FD {CLASS} → {CITY} to obtain:

```
RX3BA' { CLASS , CITY }
     KEY { CLASS }

RX3BB' { SNO , CLASS }
     KEY { SNO }
```

These relvars are both in 3NF.

So now we've seen four different examples of decompositions in which FDs are or might be lost. There's a lot more that could be said on the topic, but one clear message is: The conventional normalization procedure—in fact, the one that's often taught in practice!—is inadequate in several respects. To be specific:

- Conventional wisdom has it that FD preservation is relevant only to the step from 3NF to BCNF, but as we've seen such isn't necessarily the case.

- The FDs typically suggested by the conventional normalization procedure as the basis for decomposition aren't necessarily the best ones to use.

- That procedure also assumes the best design can be found by stepping from 1NF to 2NF to 3NF (etc.) in sequence, which again isn't necessarily the case.

Of course, the very nomenclature of "first," "second," etc. reinforces this last perception; but that nomenclature is really nothing more than a historical accident, in a way. I mean, if the first of the normal forms to be defined had been BCNF—which it easily could have been, since the definition is so conceptually simple, involving as it does no mention of FD irreducibility, nonkey attributes, subkeys, 1NF, 2NF, or 3NF—then there would really never have been any need to call out 2NF and 3NF as specific normal forms, as such, at all.[10]

A Procedure that Works

Here now is a procedure that's guaranteed to produce a decomposition in which all relvars are in 3NF (though not necessarily BCNF) and all FDs are preserved.[11] For convenience, I'll refer to it in what follows as *the 3NF procedure*. The input is a relvar *R* and what's called an *irreducible cover*, *C* say, for the FDs that hold in R. I'll explain what an irreducible cover is in a few moments—by the way, there's that word *irreducible* again—but let me state the procedure first:

1. Let *S* be a set of headings. Initialize *S* to the empty set, { }.

2. Let *X* be the left side (the determinant) of some FD in *C*; let the complete set of FDs in *C* with left side *X* be $X \rightarrow Y1, ..., X \rightarrow Yn$; and let the union of *Y1, ... Yn* be *Y*. Add the union of *X* and *Y* to *S*. Perform this step for each distinct *X*.

3. Let *U* be the set of attributes of *R* not contained in any element of *S*. If *U* is nonempty, add *U* to *S*.

4. If no element of *S* is a superkey for *R*, add some key *K* of *R* to *S*.

---

[10]In support of this contention, I'd like to quote something Codd himself had to say in the paper in which he introduced 2NF and 3NF (see Appendix D): "The basic ideas underlying [2NF and 3NF] are simple, but they have many subtle ramifications. The author has found that numerous examples are needed to explain and motivate the precise definitions of these normal forms."

[11]I give this procedure partly just for historical reasons. You can skip it if you like.

At the conclusion of this procedure, the elements of S are the headings of a set of 3NF relvars into which R can be nonloss decomposed without losing any FDs. Note in particular that the procedure makes no explicit mention of 2NF, not even as some kind of stepping stone.

So how does it work? Clearly, the notion of an irreducible cover is important. In order to explain that notion, let me first call out something I've appealed to several times already in passing: namely, the fact that *some FDs imply others*. As a simple example, the FDs $X \rightarrow Y$ and $Y \rightarrow Z$ together imply the FD $X \rightarrow Z$—by which I mean, if the first two FDs are satisfied by relation r, then the third one must be satisfied by r as well. Or, perhaps more to the point: If the first two hold in relvar R, then the third one must hold in R as well. We saw an illustration in the previous section, in connection with relvar RX3, where the FDs {CLASS} $\rightarrow$ {CITY} and {CITY} $\rightarrow$ {STATUS} both held, and so the FD {CLASS} $\rightarrow$ {STATUS} held as well.

So some FDs imply others. Given a set F of FDs, then, we can sensibly talk about a *cover* for F. Here's the definition:

> **Definition (cover):** A cover for a set F of FDs is a set C of FDs such that every FD in F is implied by the FDs in C.

As a trivial example, let F be the set:

$$\{ \ X \rightarrow Y \ , \ Y \rightarrow Z \ , \ X \rightarrow Z \ \}$$

Then the following are both covers for F:

$$\{ \ X \rightarrow Y \ , \ Y \rightarrow Z \ \}$$

$$\{ \ X \rightarrow Y \ , \ Y \rightarrow Z \ , \ X \rightarrow Z \ \}$$

This example illustrates two points right away: First, covers aren't unique, in general; second, any set of FDs is certainly a cover for itself, because among other things every FD implies itself. A third and more important point is the following: Enforcing the FDs in a cover C for a given set F will "automatically" enforce those in that set F. Thus, given some set F of FDs that need to be enforced, it's sufficient to find some cover C for F and enforce the FDs in C instead. (In fact, it's sufficient to enforce the FDs in an *irreducible* cover for F, as will quickly become clear.)

Now I can define what it means for a cover to be irreducible:

> **Definition (irreducible cover):** A cover *C* for a set *F* of FDs
> is irreducible if and only if it possesses all of the following
> properties:
>
> 1. *Singleton dependant:* Every FD in *C* has just one attribute on
>   the right side.
>
> 2. *Irreducible determinant:* Every FD in *C* is itself irreducible.[12]
>
> 3. *No redundant FDs:* No FD can be discarded from *C* without
>   losing the property that *C* is a cover for *F*.

Of course, the following question arises immediately: Given some specific set of FDs, how can we find an irreducible cover for that set? I'll answer this question properly in the next chapter. For now, let me just give an example—viz., the following set of FDs, which constitute an irreducible cover for the FDs that hold in our usual suppliers relvar S:

```
{ SNO }  → { SNAME }
{ SNO }  → { CITY }
{ CITY } → { STATUS }
```

To elaborate briefly: It's certainly the case that every FD that holds in S is implied by these three FDs taken together, so these three certainly constitute a cover. Also, each of the three has a singleton dependant; no attribute can be dropped from any of the three determinants; and none of the three FDs can be discarded. Thus, it follows that the cover is in fact an irreducible one. By contrast, the following sets of FDs are also covers for the FDs that hold in S, but they're not irreducible (in each case, why not?):

```
1. { SNO }  → { SNAME , CITY }
   { CITY } → { STATUS }
```

---

[12]I'm being sloppy here. Recall from Chapters 4 and 5 that FD irreducibility is defined only with respect to some relvar—but I haven't said anything here about the FDs in *F* as holding in any relvar, and there's thus no context that would allow us to talk legitimately about FDs being irreducible. What I mean, however, is that no attribute can be discarded from the left side of any FD in *C* without losing the property that *C* is a cover for *F*.

2. { SNO , SNAME } → { CITY }
   { SNO }   → { SNAME }
   { CITY }   → { STATUS }

3. { SNO } → { SNAME }
   { SNO } → { CITY }
   { CITY } → { STATUS }
   { SNO } → { STATUS }

Now let's get back to the 3NF procedure. In particular, let's see how it works out for the SJT example.[13] Just to remind you, the relvar had attributes S, J, and T; keys {S,J} and {S,T}; and was subject to the FD {T} → {J}. So these FDs hold:

{ S , J } → { T }
{ S , T } → { J }
{ T }   → { J }

It's easy to see, however, that the FD {S,T} → {J} is redundant here—in fact I effectively assumed as much when I first discussed this example earlier in the chapter—and hence that the other two FDs together form an irreducible cover (which I'll call C):

{ S , J } → { T }
{ T }   → { J }

Now we can apply the 3NF procedure. We start with an empty set of headings S. The second step does two things: It gathers together FDs in C that have the same left side—something that's effectively already been done in the example—and then adds the sets (actually headings)

{ S , J , T }
{ T , J }

to S. The third step has no effect, since every attribute of the original relvar is now contained in at least one element of S. The last step also has no effect, since the element {S,J,T} of S is a superkey for the original relvar. Overall, therefore, the 3NF procedure tells

---

[13]Of course SJT is already in 3NF, but we can still apply the procedure to it—and I have my reasons, which I trust will quickly become apparent, for wanting to do so.

us that relvar S can be nonloss decomposed, in an FD preserving way, into its projections on {S,J,T} and {T,J}. Points arising:

- The projection on {S,J,T} is of course identical to the original relvar!— in other words, it's an *identity projection* (see the next section), and there isn't much decomposition, as such, going on here.

- There doesn't actually seem to be much point in maintaining the second relvar (i.e., the projection on {T,J}) as well as the original one, unless we want to be able to say that, e.g., Professor Black teaches Physics without there existing, at the same time, some student who's actually being taught by Professor Black. If we don't want this ability, we probably won't want to maintain that relvar. Thus, the decomposition produced by the 3NF procedure isn't necessarily a *recommended* one—but, to repeat, it's one in which all relvars are in 3NF and all FDs are preserved.

I'll leave it as an exercise (Exercise 6.3) to show what happens when the 3NF procedure is applied to relvars RX1, RX2, and RX3. Meanwhile, I'd like to close this section with a few words regarding BCNF and a possible BCNF procedure.

First, we can add another (fifth) step to the 3NF procedure, as follows:

5. Let Z be an element of S such that the projection P of relvar R on the attributes of Z is not in BCNF; let $X \rightarrow Y$ be an FD of C that holds in P; and let X not be a superkey for P. Replace Z in S by (a) the union of X and Y and (b) the difference $Z - Y$ between Z and Y (in that order). Perform this step for each distinct Z and each distinct X.

Now, the 3NF procedure applied to relvar SJT produced a set S consisting of the headings {T,J} and {S,J,T}. The projection of SJT on {T,J} is in BCNF, but the (identity) projection of SJT on {S,J,T} isn't, because the FD {T} $\rightarrow$ {J} holds in this latter projection and {T} isn't a superkey. Applying Step 5, therefore, we delete the heading {S,J,T} and insert (a) the union of {T} and {J}—but this insertion has no effect, since that union is already an element of S—and (b) the difference between {S,J,T} and {J}, in that order. Thus, S winds up with the following headings as elements:

```
{ S , T }
{ T , J }
```

And these two headings are the headings of a set of BCNF relvars into which SJT can be nonloss decomposed (the keys for those relvars are {S,T} and {T}, respectively). Thus, adding Step 5 to the 3NF procedure converts it into a BCNF procedure, though without any guarantee that FDs will be preserved. (In fact, of course, it's impossible to provide any such guarantee, since we already know that BCNF and FD preservation can be conflicting objectives.) However, any FDs lost are ones that *can't* be preserved without violating BCNF.

Actually we can simplify matters somewhat and go straight to BCNF, bypassing 3NF entirely, using the following procedure (the input is as for the 3NF procedure—i.e., it consists of a relvar R and an irreducible cover C for the FDs that hold in R):

1. Initialize S to contain just the heading of R.

2. (*Same as Step 2 of the 3NF procedure.*) Let X be the left side (the determinant) of some FD in C; let the complete set of FDs in C with left side X be $X \rightarrow Y1, ..., X \rightarrow Yn$; and let the union of $Y1, ... Yn$ be Y. Add the union of X and Y to S. Perform this step for each distinct X.

3. (*Same as Step 5 above.*) Let Z be an element of S such that the projection P of R on the attributes of Z is not in BCNF; let $X \rightarrow Y$ be an FD of C that holds in P; and let X not be a superkey for P. Replace Z in S by (a) the union of X and Y and (b) the difference $Z - Y$ between Z and Y (in that order). Perform this step for each distinct Z and each distinct X.

At the conclusion of this procedure, the elements of S are the headings of a set of BCNF relvars into which R can be nonloss decomposed, though not necessarily without losing FDs. Note that the procedure makes no mention of either 2NF or 3NF.

Identity Decompositions

It's a bit of a digression from the main theme of this chapter, but I'd like to elaborate briefly on the concept of an identity projection. Here's a definition (I define it for relvars, but of course a precisely analogous definition applies to relations as well—and tuples too, come to that):

> **Definition (identity projection):** The identity projection of a given relvar is the projection of that relvar on all of its attributes.

Now, it should be obvious that any relvar can be nonloss decomposed, albeit trivially, into its identity projection. However, some people don't like to think of such a decomposition as being a decomposition, as such, at all (as I said in connection with the SJT example, there isn't much decomposition, as such, going on here). If you happen to be one of those people, then you might prefer the following way of looking at the matter. Let relvar R have heading H. Then it's certainly true that the FD $\{\} \rightarrow \{\}$ holds in R, where $\{\}$ is the empty set of attributes (this FD is trivial, of course, and holds in *every* relvar). By Heath's Theorem, therefore—take X, Y, and Z to be $\{\}$, $\{\}$, and H, respectively—R can be nonloss decomposed into its projections $R1$ and $R2$, where:

1. The heading XY of $R1$ is the union of $\{\}$ and $\{\}$, which reduces to just $\{\}$; i.e., $R1$ is the projection of R on no attributes at all, and its value is either TABLE_DUM, if R is empty, or TABLE_DEE otherwise.[14]

2. The heading XZ of $R2$ is the union of $\{\}$ and H, which reduces to just H; i.e., $R2$ is the projection of R on all of its attributes, or in other words the identity projection of R.

Now, I hope it's clear that this decomposition is nonloss—R is certainly equal to the join of $R1$ and $R2$. (On the other hand, it's also true that the combination of $R1$ and $R2$ fails to meet the usual requirement that both projections should be needed in the reconstruction process.)

While I'm on the subject of what might be called *identity decompositions*, let me remark that any relvar can also always be decomposed (again trivially, but this time "horizontally" instead of "vertically") into the corresponding identity *restriction*.[15] Here's a definition (again I define it for relvars, but of course an analogous concept applies to relations as well, though not this time to tuples):

> **Definition (identity restriction):** The identity restriction of a given relvar R is any restriction of R in which the restriction condition is identically true—in other words, any restriction of R that's logically equivalent to one of the following form:
>
> R WHERE TRUE

---

[14]TABLE_DUM and TABLE_DEE are pet names for, respectively, the unique relation with no attributes and no tuples and the unique relation with no attributes and one tuple (we've met these relations before, in the answer to Exercise 2.8 in Chapter 2). For further discussion, see *SQL and Relational Theory*.

[15]For precise definitions of restriction and the associated notion of a restriction condition, see the answer to Exercise 15.3 in Chapter 15.

Note: In logic, something that's identically true, such as the boolean expression CITY = CITY, is called a *tautology*. Thus, we can say the identity restriction of relvar *R* is any restriction in which the restriction condition is a tautology.

I remark in passing that any given relvar *R* also always has an *empty* restriction,[16] which we can denote thus:

```
R WHERE FALSE
```

The (disjoint!) union of the identity restriction and the empty restriction of a given relvar *R* is of course identically equal to *R*. *Note:* In logic, something that's identically false, such as the boolean expression CITY ≠ CITY, is called a *contradiction*; thus, we can say the empty restriction of relvar *R* is any restriction in which the restriction condition is a contradiction.[17]

More on the Conflict

To revert to the main theme of the chapter: By now we've seen several examples in which FDs might be lost. In most of those examples, we could avoid losing the FD by being careful; in one case, however (the SJT example), the objectives of preserving FDs and BCNF decomposition were genuinely in conflict with each other. So the obvious question arises: Can we characterize those cases where there really is a conflict? The answer is yes; in fact, it's easy to do so.

Let *R* be the relvar we're dealing with, and let *C* be an irreducible cover for the FDs that hold in *R*. Construct an *FD graph* as follows:

1. Create a node for each attribute of *R*.

2. Let $X \rightarrow Y$ be an FD in *C* for which *X* involves two or more attributes; create a "supernode" containing just the nodes for the attributes named in *X*. (If you're doing this on paper, you could draw a circle enclosing the individual attribute nodes.) Supernodes are considered to be nodes. Repeat this step for each FD in *C* for which the determinant involves two or more attributes.

---

[16]So too does any given relation *r*, of course.

[17]The term *contradiction* doesn't mean quite the same in logic as it does in ordinary discourse, but the difference isn't important for present purposes.

3. Let $X \rightarrow Y$ be an FD in C. Draw a directed arc from the node for X to the node for Y. Repeat this step for each FD in C.

4. If and only if the finished graph contains any cycles (where a cycle is a sequence of two or more directed arcs from a node to itself), then R cannot be nonloss decomposed into BCNF projections without losing an FD.

As an exercise, try applying the foregoing procedure to the various examples discussed earlier in the chapter. When you do, you'll quickly understand (if you haven't done so already) what's really going on here. To spell the point out: There's a genuine conflict only if the relvar involves a pattern of FDs akin to the pattern that obtains in the SJT example.

Independent Projections

To close this chapter, I'd like to return to the example I opened it with. Just to remind you, that example involved the nonloss decomposition of our usual suppliers relvar S into its projections SNC on {SNO,SNAME,CITY} and ST on {SNO,STATUS}. That decomposition lost the FD {CITY} $\rightarrow$ {STATUS}, with the consequence that updates to either of the projections sometimes required updates to the other, in order to enforce the constraint that each city has just one status. By contrast, the "sensible" decomposition of S into its projections SNC (on {SNO,SNAME,CITY}) and CT (on {CITY,STATUS}) suffers from no such problem—updates can be made to either projection without regard to the other.[18]

For the sake of the present discussion, let me refer to decompositions like the one into SNC and ST as *bad* and decompositions like the one into SNC and CT as *good*. As we've seen, then, the projections in a good decomposition can be updated independently of each other; for that reason, they're sometimes referred to explicitly as *independent projections*. By contrast, the projections in a bad decomposition aren't independent in that same sense. So we can say that in order to preserve FDs, we want a decomposition in which the projections are independent. And there's a theorem, due to Jorma Rissanen, that can help in this regard. Before I state that theorem, however, let me give a precise definition of what it means for two projections to be independent:

---

[18]Except that there might be a foreign key constraint, or even an equality dependency, between {CITY} in CT and {CITY} in SNC (see Chapter 3).

> **Definition (independent projections):** Projections *R1* and *R2* of relvar *R* are independent if and only if every FD that holds in *R* also holds in the join of *R1* and *R2*.

Here now is the theorem:

> **Rissanen's Theorem:** Let relvar *R*, with heading *H*, have projections *R1* and *R2*, with headings *H1* and *H2*, respectively; further, let *H1* and *H2* both be proper subsets of *H*, let their union be equal to *H*, and let their intersection be nonempty.[19] Then projections *R1* and *R2* are independent if and only if (a) their common attributes constitute a superkey for at least one of them and (b) every FD that holds in *R* is implied by those that hold in at least one of them.

Consider the "good" decomposition of S into its projections SNC and CT. Those two projections are independent, because (a) the set of common attributes is just {CITY} and {CITY} is a superkey—actually a key—for CT, and (b) every FD that holds in S either holds in one of the two projections or is implied by those that do (see the next chapter). By contrast, consider the "bad" decomposition into the projections SNC and ST. Here the projections aren't independent, because the FD {CITY} → {STATUS} can't be inferred from those holding in those projections (though it's at least true that the set of common attributes, {SNO}, is a superkey—actually a key—for both).

As a historical note, I observe that it was Rissanen's work on independent projections (which was done, or at least published, in 1977) that laid the foundation for the theory of what we now call FD preservation.

Exercises

6.1   Relvar SJT from the section "An Unfortunate Conflict" is subject to the FD {S,J} → {T}. Write a **Tutorial D** CONSTRAINT statement to express the multirelvar constraint that replaces this FD if we decompose SJT into its projections TJ and TS on {T,J} and {T,S}, respectively.

---

[19]The condition that the intersection of *H1* and *H2* be nonempty is as in Rissanen's original statement of the theorem but appears to be unnecessary.

6.2 (*Repeated from the body of the chapter.*) Suppose relvar RX2A′ from section "... And Another" is decomposed into its projections on {CLASS,STATUS} and {CITY,STATUS}. As noted in that section, an appropriate multirelvar constraint will now have to be separately stated and enforced. What does that constraint look like?

6.3 The following relvar is intended to represent a set of United States street addresses:

ADDR { STREET , CITY , STATE , ZIP }

Using **Tutorial D** syntax, a typical tuple of this relvar might look like this:

```
TUPLE { STREET '1600 Pennsylvania Ave.' ,
              CITY 'Washington' , STATE 'DC' , ZIP '20500' }
```

Assume, not entirely unrealistically, that the following FDs hold in this relvar and are irreducible:

```
{ STREET , CITY , STATE } → { ZIP }
{ ZIP }                   → { CITY , STATE }
```

How would you decompose this relvar?

6.4 Show the effects of applying the 3NF procedure to relvars RX1, RX3, and RX2 (note the sequence here!) from the body of the chapter.

6.5 Here's a predicate:

Film star S plays role R in movie M, which was directed by director D and released in year Y; further, star S was born on date B and therefore has zodiac sign Z and Chinese zodiac C, and Z and C together determine S's horoscope H.

Give a set of FDs that capture the foregoing state of affairs. State any assumptions you make regarding business rules that might be in effect. Also, apply the BCNF procedure to obtain an appropriate set of BCNF relvars. Does that procedure lose any FDs?

Answers

6.1   CONSTRAINT ... WITH (SJT := JOIN { TJ , TS }) :
                        COUNT (SJT) =
                        COUNT (SJT { S , J }) ;

Or, using the alternative style for constraints described in the answer to Exercise 4.8 in Chapter 4:

CONSTRAINT ... JOIN { TJ , TS } KEY { S , J } ;

6.2   Let LT and CT be the projections of RX2A′ on {CLASS,STATUS} and {CITY,STATUS}, respectively. Then (a) {CLASS} and {CITY} will be foreign keys in RX2B′, referencing LT and CT, respectively, and (b) the following multirelvar constraint will also hold:

CONSTRAINT ... WITH (LTX := LT RENAME { STATUS AS X } ,
                     CTY := CT RENAME { STATUS AS Y }) :
            AND (JOIN { RX2B′ , LTX , CTY } , X = Y) ;

6.3   The first of the given FDs means {STREET,CITY,STATE} is a key; the second means the relvar isn't in BCNF. However, if we use Heath's Theorem to decompose it (on the basis of the functional dependency {ZIP} → {CITY,STATE}) into BCNF projections as follows—

ZCT { ZIP , CITY , STATE }
    KEY { ZIP }

ZR { ZIP , STREET }
    KEY { ZIP , STREET }

—then we lose the FD {STREET,CITY,STATE} → {ZIP}. As a result, relvars ZCT and ZR can't be independently updated. (*Subsidiary exercise:* Develop some sample values for ZCT and ZR to illustrate this point.) Of course, if we don't perform this decomposition, there'll be some redundancy; to be specific, the fact that a given zip code corresponds to a particular city and state will appear several times. But does that redundancy cause problems? Given that the zip code for a given city and state doesn't change very often, the answer is "possibly, but not very often." (On the other hand, it's not true that zip codes *never* change.)

6.4   Here's an irreducible cover for RX1:

```
{ SNO , PNO } → { QTY }
{ SNO }        → { CITY }
{ CITY }       → { STATUS }
```

The 3NF procedure yields {SNO,PNO,QTY}, {SNO,CITY}, and {CITY,STATUS}.

Next, RX3. An irreducible cover:

```
{ SNO }   → { CLASS }
{ CLASS } → { CITY }
{ CITY }  → { STATUS }
```

The 3NF procedure yields {SNO,CLASS}, {CLASS,CITY}, and {CITY,STATUS}.

Finally RX2. Irreducible cover:

```
{ SNO }   → { CLASS }
{ SNO }   → { CITY }
{ CLASS } → { STATUS }
{ CITY }  → { STATUS }
```

The 3NF procedure yields {SNO,CLASS,CITY}, {CLASS,STATUS}, and {CITY,STATUS}. The interesting thing about this example is that (as was shown in the body of the chapter) if we decompose on the basis of the FD {SNO} → {CLASS,CITY}, we obtain {SNO,CLASS,CITY} and {CLASS,CITY,STATUS} as the 3NF projection headings, and that's *not* what we get from the 3NF procedure. In fact, the result of the 3NF procedure requires the following rather complicated multirelvar constraint (an equality dependency) to be maintained:

```
CONSTRAINT ... JOIN { SLC , LT } = JOIN { SLC , CT } ;
```

("for a given supplier, class status = city status"; SLC, LT, and CT here denote the projections of RX2 on {SNO,CLASS,CITY}, {CLASS,STATUS}, and {CITY,STATUS}, respectively). The example thus illustrates the point that although the 3NF procedure is certainly guaranteed to yield 3NF projections and not to lose any FDs, it probably shouldn't be followed too blindly.

Note: Suppose we were to name the status attributes in relvars LT and CT differently, thus:

```
LT { CLASS , CLASS_STATUS }
CT { CITY , CITY_STATUS }
```

Then the constraint that the two status values must be equal for any given supplier might be stated thus:

```
CONSTRAINT ... IS_EMPTY ( ( JOIN { SLC , LT , CT } )
                         WHERE CLASS_STATUS ≠ CITY_STATUS ) ;
```

(The **Tutorial D** expression IS_EMPTY (*rx*) returns TRUE if the relation *r* denoted by the relational expression *rx* is empty and FALSE otherwise.) Alternatively:

```
CONSTRAINT ...
   AND ( JOIN { SLC , LT , CT } ,
       CLASS_STATUS = CITY_STATUS ) ;
```

The overall message of this example might be put this way: This whole business of losing or preserving FDs in particular is really just a special case of a more general phenomenon: namely, that if we start with some design *D1* and map it into some logically equivalent design *D2*, then in general that process will involve some restructuring of constraints as well as of relvars, necessarily (as should in fact be obvious).

6.5   *Assumptions:* No star plays more than one role in any given movie; no movie has more than one director. (Are these assumptions reasonable?) FDs:

```
{ S , M } → { R }
{ M }     → { D , Y }
{ S }     → { B }
{ B }     → { Z , C }
{ Z , C } → { H }
```

If all nine attributes are combined in a single relvar, then that relvar is only in 1NF ({S,M} is a key). The BCNF procedure yields {S,M,R}, {M,D,Y}, {S,B}, {B,Z,C}, and {Z,C,H}. No FDs are lost.

CHAPTER 7

FD Axiomatization

[The] true and solid living axioms

—Francis Bacon: *The New Organon* (1620)

I've touched on the point several times already that some FDs imply others; now it's time to get more specific. First of all, however, I need to introduce some notation—notation that (a) reduces the number of keystrokes required in formal proofs and the like and (b) can also help, sometimes, to see the forest as well as the trees, as it were.

As you might recall, Heath's Theorem as I stated it in Chapter 5 included the following sentence: *Let XY denote the union of X and Y, and similarly for XZ.* The notation I want to introduce is basically just an extension of this simple idea (it's a trifle illogical, but it's very convenient). To be specific, the notation uses expressions of the form XY to mean:

- The union of $\{X\}$ and $\{Y\}$, if X and Y are individual attribute names

- The union of X and Y, if X and Y are sets of attribute names

- The union of $\{X\}$ and Y, if X is an individual attribute name and Y denotes a set of such names (or the union of X and $\{Y\}$, if the roles of X and Y are reversed)

It also allows $\{X\}$ to be abbreviated to just X (e.g., in an FD) if X denotes an individual attribute. *Note:* For convenience, I'll refer to this notation from this point forward as *Heath notation* (though I must make it clear that Heath himself didn't actually use it in his paper).

© C. J. Date 2019
C. J. Date, *Database Design and Relational Theory*, https://doi.org/10.1007/978-1-4842-5540-7_7

Armstrong's Axioms

We've seen that, formally speaking, an FD is just an expression: to be specific, an expression of the form $X \to Y$, where X and Y are sets (actually sets of attribute names, but from a formal point of view it really doesn't matter what the sets consist of). Now, suppose we're given some set (F, say) of FDs. Then we can apply certain formal *rules of inference* to derive further FDs from the ones in F—FDs that are *implied* by the ones in F, meaning that if the ones in F hold in some given relvar, then the derived ones hold in that relvar too. The rules in question were first stated by Armstrong in 1974 and for that reason are usually referred to as *Armstrong's inference rules* or (more commonly) as *Armstrong's axioms*. They can be stated in a variety of equivalent ways, of which the following is perhaps the simplest:

1. *Reflexivity:* If Y is a subset of X (i.e., $Y \subseteq X$), then $X \to Y$.

2. *Augmentation:* If $X \to Y$, then $XZ \to YZ$.

3. *Transitivity:* If $X \to Y$ and $Y \to Z$, then $X \to Z$.

Observe that these rules are intuitively reasonable, given the intended interpretation of FDs. That is, since we know what FDs "mean," we can easily see that, e.g., if the FDs $X \to Y$ and $Y \to Z$ both hold in relvar R, then the FD $X \to Z$ must do so too. (The suppliers relvar S illustrates this particular rule—the FDs {SNO} $\to$ {CITY} and {CITY} $\to$ {STATUS} both hold in that relvar, and therefore the FD {SNO} $\to$ {STATUS} does so, too.)

So the rules are reasonable. But what's more important is that they're both *sound* and *complete*. Soundness and completeness are concepts frequently encountered in connection with formal systems in general. In the particular formal system under consideration here, this is what they mean:

- *Completeness:* If an FD f is implied by the ones in the given set F, then it can be derived from the ones in F by means of the rules. (To repeat, to say that some FD f is implied by the FDs in some set F is to say that if the FDs in F hold, then f holds too.)

- *Soundness:* If an FD *f* isn't implied by the ones in the given set *F*, then it can't be derived from the ones in *F* by means of the rules.[1]

The rules thus form what's called an *axiomatization* for FDs. As a consequence, they can be used to derive what's called the *closure F^+* of any given set *F* of FDs. Here's a definition:

> **Definition (closure of a set of FDs):** Let *F* be a set of FDs. Then the closure F^+ of *F* is the set of all FDs implied by those in *F*.

What's more, the derivation process can be *mechanized*; that is, Armstrong's rules can be incorporated into (e.g.) a design tool that, given a set *F* of FDs that hold in some relvar *R*, will be able to compute the closure F^+ of that set *F*, or in other words the complete set of all FDs that hold in that relvar. The significance of this state of affairs should be obvious.

Additional Rules

Several additional inference rules can be derived from the original three, the following among them. Such additional rules can be used to simplify the practical task of computing F^+ from *F*. Here are some examples:

4. *Self determination:* $X \to X$.

5. *Union:* If $X \to Y$ and $X \to Z$, then $X \to YZ$.

6. *Composition:* If $X \to Y$ and $Z \to W$, then $XZ \to YW$.

7. *Decomposition:*[2] If $X \to YZ$, then $X \to Y$ and $X \to Z$.

---

[1] If you have a background in logic, you might like the following characterization: Soundness means all theorems are tautologies; completeness means all tautologies are theorems. Or more intuitively (and with acknowledgments to Hugh Darwen): Soundness means if you can prove it, it's true; completeness means if it's true, you can prove it.

[2] Two points: First, don't confuse this kind of decomposition with nonloss decomposition as discussed at length elsewhere in this book. Second, observe that composition and decomposition as here defined aren't quite inverses of one another; to be specific, the inverse of decomposition is that special case of composition in which *Z* is replaced by *X* and *W* is replaced by *Z*. (In other words, the inverse of decomposition isn't composition in general but rather union—union in this context being a special case of composition.)

In the next section, I'll show how these four rules can be derived from the original three. First, however, let me give a couple of examples to show how the rules (both original and additional ones) can be used in practice. By way of a first example, suppose we're given a relvar *R* with attributes *A, B, C, D, E, F*, and we're told the following FDs hold in that relvar:

$A \rightarrow BC$

$B \rightarrow E$

$CD \rightarrow EF$

I'll now show the FD $AD \rightarrow F$ also holds in *R* (a fact that, I think you'll agree, isn't immediately obvious).[3] Here's the proof:

1. $A \rightarrow BC$ (given)

2. $A \rightarrow C$ (1, decomposition)

3. $AD \rightarrow CD$ (2, augmentation)

4. $CD \rightarrow EF$ (given)

5. $AD \rightarrow EF$ (3 and 4, transitivity)

6. $AD \rightarrow F$ (5, decomposition)

For a second example, recall from Chapter 6 the notion of an *irreducible cover*. Just to remind you, (a) a cover for a given set *F* of FDs is a set *C* of FDs such that every FD in *F* is implied by those in *C*, and (b) that cover *C* is irreducible if and only if it possesses all of the following properties:

1. *Singleton dependant:* Every FD in *C* has just one attribute on the right side.

2. *Irreducible determinant:* No attribute can be discarded from the left side of any FD in *C* without losing the property that *C* is a cover for *F*.

3. *No redundant FDs:* No FD can be discarded from *C* without losing the property that *C* is a cover for *F*.

---

[3]If you'd prefer a more concrete example, take *A* as employee number, *B* as department number, *C* as manager's employee number, *D* as project number for a project directed by that manager (unique within manager), *E* as department name, and *F* as percentage of time spent by the specified manager on the specified project. The fact that the given FDs $A \rightarrow BC$, $B \rightarrow E$, and $CD \rightarrow EF$ all hold is then intuitively reasonable. (But what about the FD $AD \rightarrow F$? Myself, I still don't think it's *immediately* obvious that that one holds as well.)

Now, I assumed in the previous chapter (tacitly) that every set F of FDs had an irreducible cover. In fact, this is easy to see:

- Thanks to the decomposition rule, we can assume without loss of generality that every FD in F has a singleton right side.

- Next, for each FD in F, examine each attribute A on the left side; if deleting A from that left side has no effect on the closure F^+, delete A from that left side.

- For each FD remaining in F, if deleting that FD from F has no effect on the closure F^+, delete that FD from F.

The final version of F is irreducible and is a cover for the original version.

Here then is a concrete example to illustrate the process of actually finding an irreducible cover. Let the given set of FDs (all of which presumably hold in some relvar R with attributes A, B, C, D) be as follows:

$A \;\rightarrow\; BC$
$B \;\rightarrow\; C$
$A \;\rightarrow\; B$
$AB \;\rightarrow\; C$
$AC \;\rightarrow\; D$

Then the following procedure will produce an irreducible cover for this given set:

1. First, rewrite the FDs such that each has a singleton right side:

    $A \;\rightarrow\; B$
    $A \;\rightarrow\; C$
    $B \;\rightarrow\; C$
    $A \;\rightarrow\; B$
    $AB \;\rightarrow\; C$
    $AC \;\rightarrow\; D$

    Observe now that the FD $A \rightarrow B$ occurs twice, so one occurrence can be dropped.

2. Attribute C can be dropped from the left side of the FD $AC \rightarrow D$, because we have $A \rightarrow C$, so $A \rightarrow AC$ by augmentation, and we're given $AC \rightarrow D$, so $A \rightarrow D$ by transitivity; so the C on the left side of $AC \rightarrow D$ is redundant.

3. The FD $AB \to C$ can be dropped, because again we have $A \to C$, so $AB \to CB$ by augmentation, so $AB \to C$ by decomposition.

4. The FD $A \to C$ is implied by the FDs $A \to B$ and $B \to C$ taken together, so it can be dropped.

We're left with:

$A \to B$
$B \to C$
$A \to D$

This set is irreducible.

Proving the Additional Rules

As promised, in this section I show how to derive Rules 4-7 from the original Rules 1-3.

4. *Self determination:* $X \to X$.

    Proof: Immediate by reflexivity.

5. *Union:* If $X \to Y$ and $X \to Z$, then $X \to YZ$.

    Proof: $X \to Y$ (given), hence $X \to XY$ by augmentation; also $X \to Z$ (given), hence $XY \to YZ$ by augmentation; hence $X \to YZ$ by transitivity.

6. *Composition:* If $X \to Y$ and $Z \to W$, then $XZ \to YW$.

    Proof: $X \to Y$ (given), hence $XZ \to YZ$ by augmentation; likewise, $Z \to W$ (given), hence $YZ \to YW$ by augmentation; hence $XZ \to YW$ by transitivity.

7. *Decomposition:* If $X \to YZ$, then $X \to Y$ and $X \to Z$.

    Proof: $X \to YZ$ (given) and $YZ \to Y$ by reflexivity; hence $X \to Y$ by transitivity (and likewise for $X \to Z$).

Another Kind of Closure

To recap, the closure F^+ of a set F of FDs is the set of all FDs implied by those in F. Now, in principle we could compute F^+ from F by repeatedly applying Armstrong's rules (and/or rules derived therefrom) until they stop producing new FDs. In practice, however, there's little need to compute F^+ per se (which is just as well, perhaps, since the procedure just outlined is hardly very efficient). But now I want to show how we can compute a certain important subset of F^+: namely, that subset consisting of all FDs having a given determinant. More precisely, I'll show how, given a heading H, a subset Z of H, and a set F of FDs with respect to H, we can compute what's called the *closure* Z^+ of Z under F. Here's the definition:

> **Definition (closure of a set of attributes):** Let H be a heading, let Z be a subset of H, and let F be a set of FDs with respect to H. Then the closure Z^+ of Z under F is the maximal subset C of H such that $Z \to C$ is implied by the FDs in F.

By the way, note that we now have two kinds of closure (try not to confuse them!): closure of a set of FDs, and closure of a set of attributes under a set of FDs.[4] Note too that we use the same "superscript plus" notation for both.

Here then is a simple pseudocode algorithm for computing the closure Z^+ of Z under F:

```
Z⁺ := Z ;
do "forever" ;
    for each FD X → Y in F
        do ;
            if X is a subset of Z⁺
            then replace Z⁺ by the union of Z⁺ and Y ;
        end ;
    if Z⁺ did not change on this iteration
    then quit ; /* computation complete */
end ;
```

---

[4]Not to mention the kind of closure that applies to the operators of the relational algebra.

Let's do an example. Suppose the given heading is *ABCDEG* and we want to compute the closure *AB*⁺ of the set of attributes *AB* under the following set *F* of FDs:

$A \rightarrow BC$
$E \rightarrow CG$
$B \rightarrow E$
$CD \rightarrow EG$

Let's now step through the algorithm:

1. First of all, we initialize the result AB^+ to the set of attributes *AB*.

2. We now go round the inner loop four times, once for each of the given FDs. On the first iteration (for the FD $A \rightarrow BC$), we find that the determinant *A* is indeed a subset of AB^+ as computed thus far, so we add attributes (*B* and) *C* to the result. AB^+ is now the set *ABC*.

3. On the second iteration (for the FD $E \rightarrow CG$), we find that the determinant *E* is *not* a subset of the result as computed so far, which thus remains unchanged.

4. On the third iteration (for the FD $B \rightarrow E$), we add *E* to AB^+, which thus now has the value *ABCE*.

5. On the fourth iteration (for the FD $CD \rightarrow EG$), AB^+ remains unchanged.

6. Now we go round the inner loop four times again. On the first iteration, the result remains unchanged; on the second, it expands to *ABCEG*; on the third and fourth, it remains unchanged.

7. Now we go round the inner loop four times again. The result remains unchanged, and so the whole process terminates, with $AB^+ = ABCEG$.

Well, I hope you can see from this example that computing Z^+ given *H*, *F*, and *Z* is essentially straightforward. And the important thing is this: Given some set *F* of FDs (with respect to some heading *H*), we can easily tell whether some specific FD $X \rightarrow Y$ (with respect to that same heading *H*) is implied by *F*, because it will be so if and only if *Y* is a subset of the closure X^+ of *X* under *F*. In other words, we now have a simple way of determining whether a given FD $X \to Y$ is in the closure F^+ of F without actually having to compute F^+.

It also follows from the definition (of closure of a set of attributes) that the superkeys for a relvar R are precisely those subsets SK of the heading of R such that the closure SK^+ of SK—under the pertinent set of FDs—is the entire heading of R.

Exercises

7.1   What does it mean to say that Armstrong's rules are sound? Complete?

7.2   What's the closure of a set of FDs? Let F be the set of FDs containing just the FD {SNO,PNO} → {QTY}, which holds in relvar SP. Show the closure of that set F.

7.3   Given the definition of what it means for an FD to be satisfied, show that the reflexivity, augmentation, and transitivity rules are reasonable.

7.4   (*Try this exercise without referring back to the body of the chapter.*) Prove that the three rules of the previous exercise imply the self determination, union, composition, and decomposition rules.

7.5   The following theorem is due to Hugh Darwen:[5]

Darwen's Theorem: If $X \to Y$ and $Z \to W$, then $XV \to YW$, where $V = Z - Y$.

Prove this theorem. Which rules from the previous two exercises did you use? Which rules from those exercises can be derived as special cases of the theorem?

7.6   Find an irreducible cover for the following set of FDs:

AB → C	BE → C
C → A	CE → FA
BC → D	CF → BD
ACD → B	D → EF

---

[5]Hugh Darwen: "The Role of Functional Dependence in Query Decomposition," in C. J. Date and Hugh Darwen, *Relational Database Writings 1989-1991* (Addison-Wesley, 1992).

7.7 Consider the following set of FDs:

$A \rightarrow B$
$BC \rightarrow DE$
$AEF \rightarrow G$

Is the FD $ACF \rightarrow DG$ implied by this set?

7.8 Two sets of FDs are *equivalent* if and only if each is a cover for the other. Are the following sets equivalent?

$\{ A \rightarrow B , AB \rightarrow C , D \rightarrow AC , D \rightarrow E \}$

$\{ A \rightarrow BC , D \rightarrow AE \}$

Note that any given set *F* of FDs is certainly equivalent to any set that's an irreducible cover for *F*, and further that two sets are equivalent if and only if they have the same irreducible cover.

7.9 Relvar R has attributes A, B, C, D, E, F, G, H, I, and J, and is subject to the following FDs:

$ABD \rightarrow E$ $C \rightarrow J$
$AB \rightarrow G$ $CJ \rightarrow I$
$B \rightarrow F$ $G \rightarrow H$

Is this set reducible? What keys does R have?

Answers

7.1 See the body of the chapter.

7.2 The closure F^+ of a set *F* of FDs is the set of all FDs implied by those in *F*. The closure of the set of FDs containing just the FD $\{SNO,PNO\} \rightarrow \{QTY\}$ is given in the answer to Exercise 4.1 in Chapter 4.

7.3   The FD $X \to Y$ is satisfied if and only if whenever two tuples agree on X, they also agree on Y (I'm deliberately giving this definition in a pretty loose form). So:

- If two tuples agree on X, they certainly agree on every subset Y of X, so the reflexivity rule is reasonable.

- If two tuples agree on XZ, they certainly agree on Z. They also certainly agree on X and hence, if $X \to Y$ is satisfied, on Y as well; hence they agree on YZ, and so the augmentation rule is reasonable.

- If two tuples agree on X and $X \to Y$ is satisfied, they agree on Y. If they agree on Y and $Y \to Z$ is satisfied, they agree on Z. So the transitivity rule is reasonable.

7.4   See the body of the chapter.

7.5   Let U denote the intersection of Z and Y and let V denote the difference $Z - Y$ between Z and Y (in that order). Then:

1. $X \to Y$ (given)

2. $Z \to W$ (given)

3. $X \to U$ (1, decomposition)

4. $XV \to UV$ (3, augmentation)

5. $XV \to Z$ (simplifying 4)

6. $XV \to W$ (5, 2, transitivity)

7. $XV \to YW$ (1, 6, composition; this completes the proof)

The rules used in this proof are indicated in the comments. The following rules are all special cases of Darwen's Theorem: the union, transitivity, and augmentation rules. So too is the following useful rule:

If $X \to Y$ and $XY \to Z$, then $X \to Z$.

Note: This latter is a special case of what's sometimes called the *pseudotransitivity* rule, which in its general form looks like this:

Pseudotransitivity: If $X \to Y$ and $YW \to Z$, then $XW \to Z$.

7.6   The first step is to rewrite the given set of FDs such that every FD has a singleton right side:

1. $AB \to C$

2. $C \to A$

3. $BC \to D$

4. $ACD \to B$

5. $BE \to C$

6. $CE \to A$

7. $CE \to F$

8. $CF \to B$

9. $CF \to D$

10. $D \to E$

11. $D \to F$

Now:

- 2 implies 6, so we can drop 6.

- 8 implies $CF \to BC$ by augmentation, which with 3 implies $CF \to D$ by transitivity, so we can drop 9.

- 8 implies $ACF \to AB$ by augmentation, and 11 implies $ACD \to ACF$ by augmentation, and so $ACD \to AB$ by transitivity, and so $ACD \to B$ by decomposition, so we can drop 4.

No further reductions are possible, and so we're left with the following irreducible cover:

$AB \rightarrow C$

$C \rightarrow A$

$BC \rightarrow D$

$BE \rightarrow C$

$CE \rightarrow F$

$CF \rightarrow B$

$D \rightarrow E$

$D \rightarrow F$

Alternatively:

- 2 implies 6, so we can drop 6 (as before).

- 2 implies $CD \rightarrow AD$ by augmentation, which implies $CD \rightarrow ACD$ by augmentation again, which with 4 implies $CD \rightarrow B$ by transitivity, so we can replace 4 by $CD \rightarrow B$.

- 2 and 9 imply $CF \rightarrow AD$ by composition, which implies $CF \rightarrow ADC$ by augmentation, which with (the original) 4 implies $CF \rightarrow B$ by transitivity, so we can drop 8.

No further reductions are possible, and so we're left with the following irreducible cover:

$AB \rightarrow C$

$C \rightarrow A$

$BC \rightarrow D$

$CD \rightarrow B$

$BE \rightarrow C$

$CE \rightarrow F$

$CF \rightarrow D$

$D \rightarrow E$

$D \rightarrow F$

Observe, therefore, that there are (at least) two distinct irreducible covers for the original set of FDs. Note too that those two covers have different cardinalities.

7.7   Yes, it is. The easiest way to prove this result is to compute the closure ACF^+ of the set ACF, which turns out to be the entire set $ABCDEFG$. Alternatively, we can apply Armstrong's axioms and the other rules discussed in the body of the chapter, as follows:

1. $A \rightarrow B$ (given)

2. $ACF \rightarrow BCF$ (1, augmentation)

3. $BC \rightarrow E$ (given)

4. $BCF \rightarrow EF$ (3, augmentation)

5. $ACF \rightarrow EF$ (2, 4, transitivity)

6. $ACF \rightarrow AEF$ (5, augmentation)

7. $AEF \rightarrow G$ (given)

8. $ACF \rightarrow G$ (6, 7, transitivity)

9. $BC \rightarrow DE$ (given)

10. $BC \rightarrow D$ (9, decomposition)

11. $BCF \rightarrow DF$ (10, augmentation)

12. $BCF \rightarrow D$ (11, decomposition)

13. $ACF \rightarrow D$ (2, 12, transitivity)

14. $ACF \rightarrow DG$ (7, 13, composition)

7.8   Let's number the FDs of the first set as follows:

1. $A \rightarrow B$

2. $AB \rightarrow C$

3. $D \rightarrow AC$

4. $D \rightarrow E$

Now, 3 can be replaced by:

3. $D \rightarrow A$ and $D \rightarrow C$

Next, 1 and 2 together imply (see the "useful rule" mentioned near the end of the answer to Exercise 7.5) that 2 can be replaced by:

2. $A \rightarrow C$

But now we have $D \rightarrow A$ and $A \rightarrow C$, so $D \rightarrow C$ is implied by transitivity and can be dropped, leaving:

3. $D \rightarrow A$

The first set of FDs is thus equivalent to the following irreducible cover:

$A \rightarrow B$
$A \rightarrow C$
$D \rightarrow A$
$D \rightarrow E$

The second given set of FDs

$A \rightarrow BC$
$D \rightarrow AE$

is clearly also equivalent to this same irreducible cover. The two given sets are thus equivalent.

7.9   The set is clearly reducible, since C → J and CJ → I together imply C → I. As for keys: An obvious superkey is ABCDGJ (the combination of all attributes mentioned on the left sides of the given FDs). We can drop J from this set because C → J, and we can drop G because AB → G. Since none of A, B, C, D appears on the right side of any of the given FDs, it follows that ABCD is a key.

CHAPTER 8

Denormalization

What's normal, anyway?

—Anon.: *Where Bugs Go*

I want to say a few words about denormalization. Now, I haven't considered, so far
in this book, any level of normalization higher than BCNF (at least, not in detail). But
denormalization, if it means anything at all, can't apply just to BCNF specifically; I mean,
it can't refer just to dropping back to some level of normalization that's lower than BCNF
specifically. Rather, it has to mean dropping back from *any* given level of normalization
to some lower one.

   That said, however, I need to say too that relvars that are in BCNF and not in some
higher normal form are comparatively unusual (though not completely unknown,
I hasten to add). In practice, therefore, denormalization does usually refer quite
specifically to dropping back to some level of normalization below BCNF; hence the
inclusion of this chapter in this part of the book.

"Denormalize for Performance" (?)

Ever since SQL products first came on the market, the claim that it's necessary to
"denormalize for performance" has been widely promulgated. The (specious!)
supporting argument goes something like this:

1.   Normalization means lots of relvars.

2.   Lots of relvars means lots of stored files.

3.   Lots of stored files means lots of I/O.

C. J. Date, *Database Design and Relational Theory*, https://doi.org/10.1007/978-1-4842-5540-7_8

In the case of suppliers and parts, for example, a request to get details for suppliers who supply red parts involves two dyadic joins—suppliers to shipments first, perhaps, and then the result of that join to parts. And if the three relvars correspond to three physically separate stored files, then those two joins will require lots of I/O and will therefore perform badly.

As already noted, this argument is specious, at least in principle. The reason is that the relational model nowhere stipulates that relvars must map one for one to stored files. In the case of suppliers and parts, for example, there's no logical reason why we couldn't physically store the join of the three relvars—with the obvious redundancies factored out, possibly—as one single stored file on the disk,[1] which could reduce the amount of I/O significantly for the query under consideration. The point is irrelevant for present purposes, however, because:

- First, this area is one in which most DBMS vendors have seriously let us down; most SQL products do indeed map relvars one for one to stored files, pretty much.[2] Even the exceptions fail to provide us with as much data independence as we might like, or as much as relational systems are theoretically capable of. As a practical matter, therefore, that "specious" argument is, sadly, valid for most SQL products today.

- Second, even if relvars didn't map one for one to stored files, denormalization might still be desirable at the stored file level. Indeed, a major reason why mappings that aren't one for one would be desirable is precisely that they would permit denormalization to be done at the physical level, where it belongs, without it having to show through to—and thereby corrupt—the logical level.

So let's assume for the sake of discussion that denormalization does sometimes have to be done, at some level or other. But what *is* denormalization?

---

[1] I'm speaking pretty loosely here, of course. In particular, I'm ignoring the possibility that there might be some suppliers or some parts with no corresponding shipments.

[2] I realize the mapping from relvars to stored files isn't always exactly one to one as I'm suggesting here—for example, some products allow several relvars to share the same stored file, and some allow a single relvar to span several stored files. But such considerations don't materially affect the bigger picture, and I ignore them here for simplicity.

What Does Denormalization Mean?

Curiously, for a practice that's so widely advocated, there seems to be considerable confusion over what denormalization actually consists of. (The textbooks aren't much help, either, even the ones that specialize in design topics. Most of them don't even mention the subject, and those that do rarely offer a definition, and they certainly don't discuss the matter in much depth.) For example, some years ago now I had occasion to read a paper specifically devoted to the question of denormalization in commercial SQL products.[3] I'll refer to that paper as "the denormalization paper" in what follows. Now, the author begins by arguing *against* denormalization. To quote:

> I think the normalization principles should be treated as
> *commandments* ... unless you're faced with performance
> problems that money, hardware scalability, current SQL
> technology, network optimization, parallelization, or other
> performance techniques can't resolve [*slightly reworded, italics
> added*].

I couldn't agree more with this position. Indeed, I'm on record as saying very much the same thing myself: In a paper I wrote in 1990 on the use of SQL systems in practice,[4] I recommended denormalization as a performance tactic "only if all else fails." Unfortunately, however, the rest of the denormalization paper tends to suggest that the author doesn't really know what denormalization is; after the opening position statement quoted above, the paper goes on to give some eight examples of "designing for performance," all but one of which have absolutely nothing to do with denormalization at all!

In the author's defense, however, I say again that it does seem to be difficult to find a precise definition of denormalization in the literature. Of course, it could be argued that no such definition is needed, given that (a) denormalization, whatever else it might be, must surely be the inverse of normalization, and (b) normalization in turn certainly is precisely defined. For the record, however, I'll give some idea as to what a precise definition of denormalization might look like in just a moment. Before I do so, however, let me make it clear that I have no particular quarrel with the specific design tactics suggested in the denormalization paper; indeed, I suggested several of those same

---

[3]Sam Hamdan: "Denormalization and SQL-DBMS," *SQL Forum 4*, No. 1 (January/February 1995).
[4]"SQL Dos and Don'ts," in *Relational Database Writings 1985-1989* (Addison-Wesley, 1990).

tactics in a paper I wrote myself back in 1982.[5] My quarrel is only with the fact that the author refers to them as denormalization tactics specifically.

So here's my own definition, for what it's worth (and I apologize if it seems a little lengthy). I start with the observation that, speaking a little loosely, *normalizing* some relvar R means decreasing redundancy. To be more specific, it decreases redundancy by:

1. Replacing R by a set of projections $R1, ..., Rn$ such that at least one of $R1, ..., Rn$ is at a higher level of normalization than R, and such that also

2. For all possible values r of R, if the corresponding values $r1, ..., rn$ of $R1, ..., Rn$ (respectively) are joined back together again, then the result of that join is equal to r.

Hence the following proposed definition:

> **Definition (denormalization):** Denormalizing a set of relvars $R1$, ..., Rn means increasing redundancy by:
>
> 1. Replacing $R1, ..., Rn$ by their join R such that R is at a lower level of normalization than at least one of $R1, ..., Rn$, and such that also
>
> 2. For all possible values $r1, ..., rn$ of $R1, ..., Rn$ (respectively), the result of projecting the corresponding value r of R over the attributes of Ri is equal to ri ($i = 1, ..., n$).

Points arising from this definition:

- Observe that denormalization is a process that applies to a *set* of relvars, not to an individual relvar considered in isolation. For example, consider relvars SNC and CT, with headings {SNO,SNAME,CITY} and {CITY,STATUS}, respectively (see Figure 3-2 in Chapter 3 for some sample values). These two relvars are in BCNF. If we join them together, we get the suppliers relvar S (which is only in 2NF, not in 3NF, and therefore not in BCNF either), and so relvar S can be regarded as a denormalization of relvars SNC and CT. What's more, of course, relvar S involves more redundancy than relvars SNC and CT do.

---

[5]"A Practical Approach to Database Design," in *Relational Database: Selected Writings* (Addison-Wesley, 1986).

- If (a) $R1, ..., Rn$ were obtained by taking projections of R in the first place—in other words, if the denormalization is really undoing an earlier normalization, so to speak, as in the suppliers example in the previous bullet item—and if also (b) that earlier normalization was done purely to decrease redundancy and not to fix a logically incorrect design (see the remarks in Chapter 3 on the difference between these two possibilities), then (c) the requirement that for all possible values r of R, projecting r over the attributes of Ri must yield ri ($i = 1, ..., n$) will be met automatically.

The usual argument in favor of denormalization is basically that it makes retrievals easier to express and makes them perform better.[6] To what extent this argument might be valid I'll examine in a later section. First, however, I'd like to point out that once we make the decision to denormalize, we've embarked on a very slippery slope. The question is: Where do we stop? The situation is different with normalization, where there are clear logical reasons for continuing the process until we reach the highest possible normal form. Do we then conclude that with denormalization we should proceed until we reach the lowest possible normal form? Surely not; yet there are no logical criteria for deciding exactly where the process should stop. In choosing to denormalize, in other words, we've backed off from a position that does at least have some solid science and logical theory behind it, and replaced it by one that's purely pragmatic in nature (as well as being based, typically, on a somewhat narrow perspective on the overall problem, a point I'll elaborate on later).

What Denormalization Isn't (I)

I've said that denormalization means increasing redundancy. But it doesn't follow that increasing redundancy means denormalization! This is one of the traps the denormalization paper falls into; the design tactics it describes do increase redundancy (usually), but they're not—with, as noted earlier, one sole exception—applications of denormalization per se. (In logic, if *p implies q* is true, it doesn't follow that *q implies p* is true, and to argue otherwise is a well known example of faulty reasoning: so well known, in fact, that it enjoys a special name, *The Fallacy of False Conversion*.)

---

[6]It's also sometimes claimed to make the database easier to understand. Exercise 8.2 addresses this particular issue.

Let's examine a few of the examples from the denormalization paper. In one, we're given relvars ITEM and SALES that look like this:

```
ITEM  { INO , INAME }
      KEY { INO }

SALES { SNO , INO , QTY }
      KEY { SNO , INO }
      FOREIGN KEY { INO } REFERENCES ITEM
```

The predicates are *Item INO has name INAME* and *Quantity QTY of item INO were sold in store SNO*, respectively. For performance reasons, the paper suggests adding a TOTAL_QTY attribute to the ITEM relvar, whose value for any given item is the total sales of that item taken over all stores. But although it's true that the resulting design involves some redundancy, the fact remains that both relvars are still in BCNF (note in particular that the functional dependency {INO} → {TOTAL_QTY} holds in the revised version of relvar ITEM). In other words, there's no denormalization, as such, in this example.

A second example involves what the paper calls "an internal array":

```
EMP { ENO , JAN_PAY , FEB_PAY , ..., DEC_PAY }
    KEY { ENO }
```

The predicate is *Employee ENO was paid an amount JAN_PAY in January, FEB_PAY in February, ..., and an amount DEC_PAY in December*. And presumably, though the paper doesn't say as much explicitly, this "tuple wise" design is meant to be contrasted with—and for performance reasons, possibly preferred to—the following "attribute wise" analog:

```
EMP { ENO , MONTH , PAY }
    KEY { ENO , MONTH }
```

But both designs are in BCNF. Again, there's no denormalization here; in fact, to get ahead of myself for a moment (see Chapter 17), I would say there's no increase in redundancy, either. (On the other hand, the original "tuple wise" design is probably bad, as you'll see if you consider the query "Get employees whose salary was less than 5K in at least one month, together with the months in question.")

In connection with the foregoing example, a colleague recently drew my attention to the following excerpt from one of IBM's reference manuals for its DBMS product DB2:

First normal form: A relational entity satisfies the requirement of first normal form if every instance of an entity contains only one value, never multiple repeating attributes. Repeating attributes, often called a repeating group, are different attributes that are inherently the same. In an entity that satisfies the requirement of first normal form, each attribute is independent and unique in its meaning and its name.

Example: Assume that an entity contains the following attributes:

```
EMPLOYEE_NAME
JANUARY_SALARY_AMOUNT
FEBRUARY_SALARY_AMOUNT
MARCH_SALARY_AMOUNT
```

This situation violates the requirement of first normal form, because JANUARY_SALARY_AMOUNT, FEBRUARY_SALARY_AMOUNT, and MARCH_SALARY_AMOUNT are essentially the same attribute, EMPLOYEE_MONTHLY_SALARY_AMOUNT.

—*DB2 for z/OS Administration Guide*, IBM Form No. SC27-8844-2

Well, the writing is dire, of course, but the message it conveys—to the extent it can even be understood, that is—is arguably still worse. What can I say.

A third example involves splitting a RESELLERS relvar "horizontally" into two separate relvars, ACTIVE_RESELLERS and INACTIVE_RESELLERS. In other words, the original relvar is decomposed via *restriction* (not projection), and is reconstructed from the two restrictions via *union* (not join). So we're clearly not talking about normalization in the classical sense here at all; a fortiori, therefore, we're not talking about classical denormalization either.[7]

I'll give one more example from the denormalization paper. This one starts with STORE and EMP relvars as follows:

```
STORE { SNO , REGION , STATE , ... }
      KEY { SNO , REGION , STATE }

EMP   { ENO , SNO , REGION , STATE , ... }
      KEY { ENO }
      FOREIGN KEY { SNO , REGION , STATE } REFERENCES STORE
```

The predicates are *Store SNO is located in region REGION within state STATE* and *Employee ENO is employed at store SNO within region REGION within state STATE*. The redundancies are obvious, and so the paper suggests introducing a surrogate identifier for stores, SID say, thereby modifying the design as follows:

```
STORE { SID , SNO , REGION , STATE , ... }
      KEY { SID }
      KEY { SNO , REGION , STATE }

EMP   { ENO , SID , ... }
      KEY { ENO }
      FOREIGN KEY { SID } REFERENCES STORE
```

But this revised design not only involves no denormalization, it actually decreases redundancy![8]—because the association of a given SNO with a given REGION and STATE now appears just once, instead of once for every employee of the store in question. (To beat the point to death, there's *obviously* no denormalization here because—among other things—the one thing surely everybody agrees on is that denormalization is supposed to increase redundancy.)

---

[7]It's true that it might be possible to define a new kind of normalization, based on restriction and union instead of projection and join (I'll have a little more to say about this possibility in Chapter 15, and a lot more in Chapter 16). And if we did, well, I suppose we'd have a new kind of denormalization on our hands also. But I'm pretty sure that such considerations aren't what the denormalization paper was referring to with its RESELLERS example.

[8]Or does it? Again, see Chapter 17, which includes further discussion of the use of surrogates in particular.

By the way, I'm aware that this example might give the impression that I think surrogates are a good idea. Well, they can be—but, sadly, they aren't *always* a good idea. The fact is, surrogates, while they might solve some problems, can also introduce further problems of their own. See Exercise 8.3 at the end of the chapter, also Chapter 17, for further discussion.

In closing this section, I'd like to make it very clear that the foregoing discussions are in no way intended as an attack on the denormalization paper or its author. Indeed, the following quote from that paper makes it clear that the author and I are really on the same side on the bigger issues:

> [We should] stop criticizing the relational model and make a clear distinction between what's SQL and what's relational ... The two are totally different.

I couldn't agree more with this position, nor with the implication that the only reason we have to worry about such matters as denormalizing at the logical level is because of failures on the part of today's SQL products. As I've written elsewhere, in fact:[9] In an ideal system, we would never have to denormalize at all, at the logical level. Even in today's systems, which are typically much less than ideal, I believe we should denormalize only as a last resort. That is, we should back off from a fully normalized design only if all other strategies for improving performance have failed, somehow, to meet requirements. (Of course, I'm going along here with the usual assumption that normalization has performance implications—as indeed it does, typically, in current SQL products.)

What Denormalization Isn't (II)

So far in this chapter I've given what I think is a reasonable definition of what denormalization is, and I've given some examples of what it isn't. However, perhaps it was simply a mistake on my part to think the term ought to be used in any kind of precise or logical sense. Certainly it's not used very precisely in the industry at large; in fact, it mostly seems to be used—especially in a data warehouse context—to refer to just about anything that, as far as I'm concerned, can only be described as bad design practice.

---

[9]E.g., in *An Introduction to Database Systems* (8th edition, Addison-Wesley, 2004), also in *Go Faster! The TransRelationalTM Approach to DBMS Implementation* (Ventus Publishing, 2002, 2011, available as a free download from http://bookboon.com).

Not only that, but such bad practice is often explicitly recommended! Examples of such "recommended" bad practice include:

- Using repeating groups[10]

- Permitting duplicate rows

- Using nulls; possibly worse, allowing nulls in keys

- Mixing different kinds of information in the same column (using a separate "flag" column to specify what kind each individual value is in the column in question)

- Using a single text column to represent what ought logically to be distinct columns

I'd like to add a note here on *star schemas*, since the "star schema" concept and "denormalization" are often mentioned together.[11] The basic idea behind this concept as follows. Suppose we wish to collect a history of business transactions for analysis purposes; for example, suppose in the case of suppliers and parts that we wish to record, for each shipment, the particular time interval in which that shipment occurred. Thus, we might identify time intervals by a time interval identifier (TINO), and introduce another relvar TI to relate those identifiers to the corresponding time intervals per se. The revised shipments relvar SP and the new time intervals relvar TI might then look as shown in Figure 8-1:[12]

---

[10]Even if repeating groups are done "respectably" in the form of properly defined RVAs (see Chapter 4), they're still usually contraindicated.

[11]At least one authority claims it's misleading to refer to star schemas as denormalized, however: "[The] use of *denormalized* when describing a star [schema] implies that the design started out as normalized. Most designs are not produced in such a manner. *Not normalized* would be a better description" (from *Star Schema: The Complete Reference*, by Chris Adamson, McGraw-Hill, 2010).

[12]For simplicity I ignore here the fact that those time intervals might better be represented, not by means of FROM-TO pairs as in the figure, but by means of attributes whose values are intervals per se. Such interval valued attributes are described in a little more detail in Chapter 14. See the book *Time and Relational Theory: Temporal Databases in the Relational Model and SQL*, by C. J. Date, Hugh Darwen, and Nikos A. Lorentzos (Morgan Kaufmann, 2014) for an extended discussion of such matters.

SP

SNO	PNO	TINO	QTY
S1	P1	T13	300
S1	P1	T15	100
S1	P2	T11	200
S1	P3	T12	400
S1	P4	T11	200
S1	P5	T15	100
S1	P6	T14	100
S2	P1	T13	300
S2	P2	T14	400
S3	P2	T11	200
S3	P2	T13	200
S4	P2	T11	200
S4	P4	T13	200
S4	P5	T12	400
S4	P5	T11	400

TI

TINO	FROM	TO
TI1	t0	t1
TI2	t2	t3
TI3	t4	t5
TI4	t6	t7
TI5	t8	t9

Figure 8-1. *Sample fact table (SP) and dimension table (TI)*

In star schema terminology, SP in this example is *the fact table* and TI is *a dimension table*. The suppliers relvar S and the parts relvar P are also dimension tables (see Figure 8-2).[13] And the overall structure is referred to as a "star schema" because of a fancied resemblance of the corresponding entity / relationship diagram to a star, with the fact table being surrounded by—and connected by "rays," or "spokes," to—the dimension tables, as shown in Figure 8-2. (Those rays or spokes correspond to foreign key references, of course.)

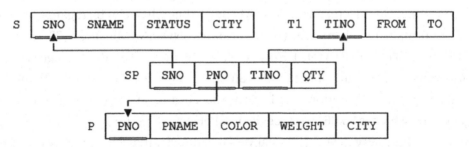

Figure 8-2. *Star schema for suppliers and parts (with time intervals)*

---

[13]For simplicity I choose to ignore here (just for the sake of the present discussion) the fact that the FD {CITY} → {STATUS} is supposed to hold in relvar S, and hence that relvar S is less than fully normalized.

Now, you might be wondering what the difference is between a star schema and a conventional relational design. In fact, a star schema for a simple example like the one under discussion is likely to be identical to a good relational design. In more complex situations, however, the dimension tables are often less than fully normalized (the objective here apparently being to avoid joins).[14] What's more, other relational design recommendations are often violated, too (see the bullet list earlier in this section).

Detailed discussion of star schemas and related matters is beyond the scope of this book; you can find a slightly more extended discussion in my book *An Introduction to Database Systems* (8th edition, Addison-Wesley, 2004).

Denormalization Considered Harmful (I)

In this section, I'd like to present an argument—a logical argument, that is, and one you might not have seen before—in support of the position that you should denormalize only as a last resort. Essentially, the argument is that while (as is well known) denormalization can be logically bad for update, *it can be logically bad for retrieval as well*, in the sense that it can make certain queries harder to formulate. (Alternatively, it can make them easier to formulate incorrectly, meaning that, if they execute, you're getting answers that might be correct in themselves but are answers to the wrong questions.) Let me illustrate.

Once again consider relvar S, with its FD {CITY} → {STATUS}. As noted earlier (in the section "What Does Denormalization Mean?"), that relvar can be regarded as the result of denormalizing relvars SNC (with attributes SNO, SNAME, and CITY) and CT (with attributes CITY and STATUS). Now consider the query "Get the average supplier city status value." Given our usual sample values (see Figure 3-2 in Chapter 3), the status values for Athens, London, and Paris are 30, 20, and 30, respectively, and so the average is 80/3, which is 26.667 to three decimal places. Here then are some attempts at formulating this query in SQL (I'll assume for simplicity that S is nonempty, so we

---

[14]In this connection, consider this advice from a book on data warehouses: "[Resist] normalization ... Efforts to normalize any of the tables in a dimensional database solely in order to save disk space [*sic!*] are a waste of time ... The dimension tables must not be normalized ... Normalized dimension tables destroy the ability to browse" (from Ralph Kimball, *The Data Warehouse Toolkit*, John Wiley & Sons, 1996).

don't have to worry about what happens in SQL if we try to apply the AVG operator to an empty set):[15]

1. SELECT AVG (STATUS) AS RESULT
    FROM   S

    Result (incorrect): 26. The problem here is that London's status and Paris's status have both been counted twice. Perhaps we need a DISTINCT inside the AVG invocation? Let's try that:

2. SELECT AVG (DISTINCT STATUS) AS RESULT
    FROM   S

    Result (incorrect): 25. No, it's distinct *cities* we need to examine, not distinct status values. We can do that by grouping:

3. SELECT CITY , AVG (STATUS) AS RESULT
    FROM   S
    GROUP BY CITY

    Result (incorrect): (Athens,30), (London,20), (Paris,30). This formulation gives average status *per city*, not the overall average. Ah, so perhaps what we want is the average of the averages?—

4. SELECT CITY , AVG (AVG (STATUS)) AS RESULT
    FROM   S
    GROUP BY CITY

    Result: Syntax error—the SQL standard quite rightly doesn't allow "set function" invocations to be nested in this manner.[16] One more attempt:

---

[15]I'll leave it as an exercise to determine the changes that would be needed to the various SQL expressions I'm about to show if we couldn't make that assumption.

[16]I say "quite rightly" only because we're in the SQL context specifically; a more orthodox language such as **Tutorial D** would certainly let us nest such invocations (or its analog of such invocations, rather). Let me explain. Consider the SQL expression SELECT SUM (QTY) AS RESULT FROM SP WHERE QTY > 100 (I deliberately switch to a different example for reasons of clarity). The argument to the SUM invocation here is really what's denoted by the expression QTY FROM SP WHERE QTY > 100, and a more orthodox language would therefore enclose that whole expression in parentheses, thus: SELECT SUM (QTY FROM SP WHERE QTY > 100) AS RESULT. But SQL doesn't do this. As a consequence, an expression of the form AVG(SUM(QTY)) has to be illegal, because SQL can't figure out which portions of the surrounding expression have to do with the AVG argument and which with the SUM argument.

5. SELECT AVG (TEMP.STATUS) AS RESULT
    FROM (SELECT DISTINCT S.CITY , S.STATUS
           FROM   S) AS TEMP

Result (correct at last): 26.667. But note how complicated this expression is compared to its analog on the fully normalized design (relvars SNC and CT):

6. SELECT AVG (STATUS) AS RESULT
    FROM   CT

Denormalization Considered Harmful (II)

I said in the previous section that the argument in favor of denormalization is that it makes retrievals easier to express and makes them perform better. But does that argument really stand up to careful analysis? Let's take a closer look.

First of all, it clearly isn't true across the board that retrievals are easier to express; the previous section presented a detailed counterexample, but the point can be made with much simpler examples. By way of illustration, consider what's involved in formulating the query "Get all supplier details" against (a) the normalized design of Figure 1-1 and (b) a denormalized design in which relvars S, SP, and P are replaced by a single "joined" relvar called, say, SSPP. Here are **Tutorial D** formulations:

a. S

b. SSPP { SNO , SNAME , STATUS , CITY }

Or if you want SQL solutions:

a. SELECT *
    FROM S

b. SELECT DISTINCT SNO , SNAME , STATUS , CITY
    FROM SSPP

The next point is that many queries are likely to perform worse, too. There are several reasons for this state of affairs. One is that denormalization leads to redundancy, which in turn can lead to a need to do duplicate elimination (in this connection, note that DISTINCT in the second of the foregoing SQL formulations). Another is as follows:

- Suppose again that the join of suppliers, shipments, and parts is represented as one single stored file. Also, assume for simplicity that any given stored file consists of a physically contiguous collection of stored records, one for each tuple currently appearing in the relvar the stored file represents.

- Let's suppose too for the sake of the argument that the query "Get details for suppliers who supply red parts" will perform reasonably well against this physical structure. OK; but the query "Get all supplier details" will perform *worse* than it would against the structure in which the three relvars map to three physically separate stored files! Why? Because in the latter design, all supplier stored records will be physically contiguous, whereas in the former design they'll effectively be spread over a wider area, and will therefore require more I/O. Analogous remarks apply to any query that accesses suppliers only, or parts only, or shipments only, instead of performing some kind of join.

- Note too that denormalization, again because it increases redundancy, will most likely lead to bigger stored records, and this fact too can lead to more I/O, not less. As a trivial example, a 4K page can hold two 2K stored records but only one 3K stored record; hence, a denormalization that increases redundancy by 50% could increase I/O by 100%. (I'm speaking pretty loosely here, of course.)

My next observation is that even if we accept the claim that denormalization makes retrievals easier to express and perform better, it certainly makes updates harder to express and perform worse. Now, this point is (as I said before) widely understood; however, what's not so widely understood is that denormalization opens the door to integrity violations, too. For example, in relvar S (as opposed to the projection relvars SNC and CT), *someone*—either the system or the user, and in current practice probably the latter—is going to have to be responsible for maintaining the FD {CITY} → {STATUS}; and if that maintenance isn't done, integrity is lost. By contrast, in the normalized two-relvar design, all that has to be done is to enforce the key constraint on CT—which will definitely be done by the system, not the user—and the fact that each city has one status will then be maintained "automatically."

One reviewer of this chapter pointed out that yet another advantage of doing a normalized design is that such a design tends to simplify the formulation of complex queries, in that it enables expressions representing such formulations to be more modular, through nesting of simple subexpressions. This is true in principle, but I feel obliged to add that, although such modular formulations can readily be constructed in a well designed language like **Tutorial D** (using that language's WITH feature, illustrated in examples elsewhere in this book), they're much harder—sometimes impossible—to formulate in SQL. Why? Because SQL's WITH feature is very much less useful than **Tutorial D**'s, owing to the fact that (a) the semantics of SQL's SELECT clause are sensitive to the presence or absence of certain other constructs in the overall expression (especially but not only GROUP BY and HAVING clauses and aggregate operator invocations), and hence owing also to the consequent fact that (b) there's nothing like a one to one mapping in SQL between semantic and syntactic constructs.

My final point is this: Regardless of whether we're talking about

a.   True denormalization, which is done at the physical level only, or

b.   The kind of denormalization we have to do in most of today's SQL products, which affects the logical level as well,

the point isn't widely appreciated enough that when people say "denormalize for performance," they're really referring to the performance *of specific applications*. As I put it earlier (in the section "What Does Denormalization Mean?"), denormalization is typically based on a somewhat narrow perspective on the overall problem. *Any* particular physical design is likely to be good for some applications but bad for others (in terms of its performance implications, that is).

Concluding Remarks

In this chapter, I've given strong arguments in favor of not denormalizing; in effect, therefore, I've given arguments in favor of normalizing. And it's certainly true that good designs are usually fully normalized. But it's important to understand that the opposite isn't necessarily true! That is, a design can be fully normalized and yet still be bad. For example, the projection ST of relvar S on attributes SNO and STATUS is certainly in

176

BCNF—in fact, it's in the highest possible normal form, as we'll see in Part IV of this book—but it's clearly not a good design, as we saw in Chapter 6.

Exercises

8.1   It's sometimes suggested that one advantage of binary relvars over the general *n*-ary relvars supported by the relational model is that binary relvars are always in BCNF (implying among other things that we don't need to worry about normalization and denormalization, perhaps). Either show that binary relvars are indeed always in BCNF, or show that the claim is incorrect by producing a counterexample.

8.2   The following is an excerpt from a published interview with a certain database consultant.[17] It begins with a statement from the consultant:

Consultant: The problems ... largely result from normalizing data across multiple [relvars] ... Many queries, however, are much easier to understand if the data is denormalized ...

Interviewer: Doesn't denormalization potentially lower data integrity and reduce flexibility in supporting unanticipated queries?

Consultant: Normalization, and its emphasis on elimination of redundant storage, is purely a transaction processing issue. When users view data, they see it in a redundant form. In order to transform data into a form that is useful to users, it must be denormalized by means of a join, which is essentially a way of dynamically denormalizing data for greater ease of use. The problem is that users can't tolerate the time and cost of joins. To address the problem, companies replicate data in an ever increasing number of decision support databases, which represent denormalized views of the data.

What if anything do you think is wrong with the opinions expressed?

---

[17]It's taken from *Data Base Newsletter 22*, No. 5 (September/October 1994).

8.3   The possibility of using surrogate identifiers or keys was mentioned in the body of the chapter. Indeed, many designers recommend the use of such artifical or surrogate keys in place of what are sometimes called "natural" keys. For example, we might add an attribute SPNO, say, to our usual shipments relvar (making sure it has the uniqueness property, of course) and then make {SPNO} a surrogate key for that relvar. (Note, however, that {SNO,PNO} would still be a key; it just wouldn't be the only one any longer.) Thus, surrogate keys are keys in the usual relational sense, but (a) they always consist of exactly one attribute and (b) their values serve solely as surrogates for the entities they stand for (i.e., they serve merely to represent the fact that those entities exist—they carry absolutely no additional meaning or baggage of any kind). Ideally, those surrogate values would be system generated, but whether they're system or user generated has nothing to do with the basic idea of surrogate keys as such. Two questions: Are surrogate keys the same thing as tuple IDs? And do you think they're a good idea?

8.4   If two designs are information equivalent, it must be possible to use operations of the relational algebra to convert them into one another. Consider, therefore, the following competing designs for an employees relvar from the body of the chapter:

```
EMP { ENO , JAN_PAY , FEB_PAY , ..., DEC_PAY }
    KEY { ENO }
```

```
EMP { ENO , MONTH , PAY }
    KEY { ENO , MONTH }
```

Using **Tutorial D** or SQL (or your own preferred database language), show how each of these designs can be converted into the other.

Answers

8.1 This exercise is (deliberately) a repeat in different words of Exercise 4.6 in Chapter 4. The claim is incorrect, as was shown in the answer to that earlier exercise.

8.2 It's truly astonishing how many erroneous statements can be made in such a tiny amount of text ... Here are some of my own responses to the views expressed:

- "Many queries are much easier to understand if the data is denormalized": I suspect that *understand* here ought really to be *formulate* (for instance, *understanding* the query "Get all supplier details" has nothing to do with how the database is designed). If I'm right, then the claim might be valid. But the opposite claim is valid too!—many queries are easier to formulate if the data isn't denormalized, as I showed in the body of the chapter.

- The interviewer suggests that denormalization can cause integrity problems and can reduce flexibility in supporting unanticipated queries. I agree with these suggestions.

- "Normalization, and its emphasis on elimination of redundant storage, is purely a transaction processing issue": Normalization is about reducing *redundancy*, not reducing redundant *storage*— though I suppose the consultant might be forgiven for conflating the two, given the implementations most widely available today. But it's categorically not "a transaction processing issue"! As I put it in Chapter 1, when we do database design in general, and when we do normalization in particular, we're concerned primarily with what the data *is*, not with how it's going to be used.

- "When users view data, they see it in a redundant form": Sometimes they do, sometimes they don't. But even if they do, that's not an argument for a denormalized design. For example, the users could be presented with a denormalized perception of the data by means of the conventional view mechanism—I'm not saying they should be, only that they could be—while the underlying database remains properly normalized.

- "In order to transform data into a form that is useful ...": This is simply a tendentious remark.

- "[Join] is essentially a way of dynamically denormalizing data for greater ease of use": The user might think of joins being done dynamically, but there's no reason in general why they can't be done statically (i.e., ahead of time)—and I believe they often would be, given a well architected DBMS.[18] It's also untrue to suggest that the result of a join must always be denormalized. "Greater ease of use" is another tendentious remark.

- "[Users] can't tolerate the time and cost of joins": Joins aren't necessarily time consuming or expensive. Again, it depends on the implementation. In any case, "can't tolerate" is, in my opinion, far too judgmental.

- "To address the problem, companies replicate data in an ever increasing number of decision support databases, which represent denormalized views of the data": This might be true, but if it is it's an indictment of current implementations, not an argument for denormalization as such.

8.3   First of all, surrogate keys are *not* the same thing as tuple IDs. For one thing (to state the obvious), surrogates identify entities and tuple IDs identify tuples, and there's certainly nothing like a one to one correspondence between entities and tuples. (Think of derived tuples in particular—for example, tuples in the result of some query. In fact, it's not at all clear that derived tuples will have tuple IDs anyway.) Furthermore, tuple IDs usually have performance connotations, but surrogates don't (access to a tuple via its tuple ID is usually assumed to be fast, but no such observation applies to surrogates). Also, tuple IDs are often concealed from the user,[19] but surrogates mustn't be, thanks

---

[18]I have in mind here, primarily, a DBMS implemented using the facilities of *The TransRelationalTM Model* (see footnote 9). *Note:* A similar remark applies to all of my uses of the phrase "well architected" throughout the present book, in Chapter 6 and elsewhere.

[19]In this connection, see the discussion of Requirement 4 in the section "Violating First Normal Form" in Chapter 4.

to *The Information Principle* (see Exercise 2.1 in Chapter 2); in other words, it's probably (and desirably!) not possible to store a tuple ID in a database relvar, while it certainly (and desirably) is possible to store a surrogate in a database relvar. In a nutshell: Surrogate keys have to do with logical design, tuple IDs have to do with physical design.

Are surrogate keys a good idea? Well, observe first that the relational model has nothing to say on this question; like the business of design in general, in fact, whether or not to use surrogate keys has to do with *how to apply* the relational model, not with the relational model as such. That said, I have to say too that the question of whether surrogate keys are good or bad is far from straightforward. There are strong arguments on both sides: so many such, in fact, that I can't possibly do justice to them here (though some of them are summarized in Chapter 17). For further details, see the paper "Composite Keys," in my book *Relational Database Writings 1989-1991* (Addison-Wesley, 1992). *Note:* The paper in question is called "Composite Keys" because surrogate keys are perhaps most likely to be useful in practice in situations in which existing keys, and corresponding foreign keys, are composite keys specifically.

8.4   I show solutions in SQL, just for a change. Defining the first in terms of the second (in outline):

```
SELECT DISTINCT EX.ENO ,
      ( SELECT PAY
        FROM   EMP AS EY
        WHERE  EY.ENO = EX.ENO
        AND    MONTH = 'Jan' ) AS JAN_PAY ,
        ...
      ( SELECT PAY
        FROM   EMP AS EY
        WHERE  EY.ENO = EX.ENO
        AND    MONTH = 'Dec' ) AS DEC_PAY
   FROM   EMP AS EX
```

Defining the second in terms of the first (again in outline):

```
SELECT ENO , 'Jan' AS MONTH , JAN_PAY AS PAY FROM EMP
UNION
  ...
UNION
SELECT ENO , 'Dec' AS MONTH , DEC_PAY AS PAY FROM EMP
```

PART III

Join Dependencies, Fifth Normal Form, and Related Matters

This part of the book does for join dependencies and fifth normal form what the previous part did for functional dependencies and Boyce/Codd normal form. It also ties up a number of loose ends having to do with normalization as a major component of design theory in general.

CHAPTER 9

JDs and 5NF (Informal)

If you can't beat 'em, join 'em.

—Anon.

Just as Boyce/Codd normal form is defined in terms of functional dependencies, so fifth normal form (5NF) is defined in terms of join dependencies (JDs);[1] as noted in Chapter 4, in fact, 5NF is *the* normal form with respect to JDs, just as BCNF is *the* normal form with respect to FDs. And the treatment of these ideas in this part of the book therefore parallels the treatment of BCNF and FDs in Part II. In other words, I plan to treat the material both formally, in Chapter 10, and informally in the present chapter.

Let me immediately add that although 5NF is indeed "the" normal form with respect to JDs, this state of affairs shouldn't necessarily be taken to mean that 5NF is the ultimate goal of the normalization process. *Au contraire*, in fact: There are at least two further normal forms that might have a better claim to that title, as we'll see in Part IV of this book. From a pedagogical point of view, however, as well as from a historical one, I think it's desirable to discuss 5NF in detail first. (I mention this point simply in order to avoid giving a false impression; one of my reviewers felt I should have presented the material in a different sequence, but I don't agree.)

Now, in previous writings I've tended to deal with JDs as if they were just a generalized kind of FD. I now realize this view of the matter is wrong, or at least misleading; rather, it's better to regard JDs as a completely different phenomenon. Of course, FDs and JDs are both dependencies (i.e., constraints), and they do resemble each other in certain respects; in particular, the fact that a certain JD holds in relvar *R* implies that *R* can be nonloss decomposed in certain ways, just as the fact that a certain

---

[1]So is 4NF, in a sense, but I'm going to ignore 4NF (for the most part, at any rate) until we get to Chapter 12.

FD holds in relvar R also implies that R can be nonloss decomposed in certain ways. It's also true that every FD implies a JD, so that if some FD *F* holds in relvar R, a certain JD *J* holds in R also. But not all JDs are implied by FDs; in fact, to speak very loosely—but I must emphasize here that what I'm about to say is *extremely* imprecise—we might say that 5NF has to do with JDs that aren't implied by FDs. That is, it's if some relvar R is in BCNF, but is subject to some JD that's not implied by FDs, that the notion of 5NF might be relevant.

Now, a relvar is in BCNF if and only if all FDs to which it's subject are implied by keys. As you'd probably expect, therefore, a relvar is in 5NF if and only if all JDs to which it's subject are implied by keys.[2] However, this latter notion—i.e., the notion of JDs being implied by keys—is a bit trickier to pin down than its FD counterpart; in fact, there's a very rich theory surrounding these ideas, as you'll soon see, and some of that theory can be a little overwhelming (not to say confusing) at first. You need to keep a clear head! As someone much more knowledgeable in these matters than I am once said to me: *JDs are very mysterious.*

So much for the preamble; now let's get down to specifics.

Join Dependencies—the Basic Idea

Most of the time in this book so far, I've been making a tacit assumption: namely, I've been assuming that when we decompose some relvar, we always do so by replacing that relvar by exactly two of its projections.[3] (Note that Heath's Theorem, which provides the formal underpinning for most of what I've had to say so far regarding nonloss decomposition, does address decomposition into exactly two projections specifically.) What's more, that assumption was fully warranted, so long as our target was only BCNF; in other words, it successfully carried us as far as that specific target. So you might be surprised to learn that there exist relvars that can't be nonloss decomposed into two projections but can be nonloss decomposed into three (or maybe more than three).

As an aside, I note that, remarkably enough, Codd gave an example in 1969, in his very first paper on the relational model (see Appendix D), that showed he was aware of the foregoing possibility. However, that example was apparently overlooked by most

---

[2]This very informal definition is the only one I'll be giving for 5NF in the present chapter.
[3]Of course, I'm referring here to one individual step in the overall process. Clearly, repeated steps—i.e., repeated individual decompositions—will, in general, eventually yield a result consisting of more than two projections, even if each individual step yields just two.

of the paper's original readers; certainly it seems to have come as a surprise to the research community when the possibility was rediscovered several years later (in 1977, to be precise).

Now, I said earlier, albeit loosely, that 5NF had to do with JDs that aren't implied by FDs. I can now add, though again speaking very loosely, that it has to do with relvars that can't be nonloss decomposed into two projections but can be nonloss decomposed into three or more. In other words, it's when these circumstances arise—i.e., when there are (a) JDs that aren't implied by FDs and (b) relvars that can only be nonloss decomposed into three or more projections—that you do really have to come to grips with JDs and 5NF.

So what exactly do we mean when we say some JD holds in some relvar? Here's a definition:

> **Definition (join dependency):** Let $X1, ..., Xn$ be subsets of the heading H of relvar R; then the join dependency (JD)—sometimes more specifically the n-ary JD—
>
> ☆ { $X1$, ... , Xn }
>
> holds in R if and only if R can be nonloss decomposed into its projections on $X1, ..., Xn$, or in other words if and only if every legal value r of R is equal to the join of its projections $r1, ..., rn$ on $X1, ..., Xn$, respectively. $X1, ..., Xn$ are said to be the components of the JD, and the JD overall can be read as "star $X1, ..., Xn$" (or sometimes "join $X1, ..., Xn$"—though I hasten to add that "join" really isn't the mot juste here, because the join operator as usually understood joins *relations*, and $X1, ..., Xn$ aren't relations but headings).

By way of a simple example, consider the suppliers relvar S once again. As we know, that relvar is subject to the FD {CITY} → {STATUS}, and so Heath's Theorem tells us it can be nonloss decomposed into its projections on {SNO,SNAME,CITY} and {CITY,STATUS}. In other words, the following binary JD holds in that relvar:

☆ { { SNO , SNAME , CITY } , { CITY , STATUS } }

Points arising:

- Note that it follows from the definition that the union of the components $X1$, ..., Xn must be equal to H (i.e., every attribute of H must appear in at least one of those components), for otherwise R couldn't possibly be equal to the join of the projections corresponding to those components.

- Different writers use different symbols to denote a JD; I use a special kind of star ("✡"), but the symbol ⋈ ("bow tie") is more frequently encountered in the research literature.[4]

- It might help to point out that to say some JD holds is equivalent to saying that if we join the corresponding projections together, we'll never get any "spurious" tuples (as I called them in Chapter 3, in Exercise 3.2).

- The following observation might also be helpful. I'll explain it in terms of a simple, though slightly abstract, example. Let relvar R have attributes A, B, C, and D (only), and let the JD ✡$\{AB,BC,CD\}$ ("Heath notation" —see Chapter 7) hold in R. Also, let me use the symbol "∈" to mean "appears in" (as in the answer to Exercise 5.4 in Chapter 5). Then to say the given JD holds in R is equivalent to saying the following:

if   EXISTS $c1$ (EXISTS $d1$ ((a , b , $c1$, $d1$) ∈ R))
         AND
         EXISTS $a2$ (EXISTS $d2$ (($a2$, b , c , $d2$) ∈ R))
         AND
         EXISTS $a3$ (EXISTS $b3$ (($a3$, $b3$, c , d) ∈ R))
then   (a , b , c , d) ∈ R

Explanation: Let there exist a tuple in R with $A = a$ and $B = b$ *and* a tuple in R with $B = b$ and $C = c$ *and* a tuple in R with $C = c$ and $D = d$. Then the tuples (a,b), (b,c), and (c,d) will appear in

---

[4]Personally I find the bow tie symbol slightly inappropriate—it looks like, and in fact originated as, a symbol for a dyadic operator specifically, whereas (as we know from Chapter 5) the join operator is actually *n*-adic, and join dependencies are accordingly *n*-ary, for arbitrary nonnegative integer *n* in both cases.

the projections of *R* on *AB*, *BC*, and *CD*, respectively, and so the tuple (*a,b,c,d*) will appear when we join these three projections together.

Moreover, the converse is clearly true as well: If the tuple (*a,b,c,d*) appears in *R*, then the tuples (*a,b*), (*b,c*), and (*c,d*) will certainly appear in those three projections (and so that ***if*** in the foregoing formal statement could in fact be replaced by ***if and only if***).

As a simple illustration of this last point, to say the following JD holds in relvar S—

☼ { { SNO , SNAME , CITY } , { CITY , STATUS } }

—is to say the tuple (*s,n,t,c*) appears in S if and only if there exists a tuple in S with SNO = *s* and SNAME = *n* and CITY = *c* ***and*** there exists a tuple in S with CITY = *c* and STATUS = *t*.

To continue with this same example for a moment, the fact that the foregoing JD holds in relvar S is a logical consequence of Heath's Theorem, as we know. In fact, we can now restate Heath's Theorem as follows:

> **Heath's Theorem** (*for relvars, restated in terms of JDs*): Let relvar *R* have heading *H* and let *X*, *Y*, and *Z* be subsets of *H* such that the union of *X*, *Y*, and *Z* is equal to *H*. Let *XY* denote the union of *X* and *Y*, and similarly for *XZ*. If *R* is subject to the FD $X \rightarrow Y$, then *R* is subject to the JD ☼{*XY,XZ*}.

As stated earlier, therefore, FDs imply JDs—but not all JDs are implied by FDs, as we'll see. Before I elaborate on this point, however, let me stress the requirement that the union of the components of a given JD must be equal to the pertinent heading. No analogous requirement applies to FDs; with FDs, the left and right sides don't have to be such that their union is equal to the pertinent heading, they only have to be subsets of that heading. This distinction might help to highlight the point (at least intuitively) that JDs and FDs really are different in kind.

Now, the JD in the foregoing example—

☼ { { SNO , SNAME , CITY } , { CITY , STATUS } }

—is binary, as I've said: It has two components, and it corresponds to a nonloss decomposition into two projections. Here by contrast is another JD that holds in relvar S:

☼ { { SNO , SNAME } , { SNO , CITY } , { CITY , STATUS } }

This one is ternary, but it's derived, in effect, by "cascading" two binary ones:

- First, as we already know, the binary JD ☼{{SNO,SNAME,CITY},{CITY, STATUS}} holds in S.

- But the FD {SNO} → {SNAME} holds in the projection of S on {SNO,SNAME,CITY} (corresponding to one of the components of that binary JD),[5] and so the binary JD ☼{{SNO,SNAME},{SNO,CITY}} holds in that projection.

It follows that the given ternary JD holds in the original relvar (and the relvar can be nonloss decomposed into three projections accordingly, though please understand that I'm not saying it should be). By contrast, in the section immediately following I'll give an example of a ternary JD that's not derived by cascading binary ones, and hence an example of a relvar that can be nonloss decomposed into three projections and not into two.

A Relvar in BCNF and Not 5NF

I'll start with a revised version—I'll call it SPJ—of our usual shipments relvar SP. The revisions consist of (a) dropping attribute QTY and (b) introducing a new attribute JNO ("project number"). The predicate is *Supplier SNO supplies part PNO to project JNO,* and a sample value is shown in Figure 9-1. Note that the relvar is "all key" and thus certainly in BCNF.

SPJ

SNO	PNO	JNO
S1	P1	J2
S1	P2	J1
S2	P1	J1
S1	P1	J1

Figure 9-1. *Relvar SPJ—sample value*

---

[5]I'm appealing here to an easily proved theorem (see Exercise 12.5 in Chapter 12): viz., given a relvar R and a projection of R whose heading includes both X and Y, the FD $X \rightarrow Y$ holds in that projection if and only if it holds in R itself.

Now suppose the following business rule (let's call it BRX) is in effect:

- If (a) supplier *s* supplies part *p* and (b) part *p* is supplied to project *j* and (c) project *j* is supplied by supplier *s*, then (d) supplier *s* supplies part *p* to project *j*.

In slightly more concrete terms, what business rule BRX says is that if (for example) all three of the following are true propositions—

a. Smith supplies monkey wrenches to some project

b. Somebody supplies monkey wrenches to the Manhattan project

c. Smith supplies something to the Manhattan project

—then the following is a true proposition as well:

d. Smith supplies monkey wrenches to the Manhattan project.

In other words, if relvar SPJ contains tuples representing propositions a., b., and c., it must also contain a tuple representing proposition d.[6] Note that this requirement is met in Figure 9-1 (take S1 to be Smith, P1 to be monkey wrenches, and J1 to be the Manhattan project).

Now, propositions a., b., and c. would normally not imply proposition d. To elaborate, if we know only that propositions a., b., and c. are true, then we know that Smith supplies monkey wrenches to some project *j*; we know that some supplier *s* supplies monkey wrenches to the Manhattan project; and we know that Smith supplies some part *p* to the Manhattan project—but we can't validly infer that *s* is Smith, we can't validly infer that *p* is monkey wrenches, and we can't validly infer that *j* is the Manhattan project. False inferences such as these are examples of what's sometimes called *the connection trap*. In the case at hand, however, business rule BRX tells us *there is no trap*; that is, we *can* validly infer proposition d. from propositions a., b., and c. in this particular case.

---

[6]I'm being a little sloppy once again. For example, consider proposition a. ("Smith supplies monkey wrenches to some project"). If "some project" here means "some *unknown* project"— i.e., there exists such a project, but no one knows what it is—then proposition a. isn't an instantiation of the predicate for SPJ, and no SPJ tuple can possibly represent it. But an SPJ tuple certainly can represent the proposition "Smith supplies monkey wrenches to some *specific* project" (e.g., the Manhattan project); what's more, the proposition so represented then implies the proposition "Smith supplies monkey wrenches to *some* project" (i.e., "there exists a known project *j* such that Smith supplies monkey wrenches to *j*"). I hope that's clear!

Now let's consider the example more carefully. Let me use SP, PJ, and JS, just for the moment, to denote the projections of SPJ on {SNO,PNO}, {PNO,JNO}, and {JNO,SNO}, respectively. Then we have the following:

- By the definitions of projection and join,

```
IF   ( s , p , j )      ∈  JOIN { SP , PJ , JS }
THEN ( s , p )          ∈  SP
AND  ( p , j )          ∈  PJ
AND  ( j , s )          ∈  JS
```

and therefore there exist s', p', and j' such that

```
     ( s  , p  , j' )  ∈  SPJ
AND  ( s  , p' , j  )  ∈  SPJ
AND  ( s' , p  , j  )  ∈  SPJ
```

- But by business rule BRX,

```
IF   ( s  , p  , j' )  ∈  SPJ
AND  ( s  , p' , j  )  ∈  SPJ
AND  ( s' , p  , j  )  ∈  SPJ
```

then we necessarily have:

```
     ( s  , p  , j  )  ∈  SPJ
```

- So if (s,p,j) appears in the join of SP, PJ, and JS, it also appears in SPJ. But the converse is obviously true as well—i.e., if (s,p,j) appears in SPJ, it certainly appears in the join of SP, PJ, and JS.

Thus (s,p,j) appears in SPJ *if and only if* it appears in the join of SP, PJ, and JS. It follows that every legal value of relvar SPJ is equal to the join of its projections on {SNO,PNO}, {PNO,JNO}, and {JNO,SNO}, and hence that the JD

☼ { { SNO , PNO } , { PNO , JNO } , { JNO , SNO } }

certainly holds in relvar SPJ.

Observe now that the foregoing JD is ternary—it has three components. What's more, it isn't implied by FDs.[7] Hence it certainly isn't implied by keys (recall from Chapter 5 that a key constraint is just a special case of an FD). As a consequence, relvar SPJ, although it's in BCNF (because it's "all key"), isn't in 5NF.

In order to understand this state of affairs a little better, it's helpful to go back to the sample SPJ value shown in Figure 9-1. Figure 9-2 shows (a) values of the projections SP, PJ, and JS corresponding to that sample value, (b) the effect of joining the SP and PJ projections (on {PNO}), and (c) the effect of joining that result and the JS projection (on {JNO,SNO}). As you can see, joining the first two projections produces a copy of the original SPJ relation plus one additional ("spurious") tuple; joining in the other projection then eliminates that additional tuple, thereby getting us back to the original SPJ relation. Moreover, the net effect is the same whatever pair of projections we choose for the first join, though the intermediate result is different in each case. *Exercise:* Check this claim.

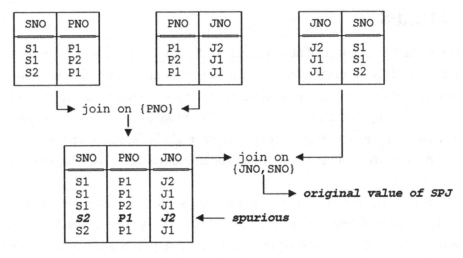

Figure 9-2. *SPJ = the join of all three of its binary projections but not of any two*

To repeat, therefore, the JD ☆{SP,PJ,JS}—if now you'll let me use the names SP, PJ, and SJ to refer not to the projections as such but to the corresponding headings—holds in relvar SPJ; in other words, that JD captures the essence, as it were, of business rule BRX. As a consequence, relvar SPJ can be nonloss decomposed accordingly. What's more,

---

[7]*Proof:* The only FDs that hold in relvar SPJ are trivial ones, and it's certainly not the case that every relation satisfying those trivial FDs also satisfies the JD. For example, the relation containing the first three but not the fourth of the tuples as shown in Figure 9-1 doesn't.

it probably should be, because it suffers from redundancy; to be specific, in terms of the sample value of Figure 9-1, the proposition that supplier S1 supplies part P1 to project J1 is represented both explicitly, by means of the tuple (S1,P1,J1), and implicitly, as a logical consequence of the JD and the propositions represented by the other three tuples.

More terminology: We say a JD like the one that applies in the SPJ example is *tuple forcing*, because if certain tuples appear, it forces certain additional tuples to appear as well. In Figure 9-1, for example, the appearance of the three tuples (S1,P1,J2), (S1,P2,J1), and (S2,P1,J1) forces the appearance of the tuple (S1,P1,J1). Note carefully that not all JDs are tuple forcing; for example, the join dependency ☼{{SNO,SNAME,CITY}, {CITY,STATUS}} holds in relvar S, as we know, but there's no question of it forcing tuples to appear. *Note:* To jump ahead of ourselves for a moment, it'll turn out later that a relvar that's subject to a tuple forcing JD can't be in 5NF (though as the SPJ example shows, it can be in BCNF).

Cyclic Rules

Observe now the cyclic nature of business rule BRX ("if *s* is connected to *p* and *p* is connected to *j* and *j* is connected back to *s* again, then *s* and *p* and *j* must all be *directly* connected, in the sense that they must all appear together in the same tuple"). Let's agree to describe that rule BRX as "3-way cyclic." Then we can say more generally that it's if an *n*-way cyclic rule exists for some *n* > 2 that we might be faced with a relvar that's (a) in BCNF and not in 5NF and therefore (b) can be nonloss decomposed into *n* projections and not into fewer.[8]

That said, I have to say too that in my experience such cyclic rules are rare in practice—which means that, in practice, most relvars, if they're in at least BCNF, are probably in 5NF as well. Indeed, it's quite unusual in practice to find a relvar that's in BCNF and not in 5NF. Unusual, but not unknown!—I've certainly encountered a few real world examples myself on occasion. In other words, the fact that such relvars are unusual doesn't mean you don't need to worry about them, or about JDs and 5NF.

---

[8]If business rule BRX had taken the slightly simpler (and noncyclic) form "if *s* is connected to *p* and *s* is connected to *j*, then *s* and *p* and *j* must all be directly connected," then we might have a relvar that's in BCNF but not in *4NF* (and hence not in 5NF either, a fortiori). See Chapter 12.

Au contraire, in fact: JDs and 5NF are tools in your designer's toolkit, as it were, and (other things being equal) you should probably try to ensure that all of the relvars in your database are in 5NF.[9]

Concluding Remarks

I'll close this chapter with a few miscellaneous observations. First, note that I'm assuming throughout this part of the book—as indeed I did throughout the previous part as well, and will continue to do until further notice—that the only operators we care about as far as relational decomposition and recomposition are concerned are projection and join (projection for decomposition and join for recomposition). Under that assumption, it's immediate from the definition of join dependency that JDs are, in a sense, the "ultimate" kind of dependency; that is, there's no "higher" kind of dependency such that JDs are just a special case of that higher kind. And it follows further that— though I haven't really defined it properly yet!—fifth normal form is the final normal form[10] with respect to projection and join (which accounts for its alternative name, *projection-join* normal form or PJ/NF).

Second, I've referred several times to relvars that are in BCNF and not 5NF; indeed, I've tacitly assumed that if relvar *R* is in 5NF, then it's certainly in BCNF. In fact this assumption is correct. Let me also state for the record that 5NF is always achievable; that is, any relvar not in 5NF can always be decomposed into a set of 5NF projections— though not necessarily without losing dependencies, of course, since we already know from Chapter 7 that preserving dependencies and decomposition to *BCNF* (let alone 5NF) can be conflicting objectives.

Third, it follows from the definition of 5NF that a relvar *R* that's in 5NF is guaranteed to be free of redundancies that can be removed by taking projections. In other words, to say *R* is in 5NF is to say that further nonloss decomposition of *R* into projections, while it might be possible, certainly won't remove any redundancies. *Note very carefully, however, that to say R is in 5NF is not to say R is free of redundancy.* (A belief to the contrary is another popular misconception. See Exercise 1.11 in Chapter 1.) The fact is, there are many kinds of redundancy that projection as such is powerless to remove— which is an illustration of the point I made in Chapter 1, in the section "The Place of

---

[9]Except as noted in Chapters 13 and 14.

[10]Well ... except for 6NF (see Chapter 14).

Design Theory," to the effect that there are numerous issues that current design theory simply doesn't address at all. By way of example, consider Figure 9-3, which shows a sample value for a relvar, CTXD, that's in 5NF and yet still suffers from redundancy. The predicate is *Teacher TNO spends DAYS days with textbook XNO on course CNO.* The sole key is {CNO,TNO,XNO}. As you can see, the fact that (e.g.) teacher T1 teaches course C1 appears twice, and so does the fact that course C1 uses textbook X1.[11]

CTXD

CNO	TNO	XNO	DAYS
C1	T1	X1	7
C1	T1	X2	8
C1	T2	X1	9
C1	T2	X2	6

Figure 9-3. *The 5NF relvar CTXD—sample value*

Let's analyze this example a little more carefully:

- Since {CNO,TNO,XNO} is a key, the relvar is subject to the following functional dependency—

  { CNO , TNO , XNO } → { DAYS }

  —which is an "arrow out of a key."

- So DAYS depends on all three of CNO, TNO, and XNO, and therefore can't appear in a relvar with anything less than all three.

- Hence there's no (nontrivial) decomposition of the relvar into projections that applies at all—the relvar is in 5NF. *Note:* A decomposition is trivial if and only if it's based on dependencies (FDs or JDs) that are themselves trivial in turn, and nontrivial if and only if it isn't trivial. Trivial FDs were discussed in Chapters 4 and 5; trivial JDs are discussed in the next chapter.

---

[11]One reviewer argued strenuously that those repetitions didn't really constitute redundancy. I disagree, but I don't want to argue the point here; I'll just remind you that I'll be examining the whole issue of exactly what does constitute redundancy in detail in Chapter 17.

- Hence there's certainly no decomposition into projections that can remove the redundancies, a fortiori.

Exercises

9.1   (*Repeated from the body of the chapter.*) Check that (a) joining any pair of the binary relations shown in Figure 9-2 yields a result containing a "spurious" tuple (i.e., a tuple not appearing in Figure 9-1) and that (b) joining the third binary relation to that intermediate result then eliminates that spurious tuple.

9.2   Write a **Tutorial D** CONSTRAINT statement to express the JD that holds in relvar SPJ as discussed in the body of the chapter.

9.3   Design a database for the following. The entities to be represented are sales representatives, sales areas, and products. Each representative is responsible for sales in one or more areas; each area has one or more responsible representatives. Each representative is responsible for sales of one or more products, and each product has one or more responsible representatives. Each product is sold in one or more areas, and each area has one or more products sold in it. Finally, if representative *r* is responsible for area *a*, and product *p* is sold in area *a*, and representative *r* sells product *p*, then *r* sells *p* in *a*.

9.4   Give an example from your own work environment, if possible, of a relvar in BCNF but not in 5NF.

Answers

9.1   Joining SP and PJ is discussed in the body of the chapter. Joining PJ and JS yields the spurious tuple (S2,P2,J1), which is then eliminated because there's no (S2,P2) tuple in SP. Joining JS and SP yields the spurious tuple (S1,P2,J2), which is then eliminated because there's no (P2,J2) tuple in PJ.

9.2   CONSTRAINT ... SPJ = JOIN { SPJ { SNO , PNO } ,
                                  SPJ { PNO , JNO } ,
                                  SPJ { JNO , SNO } } ;

Note that this constraint is an equality dependency (i.e., an EQD—see Chapter 3).

9.3   First of all, we'll presumably need three relvars for representatives, areas, and products, respectively:

R { RNO , ... } KEY { RNO }
A { ANO , ... } KEY { ANO }
P { PNO , ... } KEY { PNO }

Now, if representative *r* is responsible for area *a*, and product *p* is sold in area *a*, and representative *r* sells product *p*, then *r* sells *p* in *a*. This is a 3-way cyclic rule. So if we were to have a relvar RAP looking like this—

RAP { RNO , ANO , PNO } KEY { RNO , ANO , PNO }

(with the obvious predicate)—then the following JD would hold in that relvar:

☼ { { RNO , ANO } , { ANO , PNO } , { PNO , RNO } }

The relvar would thus be subject to redundancy. So let's replace it by its three binary projections:

RA { RNO , ANO } KEY { RNO , ANO }
AP { ANO , PNO } KEY { ANO , PNO }
PR { PNO , RNO } KEY { PNO , RNO }

(Now there are several EQDs that need to be stated and enforced—e.g., the projections RA{RNO} and PR{RNO} must always be equal—but the details are straightforward and I omit them here.)

Next, each representative is responsible for sales in one or more areas, and each area has one or more responsible representatives. But this information is already contained in relvar RA, and nothing more is necessary. Similarly, relvar AP takes care of the facts that each area has one or more products sold in it and each product is sold in one or more areas, and relvar PR takes care of the facts that each product has one or more responsible representatives and each representative is responsible for sales of one or more products. Note, however, that the user does need to be told that the join of RA, AP, and PR does *not* involve any "connection trap" (i.e., that the 3-way cyclic rule holds). Let's explore this point. First of all, the predicates for RA, AP, and PR are as follows:

- RA: *Representative RNO is responsible for area ANO.*

- AP: *Product PNO is sold in area ANO.*

- PR: *Product PNO is sold by representative RNO.*

Observe, incidentally, that a well architected DBMS—sadly, not one that's available on the market today, so far as I know!— would allow the designer to tell it about these predicates. *Note:* Telling the DBMS about the predicates would serve to tell the user too, of course. The difference is that telling the user can be done informally (in fact, it has to be done informally, in today's systems), but telling the DBMS, if it could be done at all, would have to be done formally.

Back to the 3-way rule. Clearly the designer can't just tell the user that the join of relvars RA, AP, and PR is equal to relvar RAP, because after the decomposition relvar RAP no longer exists. However, we might define that join as a view (or "virtual relvar"):

```
VAR RAP VIRTUAL ( JOIN { RA , AP , PR } )
        KEY { RNO , ANO , PNO } ;
```

And that same well architected DBMS would then be able to infer the following as a predicate for view RAP:

Representative RNO is responsible for area ANO **and** *product PNO is sold in area ANO* **and** *product PNO is sold by representative RNO.*

But this predicate is less than the truth (it doesn't capture the 3-way cyclic rule). Ideally, therefore, there ought to be a way for the designer to tell the DBMS (as well as the user) that the predicate is actually as follows:[12]

Representative RNO is responsible for area ANO **and** *product PNO is sold in area ANO* **and** *product PNO is sold by representative RNO*

and

representative RNO sells product PNO in area ANO.

Note that this latter predicate is stronger than the former, in that if a certain (RNO,PNO,ANO) triple satisfies the latter, it certainly satisfies the former, while the converse is (obviously) false.

9.4 *No answer provided.*

---

[12]This is thus one of those situations where the user (or in this case the designer) definitely knows more than the system does. Of course, the designer does need to state, and have the system enforce, the corresponding constraint. Perhaps the easiest way to state the constraint is simply as follows: RAP{RNO,ANO} = RA AND RAP{ANO,PNO} = AP AND RAP{PNO,RNO} = PR—i.e., three EQDs, in effect.

CHAPTER 10

JDs and 5NF (Formal)

After great pain, a formal feeling comes.

—Emily Dickinson:
Poem No. 341 (c. 1862):
Thomas H. Johnson (ed.):
The Complete Poems of Emily Dickinson (1960)

Just as Chapter 5 consisted of a more formal treatment of material introduced informally in Chapter 4, so this chapter consists of a more formal treatment of material introduced informally in Chapter 9. But there's rather more to cover in this chapter than there was in Chapter 5, as you'll soon see. Let me just say up front that, just as Chapter 5 had little to say about 2NF or 3NF, so this chapter has little to say about 4NF, either; like 2NF and 3NF, in fact, 4NF is—from some points of view, at least—primarily of historical interest. However, I'll discuss it in a little more detail in a later chapter (Chapter 12).

Join Dependencies Revisited

I begin with a precise and accurate definition of what a JD is, followed by some explanatory text that deliberately parallels the corresponding text in Chapter 5. (Similar remarks apply to the next section also.)

> **Definition (join dependency):** Let *H* be a heading; then a join dependency (JD) with respect to *H* is an expression of the form ✡{*X1*,...,*Xn*}, where *X1*, ..., *Xn* (the components of the JD) are subsets of *H* whose union is equal to *H*. *Note:* The phrase *JD with respect to H* can be abbreviated to just *JD*, if *H* is understood.

© C. J. Date 2019
C. J. Date, *Database Design and Relational Theory*, https://doi.org/10.1007/978-1-4842-5540-7_10

Here are some examples:

✿ { { SNO , SNAME , CITY } , { CITY , STATUS } }
✿ { { CITY , SNO } , { CITY , STATUS , SNAME } }
✿ { { SNO , SNAME } , { SNO , STATUS } , { SNAME , CITY } }
✿ { { SNO , CITY } , { CITY , STATUS } }

Note carefully that, like FDs, JDs are defined with respect to some heading, not with respect to some relation or some relvar. Of the JDs just shown, for example, the first three are defined with respect to the heading {SNO,SNAME,STATUS,CITY} and the fourth is defined with respect to the heading {SNO,STATUS,CITY}.

Note too that, again like FDs, from a formal point of view JDs are just expressions, expressions that when interpreted with respect to some specific relation become propositions that (by definition) evaluate to either TRUE or FALSE. For example, if the first two JDs shown above are interpreted with respect to the relation that's the current value of relvar S (see Figure 1-1 or Figure 3-1), then the first evaluates to TRUE and the second to FALSE. Of course, it's common informally to define ✿{X1,...,Xn} to be a JD, in some specific context, only if it evaluates to TRUE in that context. However, such a definition leaves no way of saying a given relation fails to satisfy, or in other words violates, some given JD—because, by that informal definition, a JD that isn't satisfied wouldn't be a JD in the first place. For example, we wouldn't be able to say the relation that's the current value of relvar S violates the second of the JDs shown above.

Here's another example of a JD that happens to be satisfied by the current value of relvar S (and in fact by all legitimate values of that relvar):

✿ { { SNO , SNAME , CITY } , { CITY , STATUS } , { CITY , STATUS } }

This JD corresponds to a nonloss decomposition in which one of the projections isn't needed in the reconstruction process. In fact, it's clearly equivalent to the first of the four shown previously[1]—

✿ { { SNO , SNAME , CITY } , { CITY , STATUS } }

---

[1]In general, two JDs are *equivalent* if and only if every relation that satisfies either one also
satisfies the other. I'll have more to say on this topic (equivalence of JDs) in the next chapter.

202

—implying that one of the two identical components can be dropped from the original JD without significant loss. For such reasons, I'll feel free to refer to the components of any given JD as constituting a set,[2] even though the commalist of components in the written form of that JD might contain repetitions (duplicates), which sets per se never do. (That's why that commalist is enclosed in braces, of course.)

To continue with the definitions:

> **Definition (satisfying or violating a JD):** Let relation *r* have heading *H* and let ✿{*X1*,...,*Xn*} be a JD, *J* say, with respect to *H*. If *r* is equal to the join of its projections on *X1*, ..., *Xn*, then *r* satisfies *J*; otherwise *r* violates *J*.

Observe that it's relations, not relvars, that satisfy or violate some given JD. For example, given the four JDs shown at the top of the previous page, the relation that's the current value of relvar S satisfies the first and the third—

```
✿ { { SNO , SNAME , CITY } , { CITY , STATUS } }
✿ { { SNO , SNAME } , { SNO , STATUS } , { SNAME , CITY } }
```

—but violates the second:

```
✿ { { CITY , SNO } , { CITY , STATUS , SNAME } }
```

Note that the question of that relation satisfying or violating the fourth of those JDs—

```
✿ { { SNO , CITY } , { CITY , STATUS } }
```

—doesn't arise, because that JD isn't defined with respect to the heading of that relation.

> **Definition (JD holding):** Let relvar *R* have heading *H* and let ✿{*X1*,...,*Xn*} be a JD, *J* say, with respect to *H*. Then JD *J* holds in relvar *R* (equivalently, relvar *R* is subject to JD *J*) if and only if every relation that can ever be assigned to relvar *R* satisfies *J*. The JDs that hold in relvar *R* are the JDs of *R*.

---

[2]And to the cardinality of the JD in question as being the cardinality of that set (i.e., the cardinality of the set that results after redundant duplicates, if any, have been removed). For example, I'll say the JD in the example is binary, not ternary, even though the first of the two written forms of that JD does involve three components.

Please note the terminological distinction I'm drawing here—JDs are *satisfied* (or are violated) by relations, but *hold* (or don't hold) in relvars. I'll adhere to this distinction throughout what follows. By way of example, the first of the four JDs given at the top of the previous page holds in relvar S—

✿ { { SNO , SNAME , CITY } , { CITY , STATUS } }

—but the second and third don't:

✿ { { SNO , SNAME } , { SNO , STATUS } , { SNAME , CITY } }
✿ { { CITY , SNO } , { CITY , STATUS , SNAME } }

(Contrast the examples following the previous definition.) So now, at last, we know precisely what it means for a given relvar to be subject to a given JD. And it should be clear—in fact, it's it's immediate from the definition—that relvar R can be nonloss decomposed into its projections on $X1$, ..., Xn *if and only if* it's subject to the JD ✿$\{X1,...,Xn\}$.

Fifth Normal Form

Now, when we were talking about FDs and BCNF, we got into a discussion of *trivial FDs*, and *FD irreducibility*, and *FDs implied by keys*, and various related matters. As I'm sure you'd expect by now, analogous concepts arise in connection with JDs and 5NF also, but the details are a little trickier. Well, the concept of a JD being trivial is actually quite straightforward:

> **Definition (trivial JD):** Let ✿$\{X1,...,Xn\}$ be a JD, J say, with respect to heading H. Then J is trivial if and only if it's satisfied by every relation with heading H.

From this definition, it's easy to prove the following result:

> **Theorem:** Let ✿$\{X1,...,Xn\}$ be a JD, J say, with respect to heading H. Then J is trivial if and only if some Xi $(1 \leq i \leq n)$ is equal to H (because every relation with heading H necessarily satisfies every JD with respect to H that's of the form ✿$\{...,H,...\}$).

We can regard this theorem as an operational (or "syntactic") definition, inasmuch as it provides an effective test that can easily be applied in practice. (By contrast, the formal or "semantic" definition isn't of much use in the practical problem of determining whether or not a given JD is trivial.)

I'll defer discussion of *JD irreducibility* to the next chapter. Before then, I want to explain what it means for a JD to be implied by keys:

> **Definition (JD implied by keys):** Let relvar R have heading H and let ✪{$X1,...,Xn$} be a JD, J say, with respect to H. Then J is implied by the keys of R if and only if every relation r that satisfies R's key constraints also satisfies J.

This definition requires a certain amount of elaboration. First, to say some relation satisfies some particular key constraint is to say it satisfies the applicable uniqueness requirement; and if it satisfies the uniqueness requirement for the attributes that constitute some key, it certainly satisfies the uniqueness requirement for every superset of that set of attributes (just so long as that superset is a subset of the pertinent heading, of course)—in other words, for every corresponding superkey. Thus, the phrase "satisfies R's key constraints" in the definition could be replaced by the phrase "satisfies R's superkey constraints" without making any significant difference. Likewise, the concept "implied by keys" could just as well be "implied by superkeys," again without making any significant difference.

Second, what happens if the JD J mentioned in the definition is trivial? Well, in that case, by definition, J is satisfied by every relation r with heading H, and so J is certainly satisfied by every relation r that satisfies R's key constraints a fortiori. So trivial JDs are always "implied by keys," trivially.

Third, then, consider nontrivial JDs. How do we determine whether some nontrivial JD J is implied by the keys of some relvar? This question does have a satisfactory answer, but it's a little complicated, and for that reason I'll defer it to the next section. Before then, I want to give a definition of 5NF and say something about that definition:

> **Definition (fifth normal form):** Relvar R is in fifth normal form (5NF), also known as projection-join normal form (PJ/NF), if and only if every JD of R is implied by the keys of R.

Now, it should be clear that if a JD is implied by the keys of R, it certainly holds in R (i.e., it's certainly "a JD of R"). *But the converse is false:* A JD can hold in R without being implied by the keys of R. In other words, the whole point about the 5NF definition is that the only JDs that hold in a 5NF relvar are ones we can't get rid of—which means ones implied by keys (including trivial ones as a special case).[3]

I'd like to close this section by pointing out an intuitively attractive parallelism between the BCNF and 5NF definitions:

- R is in BCNF if and only if every FD that holds in R is implied by the keys of R.

- R is in 5NF if and only if every JD that holds in R is implied by the keys of R.

However, there's a significant difference also. In the BCNF definition, we can simplify the phrase "implied by the keys" to "implied by *a* key" (meaning any key considered in isolation)—because, if relvar R has keys $K1$, ..., Kn and the FD $Ki \to Y$ holds in R for some key Ki, then the FD $Ki \to Y$ holds in R for all keys Ki $(1 \leq i \leq n)$, necessarily. By contrast, no such simplification applies to 5NF—the JDs that hold in a 5NF relvar are JDs that are implied by the keys taken in combination, *not* necessarily just by some key considered in isolation. For example, let's suppose for the moment that relvar S has two keys, {SNO} and {SNAME}. Then the following JD (a repeat of one we've seen several times already)—

☆ { { SNO , SNAME } , { SNO , STATUS } , { SNAME , CITY } }

—would hold in that relvar. (To spell the point out, every relation that satisfies the two key constraints would satisfy this JD.) But a relation that doesn't satisfy *both* of those two key constraints won't necessarily satisfy the JD either, and the JD therefore doesn't hold in the relvar, precisely because {SNAME} isn't in fact a key. *Exercise:* Invent some sample data to demonstrate the truth of these claims.

---

[3]As usual, "getting rid of" a dependency (of any kind) really means replacing it by some multirelvar constraint.

JDs Implied by Keys

So how do we determine whether a given nontrivial JD is implied by keys? It turns out there's an algorithm, the *membership algorithm* (due to Fagin), that does the job. It works like this. Let relvar R have heading H, and let ☼{$X1$,...,Xn} be a JD, J say, with respect to H. Then:

1. If two distinct components of J both include the same key K of R, replace them in J by their union.

2. Repeat the previous step until no further replacements are possible.

Then the algorithm succeeds, and the original JD is implied by the keys of R, if and only if J is now trivial—i.e., if and only if the final version of J contains H as a component.[4] (Note that trivial JDs in particular cause the algorithm to succeed, trivially.)

Let's look at a few examples. First of all, consider our usual suppliers relvar S. Here's another JD—let's call it J1—that holds in that relvar:

☼ { { SNO , SNAME } , { SNO , STATUS } , { SNO , CITY } }

We already know by repeated application of Heath's Theorem that this JD holds in S. However, observe now that the components {SNO,SNAME} and {SNO,STATUS} both include the key {SNO}. Applying the membership algorithm, therefore, we can replace them by their union {SNO,SNAME,STATUS}. J1 now looks like this:

☼ { { SNO , SNAME , STATUS } , { SNO , CITY } }

Note that (a) this revised version of J1 is itself a JD with respect to the heading of relvar S, and also that (b) relvar S is subject to it—two facts that together should give some insight as to what's going on with the algorithm (see further explanation later).

Next, the components {SNO,SNAME,STATUS} and {SNO,CITY} of this latter JD both include the key {SNO}, and so we can replace them by their union. We obtain:

☼ { { SNO , SNAME , STATUS , CITY } }

---

[4]The following implication is worth pointing out explicitly: The membership algorithm will succeed on the original JD J of R if and only if J contains a component that includes $K1$ and $K2$, a component that includes $K2$ and $K3$, .., and so on, where $K1$, $K2$, $K3$, ..., and so on are all of the keys of relvar R in some order. *Note:* In practice, of course, we might not need to go all the way to the bitter end and compute that final version of J—we can quit as soon as a component is produced that's equal to H.

This further revision of J1 is again a JD (a *unary* JD, in fact) with respect to the heading of S. However, all it says is that relvar S is equal to the "join" of just its identity projection (recall from the answer to Exercise 5.1 in Chapter 5 that the join of a single relation *r*, JOIN{*r*}, is identically equal to *r*). In other words, that further revision of J1 simply says that S can be "nonloss decomposed" into its identity projection. But this observation is trivially true: *Any* relvar can be "nonloss decomposed" into its identity projection, as we saw in Chapter 6. Indeed, the JD is now formally trivial, since it contains a component that's equal to the pertinent heading. It follows that JD J1 as originally stated is implied by the keys of relvar S.

By way of a counterexample, consider now the following JD—let's call it J2—which also holds in relvar S:

☼ { { SNO , SNAME , CITY } , { CITY , STATUS } }

Since the sole key, {SNO}, of the relvar is certainly not included in both components of this (binary) JD, the membership algorithm has no effect on it. Thus, the output from that algorithm is equal to the input (i.e., it consists of the original JD J2, unchanged); no component of that output is equal to the entire heading, and so J2 isn't implied by keys (and relvar S isn't in 5NF, therefore).

Finally, let's consider some more abstract examples. Let relvar *R* have attributes *A*, *B*, *C*, *D*, *E*, and *F* (only), and let *R* have keys {*A*}, {*B*}, and {*C,D*} (only). Further, let *AB* denote the set of attributes {*A,B*}, and similarly for other attribute name combinations ("Heath notation"—see Chapter 7). Now consider the following JDs:

1. ☼ { AB , ACDE , BF }

2. ☼ { ABC , ACD , BEF }

3. ☼ { AB , AC , ADEF }

4. ☼ { ABC , CDEF }

5. ☼ { ABD , ACDE , DF }

Try applying the membership algorithm to these JDs for yourself before reading any further. If you do, you'll find that Nos. 1-3 are implied by keys (and *R* is therefore subject to them, necessarily), while Nos. 4-5 aren't. To elaborate briefly:

- Nos. 1 and 2 are both implied by the pair of keys {A} and {B} taken together, but not by any individual key.

- By contrast, No. 3 is implied by the key {A} considered in isolation.

- No. 4 would be implied by keys—actually by an individual key—if and only if {C} were a key, but it isn't; what's more, that JD can't possibly hold in R, because if it did, then {C} would have to be a key after all (think about it!).

- As for No. 5, it clearly isn't implied by the keys; it might or might not hold in R, but if it does, then R can't be in 5NF.

So what exactly is going on in these examples? Let me try to explain the intuition behind what I've been saying (you might like to try working through what follows in terms of the suppliers relvar S and the JD ☆{{SNO,SNAME},{SNO,STATUS},{SNAME,CITY}}, under the assumption once again that {SNO} and {SNAME} are both keys for that relvar):

- Let $X1$, ..., Xn be subsets of the heading H of relvar R, such that the union of $X1$, ..., Xn is equal to H.

- Let J be the JD ☆{$X1$,...,Xn}, and let J be implied by the keys of R.

- Let r be the relation that's the current value of R.

- Choose, arbitrarily, two distinct elements (components) of the set {$X1$,...,Xn}, say $X1$ and $X2$.

- Let $r1$ and $r2$ be the projections of r on $X1$ and $X2$, respectively.

Now, if $X1$ and $X2$ both include the same key K of R, then the join $r12$ of $r1$ and $r2$—whose heading $X12$ will be the union of $X1$ and $X2$—will be a strict one to one join, and so $r1$ and $r2$ can be replaced by $r12$ without loss of information. (At the same time, $X1$ and $X2$ can be replaced in J by $X12$.) Since (as stated) the original version of J was implied by the keys of R, performing such replacements repeatedly will, by definition, eventually yield a relation (a) that's equal to the original relation r, and in particular (b) will therefore have a heading equal to the entire heading H.

Let me now point out that everything I've said so far becomes much simpler in the common special case where the pertinent relvar R has just one key K. In that case, the JD ✫$\{X1,...,Xn\}$ is implied by keys if and only if the following are both true:

a.   Every attribute of R is included in at least one of $X1$, ..., Xn. (This requirement always applies, of course, in the general case as well as in this special one.)

b.   The sole key K of R is included in each of $X1$, ..., Xn—in other words, each of $X1$, ..., Xn is a superkey.

So if R has just one key K, then R is in 5NF if and only if every component of every JD that holds in R includes that key K.[5] However, please note that—**this is important!**—I'm assuming here that the only JDs under consideration are ones that are irreducible with respect to R. See Chapter 11 for further explanation.

By way of an example of the foregoing point, consider the parts relvar P. The only irreducible JDs ✫$\{X1,...,Xn\}$ that hold in that relvar are such that each Xi ($i = 1$, ..., n) includes the sole key $\{PNO\}$. Those JDs are clearly all implied by that sole key, therefore, and relvar P is thus in 5NF. Here's one of the JDs in question:

✫ { { PNO , PNAME , COLOR } , { PNO , WEIGHT , CITY } }

Thus, relvar P can be nonloss decomposed into its projections on the components of this JD. (Whether we would actually want to perform that decomposition is another matter, of course. We know we could if we wanted to, that's all.)

Let me close this section by revisiting the SPJ example from Chapter 9. For convenience, a sample value of that relvar is shown in Figure 10-1 (a repeat of Figure 9-1). The predicate is *Supplier SNO supplies part PNO to project JNO*, and the following business rule (BRX) is in effect:

• If supplier s supplies part p and part p is supplied to project j and project j is supplied by supplier s, then supplier s supplies part p to project j.

---

[5]Note that this isn't the case with our usual relvar S as defined in Chapters 1 and 2: That relvar is subject to at least one JD—viz., the JD ✫$\{\{SNO,SNAME,CITY\},\{CITY,STATUS\}\}$—in which at least one component fails to include the sole key $\{SNO\}$, and the relvar is therefore not in 5NF.

SPJ

SNO	PNO	JNO
S1	P1	J2
S1	P2	J1
S2	P1	J1
S1	P1	J1

Figure 10-1. *Relvar SPJ—sample value*

Now, we know from Chapter 9 that (as I put it in that chapter) the following JD captures the essence of business rule BRX and so holds in relvar SPJ:

☆ { { SNO , PNO } , { PNO , JNO } , { JNO , SNO } }

Now we can see that this JD isn't implied by the sole key (viz., {SNO,PNO,JNO}) of the relvar, because the membership algorithm fails, and so SPJ isn't in 5NF. So it can be nonloss decomposed into its three binary projections, and probably should be, if we want to reduce redundancy. Those three projections are all in 5NF (no JDs hold in them at all apart from trivial ones).

A Useful Theorem

I said in Chapter 9 that in practice it's quite unusual to find a relvar that's in BCNF and not in 5NF. In fact, there's a theorem that addresses this issue:

> **Theorem:** Let R be a BCNF relvar and let R have no composite keys; then R is in 5NF.

(Recall from Chapter 1 that a composite key is a key consisting of two or more attributes.)

This theorem is quite useful. What it says is, if you can get to BCNF (which is easy enough), and if there aren't any composite keys in your BCNF relvar (which is often but not always the case), then you don't have to worry about the complexities of JDs and 5NF in general—you know without having to think about the matter any further that the relvar simply *is* in 5NF. *Note:* Actually the theorem applies to *3NF*, not BCNF; that is, it really says a *3NF* relvar with no composite keys is in 5NF. But every BCNF relvar is in 3NF, and in any case BCNF is much more important than 3NF, pragmatically speaking (as well as being conceptually simpler).

I don't know why, but people often misinterpret the foregoing theorem. To be specific, given that a BCNF relvar with no composite keys is "automatically" in 5NF, people often seem to think that simply introducing a surrogate key (noncomposite by definition) into a BCNF relvar "automatically" means the relvar is now in 5NF. But it doesn't mean that at all! If the relvar wasn't in 5NF before the surrogate was introduced, it won't be in 5NF afterward. In particular, if it had a composite key before the surrogate was introduced, it'll still have one afterward.

FDs Aren't JDs

Statements to the effect that every FD is a JD, or that (as I put it in Chapter 9) JDs are a kind of generalized FD, are quite common in the less formal parts of the literature; indeed, I've said such things myself in previous books and other previous writings. But such talk is strictly incorrect. It would be better to say that every FD *implies* a JD (which in fact is something we already know to be the case from Heath's Theorem). In other words, if R is subject to a certain FD, F say, then it's certainly subject to a certain JD, J say. However, the converse is false—R can be subject to that same JD J without being subject to that same FD F, as I now show:

- Let relvar R have attributes A, B, and C (only), let F be the FD $AB \to C$, and let R be subject to F (Heath notation once again).

- By Heath's Theorem, then, R is subject to the JD ☆$\{ABC, AB\}$. (With reference to the formulation of Heath's Theorem given in Chapter 9, take X to be AB, Y to be C, and Z to be the empty set of attributes.) Call this JD J.

- But this JD J is trivial—it holds in every relvar R that has heading ABC, regardless of whether that relvar is subject to the FD $AB \to C$.

Update Anomalies Revisited

In Chapter 3, we took a brief look at certain update anomalies that can be caused by FDs: specifically, FDs that hold in a relvar that's not in BCNF. To be frank, however, the update anomaly concept was never very precisely defined (at least, not in that context); probably the best that could be said about it is that the update anomaly problem is just the redundancy problem looked at from another point of view. So what about JDs?—specifically, JDs that hold in a relvar that's not in 5NF? Such JDs do cause redundancy, as we've seen, and so we can expect them to give rise to update anomalies as well. And indeed they do; what's more, the concept can be (or at any rate, is) more precisely defined in that context, as we'll see.

Consider Figure 10-2, which shows two possible values for relvar SPJ; the one on the left is a repeat of the relation from Figure 10-1, the one on the right is obtained from the one on the left by removing two tuples.

possible value 1

SNO	PNO	JNO
S1	P1	J2
S1	P2	J1
S2	P1	J1
S1	P1	J1

possible value 2

SNO	PNO	JNO
S1	P1	J2
S1	P2	J1

Figure 10-2. *Two possible values for relvar SPJ*

Recall now that the following JD holds in relvar SPJ:

✫ { { SNO , PNO } , { PNO , JNO } , { JNO , SNO } }

It follows that:

- If the current value of the relvar is the relation on the left of the figure ("possible value 1"), there's a *deletion anomaly*: We can't delete just the tuple (S1,P1,J1), because what results after that deletion violates the JD and is thus not a legal value for SPJ.

- Likewise, if the current value of the relvar is the relation on the right of the figure ("possible value 2"), there's an *insertion anomaly*: We can't insert just the tuple (S2,P1,J1), because what results after that insertion is—again, and for the same reason—not a legal value for SPJ.

213

Now, the JD in this example is *tuple forcing*. (Recall from Chapter 9 that a JD is tuple forcing if it's such that, if certain tuples appear, certain additional tuples are forced to appear as well.) And the notion of tuple forcing JDs—or the intuition behind that notion, rather—allows us to give definitions of the kinds of update anomalies that can occur in the presence of such a JD, definitions that are more precise than their FD counterparts (such as they are).[6] To be specific:

> **Definition (deletion anomaly with JDs):** Let the JD J hold in relvar R. Then R suffers from a deletion anomaly with respect to J if and only if there exist a relation r and a tuple t, each with the same heading as R, such that:
>
> a. r satisfies J, and
>
> b.   The relation r' whose body is obtained from that of r by removing t violates J.

> **Definition (insertion anomaly with JDs):** Let the JD J hold in relvar R. Then R suffers from an insertion anomaly with respect to J if and only if there exist a relation r and a tuple t, each with the same heading as R, such that:
>
> a. r satisfies J, and
>
> b.   The relation r' whose body is obtained from that of r by appending t satisfies R's key constraints but violates J.

Points arising:

- Note that (a) the foregoing anomalies are specifically defined in terms of some JD J, and (b) they can certainly both occur in the same relvar R, as the SPJ example illustrates. In Chapter 13, however, we'll see that it's also possible, if JD J holds in relvar R, for R to suffer from an insertion anomaly and not a deletion anomaly (with respect to J in both cases).

---

[6]They might be more precise, but they're also very slightly suspect, in a sense, inasmuch as they talk about removing or appending individual tuples and (as explained in *SQL and Relational Theory*) DELETE and INSERT really "remove" or "append" entire relations, not individual tuples. However, the definitions can clearly be refined in such a way as to take care of this minor quibble.

- Although they're more precisely defined than their FD counterparts, the foregoing anomalies can still be regarded as the redundancy problem looked at from another point of view—though here, of course, we're referring to redundancy that's caused by a JD, not by an FD.

- If relvar *R* is subject to update anomalies and those anomalies are caused by a JD (tuple forcing or otherwise), then replacing *R* by a set of 5NF projections will solve the problem. That is, such anomalies can't occur with a 5NF relvar.

Please note carefully, however, that not all update anomalies are caused by FDs or JDs. In fact, it's probably true to say that most integrity constraints (perhaps all?) can give rise to an insertion anomaly, in the sense that there always exists a tuple whose insertion would cause the constraint in question to be violated. (As a simple example, suppose there's a constraint to the effect that supplier status values must lie in the range 1 to 100, inclusive.) By contrast, comparatively few constraints can give rise to a deletion anomaly. (One that can would be a constraint to the effect that there must always be at least two distinct suppliers. Another is a foreign key constraint; in the suppliers-and-parts database, for example, deleting a supplier can't be done if it causes the foreign key constraint from SP to S to be violated.[7])

Exercises

10.1   The following questions are repeated from Chapter 1, but you should have a better chance of answering them now (assuming you couldn't do so before, that is):

a.   (*Exercise 1.6.*) Is it true that every "all key" relvar is in 5NF?

b.   (*Exercise 1.7.*) Is it true that every binary relvar is in 5NF?

---

[7]Note, however, that (by definition) the foreign key constraint from SP to S is a multirelvar constraint. By contrast, JDs are always single-relvar constraints specifically (where a single-relvar constraint is any constraint that can be tested by examining the pertinent relvar in isolation, i.e., without having to examine any other relvar in the database). Even the generalized update anomaly definitions to be discussed in Chapter 15 have to do with single-relvar constraints only and have nothing to say about multirelvar constraints.

    c. (*Exercise 1.8.*) Is it true that if a relvar has just one key and just one other attribute, then it's in 5NF?

    d. (*Exercise 1.9.*) Is it true that if a relvar is in BCNF but not 5NF, then it must be all key?

    e. (*Exercise 1.10.*) Can you give a precise definition of 5NF?

    f. (*Exercise 1.11.*) Is it true that 5NF relvars are redundancy free?

10.2 Give as precise a definition as you can of what it means for a relvar to be subject to a join dependency.

10.3 How many JDs hold in the shipments relvar SP?

10.4 What does it mean to say a JD is implied by superkeys?

10.5 What's a trivial JD? Is a trivial FD a special case?

10.6 Give an example of a JD that's (a) tuple forcing, (b) not tuple forcing.

10.7 Consider (either base relvar or view) RAP as discussed in the answer to Exercise 9.2 in Chapter 9. Give examples of an insertion anomaly and a deletion anomaly that can occur with that relvar.

10.8 The following is a lightly edited quote from a certain database textbook:

Fifth normal form concerns dependencies that are rather obscure. It has to do with relations that can be divided into subrelations ... but then cannot be reconstructed. The condition under which this situation arises has no clear, intuitive meaning. We do not know what the consequences of such dependencies are or even if they have any practical consequences.

Do *you* have any comments?

10.9   The following is a lightly edited quote from my own textbook *An Introduction to Database Systems* (8th edition, Addison-Wesley, 2004):

Relvar *R* is in 5NF if and only if every nontrivial JD that holds in *R* is implied by the keys of *R*, where:

    a.   The JD ✩{*A*, *B*, ..., *Z*} is trivial (with respect to *R*) if and only if at least one of *A*, *B*, ..., *Z* is the heading of *R*.

    b.   The JD ✩{*A*, *B*, ..., *Z*} is implied by the keys of *R* if and only if each of *A*, *B*, ..., *Z* is a superkey for *R*.

Do you have any comments?

Answers

10.1   No (see the discussion of relvar SPJ in the body of the chapter for a counterexample). b. No (in fact, as was shown in the answer to Exercise 4.6 in Chapter 4, a binary relvar isn't necessarily even in BCNF, or even 2NF). c. No (see Chapter 13). d. No (again, see Chapter 13). e. See the body of the chapter. f. No (see relvar CTXD in Chapter 9 for a counterexample; see also Chapter 17).

10.2   See the body of the chapter.

10.3   First, I assume no JD has any repeated components, for otherwise the number of JDs would literally be infinite (though at least the number of *logically distinct* JDs would of course always be finite). Second, relvar SP is in 5NF, and in fact in 6NF; we haven't discussed 6NF yet (see Chapter 14), but I can at least say for now that if a relvar is in 6NF, then all of the JDs that hold in that relvar will be trivial ones. So the question becomes: How many trivial JDs hold in relvar SP? Well, all such JDs take the form ✩{*H*,*X1*,...,*Xn*}, where *H* denotes the entire heading and {*X1*,...,*Xn*} is a set—possibly empty—of proper subsets of *H*. Since *H* is of degree three, it has eight subsets, of which all but one are proper. So how many distinct sets are there whose elements are some subset of a prescribed set of seven elements? Well, there's one such set with no elements at all; there are seven such sets with just one element; and, more generally, there are "7 pick i" such sets with i elements ($i = 0, 1, ..., 7$).[8] So the total number of sets of proper subsets of H = (7 pick 0) + (7 pick 1) + (7 pick 2) + ... + (7 pick 7) = 1 + 7 + 21 + 35 + 35 + 21 + 7 + 1 = 128. So there are 128 trivial JDs altogether that hold in relvar SP. *Note:* Of those 128, 64 involve an empty component, which might reasonably be ignored—for example, the JDs ✸{H,{ }} and ✸{H} are clearly equivalent[9]—thereby reducing the total count to 64.

10.4   See the body of the chapter.

10.5   For the definition, see the body of the chapter. Since an FD isn't a JD but merely implies one, a trivial FD isn't a special case. However, the JD implied by a trivial FD is indeed itself trivial in turn. For example, the trivial FD {CITY,STATUS} → {STATUS} holds in the suppliers relvar S. Applying Heath's Theorem, therefore, we see the trivial JD ✸{AB,AC} holds in S, where A is {CITY,STATUS}, B is {STATUS}, and C is {SNO,SNAME} (the JD is trivial because AC is equal to the entire heading).

10.6   For an example of a tuple forcing JD, see the SPJ example in the body of the chapter. As for one that's not tuple forcing, consider, e.g., the JD ✸{{SNO,SNAME,CITY},{CITY,STATUS}} that holds in relvar S (which fails to be tuple forcing, observe, precisely because it has a component that's a superkey for the pertinent relvar).

10.7   Examples can be obtained from the examples given in the body of the chapter in connection with relvar SPJ by systematically replacing supplier numbers by RNO values, part numbers by ANO values, and project numbers by PNO values. *No further answer provided.*

10.8   Well, obviously I don't know whether you have any comments, but I certainly do. However, I don't think it would be polite to air them here, so I won't.

---

[8]In general, the expression "n pick r" denotes the number of ways of picking r elements from a set of n elements.

[9]*Proof:* For all relations r, JOIN{$r\{H\}$,r\{ \}} = JOIN{$r\{H\}$} = JOIN{r} = r.

10.9   The given "definition" is not only embarrassingly sloppy, it's wrong! To be more specific:

- "*R* is in in 5NF if and only if every nontrivial JD that holds in *R* is implied by the keys of *R*" is correct.

However:

- The triviality or otherwise of a given JD should be defined with respect to a heading, not a relvar.

- For the JD ✲{*A*, *B*, ..., *Z*} to hold in *R*, it's necessary, but obviously not sufficient, that the union of *A*, *B*, ..., *Z* be equal to the entire heading of *R*.

- But even if the foregoing condition is satisfied, then the fact that each of *A*, *B*, ..., *Z* is a superkey for *R* is *not* sufficient for the JD in question to be implied by the keys of *R*. (On the other hand, it *is* sufficient in the simple special case in which *R* has just one key.)

See Chapter 13 for further discussion.

CHAPTER 11

Implicit Dependencies

What are you implying?

—20th century catchphrase

We've seen several illustrations in previous chapters of the idea that certain dependencies imply others. To be specific, we saw in Chapter 7 how some FDs are implied by other FDs, and we saw in Chapters 9 and 10 how some JDs are implied by FDs. It's time to take a closer look at such matters. Note that if we need to tell what normal form some given relvar is in, we do need to know all of the dependencies, implicit ones as well as explicit ones, that hold in that relvar. In this chapter, therefore, I plan to discuss among other things:

- Irrelevant JD components

- Combining JD components

- Irreducible JDs

- Adding JD components

These various discussions will pave the way for an explanation of what's called *the chase*, to be described in the penultimate section of the chapter.

221

© C. J. Date 2019
C. J. Date, *Database Design and Relational Theory*, https://doi.org/10.1007/978-1-4842-5540-7_11

Irrelevant Components

Once again consider relvar S, with its FD {CITY} → {STATUS}. As we know from previous chapters:

- That relvar can be nonloss decomposed into its projections on {SNO,SNAME,CITY} and {CITY,STATUS}.

- It can also clearly be nonloss decomposed into those same two projections *together with* the projection on (say) {SNAME,CITY}.

- However, that third projection is irrelevant, in the sense that it clearly isn't needed in the process of reconstructing the original relvar.

Now let me restate the foregoing example in terms of JDs, as follows: Relvar S is subject to the JD

☆ { { SNO , SNAME , CITY } , { CITY , STATUS } }

and also to the JD

☆ { { SNO , SNAME , CITY } , { CITY , STATUS } , { SNAME , CITY } }

In this latter JD, however, the {SNAME,CITY} component is irrelevant: It's a proper subset of another component, and for that reason the corresponding projection isn't needed in the process of reconstructing the original relvar.

With the foregoing example by way of motivation, I can now give a precise definition of what it means for some component to be irrelevant in some JD:

> **Definition (irrelevant component):** Let ☆{$X1$,..., Xn} be a JD, J say; then Xi is irrelevant in J if and only if (a) there exists some Xj in J such that Xi is a proper subset of Xj (in symbols, $Xi \subset Xj$) or (b) there exists some Xj in J ($j < i$) such that $Xj = Xi$.[1]

The reason for my choice of the term *irrelevant* here should be clear: If Xi is irrelevant in J, then every relation that satisfies J also satisfies J', where J' is derived from J by dropping Xi. What's more, the converse is true too: Every relation that satisfies J' also satisfies J. In other words, the JDs J and J' are *equivalent*: Each implies the other, and every relation that satisfies either necessarily satisfies the other as well. It follows that not only can irrelevant components always be dropped, they can always be added too, without significant effect.

---

[1]If we can assume the components $X1$, ..., Xn are all distinct, then we can drop part (b) of this definition.

Combining Components

So now we've seen that some JDs imply others, just as some FDs imply others. But irrelevant components are far from being the end of the story. The next point is as follows (I've labeled it a theorem, but it's very obvious and scarcely merits such a grand designation):

> **Theorem:** Let J be a JD and let J' be derived from J by replacing two components by their union. Then J implies J' (that is, every relation that satisfies J also satisfies J').

By way of example, every legal value of relvar S satisfies the following JD (it's the JD from the previous section, the one with an irrelevant component)—

☼ { { SNO , SNAME , CITY } , { CITY , STATUS } , { SNAME , CITY } }

—and therefore satisfies this one too:

☼ { { SNO , SNAME , CITY } , { CITY , STATUS , SNAME } }

Exercise: Check the validity of the foregoing claim for yourself—perhaps even try to prove it, formally—if it isn't immediately obvious. (Also, how many distinct JDs can be derived from the given one by combining components in this manner?) Points arising:

- I made use of the foregoing theorem, tacitly, when I explained the intuition behind the membership algorithm (i.e., the algorithm for testing whether a JD is implied by keys) in Chapter 10.

- Observe that the theorem involves an implication, not an equivalence: J implies J', but the converse isn't true—J' doesn't imply J, in general, and so J and J' aren't equivalent (again, in general).

  Note: In fact this point is easy to see: If we keep on replacing components by their union, we'll eventually obtain one that's equal to the entire heading, and the resulting JD J' will be trivial— and it's clearly not the case that every JD is equivalent to some trivial JD.

- Although it's true that the second of the two JDs shown above (the binary one) holds in relvar S, nonloss decomposing that relvar on the basis of that JD would *not* be a good idea.

Note: Exercise 11.4 asks you to explain this observation further, but you might like to take a moment now to convince yourself that it's true. Also—to get ahead of myself for a moment—I can say the JD in question, the binary one, is in fact *irreducible* with respect to S (see the section immediately following). What the example shows, therefore, is that although irreducible JDs are important, they don't necessarily correspond to good decompositions. Informally, in other words, we need to distinguish between "good" and "bad" JDs, where "good" and "bad" refer to the quality of the corresponding decompositions. For further discussion of such matters, see Chapter 16.

Irreducible JDs

So far the notion of one JD implying another has been more or less syntactic in nature—I haven't really paid much attention to the question of whether the JDs we're talking about actually hold in some given relvar. (Observe that neither the definition of irrelevant components, nor the theorem about replacing components by their union, made any mention of a relvar, nor even of a heading.) Now, however, let's consider JDs that do actually hold in some relvar. Then we have the following theorem:

> **Theorem:** Let JD *J* hold in relvar *R*; then *J* is equivalent to some irreducible JD (not necessarily unique) that also holds in *R*.

I'll explain exactly what it means for a JD to be irreducible in a moment. Note first, however, that the concept of equivalence (i.e., of JDs) has to be understood in the context of some particular relvar; that is, it's possible for two JDs to be such that both hold in one relvar while just one holds in another. In such a case, the two JDs might or might not be equivalent with respect to the first relvar, but they're certainly not equivalent with respect to the second.

Now to JD equivalence as such. Let me begin by reminding you of something from Part II of this book regarding FDs: namely, that every FD that holds in relvar *R* implies some irreducible FD that also holds in relvar *R*. (This is easy to see: Just keep dropping attributes from the determinant until what remains is an FD that no longer holds.) Similarly, every JD that holds in relvar *R* implies—in fact (a stronger statement), is equivalent to—some irreducible JD that also holds in relvar *R*.

So what does it mean for a JD to be irreducible? Here's a definition:

> **Definition (irreducible JD):** Let ☼{*X1*,...,*Xn*} be a JD, *J* say, that
> holds in relvar *R*, and let there be no proper subset {*Y1*,...,*Ym*}
> of {*X1*,...,*Xn*} such that the JD ☼{*Y1*,...,*Ym*} also holds in *R*.
> Then *J* is irreducible with respect to *R* (or just irreducible, if *R* is
> understood).

Points arising:

- It's easy to see that every JD that holds in relvar *R* implies an irreducible JD that also holds in relvar *R*: Just keep dropping components from the given JD until what's left is a JD that no longer holds in *R*, and then the last one that does hold is irreducible.

- It's also easy to see that the implication goes the other way, too: Start with the irreducible JD and add the dropped components back in one by one until the original JD is reached. At each step in this process, the current version of the JD will be a JD that holds in *R*.

  Note: From this point and the previous point taken together, it follows that (a) every JD that holds in *R* is equivalent to some irreducible JD that holds in *R* (as previously stated, in fact), and hence that (b) the irreducible JDs that hold in *R* in fact imply all of the JDs that hold in *R*.

- If some component *Xi* is irrelevant in *J*, then *J* is certainly reducible with respect to every relvar in which it holds (because *Xi* can be dropped without significant loss). However, *J* can still be reducible with respect to some relvar even if all components are relevant, as I now show.

Consider the suppliers relvar S once again. For simplicity, however, let's agree to ignore attribute SNAME; what's more, let's agree to take the name "S" to refer to this reduced version of the relvar, until further notice. Now consider the following JD:

☼ { { SNO , CITY } , { CITY , STATUS } , { SNO , STATUS } }

This JD—let's call it J1—clearly has no irrelevant components. However, I'll show that (a) it holds in relvar S but that (b) it's reducible with respect to that relvar, because the {CITY,STATUS} component can be dropped and what's left is still a JD of S.

Note: Actually the reducibility in this example is intuitively obvious, because (to state the matter precisely) the projection on {CITY,STATUS} of S is clearly equal to the projection on {CITY,STATUS} of the join of S{SNO,CITY} and S{SNO,STATUS}. As a consequence, the {CITY,STATUS} component adds nothing, as it were. To repeat, therefore: The reducibility is "obvious"—but now I want to *prove* it.

a. First, then, suppose the following tuples appear in S:

> *s1   c1   t2*
> *s2   c1   t1*
> *s1   c2   t1*

(I'm using an obvious simplified notation for tuples here; *s1* and *s2* denote supplier numbers, *c1* and *c2* denote supplier cities, and *t1* and *t2* denote status values. Note how each of the three tuples corresponds to one component of JD J1.)

Now, because {SNO} is a key, the following FDs hold in S:

> { SNO } → { CITY }
> { SNO } → { STATUS }

We can therefore conclude that *c1* = *c2* and *t1* = *t2*, and so the tuple

> *s1   c1   t1*

appears in S, necessarily, because in fact it's identical to the first (or, equally, the third) in the original list of tuples as shown above. But to say the original "three" tuples cause this "fourth" tuple to appear—if you see what I mean—is to say, precisely, that JD J1 holds (I mean, that's what J1 says). So J1 does hold in S.

b. Now appealing to either of the FDs {SNO} → {CITY} and {SNO} → {STATUS} (both of which hold in S, as we know) and to Heath's Theorem, we see that the following JD—let's call it J2—certainly holds in relvar S:

> ☼ { { SNO , CITY } , { SNO , STATUS } }

But the components of J2 form a proper subset of those of J1. It follows that J1 is reducible with respect to S. To be specific, the component {CITY,STATUS} can be dropped from J1 without loss, in the sense that what remains is still a JD of S.

Observe now that the foregoing proof made no use of the fact that the functional dependency {CITY} → {STATUS} holds in S (indeed, the result would still be valid even if that FD didn't hold). But now let's do another example that does make use of that FD:

- First, we know from the previous example that the following JD (J1 from that example) holds in S:

  ☼ { { SNO , CITY } , { CITY , STATUS } , { SNO , STATUS } }

- But the FD {CITY} → {STATUS} also holds, and so by Heath's Theorem the following JD—let's call it J3—holds as well:

  ☼ { { CITY , STATUS } , { CITY , SNO } }

- The components of J3 form a proper subset of those of J1, and so it follows once again that J1 is reducible with respect to S. To be specific, the component {SNO,STATUS} can be dropped from J1 without loss, in the sense that what remains is still a JD of S.

Observe, therefore, that the original JD J1 is equivalent, with respect to relvar S, to two distinct JDs: namely, J2 and J3.

In general, of course, the question is: Given relvar R and a JD J that holds in R, how can we find an irreducible equivalent (meaning, to be more precise about the matter, a JD that's both equivalent to J and irreducible, where *equivalent* and *irreducible* are both understood as being with respect to R)? Well:

- If some component is irrelevant in J, that component can clearly be dropped.

- If all components are relevant, we can only try dropping one, and then:

  a. If what's left is still a JD of R, we drop another component and repeat the process.

  b. If what's left isn't a JD of R, we reinstate the dropped component and try dropping another one.

Eventually, we'll arrive at a JD that's equivalent to the original one and is irreducible.

And how do we tell whether some JD is in fact a JD of *R*? Well, if it's one that's been explicitly declared as such, there's clearly no problem; but if not, we can use the *chase*, which I'll be describing in the next section but one.

Summary So Far

Let me summarize where we are. The general point is that some JDs imply others. As specific illustrations of this point, we've discussed:

- *Irrelevant components:* Any given JD *J* is equivalent to every JD *J'* that can be obtained from *J* by adding or dropping irrelevant components.

- *Combining components:* Any given JD *J* implies every JD *J'* that can be obtained from *J* by replacing two or more components by their union.

- *Irreducibility:* Any given JD *J* that holds in relvar *R* is equivalent to at least one JD *J'*—not necessarily distinct from *J*—that holds in *R* and is irreducible (where *equivalent* and *irreducible* must both be understood as being with respect to *R*). It follows that *R*'s irreducible JDs in fact imply all of *R*'s JDs.

The following observations are also valid (I haven't discussed them in detail, but they're intuitively obvious):

- *Adding attributes:* If JD *J* holds in relvar *R*, then so does every JD *J'* that can be obtained from *J* by adding some attribute of *R* to some component of *J*.

- *Adding components:* If JD *J* holds in relvar *R*, then so does every JD *J'* that can be obtained from *J* by adding any subset of the heading of *R* as another component.

In both of these latter cases, however, we're talking about implication, not equivalence. For example, in relvar S (but ignoring SNAME once again, for simplicity), the JD

☼ { { SNO , STATUS } , { SNO , CITY } }

holds, and therefore the following JD, with an added component, holds as well:

☼ { { SNO , STATUS } , { SNO , CITY } , { CITY , STATUS } }

However, the converse is false—if the latter JD holds, it doesn't follow that the former one does.[2]

We can also say the following: If (a) *J* is a JD that holds in relvar *R* and *J* implies another JD *J'* (which therefore also holds in *R*, by definition), and (b) *J'* is obtained from *J* by dropping attributes from components of *J* and/or dropping entire components from *J*, then *J* is certainly a "bad" JD (see the remarks on the topic of good vs. bad JDs at the end of the section "Combining Components"). However, a JD *J* can still be "bad" even if it implies no such JD *J'*, as we'll see; that is, not all "bad" JDs conform to the foregoing simple pattern.

Now I'd like to generalize the discussion somewhat. First of all, from this point forward I'll take the term *dependencies* to mean either FDs or JDs or both, as the context demands.[3] Now, throughout this book so far, whenever I've considered the question of dependencies being implied by others, I've mostly, albeit tacitly, limited my attention to ones that are implied by an *individual* dependency. More generally, however, it turns out that certain *combinations* of dependencies can imply others. Let me give an example.

Consider a relvar SPT, with attributes SNO, PNO, and STATUS (only), where the attributes have their usual meanings. Suppose we're told, not entirely unreasonably, that the following dependencies (one FD and one JD) both hold in this relvar:

```
{ SNO , PNO } → { STATUS }

☼ { { SNO , PNO } , { SNO , STATUS } }
```

Now, given the semantics of the situation, it's intuitively obvious that (a) {SNO} isn't a key for SPT and yet (b) the FD {SNO} → {STATUS} holds in SPT implicitly (and so SPT isn't in 2NF, incidentally). Note that I say *implicitly*—we haven't been told explicitly that the FD holds. The question is: Can we *prove* (a) and (b), given only that the stated FD and JD hold? That is, can we show that (a) and (b) are valid *formally*, without paying any regard to semantics? (After all, that's what the system would have to do, if we wanted it to be able to infer dependencies. The system doesn't know anything about semantics, as I'm using that term here.)[4]

---

[2]Of course, both JDs do hold in our running example, but that's not because the ternary one implies the binary one (it doesn't); rather, it's because the FD {CITY} → {STATUS} also holds.

[3]As we know, other kinds of dependencies do exist, but I'm deliberately excluding them from consideration at this time.

[4]I note in passing that a proof of part (b) follows immediately from what Exercise 11.3, q.v., refers to as the converse of an extended version of Heath's theorem.

So let's give it a try. First of all, suppose the following tuples appear in SPT—

s1   p1   t1
s1   p2   t2

—where *p1* ≠ *p2*. Now what we need to do, in order to show that the FD {SNO} →
{STATUS} holds, is to show that *t1* and *t2* must be equal. We begin by writing down
the projections of the two tuples corresponding to the components of the given JD
✳{{SNO,PNO},{SNO,STATUS}}:

s1   p1   *s1   t1*
s1   p2   *s1   t2*

Joining these projections together, we obtain the original two tuples plus two extra
ones (shown below in **bold**):

s1   p1   t1
s1   p1   t2
s1   p2   t1
s1   p2   t2

Since the given JD holds, the two extra tuples must in fact appear in the relvar along
with the original two. But the FD {SNO,PNO} → {STATUS} holds also; it follows that
t1 = *t2*, and hence that the FD {SNO} → {STATUS} holds (every tuple that has SNO *s1*
also has STATUS *t1*). This is part (b) of what was to be proved. At the same time, by our
assumption we have *p1* ≠ *p2*—note that nothing in the argument so far invalidates that
assumption—from which it follows that the FD {SNO} → {PNO} *doesn't* hold, and so
{SNO} isn't a key; and this is part (a) of what was to be proved.

So we see that any given relvar is subject to both explicit dependencies (these are
the ones explicitly declared) and implicit dependencies (these are the ones implied by
the explicitly declared ones). For the record, let me bring these points together into an
appropriate definition:

> **Definition (explicit vs. implicit dependencies):** Let *R* be a relvar.
> Associated with *R* are two sets of explicit dependencies: a set
> *XFD* of explicit FDs that hold in *R* and a set *XJD* of explicit JDs
> that hold in *R*. The FDs in *XFD* together with the JDs in *XJD* are
> the explicit dependencies of *R*. The FDs and JDs that aren't in
> *XFD* or *XJD* but are logical consequences of the ones in *XFD* and

XJD are the implicit dependencies of *R*. The explicit and implicit dependencies of *R* taken together are the dependencies of *R*. A relation *r* can be assigned to *R* only if that relation *r* satisfies all of the dependencies of *R*.

The Chase Algorithm

From everything we've seen in this chapter so far, the obvious question presents itself:

> ***Given some set D of dependencies (FDs or JDs or a mixture), what dependencies d are implied by those in that set?***

A partial answer to this question is provided by *the chase algorithm*, which is, precisely, an algorithm for testing whether some given dependency *d* is implied by some given set of dependencies *D*.[5] More specifically, given such a set *D* and such a dependency *d*, the chase will either:

a. Show that *d* is implied by *D*, or

b. Show that it isn't, by providing an explicit counterexample—that is, a relation that satisfies all of the dependencies in *D* and yet violates *d*.

As a matter of fact we've already seen some examples of the chase in action, as it were. In the previous section, I showed how a given FD and JD together implied a certain FD and not another (the latter was actually a key constraint, which is a special case of an FD constraint, of course). And in the section before that, I gave two examples in which a given FD and JD together implied a certain JD (thereby showing the given JD was reducible, incidentally). All of these examples were in fact applications of the chase. But now let's get more specific. In order to do that, I first need to introduce a little more terminology:

- Consider FDs. Abstractly (though of course very loosely), an FD takes the form "If certain tuples *t1*, ..., *tn* appear, then certain attributes within those tuples must have equal values." For this reason, FDs are sometimes said to be *equality generating* dependencies.

---

[5]See David Maier, Alberto O. Mendelzon, and Yehoshua Sagiv: "Testing Implications of Data Dependencies," *ACM Transactions on Database Systems 4*, No. 4 (December 1979).

- Now consider JDs. Abstractly, but again very loosely, a JD takes the form "If certain tuples *t1, ..., tn* appear, then a certain tuple *t* must appear." JDs are therefore sometimes said to be *tuple generating* dependencies.

Before going any further, I must caution you not to confuse tuple generating and tuple *forcing* dependencies.[6] A tuple *forcing* dependency is a JD with the property that if tuples *t1, ..., tn* appear, then some tuple *t* is forced to appear that's distinct from each of *t1, ..., tn*. By contrast, a tuple *generating* dependency (a) doesn't require the "generated" tuple to be distinct from the given tuples and (b) doesn't in fact have to be a JD, as such, at all. (However, the only tuple generating dependencies discussed in this book are indeed JDs specifically. For present purposes, therefore, you can take "tuple generating dependency" to mean a JD; thus, we can say that all tuple forcing dependencies are tuple generating, but some tuple generating dependencies aren't tuple forcing.)

Equality generating and tuple generating dependencies both involve a set of *premises*—viz., the given tuples *t1, ..., tn*—and a *conclusion*. For a tuple generating dependency, the conclusion is the generated tuple *t*; for an equality generating dependency, it's the fact that a certain equality holds.

Now I can explain the chase algorithm as such. Perhaps I should say first that it's essentially common sense; in fact, it tends to be easier to illustrate than to describe. In outline, however, it works like this. We're trying to determine whether the dependency *d* follows from the dependencies in the set *D*. We proceed as follows:

1. We write down tuples representing the premises of *d*.

2. We apply the dependencies in *D* to those tuples (possibly generating additional tuples), and keep repeating this process until no further change occurs.

This procedure overall will eventually yield either:

a. A representation of the conclusion of *d*, in which case *d* does follow from *D*, or

b. A relation that satisfies *D* but not *d*, in which case *d* doesn't follow from *D*.

---

[6]By the same token, don't confuse *equality generating* dependencies and *equality* dependencies, which were described in Chapter 3.

Let's do an example. Let the given set of dependencies be as follows:

$\{ A \rightarrow C , B \rightarrow C , C \rightarrow D , CE \rightarrow A , DE \rightarrow C \}$

(Actually they're all FDs, as you can see.) Consider also the following JD (call it *J*):

☆ { *AB* , *AD* , *AE* , *BE* , *CDE* }

I'll now show that the given FDs do in fact imply *J* (a state of affairs that, I'll think you agree, is far from immediately obvious).

The first step is to write down tuples representing the premises of the JD *J*. Now, let me spell out exactly what that JD says:

- If all of the following are the case—

    a tuple appears with $A = a$ and $B = b$

    a tuple appears with $A = a$ and $D = d$

    a tuple appears with $A = a$ and $E = e$

    a tuple appears with $B = b$ and $E = e$

    a tuple appears with $C = c$ and $D = d$ and $E = e$

    —then the following must also be the case:

    a tuple appears with $A = a$ and $B = b$ and $C = c$ and $D = d$ and $E = e$.

However, it turns out to be more convenient in what follows to use, not *a, b, c, d,* and *e* as such, but rather suffixed *x*'s and *y*'s to denote attribute values. To be specific, I'll use *x1-x5* in place of *a-e*, respectively, and I'll use *y*'s in all other positions; e.g., I'll use *y23* to denote the "third" (i.e., *C*) value in the "second" premise tuple. So the premise tuples look like this:[7]

x1	*x2*	*y13*	*y14*	*y15*
x1	*y22*	*y23*	*x4*	*y25*
x1	*y32*	*y33*	*y34*	*x5*
y41	*x2*	*y43*	*y44*	*x5*
y51	*y52*	*x3*	*x4*	*x5*

---

[7]Strictly speaking, the premise tuples aren't really tuples at all, because they contain variables instead of values. Likewise, the premise tuples taken together don't really constitute a relation, either. I propose to overlook these points from here on, but I should at least mention that—partly for such reasons—the research literature typically refers to the initial set of premise "tuples," and all other such sets appearing subsequently during the chase process, as constituting not relations but *tableaux*.

If (and only if) the JD is implied by the five FDs, then, these tuples will "generate" the following tuple:

$x1$ $x2$ $x3$ $x4$ $x5$

So let's see if it does; i.e., let's apply the given dependencies.

- From $A \rightarrow C$, we have $y13 = y23 = y33$; likewise, from $B \rightarrow C$, we have $y13 = y43$. So we can replace each of $y23$, $y33$, and $y43$ by $y13$. The premise tuples become (replacements shown in **bold**):

$x1$	$x2$	$y13$	$y14$	$y15$
$x1$	$y22$	**$y13$**	$x4$	$y25$
$x1$	$y32$	**$y13$**	$y34$	$x5$
$y41$	$x2$	**$y13$**	$y44$	$x5$
$y51$	$y52$	$x3$	$x4$	$x5$

- From $C \rightarrow D$, we have $y14 = y34 = y44 = x4$. Make the replacements:

$x1$	$x2$	$y13$	**$x4$**	$y15$
$x1$	$y22$	$y13$	$x4$	$y25$
$x1$	$y32$	$y13$	**$x4$**	$x5$
$y41$	$x2$	$y13$	**$x4$**	$x5$
$y51$	$y52$	$x3$	$x4$	$x5$

- From $CE \rightarrow A$, we have $y41 = x1$. Make the replacements:

$x1$	$x2$	$y13$	$x4$	$y15$
$x1$	$y22$	$y13$	$x4$	$y25$
$x1$	$y32$	$y13$	$x4$	$x5$
$x1$	$x2$	$y13$	$x4$	$x5$
$y51$	$y52$	$x3$	$x4$	$x5$

- From $DE \rightarrow C$, we have $y13 = x3$. Make the replacements:

$x1$	$x2$	**$x3$**	$x4$	$y15$	
$x1$	$y22$	**$x3$**	$x4$	$y25$	
$x1$	$y32$	**$x3$**	$x4$	$x5$	
$x1$	$x2$	**$x3$**	$x4$	$x5$	Success: all x's !!!
$y51$	$y52$	$x3$	$x4$	$x5$	

- The "fourth" tuple here is all x's, and so the JD J does indeed follow from the given FDs.

Let's look at another example. Let the given set of dependencies consist of just the JD {AB,AC}. Does this set imply the FD $A \rightarrow B$? *Note:* We already know the answer is no, because what we're talking about here is the converse of Heath's Theorem, and we know from Exercise 5.4 that the converse of Heath's Theorem is false. But let's see what the chase tells us:

- Premise tuples:

  x1   y12   y13
  x1   y22   y23

If and only if the FD is implied by the JD, then applying the JD to these tuples will have to make *y12* and *y22* equal. Does it do so? Well:

- The given JD "generates" tuples as follows:

  x1   y12   y23
  x1   y22   y13

- The four tuples taken together satisfy the JD but not the FD; in particular, they don't require that *y12* = *y22*. So the FD doesn't follow from the JD.

Concluding Remarks

In this chapter, we've seen JDs implying JDs; a JD and an FD together implying an FD; FDs implying a JD; and, in earlier chapters, FDs implying FDs. However, note carefully that all the chase lets us do is determine whether a *specific* dependency follows from given dependencies. What it doesn't do is let us *infer*, or *generate*, new dependencies from the given set (that's why I said, near the beginning of the previous section, that the chase provided only a partial answer to the question). For that, we'd need an axiomatization for FDs and JDs. And while Armstrong's rules provide a sound and complete axiomatization for FDs by themselves, it's unfortunately a known fact that no such axiomatization exists for FDs and JDs considered together.[8]

Exercises

11.1   Consider the parts relvar P from the suppliers-and-parts database. For simplicity, let's rename attributes PNO, PNAME, COLOR, WEIGHT, and CITY as A, B, C, D, and E, respectively, and let's use Heath notation once again. Then the following JDs are all defined with respect to the heading of P:

a. ☼{ AC , ABDE }

b. ☼{ ACD , ABDE }

c. ☼{ AE , ABCD }

d. ☼{ AB , ACD , CE }

e. ☼{ AB , ACD , AE }

f. ☼{ AB , BCD , DE }

g. ☼{ ABC , ACDE , CE }

h. ☼{ ABCD , BDE , BCE }

i. ☼{ AB , ABC , BCD , CDE , AD }

j. ☼{ AB , BC , CD , DE , AD }

k. ☼{ ABD , CDE , ABC , BE , ABE }

l. ☼{ A , AB , ABC , ABD , ACE }

Which of these JDs are trivial? Which ones involve irrelevant components? Which imply which others in the list? Which pairs are equivalent to one another? Which are satisfied by the sample value of relvar P shown in Figure 1-1? Which hold in relvar P? Which are irreducible with respect to P?

---

[8]See for example the book *Foundations of Databases*, by Serge Abiteboul, Richard Hull, and Victor Vianu (Addison-Wesley, 1995).

11.2   The dependencies in this exercise are all defined with respect to a heading consisting of attributes *ABCD*.

   a.   Does the set of FDs {$A \rightarrow B, A \rightarrow C$} imply the JD ✿{*AD,ABC*}?

   b.   Does the set of FDs {$C \rightarrow D, B \rightarrow C$} imply the JD ✿{*AB,BC,CD*}?

   c.   Does the set of FDs {$A \rightarrow B, B \rightarrow C$} imply the JD ✿{*AB,BC,CD*}?

   d.   Does the the JD ✿{*BC,ABD*} imply the JD ✿{*AB,BC,CD*}?

11.3   We know from Exercise 5.4 in Chapter 5 that the converse of Heath's Theorem is false. However, there's an extended version of that theorem whose converse is true. Here it is:

Heath's Theorem (*extended version*): Let relvar *R* have heading *H* and let *X*, *Y*, and *Z* be subsets of *H* such that the union of *X*, *Y*, and *Z* is equal to *H*. Let *XY* denote the union of *X* and *Y*, and similarly for *XZ*. If *R* is subject to the FD $X \rightarrow Y$, then (a) *R* is subject to the JD ✿{*XY,XZ*}, and (b) *XZ* is a superkey for *R*.

Prove part (b) of this theorem. Prove also that (a) and (b) together imply that $X \rightarrow Y$ holds (the converse of the extended theorem).

11.4   Consider the following JDs, both of which hold in relvar S:

   ✿ { { SNO , SNAME , CITY } , { CITY , STATUS } , { SNAME , CITY } }

   ✿ { { SNO , SNAME , CITY } , { CITY , STATUS , SNAME } }

I pointed out in the body of the chapter (in the section "Combining Components") that (a) the first of these JDs implied the second but that (b) decomposing S on the basis of that second JD (even though it's irreducible) wouldn't be a good idea. Why not?

11.5   Can a JD be both trivial and irreducible?

Answers

11.1.   *Which JDs are trivial?* None. *Which ones involve irrelevant components?* i., k., and l. *Which imply others?* a. implies b.; d. implies g. and h.; e. implies g.; f. implies h. and i.; j. implies k. *Which pairs are equivalent?* None. *Which are satisfied by the sample value in Figure 1-1?* a., b., c., d., e., g., and l. *Which hold in relvar P?* a., b., c., e., and l. *Which are irreducible?* a., b., c., and e.

11.2.

a. By Heath's Theorem, the answer is obviously yes (take X as A, Y as BC, and Z as D). But let's see if we can prove this result using the chase. Premise tuples:

```
x1   y12   y13    x4
x1    x2    x3   y24
```

From the FD $A \rightarrow B$, we have $y12 = x2$; from the FD $A \rightarrow C$, we have $y13 = x3$. Make the replacements:

```
x1    x2    x3    x4
x1    x2    x3   y24
```

Now we have a tuple of all x's, and the desired result follows: The given JD does follow from the given JDs.

b. Premise tuples:

```
 x1    x2   y13   y14
y21    x2    x3   y24
y31   y32    x3    x4
```

The FDs imply $y24 = x4$ and $y13 = x3$. Make the replacements:

```
 x1    x2    x3   y14
y21    x2    x3    x4
y31   y32    x3    x4
```

The FD $C \rightarrow D$ now implies $y14 = x4$; making the replacement gives us a tuple of all x's, and so the result follows: The given JD does follow from the given FDs. Note that we had to use one

of the FDs twice in the chase in this example. Note too that
we could have obtained the same result by applying Heath's
Theorem twice: The FD $C \to D$ implies the JD $☆\{CD,CAB\}$, which
in turn implies the JD $☆\{CD,BC,BA\}$, thanks to the FD $B \to C$.

c. I leave it to you to show the answer here is *no*.

d. Premise tuples:

x1	x2	y13	y14
y21	x2	x3	y24
y31	y32	x3	x4

Applying the JD $☆\{BC,ABD\}$ to the tuples with a common B
value (viz., *x2*) generates the following tuples:

x1	x2	x3	y24
y21	x2	y13	y14

We don't obtain a tuple of all *x*'s, and so the "target" JD doesn't
follow from the given one; in fact, we now have a sample relation
(of five tuples) that satisfies the latter and not the former.

11.3. Here first is a proof of part (b) of the extended theorem:

1. $X \to Y$ (given)

2. $XZ \to YZ$ (augmentation)

3. $XZ \to XZ$ (self determination)

4. $XZ \to XYZ$ (2 and 3, union)

Hence XZ is a superkey for R.

As for the converse, suppose relvar R contains the following tuples:

x	y1	z1
x	y2	z2

Thanks to the JD $☆\{XY,XZ\}$, the following tuples must then also appear:

x	y1	z2
x	y2	z1

But XZ is a superkey and so $XZ \to Y$ holds, so $y1 = y2$; hence $X \to Y$ holds.

11.4. This exercise is discussed further in Chapter 16, but I give
a preliminary discussion here. First of all, suppose such a
decomposition (i.e., on the basis of the second JD) were done.
Let the projections so obtained be labeled SNC and CTN in
the obvious way. Then the projections of SNC and CTN on
{SNAME,CITY} are clearly equal; that is, the following equality
dependency (EQD) holds—

```
CONSTRAINT ... SNC { SNAME , CITY } = CTN { SNAME , CITY } ;
```

—and relvars SNC and CTN thus suffer from redundancy.

Observe further that the FD {CITY} → {STATUS} holds in CTN. By
Heath's Theorem, therefore, we can decompose CTN into its
projections CT and CN on {CITY,STATUS} and {CITY,SNAME},
respectively. It follows that the JD

```
☼ { { SNO , SNAME , CITY } , { CITY , STATUS , SNAME } }
```

implies the JD

```
☼ { { SNO , SNAME , CITY } , { CITY , STATUS } , { CITY , SNAME } }
```

In this latter JD, however, the {CITY,SNAME} component is clearly
irrelevant, since it's a proper subset of the {SNO,SNAME,CITY}
component; it can therefore be dropped without significant loss.
(In fact, of course, this latter JD is identical to the first of the two
JDs as given in the original exercise.)

11.5. Yes! To be specific, every relvar R is subject to the trivial
and irreducible JD {H}, where H is the heading of R. (The
corresponding decomposition is into the pertinent identity
projection.)

CHAPTER 12

MVDs and 4NF

Who's on first, What's on second, I Don't Know's on third.

—Bud Abbott and Lou Costello: *The Naughty Nineties* (1945)

In Chapter 10, I said that 4NF, like 2NF and 3NF, is mostly of historical interest. However, that characterization is possibly a little unfair, because:

- First of all, 4NF is *the* normal form with respect to what are called multivalued dependencies or MVDs. Now, MVDs are really just a special kind of JD; so if you know about JDs in general, you know about MVDs as well, in a sense. Nevertheless, MVDs are still worth studying in their own right (for one thing, they're probably more common in practice than JDs that aren't MVDs).

- Second, MVDs have a more intuitive real world interpretation than JDs in general do, and therefore tend to be a little easier to understand.

- Third, MVDs, unlike JDs in general, do have an axiomatization, as we'll see.

So let's take a closer look.

© C. J. Date 2019
C. J. Date, *Database Design and Relational Theory*, https://doi.org/10.1007/978-1-4842-5540-7_12

An Introductory Example

In this section and the next, I'll examine MVDs from a comparatively informal point of view; in the section after that I'll consider them again, but more formally, and use that more formal understanding to lead up to 4NF. I'll begin with a definition:

> **Definition (multivalued dependency as a JD):** A multivalued dependency (MVD) is a join dependency with exactly two components.

It follows from this definition that a nonloss decomposition on the basis of an MVD always yields exactly two projections (recall that JDs in general are n-way for some positive integer n, where n can be greater than two; by contrast, MVDs are always exactly 2-way). It follows further that the following JD (for example) is in fact an MVD:

✩ { { SNO , SNAME , CITY } , { CITY , STATUS } }

Now, we've seen this particular JD repeatedly in this book; it holds in relvar S. But didn't I say in Chapter 9 that this particular JD was implied by a *functional* dependency: viz., the FD {CITY} → {STATUS}? Indeed I did; what the example shows, therefore, is that some MVDs are implied by FDs. But not all are, and as you'd probably expect it's the ones that aren't that are the interesting ones, in a sense. So let's take a look at an example of one of those "interesting ones." Consider Figure 12-1, which shows a sample value for a relvar called CTX.[1] The predicate is *Course CNO can be taught by teacher TNO and uses textbook XNO.*

CTX

CNO	TNO	XNO
C1	T1	X1
C1	T1	X2
C1	T2	X1
C1	T2	X2

Figure 12-1. *Relvar CTX—sample value*

---

[1]The example is a modified version of the CTXD example from Chapter 9.

Now, relvar CTX is "all key" and is thus certainly in BCNF. Yet it suffers from redundancy, as you can see; for example, the fact that teacher T1 can teach course C1 appears twice, and so does the fact that course C1 uses textbook X1. (It therefore suffers from certain update anomalies also. See Exercise 12.3 at the end of the chapter.) And the reason for these redundancies is that I'm assuming, perhaps not very realistically, that teachers and textbooks are quite independent of one another—that is, no matter who actually teaches any particular offering of some particular course, the same textbooks are used. I also assume a given teacher or given textbook can be associated with any number of courses. Thus:

- Each course c has a set T of teachers who can teach it and a set X of textbooks that it uses.

- And, for each such course c, there's a tuple in CTX for every possible combination of a teacher t from T and a textbook x from X. (Loosely speaking, in other words, each CNO value appears together with the *cartesian product* of all of the TNO and XNO values that are associated with that CNO value.)

To state the matter more precisely, the following constraint holds in relvar CTX (recall that from Chapter 9 that the symbol "∈" means "appears in"):

```
IF    ( c , t1 , x1 )  ∈  CTX AND
      ( c , t2 , x2 )  ∈  CTX
THEN ( c , t1 , x2 )  ∈  CTX AND
      ( c , t2 , x1 )  ∈  CTX
```

But to say this constraint holds is equivalent to saying that the following join dependency holds:

☆ { { CNO , TNO } , { CNO , XNO } }

It follows that CTX is subject to this JD, and it further follows that the relvar can, and probably should, be decomposed into its projections on {CNO,TNO} and {CNO,XNO}. *Exercise:* Show the values of these projections corresponding to the sample value of relvar CTX in Figure 12-1, and check that the redundancies disappear. (But what multirelvar constraint now needs to be enforced?)

I remark that the constraint shown above could be reduced from four lines to three without loss, by simply dropping the last line. What I mean is this: If tuples (*c,t1,x1*) and (*c,t2,x2*) both appear, then the tuple (*c,t1,x2*) must appear (as the third line says); so, switching the first two tuples around, it follows that if (*c,t2,x2*) and (*c,t1,x1*) appear, then (*c,t2,x1*) must appear as well (as the fourth line says). But the four-line version of the constraint is more symmetric and aesthetically more satisfying, as well as perhaps being easier to understand.

By the way, you might be thinking the redundancies in CTX are unnecessary; more specifically, you might be thinking the relvar doesn't need to show all possible TNO / XNO combinations for a given CNO. For example, two tuples would clearly suffice to represent the information that course C1 has two teachers and two textbooks. The problem is, *which* two tuples? Any specific choice leads to a relvar having a very unobvious interpretation and very strange update behavior. (Try stating the predicate for such a relvar!—i.e., try stating the criteria for deciding whether or not some given tuple logically belongs in that relvar. If you try this exercise, I think you'll see why the redundancies in CTX are necessary after all.)

Multivalued Dependencies (Informal)

The existence of "problem" BCNF relvars like CTX was recognized very early on, and the way to deal with them was also recognized at that time, at least intuitively (see Exercise 12.8). However, it wasn't until 1977 that these intuitive ideas were put on a sound theoretical footing by Fagin's introduction of the notion of MVDs.[2] Let me elaborate.

Relvar CTX is subject to the JD ☆{{CNO,TNO},{CNO,XNO}}. However, we can equally well say it's subject to the following *pair of MVDs*:

```
{ CNO } →→ { TNO }
{ CNO } →→ { XNO }
```

Note: The MVD $X \to\to Y$ can be read as "X multidetermines Y" or "Y is multidependent on X," or more simply just as "X double arrow Y."

---

[2]Fagin's work on MVDs predated the widespread adoption of the concept of JDs in general, which is why MVDs were initially treated as a separate phenomenon in their own right.

Taken together, what the foregoing MVDs mean, intuitively, is this: Courses don't have just one teacher or just one textbook (i.e., the FDs {CNO} → {TNO} and {CNO} → {XNO} don't hold)—but they do have a *set* of teachers and a *set* of textbooks (where both of those sets are nonempty). What's more, for a given course, the set of teachers and the set of textbooks are completely independent of one another. (As I put it earlier, it doesn't matter who actually teaches some specific offering of some course, the same textbooks are used. Likewise, it doesn't matter, with respect to some course, which textbooks are actually used—the same teachers can teach it.) So we can say the following:

- For a given course c and a given textbook x, the set T of teachers associated with that (c,x) pair depends on c alone—it makes no difference which particular x we choose.

- Likewise, for a given course c and a given teacher t, the set X of textbooks associated with that (c,t) pair also depends on c alone—it makes no difference which particular t we choose.

Note that the sample value of relvar CTX shown in Figure 12-1 does indeed abide by these two rules.

To repeat, relvar CTX is subject to a *pair* of MVDs. In general, in fact, it's easy to show (see the next section) that, given relvar R with heading H and subsets X, Y, and Z of H such that the union of X, Y, and Z is equal to H, the MVD $X \rightarrow\rightarrow Y$ holds in R if and only if the MVD $X \rightarrow\rightarrow Z$ also holds in R. MVDs always go together in pairs in this way. For that reason it's usual to write them as a "one liner," thus:

$X \rightarrow\rightarrow Y \mid Z$

("X double arrow Y bar Z"). In the case of relvar CTX, for example, we have:

```
{ CNO } →→ { TNO } | { XNO }
```

Now, we might say, *very* loosely, that an MVD is like an FD, except that instead of "For one of these, there's one of those," it's "For one of these, there's a *set* of those" (it's this informal characterization that makes MVDs a little easier to understand than JDs in general). But the point about always going in pairs is important (note that nothing analogous applies to FDs). Indeed, if the MVD concept is defined *too* imprecisely—as I've just done, in fact!—one could incorrectly conclude that for *every* pair of subsets X and Y of the heading of the pertinent relvar, there's an MVD from X to Y. For example, in the shipments relvar SP, there's certainly a set of quantities for each supplier number, but the MVD {SNO} →→ {QTY} does *not* hold—it's not the case that for a given supplier number *s* and given part number *p*, the set *Q* of quantities associated with that (*s*,*p*) pair depends on *s* alone.

Multivalued Dependencies (Formal)

The definitions in this section parallel those given in earlier chapters for FDs and JDs and are therefore presented with little by way of further commentary.

> **Definition (multivalued dependency):** Let *H* be a heading; then a multivalued dependency (MVD) with respect to *H* is an expression of the form $X \rightarrow\rightarrow Y$, where *X* (the determinant) and *Y* (the dependant) are both subsets of *H*. The phrase *MVD with respect to H* can be abbreviated to just *MVD*, if *H* is understood.

Note carefully that, like FDs and JDs, MVDs are defined with respect to some heading, not with respect to some relation or some relvar. Note too that from a formal point of view (again like FDs and JDs), MVDs are just expressions—expressions that, when interpreted with respect to some specific relation, become propositions that (by definition) evaluate to either TRUE or FALSE.

> **Definition (satisfying or violating an MVD):** Let relation *r* have heading *H*; let $X \rightarrow\rightarrow Y$ be an MVD, *M* say, with respect to *H*; and let *Z* be the attributes of *H* not contained in either *X* or *Y*. (In other words, (a) *Z* is the complement with respect to *H* of the union of *X* and *Y*, and (b) the union of *X*, *Y*, and *Z* is thus equal to *H*.) If *r* satisfies the JD ✿{*XY*,*XZ*}, then *r* satisfies *M*; otherwise *r* violates *M*.

Note that the foregoing definition is symmetric in *Y* and *Z*, whence it follows that *r* satisfies the MVD $X \rightarrow\rightarrow Y$ if and only if it satisfies the MVD $X \rightarrow\rightarrow Z$ (and we can therefore write them as a "one liner," as noted in the previous section).

> **Definition (MVD holding):** The MVD *M* holds in relvar *R* (equivalently, relvar *R* is subject to the MVD *M*) if and only if every relation that can ever be assigned to relvar *R* satisfies *M*. The MVDs that hold in relvar *R* are the MVDs of *R*.

From this definition and the previous one, it follows that R is subject to the MVD $X \rightarrow\rightarrow Y$ if and only if it's subject to the MVD $X \rightarrow\rightarrow Z$.

> **Fagin's Theorem:**[3] Relvar R can be nonloss decomposed into its projections on XY and XZ if and only if the MVDs $X \rightarrow\rightarrow Y \mid Z$ hold in R.

Fagin's Theorem is the "stronger form of Heath's Theorem" that I promised in Chapter 5. That is, where Heath's Theorem gives only a sufficient condition for a relvar to be nonloss decomposable into two projections, Fagin's Theorem gives both necessary and sufficient conditions. Of course, Fagin's Theorem is "obvious," given what we now know about JDs in general; with hindsight, there would never have been any formal need to define MVDs at all if JDs in general had been defined and properly investigated first. But Fagin's Theorem was proved before JDs in general had been properly investigated, and it was a new and important result at the time; what's more, it still has practical significance, inasmuch as MVDs do correspond to a fairly common kind of business rule, whereas the same probably can't be said for "cyclic" n-way JDs for $n > 2$ as discussed in Chapters 9 and 10.

Fourth Normal Form

You won't be surprised to hear there's such a thing as a trivial MVD:

> **Definition (trivial MVD):** Let $X \rightarrow\rightarrow Y$ be an MVD, M say, with respect to heading H. Then M is trivial if and only if it's satisfied by every relation with heading H.

From this definition, it's easy to prove the following theorem (see Exercise 12.7):

> **Theorem:** Let $X \rightarrow\rightarrow Y$ be an MVD, M say, with respect to heading H. Then M is trivial if and only if either (a) Y is a subset of X or (b) the union of X and Y is equal to H.

---

[3]Actually this is just one of literally scores of theoretical results in computing (not just in the field of database design theory as such) that could all justifiably be called "Fagin's Theorem."

You probably won't be surprised by the next definition, either:

> **Definition (MVD implied by keys):** Let relvar R have heading H
> and let $X \rightarrow\rightarrow Y$ be an MVD, M say, with respect to H. Then M is
> implied by the keys of R if and only if every relation r that satisfies
> R's key constraints also satisfies M.

As with FDs and JDs, "implied by keys" here could just as well be "implied by superkeys" without making any significant difference. Also, if M is trivial, it's satisfied by every relation r with heading H, and so it's satisfied by every relation r that satisfies R's key constraints a fortiori. Thus, trivial MVDs are always "implied by keys," trivially. So suppose M is nontrivial. Then it's easy to prove the following theorem:

> **Theorem:** Let M be a nontrivial MVD that holds in relvar R. Then
> M is implied by the keys of R if and only if it reduces to an *FD*
> out of a superkey of R—i.e., the double arrow reduces to a single
> arrow, as it were, and the determinant is a superkey.

And now I can define 4NF:

> **Definition (fourth normal form):** Relvar R is in fourth normal
> form (4NF) if and only if every MVD of R is implied by the keys
> of R.

However, given the various definitions and theorems already discussed in this section, we can see that the following operational definition (or theorem) is valid too:

> **Definition (fourth normal form):** Relvar R is in fourth normal
> form (4NF) if and only for every nontrivial MVD $X \rightarrow\rightarrow Y$ that
> holds in R, X is a superkey for R (in other words, every such MVD
> reduces to "an *FD* out of a superkey").

Of course, if an MVD is implied by the keys of R, it certainly holds in R—i.e., it's certainly "an MVD of R." However, the converse is false: An MVD can hold in R without being implied by the keys of R (as relvar CTX illustrates). Thus, the whole point about the 4NF definition is that the only MVDs that hold in a 4NF relvar are ones we can't get rid of—which means ones implied by keys (including trivial ones as a special case).[4]

---

[4]As usual, "getting rid of" a dependency here really means replacing it by some multirelvar
 constraint.

Recall now from Chapter 10 the parallelism between the BCNF and 5NF definitions. In fact, that parallelism extends to the 4NF definition, too. That is, we have the following:

- *R* is in BCNF if and only if every FD that holds in *R* is implied by the keys of *R*.

- *R* is in 4NF if and only if every MVD that holds in *R* is implied by the keys of *R*.

- *R* is in 5NF if and only if every JD that holds in *R* is implied by the keys of *R*.

Now, in the BCNF and 4NF definitions, we can simplify "implied by the keys" to just "implied by some key"; as noted in Chapter 10, however, the same is not true for the 5NF definition. In that sense, 4NF resembles BCNF more than it does 5NF. On the other hand, 4NF also resembles 5NF more than it does BCNF, in the sense that the 4NF and 5NF definitions both rely on context—by which I mean that the MVDs and JDs that hold in a 4NF or 5NF relvar involve, at least implicitly, all of the attributes of that relvar, whereas the same is not true for BCNF. (As I said earlier, the point about MVDs always going in pairs is important. Nothing analogous applies to FDs.)

Recall now from Chapter 6 the concept of FD preservation. Essentially, the idea was as follows: If the FD $X \to Y$ holds in relvar *R*, then the recommendation is to decompose *R*—assuming that decomposition is desired at all, and assuming further that it's done on the basis of some FD other than $X \to Y$ itself—in such a way that *X* and *Y* are kept together in the same projection. Well, that concept extends to MVDs too—that is, the recommendation still applies if we replace the FD $X \to Y$ by the MVD $X \to\to Y$ throughout.

In closing this section, let me state explicitly that:

a. If relvar *R* is in 5NF, it's certainly in 4NF; likewise, if relvar *R* is in 4NF, it's certainly in BCNF.

b. A relvar can be in 4NF without being in 5NF (see Exercise 12.4 at the end of the chapter).

c. 4NF is always achievable. (In fact, of course, we know this already, because we know that 5NF is always achievable, and now we also know that 5NF implies 4NF.)

MVD Axiomatization

As I mentioned near the beginning of this chapter, MVDs, unlike JDs in general, do have an axiomatization, or in other words a sound and complete set of rules for generating "new" MVDs from given ones. The rules in question are as follows:

1. *Reflexivity:* If Y is a subset of X, then $X \twoheadrightarrow Y$.

2. *Augmentation:* If $X \twoheadrightarrow Y$ and Z is a subset of W, then $XW \twoheadrightarrow YZ$.

3. *Transitivity:* If $X \twoheadrightarrow Y$ and $Y \twoheadrightarrow Z$, then $X \twoheadrightarrow Z - Y$.

4. *Complementation:* If (a) the union of X, Y, and Z is equal to the pertinent heading H and (b) the intersection of Y and Z is a subset of X, then (c) $X \twoheadrightarrow Y \,|\, Z$.

Now, these four rules aren't nearly as easy to understand or remember as Armstrong's rules are for FDs (or so it seems to me, at any rate). Partly for that reason, I won't attempt to justify them here, nor will I show them in action. However, I will at least say that further rules can be derived from the original four, the following among them:

5. *Pseudotransitivity:* If $X \twoheadrightarrow Y$ and $YZ \twoheadrightarrow W$, then $XZ \twoheadrightarrow W - YZ$.

6. *Union:* If $X \twoheadrightarrow Y$ and $X \twoheadrightarrow Z$, then $X \twoheadrightarrow YZ$.

7. *Decomposition:* If $X \twoheadrightarrow YZ$ and W is the intersection of Y and Z, then $X \twoheadrightarrow Y - Z$, $X \twoheadrightarrow Z - Y$, and $X \twoheadrightarrow W$.

The following rules involve both MVDs and FDs:

8. *Replication:* If $X \rightarrow Y$, then $X \twoheadrightarrow Y$.

9. *Coalescence:* If (a) $X \twoheadrightarrow Y$, (b) $Z \rightarrow W$, (c) W is a subset of Y, and (d) the intersection of Y and Z is empty, then (e) $X \rightarrow W$.

And the following is an additional derived rule:

10. *Mixed pseudotransitivity:* If $X \twoheadrightarrow Y$ and $XY \rightarrow Z$, then $X \rightarrow Z - Y$.

Embedded Dependencies

Recall relvar CTXD from Chapter 9, with attributes CNO, TNO, XNO, and DAYS; sole key {CNO,TNO,XNO}; and predicate *Teacher TNO spends DAYS days with textbook XNO on course CNO.*[5] (This relvar can be regarded as an extended version of relvar CTX as discussed earlier in this chapter.) A sample value, repeated from Figure 9-3, is shown in Figure 12-2:

CTXD

CNO	TNO	XNO	DAYS
C1	T1	X1	7
C1	T1	X2	8
C1	T2	X1	9
C1	T2	X2	6

Figure 12-2. *The 5NF relvar CTXD—sample value*

As we saw in Chapter 9, this relvar suffers from redundancy;[6] yet it's in 5NF, which means that no JDs (and therefore no MVDs, a fortiori) hold apart from ones implied by the sole key. In particular, therefore, the MVDs

{ CNO } →→ { TNO } | { XNO }

do *not* hold.[7] However, observe that, by contrast, they do hold in the projection of CTXD on {CNO,TNO,XNO} (right?). For that reason, those MVDs are said to be *embedded* dependencies (embedded, that is, with respect to the original relvar CTXD). In general, given some relvar *R* with heading *H*, an embedded dependency with respect to *R* is a dependency that doesn't hold in *R* itself but does hold in the projection of *R* on some proper subset of *H*. As the example illustrates, therefore (and as was noted in Chapter 9,

---

[5]This is the predicate I gave in Chapter 9, but a more accurate version might be: *Course CNO can be taught by teacher TNO and uses textbook XNO, and teacher TNO spends DAYS days with textbook XNO on course CNO* (see Chapter 17). And we might want to add *DAYS is greater than zero* as well.

[6]As also noted in Chapter 9, however, one of my reviewers disputed this claim. Again, see Chapter 17 for further discussion.

[7]I'm being a little sloppy here; by the definitions given earlier in the chapter, the MVDs {CNO} →→ {TNO} | {XNO} can't possibly hold in relvar CTXD, since they fail to mention the DAYS attribute—but I think you see what I mean. For further discussion of such matters, see Exercise 12.10.

in fact, albeit in different words), embedded dependencies cause redundancy, but that redundancy can't be eliminated by taking projections. Such redundancies thus correspond to constraints that must be separately stated and enforced (see Exercise 12.2).

Observe, incidentally, that the foregoing notion of embedding applies to JDs (and therefore to MVDs)[8] but not to FDs. That is, given some relvar R and a projection of R whose heading includes both X and Y, the FD $X \rightarrow Y$ holds in that projection if and only if it holds in R itself (see Exercise 12.5). For example, the FD $\{CITY\} \rightarrow \{STATUS\}$ holds in relvar S as such and also in every projection of that relvar that retains both of those attributes.

Exercises

12.1   Give (a) an example of a relvar of degree at least three that's in BCNF but not 4NF and (b) an example of a binary relvar that's in BCNF but not 4NF.

12.2   Write **Tutorial D** CONSTRAINT statements to express (a) the MVDs that hold in relvar CTX and (b) the embedded MVDs that hold in relvar CTXD, where relvars CTX and CTXD are as discussed in the body of the chapter.

12.3   Consider relvar CTX from the body of the chapter. What kinds of update anomalies can occur with that relvar?

12.4   Give an example of a relvar that's in 4NF but not 5NF.

12.5   Prove that, given some relvar R and a projection of R whose heading includes both X and Y, the FD $X \rightarrow Y$ holds in that projection if and only if it holds in R itself (see the section "Embedded Dependencies" in the body of the chapter, also footnote 5 in Chapter 9).

---

[8]For an example of an embedded JD that's not an embedded MVD, suppose relvar SPJ from Chapter 9 is extended to include a quantity attribute, QTY, thereby forming a new relvar SPJQ. Suppose the FD $\{SNO,PNO,JNO\} \rightarrow \{QTY\}$ holds in SPJQ (i.e., $\{SNO,PNO,JNO\}$ is a key). Then ✡$\{\{SNO,PNO\},\{PNO,JNO\},\{JNO,SNO\}\}$ is a JD that holds in the projection of SPJQ on $\{SNO,PNO,JNO\}$ but not in SPJQ itself. *Note:* This example is discussed in more detail near the end of Chapter 13.

12.6   Show that if relvar R is subject to the FD $X \to Y$, it's also subject to the MVD $X \to\to Y$.

12.7   Let $X \to\to Y$ be an MVD, M say, with respect to heading H. Prove that M is trivial if and only if either (a) Y is a subset of X or (b) the union of X and Y is equal to H. Incidentally, note that it follows from this result that, given the pair of MVDs $X \to\to Y \mid Z$ (defined with respect to heading H, where H is equal to the union of X, Y, and Z), $X \to\to Y$ is trivial if and only if $X \to\to Z$ is trivial.

12.8   The following rule of thumb is often adopted in practice:

Let relvar R have heading H and let the heading H of R be partitioned into disjoint subsets X, Y, and Z. Further, let X be the sole key and let Y and Z both be relation valued. Then, using Heath notation once again, R should be replaced by $R1$ and $R2$, where $R1 = (R\{XY\})$ UNGROUP (Y) and $R2 = (R\{XZ\})$ UNGROUP (Z), respectively.[9]

How does this informal rule relate to the topics discussed in the present chapter?

12.9   (*Modified version of Exercise 9.3.*) Design a database for the following. The entities to be represented are sales representatives, sales areas, and products. Each representative is responsible for sales in one or more areas; each area has one or more responsible representatives. Each representative is responsible for sales of one or more products, and each product has one or more responsible representatives. Each product is sold in each area; however, no two representatives sell the same product in the same area. Each representative sells the same set of products in each area for which that representative is responsible.

12.10 The following dependencies are defined with respect to a heading consisting of attributes $ABCD$:

$B \to D$
$A \to\to B \mid C$

---

[9]UNGROUP is an operator of **Tutorial D**. I used it in the answer to Exercise 4.14 in Chapter 4. It's discussed in detail in *SQL and Relational Theory* and elsewhere.

Use the chase to show these dependencies imply the MVDs
$A \rightarrow\rightarrow C \mid D$. *Note:* I'm making use of a certain shorthand notation
here, according to which $A \rightarrow\rightarrow B \mid C$ and $A \rightarrow\rightarrow C \mid D$ denote,
respectively, $A \rightarrow\rightarrow B \mid CD$ and $A \rightarrow\rightarrow C \mid BD$. See the answer to
this exercise for further explanation.

12.11 Let relvar SCP have attributes SNO, PNO, and CITY and predicate
Supplier SNO and part PNO are both located in city CITY. Can SCP
be derived from our usual relvars S, P, and SP? What normal form
is it in? Can you think of any conventional wisdom this example
might fly in the face of?

Answers

12.1. (a) Relvar CTX in the body of the chapter is an example, of course,
but it would be better if you could come up with an example from
your own work environment. (b) Let C be a certain club, and let
relvar $R\{A,B\}$ be such that the tuple (a,b) appears in R if and only
if a and b are both members of C. Then R is equal to the cartesian
product of its projections $R\{A\}$ and $R\{B\}$; thus, it's subject to the
JD ✩$\{A,B\}$ and, equivalently, to the following MVDs:

```
{ } →→ A | B
```

These MVDs aren't trivial, since they certainly don't hold in
all binary relvars, and they're not implied by a superkey either
(the only key in R is the entire heading). It follows that R isn't in
4NF. However, it's certainly in BCNF, because it's "all key."

12.2. Possible formulations (note that these are equality
dependencies, EQDs):

```
a. CONSTRAINT ... CTX = JOIN { CTX { CNO , TNO } ,
                               CTX { CNO , XNO } } ;
b. CONSTRAINT ... CTXD { CNO , TNO , XNO } =
              JOIN { CTXD { CNO , TNO } , CTXD { CNO , XNO } } ;
```

12.3. (a) Suppose the current value of CTX is as given in Figure 12-1. Then none of the four tuples shown can be deleted in isolation: a deletion anomaly. (b) Suppose the current value of CTX contains just "the first two" of the tuples shown in Figure. 12-1. Then neither "the third" nor "the fourth" tuple shown can be inserted in isolation: an insertion anomaly.

12.4. Relvar SPJ from Chapter 9 is an example (no MVDs hold in that relvar at all, apart from trivial ones, and so the relvar is certainly in 4NF).

12.5. The following proof might be thought to make very heavy weather of such an obvious point. Let the projection in question be R'. The FD $X \to Y$ holds in R' if and only if, whenever tuples $t1'$ and $t2'$ of R' have the same X value, they also have the same Y value. Let $T1$ and $T2$ be, respectively, the set of tuples in R from which $t1'$ is derived and the set of tuples in R from which $t2'$ is derived. By the definition of projection, every tuple $t1$ in $T1$ has the same X and Y values as $t1'$; likewise, every tuple $t2$ in $T2$ has the same X and Y values as $t2'$. It follows that whenever such tuples $t1$ and $t2$ have the same X value, they also have the same Y value; thus the FD $X \to Y$ holds in R. And it further follows that $X \to Y$ holds in R' if and only if it holds in R.

12.6. This result is immediate from Heath's Theorem: If R is subject to the FD $X \to Y$, it's also subject to the JD $\Join\{XY,XZ\}$, where Z is "the other" attributes of R, and therefore it's subject to the MVDs $X \to\to Y \mid Z$.

12.7. The JD $\Join\{XY,XZ\}$ is trivial if and only if $XY = H$ or $XZ = H$. If $XY = H$, we have Case (b). If $XZ = H$, then (noting that Y and Z are disjoint by definition) it must be the case that Y is a subset of X, and so we have Case (a).

12.8. The rule amounts to saying: If we start with a relvar with two or more independent relation valued attributes (RVAs) and we want to eliminate them—which we usually but not invariably do want to do (see the answer to Exercise 4.11 in Chapter 4)—then the first thing we should do is separate those RVAs. Using the notation of the exercise, this step will give us relvars with headings XY and XZ, respectively. The next thing we should do is ungroup the RVA in each of those relvars. Suppose the relations in *Y* and *Z* have headings *A* and *B*, respectively; then the relvars that result from those ungroupings will have headings *XA* and *XB*, respectively.[10] Now normalize those relvars in the usual way, replacing them by BCNF projections. Then those BCNF projections will "automatically" be in 4NF. In other words, MVDs that cause a relvar *not* to be in 4NF shouldn't arise in practice, if the foregoing procedure is followed.

It's interesting to note, incidentally, that in his famous 1970 paper on the relational model (see Appendix D), Codd gave an example in which he actually followed the foregoing procedure. He touched on it again, briefly, in another paper the following year ("Normalized Data Base Structure: A Brief Tutorial," Proc. 1971 ACM SIGFIDET Workshop on Data Description, Access, and Control, San Diego, Calif., November 11th-12th, 1971; see Appendix D once again). But I don't think he ever mentioned it subsequently, at least not in writing (because it was so intuitively obvious, perhaps).

Note In case you find the foregoing discussion too abstract, take *R* to be a relvar with heading {CNO,T,X}, where T and X are relation valued and contain relations with headings {TNO} and {XNO}, respectively. Separating the RVAs gives us relvars with headings {CNO,T} and {CNO,X}, respectively. Ungrouping then gives us relvars with headings {CNO,TNO} and {CNO,XNO}, respectively— which is precisely what we want, of course, in the CTX example.

12.9. First of all, we'll presumably need three relvars for representatives, areas, and products, respectively:

```
R { RNO , ... } KEY { RNO }
A { ANO , ... } KEY { ANO }
P { PNO , ... } KEY { PNO }
```

---

[10]We might have to do some attribute renaming first, if some attribute in either *A* or *B* has the same name as some attribute in *X*.

Next, we can represent the relationships (a) between sales representatives and sales areas and (b) between sales representatives and products by relvars like this:

```
RA { RNO , ANO } KEY { RNO , ANO }
RP { RNO , PNO } KEY { RNO , PNO }
```

Every product is sold in every area. So if we introduce a relvar

```
AP { ANO , PNO } KEY { ANO , PNO }
```

to represent the relationship between areas and products, then we have the following constraint (an EQD):

```
CONSTRAINT C1 AP = JOIN { A { ANO } , P { PNO } } ;
```

(The join here is actually a cartesian product.) Note that this constraint implies that AP isn't in 4NF. In fact, AP doesn't give us any information we can't obtain from the other relvars. To be precise, the following EQDs hold:

```
AP { ANO } = A { ANO }
AP { PNO } = P { PNO }
```

But let's assume for the moment that relvar AP is included in our design anyway.

No two representatives sell the same product in the same area. In other words, given an {ANO,PNO} combination, there's exactly one responsible sales representative, RNO, and so we can introduce a relvar

```
APR { ANO , PNO , RNO } KEY { ANO , PNO }
```

in which (to state it explicitly) the following FD holds:

```
{ ANO , PNO } → { RNO }
```

(Specification of {ANO,PNO} as a key is sufficient to express this FD.) However, relvars RA, RP, and AP are now all redundant, since they're all projections of APR; they can therefore all be dropped. In place of constraint C1 we now need constraint C2 (another EQD):

```
CONSTRAINT C2 APR { ANO , PNO } =
              JOIN { A { ANO } , P { PNO } } ;
```

This constraint must be separately and explicitly stated, since it isn't "implied by keys."

Also, since every representative sells all of that representative's products in all of that representative's areas, we have the additional constraint C3 on relvar APR:

```
{ RNO } →→ { ANO } | { PNO }
```

(These MVDs are nontrivial and not implied by keys, and relvar APR is thus not in 4NF.)[11] Again the constraint must be separately and explicitly stated.

Thus the final design consists of the relvars R, A, P, and APR, together with the constraints C2 and C3 (both of which are in fact EQDs once again):

```
CONSTRAINT C2 APR { ANO , PNO } =
              JOIN { A { ANO } , P { PNO } } ;

CONSTRAINT C3 APR = JOIN { APR { RNO , ANO } ,
                           APR { RNO , PNO } } ;
```

(There are also some foreign key constraints from APR to the other three relvars, but the details are straightforward and I omit them here.)

This exercise illustrates very nicely the point that, in general, normalization might be adequate to represent some of the semantic aspects of a given problem (basically, FDs, MVDs, and JDs that are implied by keys), but explicit statement of additional

---

[11]Note, therefore, that relvar APR gives the lie to another popular misconception: viz., that a relvar consisting of a single key and a single nonkey attribute is necessarily in 4NF. See also the answer to Exercise 12.11.

constraints will almost certainly be needed for other aspects. It also illustrates the point that it might not always be desirable to normalize "all the way" (relvar APR is in BCNF but not in 4NF).

As a subsidiary exercise, you might like to consider whether a design involving RVAs might be appropriate for the problem under consideration. Might such a design mean that some of the comments in the previous paragraph no longer apply?

12.10.   The first point to note here is that the MVDs $A \rightarrow\rightarrow B \mid C$ and $A \rightarrow\rightarrow C \mid D$ make no mention of attributes D and B, respectively. But didn't I say that, given the generic pair of MVDs $X \rightarrow\rightarrow Y \mid Z$, the union of X, Y, and Z had to be equal to the heading? Well, yes, I did—but I must now explain that we allow a certain shorthand notation to be used as well, one that's illustrated in this exercise. For definiteness, let's focus on the expression $A \rightarrow\rightarrow B \mid C$. By definition, this expression means $A \rightarrow\rightarrow B$ and $A \rightarrow\rightarrow C$; and $A \rightarrow\rightarrow B$ implies $A \rightarrow\rightarrow CD$, and $A \rightarrow\rightarrow C$ implies $A \rightarrow\rightarrow BD$. Moreover, since A, B, C, and D are single attributes and hence mutually disjoint, the decomposition rule for MVDs allows us to infer $A \rightarrow\rightarrow D$ from either $A \rightarrow\rightarrow CD$ or $A \rightarrow\rightarrow BD$. Putting this all together, we see that $A \rightarrow\rightarrow B \mid C$ is shorthand for either or both of $A \rightarrow\rightarrow B \mid CD$ and $A \rightarrow\rightarrow BD \mid C$. Given this state of affairs, moreover, we adopt a shorthand according to which $A \rightarrow\rightarrow B \mid CD$ and $A \rightarrow\rightarrow BD \mid C$ can both be written thus: $A \rightarrow\rightarrow B \mid C \mid D$—and this latter expression in turn can also be thought of as shorthand for the following *three* MVDs in combination: $A \rightarrow\rightarrow B$, $A \rightarrow\rightarrow C$, and $A \rightarrow\rightarrow D$.[12]

Now let's try the chase. Here are premise tuples for $A \rightarrow\rightarrow C \mid D$, which as we've just seen is equivalent to $A \rightarrow\rightarrow BC \mid D$:

x1   x2   x3   y14
x1   y22   y23   x4

---

[12]If you'd like to see a concrete example illustrating the ideas in this paragraph, consider a relvar CTXS, with attributes CNO, TNO, XNO, and SNO and predicate *Student SNO is enrolled on course CNO, which can be taught be teacher TNO and uses textbook XNO.* Taking A, B, C, and D to be {CNO}, TNO}, {XNO}, and {SNO}, respectively, it would be perfectly reasonable to expect the MVDs $A \rightarrow\rightarrow B \mid C \mid D$ to hold in this relvar.

Applying $A \rightarrow\rightarrow B \mid CD$ generates:

```
x1    x2   y23    x4
x1   y22    x3   y14
```

Applying $B \rightarrow D$ gives $y14 = x4$. Replacing:

```
x1    x2    x3    x4
x1   y22   y23    x4
x1    x2   y23    x4
x1   y22    x3    x4
```

And now we have a tuple of all x's, so the given dependencies do imply the target MVDs.

12.11. SCP can be define as a view (or "virtual relvar"), thus:

```
VAR SCP VIRTUAL ( ( JOIN { S , SP , P } ) { SNO , PNO , CITY } ) ;
```

The following FD holds in this view:

```
{ SNO , PNO } → { CITY }
```

In fact, {SNO,PNO} is a key, and could be declared as such, thus:[13]

```
VAR SCP VIRTUAL ( ( JOIN { S , SP , P } ) { SNO , PNO , CITY } )
        KEY { SNO , PNO } ;
```

The following (nontrivial) MVDs also hold:

```
{ CITY } →→ { SNO } | { PNO }
```

Because of these MVDs, relvar SCP isn't in 4NF, though it is in BCNF. As for "conventional wisdom," this example gives the lie to another popular misconception: viz., that a relvar consisting of a single key and a single nonkey attribute is necessarily in 5NF (see Exercises 1.8 and 10.1).

---

[13]Unlike SQL, **Tutorial D** does allow keys (and foreign keys) to be specified for views.

PART IV

Further Normal Forms

Together, Parts II and III of this book have covered all of the normal forms included in what Chapter 3 called "a first take" on the normal form hierarchy (see Figure 3-3); to be specific, they've discussed, in detail, the classical normal forms 1NF, 2NF, 3NF, BCNF, 4NF, and 5NF, with the emphasis on BCNF and 5NF as the most significant ones. But those six normal forms aren't the end of the story!—there are several more, and they constitute the primary subject matter of this part of the book.

Perhaps I should add that, of the three chapters in this part of the book, Chapter 14 is probably the most important. The other two are included mainly as an attempt on my part at some kind of completeness.

CHAPTER 13

ETNF, RFNF, SKNF

The essential thing in form is to be free in whatever form is used.

—Wallace Stevens: *A Note on Poetry* (1937)

Other things being equal, we generally want our databases to be as free of redundancy as possible, where by *redundancy* I mean more specifically—at least as far as the present chapter is concerned—any redundancy that can be removed by taking projections. And of course we use the discipline of further normalization, or just normalization for short, to help us reach that goal. Now, for many years it was believed that a relvar had to be in fifth normal form (5NF, also known as projection-join normal form or PJ/NF) in order for it to be free of redundancy in the foregoing sense. Somewhat surprisingly, however, it turns out that this belief was incorrect—that is, it turns out that several other normal forms can be defined, all of them both weaker than 5NF and stronger than fourth normal form (4NF), and all of them just as effective as 5NF at eliminating redundancy. The normal forms in question are:

- Essential tuple normal form, ETNF

- Redundancy free normal form, RFNF (also known as key complete normal form, KCNF)

- Superkey normal form, SKNF

What's more, using the symbol "⇒" to denote logical implication, there's a theorem to the effect that 5NF ⇒ SKNF ⇒ RFNF ⇒ ETNF ⇒ 4NF, while none of the reverse implications holds; that is, a relvar in any one of the normal forms listed here (a) is necessarily also in the normal form immediately to its right in the sequence, but (b) is *not* necessarily also in the normal form immediately to its left. Refer to Figure 13-1 (an extended version of Figure 3-3 from Chapter 3).

© C. J. Date 2019
C. J. Date, *Database Design and Relational Theory*, https://doi.org/10.1007/978-1-4842-5540-7_13

```
                  1NF
                  2NF
                  3NF
                  BCNF
                  4NF
                  ETNF
            RFNF / KCNF
                  SKNF
                  5NF
```

Figure 13-1. *The normal form hierarchy (II)*

The remainder of the chapter describes these new normal forms—i.e., ETNF, RFNF (or KCNF), and SKNF—and various related matters in some depth. Please note, however, that the chapter is intended to serve at least as much as a reference piece as it is a tutorial; the details are subtle and quite confusing, and they can be difficult to remember, and I certainly don't expect you to absorb them all on just one or two readings. Nor do I think you need to, for the most part. However, let me at least give you some idea of the structure of the discussion to come, so that you can have some idea of how the argument proceeds overall before we start delving into detail.

The chapter contains four main sections. The first, "5NF Is Too Strong," provides some motivational material, and the next three then deal with ETNF, RFNF, and SKNF, respectively. In particular:

- The section on ETNF—easily the longest, by the way—provides examples of (a) a relvar that's in ETNF and not in 5NF and (b) a relvar that's in 4NF and not in ETNF.

- The section on RFNF provides examples of (a) a relvar that's in RFNF and not in 5NF and (b) a relvar that's in ETNF and not in RFNF.

- The section on SKNF provides examples of (a) a relvar that's in SKNF and not in 5NF and (b) a relvar that's in RFNF and not SKNF.

Taken together, therefore, these examples illustrate among other things the claim—or theorem, rather—that 5NF $\Rightarrow$ SKNF $\Rightarrow$ RFNF $\Rightarrow$ ETNF $\Rightarrow$ 4NF, while none of the reverse implications holds.

5NF Is Too Strong

This section presents two examples. The first serves as a reminder of the redundancy problem that 5NF is intended to address; the second shows that maybe 5NF isn't the best solution to that problem after all.

The First Example: What 5NF Does

The first example is just a repeat of the SPJ example from Chapters 9 and 10. As I'm sure you'll recall, relvar SPJ is all key (and thus certainly in BCNF)—its attributes are SNO, PNO, and JNO, and the predicate is *Supplier SNO supplies part PNO to project JNO*. In addition, the following business rule (BRX) is in effect:

- If supplier *s* supplies part *p* and part *p* is supplied to project *j* and project *j* is supplied by supplier *s*, then supplier *s* supplies part *p* to project *j*.

The following join dependency (JD) captures the essence of business rule BRX and therefore holds in relvar SPJ:

☆ { { SNO , PNO } , { PNO , JNO } , { JNO , SNO } }

In case your memory needs jogging regarding join dependencies, what this JD says is that, at any given time, the current value of SPJ is equal to the join of its projections on {SNO,PNO}, {PNO,JNO}, and {JNO,SNO}. Note, however, that this JD isn't implied by the sole key of relvar SPJ—see Chapter 10 if you need to be reminded what it means for a JD to be implied by keys—and the relvar is thus not in 5NF. What's more, it suffers from redundancy. To be specific, suppose it contains the following three tuples:

```
t1 :  s1  p1  j2
t2 :  s1  p2  j1
t3 :  s2  p1  j1
```

(Here *s1* and *s2* denote supplier numbers; *p1* and *p2* denote part numbers; *j1* and *j2* denote project numbers; and *t1*, *t2*, and *t3* are just labels for the three tuples, used in what follows for convenience. Also, I assume until further notice that $s1 \neq s2$, $p1 \neq p2$, and $j1 \neq j2$.) Thanks to the JD, then, the following tuple must also appear in relvar SPJ:

```
t4 :  s1  p1  j1
```

So we can say that the fact that tuples *t1-t3* appear forces tuple *t4* to appear as well (and the JD is thus a tuple forcing JD specifically). In other words, the relvar does indeed suffer from redundancy as claimed, because the proposition "*s1* supplies *p1* to *j1*" is represented both explicitly (by tuple *t4*) and implicitly (as a logical consequence of the JD together with the propositions represented by tuples *t1-t3*). For that reason, the principles of normalization would suggest we decompose the relvar into its projections SP on {SNO, PNO}, PJ on {PNO,JNO}, and JS on {JNO,SNO}. That decomposition is nonloss (SPJ is equal to the join of SP, PJ, and JS); SP, PJ, and JS are each in 5NF; and the redundancy disappears.

By the way, the redundancy displayed by relvar SPJ has certain interesting implications (and these observations should prove helpful later). Let tuples *t1-t4* be as before, and assume again that $s1 \neq s2$, $p1 \neq p2$, and $j1 \neq j2$. Then:

- If the relvar contains all four tuples *t1-t4*, then an attempt to delete just tuple *t4* must clearly fail, because of the JD. In other words, as explained in Chapter 10, relvar SPJ suffers from a deletion anomaly with respect to that JD.

- Alternatively, if the relvar contains just tuples *t1* and *t2*, then an attempt to insert just tuple *t3* must also fail, again because of the JD. As also explained in Chapter 10, therefore, we can say that relvar SPJ suffers from an insertion anomaly with respect to that JD.

The decomposition of SPJ into its projections SP, PJ, and JS eliminates these anomalies.

The Second Example: Why 5NF Does Too Much

Now I turn to the promised second example. Suppose we have another relvar SPJ', where SPJ' is identical to SPJ except that it's subject to the following additional business rule (BRY):

- Any given supplier *s* supplies a given part *p* to at most one project *j*.

The following functional dependency (FD) captures the essence of rule BRY and therefore holds in relvar SPJ':

{ SNO , PNO } → { JNO }

In other words, {SNO,PNO} is a key for SPJ'. What's more, it can be shown that no other FDs hold in SPJ' apart from the one just shown (and trivial ones), and SPJ' is thus, like SPJ, in BCNF. However, it's not in 5NF, because the JD shown previously holds in SPJ' just as it did in SPJ, again without being implied by the keys.

The example thus gives the lie to two popular misconceptions—first, that a BCNF relvar that's not in 5NF must be all key (see Exercise 1.8); second, that a relvar with just one key and just one nonkey attribute must be in 5NF (see Exercise 1.9).

Now suppose as we did with SPJ that relvar SPJ' contains the following three tuples:

```
t1  :  s1  p1  j2
t2  :  s1  p2  j1
t3  :  s2  p1  j1
```

Thanks to the JD, then, the following tuple also has to appear:

```
t4  :  s1  p1  j1
```

But {SNO,PNO} is a key; it follows that tuples $t1$ and $t4$, since they have the same value for that key, are in fact one and the same (and hence that $j1 = j2$, so now we have to drop at least part of our original assumption that $s1 \neq s2$, $p1 \neq p2$, and $j1 \neq j2$). Hence, the kind of redundancy we observed with SPJ doesn't occur with SPJ'. (To be specific, tuple $t4$ in this case isn't an "additional" tuple, because it already exists.) In other words, SPJ', even though it's not in 5NF, doesn't ***and in fact can't*** suffer from the kind of redundancy that 5NF is intended to address. Thus, it looks as if 5NF might be, in a certain sense, too strong for the purpose.

Essential Tuple Normal Form

Essential tuple normal form (ETNF) was first described in a 2012 paper—referred to hereinafter as "the ETNF paper"—by Ron Fagin, Hugh Darwen, and myself.[1] I'll begin the discussion by giving a brief and somewhat informal summary of the main results from that paper (please note, however, that the following summary isn't meant to stand on its own—it's provided purely as a convenient overview):

- Loosely, to say that relvar R is free from redundancy is to say that no tuple t currently appearing in R represents information that can be derived from other tuples distinct from t but also currently appearing in R.

- Relvar R is in essential tuple normal form (ETNF) if and only if it's free from redundancy in the foregoing sense.

- Relvar R is in ETNF if and only if it's in BCNF and, for every JD J that holds in R, at least one component of J is a superkey for R.

- 5NF $\Rightarrow$ ETNF $\Rightarrow$ 4NF, while the reverse implications don't hold (in other words, ETNF falls strictly between 4NF and 5NF).

- If relvar R is in BCNF and has a noncomposite key, then it's in ETNF.

Definitions and Theorems

Now I present a series of definitions and theorems (with supporting discussion) that together constitute the principal results of the ETNF paper. First let me give—not before time, you might be thinking—a precise definition of the concept of a tuple forcing JD:

---

[1] Hugh Darwen, C. J. Date, and Ronald Fagin: "A Normal Form for Preventing Redundant Tuples in Relational Databases," Proc. 15th International Conference on Database Theory, Berlin, Germany, March 26th-29th, 2012. Available at www.almaden.ibm. *com/cs/people/fagin/icdt12. pdf.* Be aware, however, that this paper uses terminology that differs in several respects from the terminology used in the present chapter (and, more generally, in this book). To be specific, it uses terminology that conforms more closely to that found in the bulk of the research literature in this field; for instance, it nowhere mentions the crucial but nonstandard term *relvar.*

Definition (tuple forcing JD): Let *J* be a JD with respect to heading *H*, and let *J* hold in relvar *R*. Then *J* might or might not have the consequence that if certain tuples *t1*, ..., *tn* appear in *R*, a certain additional tuple *t* is forced to appear in *R* as well (where the term *additional* means that *t* is distinct from each of *t1*, ..., *tn*). If and only if it does have that consequence, then *J* is tuple forcing with respect to *R*.

Given this definition, it's easy to see that if *J* is indeed tuple forcing with respect to *R*, it must be (a) nontrivial, (b) not implied by the keys of *R*, and (c) not implied by any FD of *R*.[2] (Thanks to (a) and (b) here, it also follows that *R* can't possibly be in 5NF.)

Next, it's convenient to introduce the terms *FD redundant* and *JD redundant*:

Definition (FD redundancy): Relvar *R* is FD redundant if and only if it's not in BCNF.

Definition (JD redundancy): Relvar *R* is JD redundant if and only if some tuple forcing JD holds in *R*.

Note that neither of these kinds of redundancy implies the other; that is, a relvar can be FD redundant without being JD redundant, and JD redundant without being FD redundant. For example:

- Relvar SPJ from the section "5NF Is Too Strong"—with attributes SNO, PNO, and JNO; key {SNO,PNO,JNO}; and JD ☼{{SNO,PNO}, {PNO,JNO},{JNO,SNO}}—is in BCNF and hence not FD redundant, but it's clearly JD redundant, because that JD is tuple forcing.

- Relvar S from Chapter 1—with attributes SNO, SNAME, STATUS, and CITY; key {SNO}; and FD {CITY} → {STATUS}—isn't in BCNF and is therefore FD redundant. But no tuple forcing JDs hold in that relvar, and so the relvar isn't JD redundant.

---

[2]You might think the third of these conditions is a logical consequence of the second, but it's not. For example, consider a relvar *R* with attributes *A*, *B*, *C*, and *D* and keys *A* and *B*. Let no FDs hold in *R* except ones implied by those keys. Then it's easy to see that the JD ☼{AB,AC,BD} holds in *R*, because that JD is implied by those keys taken together. However, it isn't implied by either key taken individually, and so it isn't implied by any FD that holds in *R*. *Note:* See the discussion of Heath's Theorem in Chapter 9 if you need to refresh your memory regarding the notion of a JD being implied by an FD.

To continue with the definitions:

> **Definition (redundancy free):** Relvar R is redundancy free if and only if it's neither FD redundant nor JD redundant.[3]

Note that a 5NF relvar is certainly redundancy free by this definition. As I'll show, however, it turns out that a relvar doesn't have to be in 5NF in order to be redundancy free; rather, it's sufficient that it just be in ETNF. In fact, that's the definition of ETNF:

> **Definition (essential tuple normal form):** Relvar R is in essential tuple normal form (ETNF) if and only if it's redundancy free.[4]

In other words, relvar R is in ETNF if and only if it's neither FD redundant nor JD redundant—equivalently, if and only if it's in BCNF and no tuple forcing JD holds.

Of course, while the foregoing definition is both precise and accurate, it's of little practical use, because it doesn't help much with the question of determining whether a given relvar is indeed in ETNF. But the following theorem does help in this regard:

> **Theorem:** Relvar R is in ETNF if and only if it's in BCNF and, for every explicit JD J that holds in R, some component of J is a superkey for R.

This theorem provides both necessary and sufficient conditions for a relvar to be in ETNF. We can therefore take it as a useful, usable test—in effect, as a valid *definition* of ETNF. (To put it another way, the original definition is a semantic definition, while the theorem provides an operational or syntactic definition. See the explanatory remarks on such matters in Chapter 5.)

By the way, the theorem refers to *explicit* JDs of R, but in fact we could drop that "explicit" qualifier and what would be left would still be true (i.e., R is in ETNF if and only if *every* JD that holds in R has a superkey component).[5] However, including the qualifier makes the theorem "tighter," in a sense. In particular, it means there's no need to check a relvar's implicit JDs in order to test whether the relvar in question is in ETNF.

---

[3]But I must repeat and emphasize that I'm using the term *redundancy* here in a very special sense.

[4]For obvious reasons we originally called this new normal form not ETNF but RFNF (redundancy free normal form). Subsequently, however, we discovered that this name had already been taken, and so we had to choose another. See (a) the subsection "Our Choice of Name" at the end of the present section and (b) the next section, "Redundancy Free Normal Form," for further discussion and explanation.

[5]Just to remind you, explicit JDs are the ones explicitly declared, and implicit JDs are the ones not explicitly declared but implied by those that are. Similarly for FDs, of course.

The next theorem provides another simple and useful test:

> **Theorem:** Relvar *R* is in ETNF if it's in BCNF and has at least one noncomposite key (where a noncomposite key is one that isn't composite, and a composite key is one that consists of two or more attributes).

This theorem provides a sufficient condition, though not a necessary one, for a relvar to be in ETNF. By the way, it's worth noting that the condition in question has the attractive property that it talks in terms of keys only, not JDs and not FDs (at least, not explicitly).

The next theorem shows that ETNF does indeed fall strictly between 4NF and 5NF:

> **Theorem:** 5NF ⇒ ETNF ⇒ 4NF, while neither of the reverse implications holds.

Finally, here's another theorem giving a sufficient condition, though not a necessary one, for a relvar to be in ETNF:

> **Theorem:** Relvar *R* is in ETNF if it's in 3NF and has no composite key.

This result is immediate because the stated conditions in fact imply that relvar *R* is in 5NF.[6] Hence it's in ETNF a fortiori.

A Relvar in ETNF and Not 5NF

Relvar SPJ′, the second example from the previous section ("5NF Is Too Strong"), provides a concrete example of a relvar that's in ETNF and not in 5NF. Just to remind you, that relvar has attributes SNO, PNO, and JNO; it has just one key, viz., {SNO,PNO}; it's in BCNF; the predicate is *Supplier SNO supplies part PNO to project JNO*; and the following JD holds (but no others do, apart from ones that are logical consequences of this JD and/or the sole key):

☼ { { SNO , PNO } , { PNO , JNO } , { JNO , SNO } }

---

[6]See C. J. Date and Ronald Fagin: "Simple Conditions for Guaranteeing Higher Normal Forms in Relational Databases," *ACM Transactions on Database Systems 17*, No. 3 (September 1992), also published in C. J. Date and Hugh Darwen, *Relational Database Writings 1989-1991* (Addison-Wesley, 1992).

As noted earlier, this relvar isn't in 5NF, precisely because the foregoing JD isn't implied by the sole key. However, it *is* in ETNF, because the only explicit JD—i.e., the one just shown—that holds in the relvar has a component that's a superkey (viz., the component {SNO,PNO}). In other words, the relvar, even though it's not in 5NF, is nevertheless neither FD redundant nor JD redundant, and is thus redundancy free, and hence in ETNF.

Suppose now that the relvar contains just these two tuples:

```
t1  :  s1  p1  j2
t2  :  s1  p2  j1
```

(where, let's assume, $p1 \neq p2$ and $j1 \neq j2$). Suppose we now insert the following tuple:

```
t3  :  s2  p1  j1
```

(where $s2 \neq s1$). The JD then implies that the following tuple must appear as well:

```
t4  :  s1  p1  j1
```

As we saw earlier, however, tuples *t1* and *t4* here must in fact be one and the same, since they have the same key value. It follows that $j1 = j2$, contradicting one of the original assumptions. Hence, if tuples *t1* and *t2* appear, then an attempt to insert tuple *t3* must fail, precisely because it leads to that contradiction. Moreover, since an attempt to insert tuple *t4* directly must also fail (either on a key uniqueness violation or because it implies $j1 = j2$, take your pick), it follows that the following somewhat bizarre business rule must also be in effect:

- If (a) supplier *s1* supplies part *p1* to project *j2* and (b) supplier *s1* supplies part *p2* to project *j1* ($p1 \neq p2$, $j1 \neq j2$), then (c) no supplier, not even *s1*, can supply part *p1* to project *j1*.

As a matter of fact, it turns out that the following equally bizarre rules must be in effect as well (note the symmetry):[7]

- If (a) supplier *s1* supplies part *p1* to project *j2* and (b) supplier *s2* supplies part *p1* to project *j1* ($s1 \neq s2$, $j1 \neq j2$), then (c) no part, not even *p1*, can be supplied by supplier *s1* to project *j1*.

---

[7] The symmetry displayed by these three rules is a consequence of the symmetry of the roles played by SNO, PNO, and JNO in the JD ✡{{SNO,PNO},{PNO,JNO},{JNO,SNO}}.

- If (a) supplier *s1* supplies part *p2* to project *j1* and (b) supplier *s2* supplies part *p1* to project *j1* (*s1* ≠ *s2*, *p1* ≠ *p2*), then (c) no project, not even *j1*, can be supplied by supplier *s1* with part *p1*.

Actually these three rules can be combined into one, as follows. Let's agree to say that each tuple of relvar SPJ′ represents a shipment (by some supplier of some part to some project). Then there can't exist three distinct shipments *x*, *y*, and *z* such that *x* and *y* involve the same supplier, *y* and *z* involve the same part, and *z* and *x* involve the same project.

There's another point to make (an important one) in connection with the SPJ′ example. Refer once more to the analysis that led to the three "bizarre" business rules discussed above (the first of those rules in particular). That analysis showed that tuple *t3* can't appear in the relvar together with tuples *t1* and *t2*. It follows, therefore, that SPJ′, although it's in ETNF, nevertheless does suffer from an insertion anomaly. (By contrast, it doesn't suffer from a deletion anomaly—assuming, that is, that the only constraints that hold are the stated JD and the stated key constraint and logical consequences thereof.) So one distinction between 5NF and ETNF is as follows:

- Even though both are redundancy free, 5NF guarantees "no insertion anomalies" while ETNF doesn't—assuming, again, that FDs and JDs are the only kinds of constraints under consideration.[8]

Of course, it's tempting to conclude from the SPJ′ example that relvars that are in ETNF and not in 5NF are likely to be rare in practice. Nevertheless, there's a clear logical difference between the two, and so—from the point of view of reducing redundancy, at least—it's ETNF, not 5NF, that ought to be the target to be aimed for.

As a matter of fact, the SPJ′ example reinforces this latter claim in another way also. Since the relvar satisfies the ternary JD ☆{{SNO,PNO},{PNO,JNO},{JNO,SNO}}, it can be nonloss decomposed into its projections on {SNO,PNO}, {PNO,JNO}, and {JNO,SNO}, respectively. Those projections are each all key, and each in fact is in 5NF. However, that decomposition "loses" the FD {SNO,PNO} → {JNO}! As we saw in Part II of this book, losing dependencies in such a manner is generally not recommended; hence relvar SPJ′ illustrates the point that not only is 5NF sometimes too strong, but it might sometimes be positively contraindicated.

---

[8]To put the point another way, 5NF and domain-key normal form, DK/NF (see Chapter 15), coincide in the case where the only constraints that apply are FDs and JDs specifically.

A Relvar in 4NF and Not ETNF

As we've seen, relvar SPJ' is in ETNF and not in 5NF. It is, however, in 4NF (though not BCNF), because no nontrivial MVDs hold in that relvar at all. So what about a relvar that's in 4NF and not in ETNF? In fact relvar SPJ (not SPJ') provides an example. Just to recap, that relvar has attributes SNO, PNO, and JNO; is all key; and is subject to a certain ternary JD. No nontrivial MVDs—equivalently, no nontrivial binary JDs—hold in that relvar at all, however, and so it's certainly in 4NF. But it's not in ETNF (as we know), because no component of that ternary JD is a superkey. Nor is it in 5NF, of course, a fortiori.

Our Choice of Name

After Fagin, Darwen, and I had completed the bulk of our work on what became ETNF, our attention was drawn to a paper by Millist Vincent,[9] and in particular to the fact that our original name "redundancy free normal form" (RFNF) had already been used by Vincent to refer to something else. Since that name had been taken, therefore, we had to choose a different one, and of course we settled on "essential tuple normal form" (ETNF). Here's the rationale for our choice. Let R be a relvar, let r be a value of R, and let t be a tuple in r. Then we define what it means for t to be either *partly* or *fully* redundant in r, thus:

> **Definition (partly redundant tuple):** Tuple t is partly redundant in r if and only if an FD $X \rightarrow Y$ holds in R and there exists a tuple t' in r $(t \neq t')$ such that $t\{X\} = t'\{X\}$.

> **Definition (fully redundant tuple):** Tuple t is fully redundant in r if and only if there exists a set s of tuples in r $(t \notin s)$ such that, per some JD of R, the tuples in s force t to appear in r.

---

[9]Millist W. Vincent: "Redundancy Elimination and a New Normal Form for Relational Database Design," in B. Thalheim and L. Libkin (eds.), *Semantics in Databases*, Vol. 1358 of *Lecture Notes in Computer Science* (Springer, 1998).

Then we go on to define *t* to be redundant in *r* if and only if it's either partly or fully redundant in *r*. Now, it should be immediately obvious that:

a. Such an *r* and *t* exist, and *t* is partly redundant in *r*, if and only if *R* is FD redundant.

b. Such an *r* and *t* exist, and *t* is fully redundant in *r*, if and only if *R* is JD redundant.[10]

Thus, taking *essential* to be an antonym of *redundant*, we define (a) *t* to be essential in *r* if and only if it's not redundant in *r*, and (b) *R* to be in ETNF if and only if every relation *r* that's a legitimate value for *R* is such that every tuple in *r* is essential in the foregoing sense.[11]

Redundancy Free Normal Form

Now I turn to Vincent's RFNF. Consider our usual suppliers relvar S, with attributes SNO, SNAME, STATUS, and CITY; sole key {SNO}; and explicit FD {CITY} → {STATUS}. A sample value is shown in Figure 13-2 (basically just a repeat of Figure 3-1 from Chapter 3):

SNO	SNAME	STATUS	CITY
S1	Smith	20	London
S2	Jones	30	Paris
S3	Blake	30	Paris
S4	Clark	20	London
S5	Adams	30	Athens

Figure 13-2. The suppliers relvar—sample value

---

[10]Note, therefore, that "fully redundant" is not a special case of "partly redundant"; in fact, a tuple can be partly redundant in *r* without being fully so or the other way around.

[11]Our use of the term *essential* in this context was influenced by Codd's notion of essentiality, introduced by Codd in his paper "Interactive Support for Nonprogrammers: The Relational and Network Approaches," Proc. ACM SIGMOD Workshop on Data Description, Access, and Control, Vol. II, Ann Arbor, Michigan (May 1974). Briefly, to say some data construct is essential in Codd's sense is to say its loss would cause a loss of information. As already indicated (in effect), every tuple in every relation that's a possible value for an ETNF relvar is clearly essential in this sense.

Now, the tuple for supplier S1 in the figure has city London and status 20. As a consequence, the tuple for supplier S4, which also has city London, *must* have status 20, for otherwise the FD {CITY} → {STATUS} would be violated. In a sense, therefore, the occurrence of that status value 20 in the tuple for supplier S4 is redundant, because there's nothing else it could possibly be—it's a logical consequence of, and is fully determined by, the values appearing elsewhere in the overall relation.

Examples like the foregoing provide the motivation for the following intuitively attractive definition (due to Vincent but considerably paraphrased here):

> **Definition (redundancy per Vincent):** Let relation *r* be a value of relvar *R*, let *t* be a tuple in *r*, and let *v* be an attribute value within *t*. Then that occurrence of *v* within *t* is redundant in *r*, and *R* is subject to redundancy, if and only if replacing that occurrence of *v* by an occurrence of *v'* (*v'* ≠ *v*), while leaving everything else unchanged, causes some dependency[12] of *R* to be violated.

In other words, Vincent's kind of redundancy exists if the attribute value occurrence in question *must* be *v* and nothing else. Note incidentally that a relation that contains a partly redundant tuple (according to our definition of that term) certainly displays Vincent's kind of redundancy.

Even though I said the foregoing definition is intuitively attractive (and I think it is), I should point out that in at least one respect it's a little strange, too. Again consider the example of Figure 13-2, in which the tuple for supplier S4 has to have status value 20 because the tuple for supplier S1 has status value 20. Observe now that the reverse argument holds equally well: The tuple for supplier S1 has to have status value 20 because the tuple for supplier S4 has status value 20! Now, it surely makes no sense to say those 20's are *both* redundant (does it?)—but that's what the definition says if we take it literally. Thus, it seems to me that the definition is slightly weak and could do with a little tightening up. I'll leave as an exercise for you to come up with such a tightened up definition, if you're interested.

---

[12]Here the term *dependency* must be understood as referring to dependencies in general, not necessarily to FDs or JDs as such.

Be all that as it may, let's agree to refer to redundancy as just defined as "redundancy by Vincent's definition." Then we can define a new normal form, as follows:

> **Definition (redundancy free normal form):** Relvar *R* is in redundancy free normal form (RFNF) if and only if it's not subject to redundancy by Vincent's definition.[13]

Now, I hope it's obvious that a relvar that's not in 4NF isn't in RFNF as just defined.[14] But what about one that's in ETNF? Well, consider the example of relvar SPJ′ from the previous section (on ETNF) once again. As you'll recall, that relvar suffers from neither FD redundancy nor JD redundancy and is thus in ETNF (though not in 5NF). Now, we saw in that earlier section that if the relvar contains the following three tuples—

```
t1  :  s1  p1  j2
t2  :  s1  p2  j1
t3  :  s2  p1  j1
```

—then the following tuple has to appear as well:

```
t4  :  s1  p1  j1
```

But {SNO,PNO} is a key; it follows that (a) tuples *t1* and *t4*, since they have the same key value, are in fact one and the same, and hence that (b) *j1* = *j2*. Observe now, however, that the very fact that *j2*, in tuple *t1*, must be equal to *j1* means the relvar is subject to redundancy by Vincent's definition![15] It follows that RFNF and ETNF are logically distinct; in fact, RFNF is strictly stronger than ETNF, in the sense that a relvar can be in ETNF—and hence redundancy free, by our definition—without being in RFNF, while the converse isn't so. In fact, the ETNF paper proves the following stronger result:

> **Theorem:** 5NF ⇒ RFNF ⇒ ETNF ⇒ 4NF, while none of the reverse implications hold.

---

[13]Note that (perhaps fortunately) the weakness referred to in the aside has no impact on this definition.

[14]By way of example, consider Fig. 12.1 in Chapter 12, which shows a sample value for the non4NF relvar CTX. Let X3 ≠ X1. Then replacing the tuple (C1,T1,X1) in that sample value by the tuple (C1,T1,X3) would certainly cause the MVD {CNO} →→ {XNO} that's supposed to hold in that relvar to be violated.

[15]You might be thinking the redundancy in question is caused by a JD and the relvar is thus not in ETNF in the first place, let alone RFNF. But the point is, that JD isn't a *tuple forcing* one, and so the relvar is indeed in ETNF as previously claimed.

Note, therefore, that ETNF falls strictly between 4NF and RFNF. Vincent also proves the following useful result:

> **Theorem:** Relvar R is in RFNF if and only if it's in BCNF and, for every JD J that holds in R, the union of those components of J that are superkeys for R is equal to the heading of R.

What Vincent actually does here is this: He defines relvar R to be in yet another normal form that he calls key complete normal form (KCNF) if and only if it satisfies the stated conditions (i.e., if and only if R is in BCNF and, for every JD J that holds in R, the union of those components of J that are superkeys for R is equal to the heading of R). Then he goes on to prove that KCNF and RFNF are in fact one and the same. In other words, his original RFNF definition is a semantic definition, while his KCNF definition—in effect, the foregoing theorem—is an operational or syntactic one.

A Relvar in RFNF and Not 5NF

We can construct an example of a relvar that's in RFNF and not in 5NF by taking relvar SPJ′ with its two dependencies as discussed earlier in this chapter—

```
{ SNO , PNO } → { JNO }
```

```
☼ { { SNO , PNO } , { PNO , JNO } , { JNO , SNO } }
```

—and adding another:

```
{ PNO , JNO } → { SNO }
```

This additional dependency (which implies, of course, that {PNO,JNO} is another key for the relvar) corresponds to an additional business rule (BRZ):

- Any given part p is supplied to a given project j by at most one supplier s.

Let me refer to this revised version of SPJ′ as SPJ′′, and to the given ternary JD as J. Then the {SNO,PNO} and {PNO,JNO} components of J are both superkeys for SPJ′′; their union is equal to the heading of SPJ′′; and so—since it can be shown that no other irreducible JDs hold—it follows that SPJ′′ is in RFNF. Yet it's not in 5NF, because the membership algorithm fails on that ternary JD J.

A Relvar in ETNF and Not RFNF

Relvar SPJ'—not SPJ''!—is an example of a relvar that's in ETNF and not in RFNF, as already noted. Just to spell the point out, however: Once again, that ternary JD holds. But since the only component of this JD that's a superkey is {SNO,PNO}, the union of all superkey components is certainly not equal to the heading, and the relvar is thus not in RFNF.

Superkey Normal Form

While Fagin, Darwen, and I were working on what became ETNF, our attention was drawn to yet another paper, this one by Ragnar Normann,[16] that dealt with issues related to our work. That paper doesn't describe anything equivalent to our ETNF, however, nor to Vincent's RFNF; rather, its focus is on showing that certain textbook definitions of 5NF are incorrect.[17] It does this by defining what it calls *minimal lossless decompositions* (which are basically decompositions that correspond to irreducible JDs as defined in the present book), and then using that notion as a basis for defining a new normal form:[18]

> **Definition (superkey normal form):** Relvar R is in superkey normal form (SKNF) if and only if, for every irreducible JD ✧{$X1,...,Xn$} that holds in R, each of $X1, ..., Xn$ is a superkey for R.

The paper also proves that 5NF ⇒ SKNF ⇒ 4NF and that the reverse implications don't hold. It doesn't show that SKNF is redundancy free (neither as I've defined that term nor in Vincent's sense), though in fact it is.[19]

---

[16]Ragnar Normann: "Minimal Lossless Decompositions and Some Normal Forms between 4NF and PJ/NF," *Information Systems 23, No. 7* (1998).

[17]Including, sadly, the one given in various editions of my own Addison-Wesley book *An Introduction to Database Systems*. See Exercise 10.9 in Chapter 10. In fact, it was realizing that I'd made this mistake that served as the initial impetus that led Darwen, Fagin, and myself to develop the concept of ETNF.

[18]Normann's definition is essentially equivalent to the one that follows (I've rephrased it to use our own terminology) but uses SNF, not SKNF, as the abbreviated form of the name.

[19]Despite this state of affairs, SKNF doesn't really seem to be all that interesting in its own right.

To repeat, Normann's paper proves that 5NF $\Rightarrow$ SKNF $\Rightarrow$ 4NF. However, the ETNF paper actually proves the following stronger result:

> **Theorem:** 5NF $\Rightarrow$ SKNF $\Rightarrow$ RFNF $\Rightarrow$ ETNF $\Rightarrow$ 4NF, while none of the reverse implications holds.

Note, therefore, that SKNF falls strictly between RFNF and 5NF.

A Relvar in SKNF and Not 5NF

Here then is an example of a relvar that's in SKNF and not in 5NF. Let relvar R have attributes A, B, and C; using Heath notation, let AB, BC, and CA each be keys of R; and let the JD ☼{AB,BC,CA}—call it J—hold in R. Then it can be shown that this relvar is in SKNF;[20] yet it's not in 5NF, because the membership algorithm fails on J. *Note:* To make the example a little more concrete, let the predicate be *There exists a person whose favorite color is A, favorite restaurant is B, and favorite composer is C,* and let there be business rules to the effect that (a) no two distinct persons can have more than one favorite in common and (b) no three distinct persons can be such that, for each favorite, two of those three persons have it in common.

A Relvar in RFNF and Not SKNF

The example given in the previous section under the heading "A Relvar in RFNF and not 5NF" serves here also, since the relvar in question is indeed not in SKNF, though it is in RFNF.

Concluding Remarks

To repeat something I warned you about in the introduction, the details of everything we've been covering in this chapter are subtle and confusing and can be difficult to remember—indeed, I'd be very surprised if you didn't agree with these remarks by now!—and I don't expect you to absorb all of those details on just one or two readings.

---

[20]The details are a little complicated and I omit them here, but you can find them in the ETNF paper if you're interested.

However, the following brief summary, highlighting the most significant logical differences between the various new normal forms, might help a little:

- Relvar *R* is in ETNF if and only if it's in BCNF and, for every JD *J* that holds in *R*, some component of *J* is a superkey for *R*.

- Relvar *R* is in RFNF if and only if it's in BCNF and, for every JD *J* that holds in *R*, the union of those components of *J* that are superkeys for *R* is equal to the heading of *R*.

- Relvar *R* is in SKNF if and only if it's in BCNF and, for every JD *J* that holds in *R*, every component of *J* is a superkey for *R*.

Let me close the chapter by pointing out that a relvar can be in 5NF—and hence in any or all of the new normal forms discussed in this chapter—and yet still be subject to redundancy that, while not exactly identical to redundancy in any of the various senses in which I've used that term in this chapter, is nevertheless very close to it.[21] Consider a relvar SPJQ, with attributes SNO, PNO, JNO, and QTY (only) and predicate *Supplier SNO supplies part PNO to project JNO in quantity QTY*. The sole key is {SNO,PNO,JNO}, and the relvar is in BCNF. Note carefully that the JD ✿{{SNO,PNO},{PNO,JNO},{JNO,SNO}} does *not* hold in this relvar. However, it does hold in the projection of the relvar on {SNO,PNO,JNO} (actually it's an example of an embedded dependency—see Chapter 12). Now suppose the relvar contains the following tuples (only):

```
s1   p1   j2   100
s1   p2   j1   200
s2   p1   j1   300
s1   p1   j3   400
```

Thanks to the embedded dependency, then, we must have $j3 = j1$. Thus, relvar SPJQ is certainly subject to redundancy, of a kind. Nevertheless, the relvar is in ETNF, RFNF, SKNF, and indeed 5NF. The point is, the kind of redundancy discussed in this chapter has to do with *the FDs and JDs* (only) that hold in the relvar in question. Sadly, that definition has nothing whatsoever to say about any other constraints—embedded dependencies or any other kinds of constraints—that might also happen to hold.

---

[21]This example was mentioned in passing in Chapter 12, footnote 8.

Exercises

13.1   Draw the normal form hierarchy ("Version II") from memory. Your drawing should include at least nine normal forms.

13.2   Define (a) FD redundancy; (b) JD redundancy; (c) ETNF.

13.3   In the body of the chapter, I said among other things that a relvar could be in SKNF and not in 5NF, and I proposed the following as an example of such a relvar:

Let relvar R have attributes A, B, and C; using Heath notation, let AB, BC, and CA each be keys of R; and let the JD ✡{AB,BC,CA}— call it J—hold in R.

But you might not unreasonably be a little suspicious of this example. To be more specific, you might be wondering whether a relvar could even exist that's subject to exactly the specified key constraints and the specified JD (despite the fact that I did go on to give a slightly more concrete version of the example). Show that the example is reasonable after all by demonstrating that in fact all possible sets of dependencies (FDs and JDs) are consistent, in the sense that at least one relation can always be found that satisfies all of the dependencies in the set.

13.4   Relvar SPJ' from the section "5NF Is Too Strong" was subject to what might be called a "symmetric" JD—viz., the JD ✡{{SNO,PNO},{PNO,JNO},{JNO,SNO}}—and yet displayed some asymmetry also, in that just one of the three components of that JD corresponded to a key. Intuitively, you might expect the other two components to correspond to keys as well. Show that such isn't necessarily the case.

13.5   With regard to relvar SPJ' from the body of the chapter, show that the following business rules must be in effect as claimed:

- If supplier *s1* supplies part *p1* to project *j2* and supplier *s2* supplies part *p1* to project *j1* (*s1* ≠ *s2*, *j1* ≠ *j2*), then no part, not even *p1*, can be supplied by supplier *s1* to project *j1*.

- If supplier *s1* supplies part *p2* to project *j1* and supplier *s2* supplies part *p1* to project *j1* (*s1* ≠ *s2*, *p1* ≠ *p2*), then (c) no project, not even *j1*, can be supplied by supplier *s1* with part *p1*.

13.6   Again with regard to relvar SPJ′ from the body of the chapter, give a **Tutorial D** CONSTRAINT statement corresponding to the following business rule:

- If (a) supplier *s1* supplies part *p1* to project *j2* and (b) supplier *s1* supplies part *p2* to project *j1* (*p1* ≠ *p2*, *j1* ≠ *j2*), then (c) no supplier, not even *s1*, can supply part *p1* to project *j1*.

Answers

13.1   See Figure 13-1.

13.2   See the body of the chapter.

13.3   Let relation *r* have heading *H*. Then *r* will certainly satisfy all possible FDs and JDs that can be defined with respect to *H* if *r* has cardinality either one or zero. It follows that all possible sets of dependencies (FDs and JDs) are consistent, though some such sets might have the implication that any relation that satisfies them can have cardinality at most one. (Note, incidentally, that a relvar of cardinality at most one has the empty set { } as its sole key—see the answer to Exercise 4.10 in Chapter 4—and is necessarily in 5NF.)

13.4   The following is certainly a legitimate value for relvar SPJ′—

```
s1   p1   j1
s2   p1   j1
```

(*s1* ≠ *s2*)—so {PNO,JNO} isn't a key. Likewise, the following is also a legitimate value for SPJ′—

```
s1   p1   j1
s1   p2   j1
```

(*p1* ≠ *p2*)—so {JNO,SNO} isn't a key either.

13.5   With respect to the first of the rules as stated, suppose relvar SPJ′
contains the following tuples (note that "the third" tuple directly
violates the rule):

```
s1   p1   j2
s2   p1   j1
s1   px   j1
```

(*s1* ≠ *s2*, *j1* ≠ *j2*). Here then are the corresponding binary
projections:

```
s1   p1       p1   j2       j2   s1
s2   p1       p1   j1       j1   s2
s1   px       px   j1       j1   s1
```

Joining the two leftmost projections gives:

```
s1   p1   j2
s1   p1   j1
s2   p1   j2
s2   p1   j1
s1   px   j1
```

Joining this result with the third projection gives:

```
s1   p1   j2
s1   p1   j1
s2   p1   j1
s1   px   j1
```

But {SNO,PNO} is a key, so from "the first two tuples" it follows
that *j1* = *j2*: Contradiction. So the first rule must indeed be in
effect.

Proving that the second rule is in effect as well follows the same
general pattern.

13.6 CONSTRAINT ...
```
    WITH ( T1 := SPJ' RENAME { PNO AS Y1 , JNO AS Z1 ) ,
           T2 := SPJ' RENAME { PNO AS Y2 , JNO AS Z2 ) ,
           T3 := JOIN { T1 , T2 } ,
           T4 := T3 WHERE Y1 ≠ Y2 AND Z1 ≠ Z2 ,
           T5 := T4 { Y1 , Z2 } ,
           T6 := T5 RENAME { Y1 AS PNO , Z2 AS JNO } ,
           T7 := JOIN { SPJ' , T6 } ) :
    IS_EMPTY ( T7 ) ;
```

Here for interest is a formulation of the foregoing constraint in
relational calculus (**Tutorial D** is based on relational algebra, of
course). Let *t1*, *t2*, *t3* be range variables ranging over relvar SPJ'.
Then we have:

```
CONSTRAINT ...
    FORALL t1 FORALL t2 FORALL t3
    ( IF   t1.SNO = t2.SNO AND t1.PNO ≠ t2.PNO AND t1.JNO ≠ t2.JNO
      THEN t3.PNO ≠ t1.PNO OR  t3.JNO ≠ t2.JNO ) ;
```

CHAPTER 14

6NF

Why, sometimes I've believed
as many as six impossible things before breakfast.

—Lewis Carroll: Alice's Adventures in Wonderland (1865)

To paraphrase something I said in Chapter 9, I've assumed throughout this book so far that the only normal forms we care about are ones that involve projection as the decomposition operator and join as the corresponding recomposition operator. I also said in that same chapter that, given that assumption, it followed that 5NF was the final normal form. However, I did also say in a footnote to that chapter that there was something called *sixth* normal form or 6NF,[1] and that's what the present chapter is all about.

So what happens if we depart from those usual assumptions regarding the decomposition and recomposition operators? Well, in our book *Time and Relational Theory: Temporal Databases in the Relational Model and SQL* (Morgan Kaufmann, 2014)—referred to throughout what follows just as "the temporal book"—Hugh Darwen, Nikos Lorentzos, and I define:

    a.   Generalized versions of the relational operators, including generalized versions of projection and join in particular, and hence

---

[1]Hardly a very appropriate name, you might think, since there are at least nine normal forms, and arguably as many as eleven, that are strictly weaker than it! But we called it sixth because it really does represent the next step along the normalization road after 5NF—i.e., it deserves to be called sixth exactly as much as 5NF deserves to be called fifth.

b. On the basis of those generalized version of projection and join, a generalized kind of join dependency, and hence

c. A new normal form (viz., 6NF).[2]

As the title of the book in which they're described suggests, these developments turn out to be particularly important in connection with temporal data specifically. However, 6NF as such can be defined in such a way as (a) not to rely on those generalized concepts, and thereby (b) to be applicable—and, dare I say it, important—for ordinary or "regular" (i.e., nontemporal) data as well. And that's what the next section is all about.

Sixth Normal Form for Regular Data

Here then is a definition:

> **Definition (sixth normal form for regular data):** Relvar R is in sixth normal form (6NF) if and only if the only JDs that hold in R are trivial ones; in other words, the only JDs that hold in R are of the form ☆{ ..., H, ... }, where H is the heading of R.

Of course, we can never get rid of trivial dependencies; thus, a relvar in 6NF can't be nonloss decomposed at all, other than trivially.[3] For that reason, a 6NF relvar is sometimes said to be *irreducible* (yet another kind of irreducibility, observe). Our usual shipments relvar SP is in 6NF, and so is relvar CTXD from Chapter 9; by contrast, our usual parts relvar P is in 5NF but not in 6NF. (Our usual suppliers relvar S isn't even in 3NF, of course.)

Now, it follows immediately from the definition that every 6NF relvar is certainly in 5NF—i.e., 6NF implies 5NF. What's more, 6NF is always achievable. It's also intuitively attractive for the following reason:

> If relvar R is replaced by its 6NF projections $R1$, ..., Rn, then the predicates for $R1$, ..., Rn are all simple, and the predicate for R overall is the conjunction of those simple predicates (i.e., it's a *conjunctive predicate*).

---

[2]So we're not really departing from our usual assumptions regarding dependencies and decomposition and recomposition operators after all; rather, we're just generalizing the concepts on which those assumptions are based.

[3]Recall from Chapter 9 that a decomposition is trivial if and only if it's based on dependencies that are themselves trivial in turn.

Let me immediately explain what I mean by these remarks:

Definition (simple vs. compound predicate): A predicate is simple if and only if it involves no connectives. A predicate is composite (or compound) if and only if it's not simple.

Definition (connective): A connective is a logical operator such as AND, OR, or NOT.

Definition (conjunctive predicate): A conjunctive predicate is the logical AND of two or more other predicates.[4]

For example, suppose we replace relvar P by its projections PN, PL, PW, and PC on attributes {PNO,PNAME}, {PNO,COLOR}, {PNO,WEIGHT}, and {PNO,CITY}, respectively. Then the predicates for these projections are as follows (and note that these predicates are all simple ones):

- PN: *Part PNO is named PNAME.*

- PL: *Part PNO has color COLOR.*

- PW: *Part PNO has weight WEIGHT.*

- PC: *Part PNO is stored in city CITY.*

And the predicate for P itself is the logical AND of these four.[5] As the example shows, therefore, relvars in 6NF can be thought of as breaking the meaning of the data down into pieces that can't be broken down any further (they represent what are sometimes called "atomic facts" or, perhaps preferably, "irreducible facts"). Loosely, we might say the predicate for a 6NF relvar doesn't involve any ANDs.

---

[4]This definition is a trifle loose, but it's good enough for present purposes.

[5]In fact, of course, every part has *exactly one* name, color, weight, and city, and it's precisely this state of affairs that means we don't actually need to decompose relvar P into projections PN, PL, PW, and PC if we don't want to—the single 5NF relvar P, with its sole key {PNO}, can effectively serve as shorthand for the combination (in fact, the join) of those four 6NF relvars.

In this connection, let me briefly remind you of relvars CTX and SPJ from Chapters 12 and 9 respectively. For CTX, the predicate was certainly conjunctive—*Course CNO can be taught by teacher TNO* **AND** *course CNO uses textbook XNO*—and decomposing the relvar into its binary (and in fact 6NF) projections on {CNO,TNO} and {CNO,XNO} effectively eliminated that AND. As for SPJ, the predicate there was conjunctive too, even though it might not have appeared so in the simplified form in which I stated it. Here's a more complete version: *Supplier SNO supplies part PNO* **AND** *part PNO is supplied to project JNO* **AND** *project JNO is supplied by supplier SNO* **AND** *supplier SNO supplies part PNO to project JNO.* Again, decomposing the relvar into its three binary (and in fact 6NF) projections effectively eliminates those ANDs.

Here now is a nice characterization of 6NF (in fact, it's a theorem):

> **Theorem:** Relvar R is in 6NF if and only if (a) it's in 5NF, (b) it's of degree n, and (c) it has no key of degree less than $n - 1$.

For example, let PLUS be a relvar with attributes A, B, and C (so the degree is three), and let the relvar predicate be $A + B = C$. Then PLUS is in 5NF, and it has three keys (viz., AB, BC, and CA, to use Heath notation once again); however, none of those keys is of degree less than two, and PLUS is thus also in 6NF.

By the way, please don't misunderstand me here—I'm *not* saying that relvars should always be in 6NF, or that normalization should always be carried as far as 6NF. Sometimes some lower normal form (5NF, say) is at least adequate. What's more, to repeat something I said in Chapter 8, a design can be fully normalized (meaning the relvars are all in 5NF, or even 6NF) and yet still be bad. For example, the projections of the suppliers relvar S on {SNO,SNAME}, {SNO,STATUS}, and {SNO,CITY} are all in 6NF, and yet a design consisting of those three projections is probably not a good one, because (as we saw in Chapter 6) it loses an FD.

Another point to consider is that replacing a 5NF relvar by 6NF projections will probably lead to the need to maintain certain equality dependencies (EQDs). Recall from Chapter 3 that an EQD is a constraint to the effect that certain projections of certain relvars must be equal (speaking a trifle loosely). For example, if we decompose relvar P as discussed above into its projections PN, PL, PW, and PC, then the following EQDs will probably apply:[6]

```
CONSTRAINT ... PL { PNO } = PN { PNO } ;
CONSTRAINT ... PW { PNO } = PN { PNO } ;
CONSTRAINT ... PC { PNO } = PN { PNO } ;
```

On the other hand, as explained elsewhere,[7] decompositions like the one under discussion can be a good basis for dealing with missing information. Suppose every part does always have a known name but doesn't necessarily have a known color, weight, or city. Then a part with no known color will simply have no tuple in relvar PL (and similarly for weights and cities and relvars PW and PC, respectively). Of course, the equality dependencies will then become *inclusion* dependencies (actually foreign key constraints), from PL to PN, PW to PN, and PC to PN, respectively.

The net of the foregoing discussion is as follows (I'll express it in terms of the parts example, just for definiteness): If there are two or more properties, say name and color, that every part always has, then separating those two properties into distinct projections is probably a bad idea; but if some property is "optional"—in other words, if it has the potential to be "missing" or unknown for some reason—then placing that property in a relvar of its own is probably a good idea.

Sixth Normal Form for Temporal Data

Temporal data is a huge subject in its own right, of course, and I can give only a very superficial introduction to it here; however, I'd like to cover enough to explain, at least informally, what the generalized version of 6NF is all about. Consider Figure 14-1, which shows a sample value for a relvar called S_DURING, with predicate as follows:

Supplier SNO was under contract throughout interval DURING.

---

[6]These three EQDS might more succinctly expressed as follows: IDENTICAL{PN{PNO},PL{PNO}, PW{PNO},PC{PNO}}. See Chapter 17 for further explanation.

[7]See either *SQL and Relational Theory* or the book *Database Explorations: Essays on The Third Manifesto and Related Topics*, by Hugh Darwen and myself (Trafford, 2010). See also the further discussion of such matters in Chapter 16 of the present book.

For example, we see from the figure that (among other things) supplier S1 was under contract throughout the interval from "day 4" (*d04*) to "day 7" (*d07*), inclusive.

SNO	DURING
S1	[d04:d07]
S1	[d05:d10]
S1	[d09:d09]
S2	[d05:d06]
S2	[d03:d03]
S2	[d07:d08]

Figure 14-1. *Relvar S_DURING—sample value*

As the example suggests, intervals are crucial to temporal data support. However, the interval notion is actually of much wider applicability, cropping up as it does in a huge variety of practical situations. For example, tax brackets (e.g., $50,000–$75,000) can be thought of as intervals, intervals that involve money values instead of date or time values. Despite the fact that the title of the present section refers to temporal data as such, therefore, please be aware that all of the concepts to be discussed—not just the interval concept as such, but all of the various related concepts—are of much more general applicability and usefulness. (As a matter of fact I toyed with the idea of naming the section "Sixth Normal Form for Interval Data," a title that would really be more appropriate in some ways, though perhaps less imediately understandable.)

Now, the relation in Figure 14-1 clearly exhibits some redundancy; for example, it tells us twice that supplier S1 was under contract on day 6. It also exhibits a kind of *circumlocution*; for example, it takes three tuples to tell us what it could have told us with just one, viz., that supplier S1 was under contract throughout the interval [*d04:d10*].[8] By contrast, the relation shown in Figure 14-2 contains the same information

---

[8] I assume for present purposes that circumlocution, like redundancy, is generally undesirable and better eliminated if possible. For detailed arguments in support of this position (if you need them), please refer to the temporal book.

as—i.e., is *information equivalent* to[9]—the one in Figure 14-1 but exhibits no such redundancy or circumlocution:

SNO	DURING
S1	[d04:d10]
S2	[d03:d03]
S2	[d05:d08]

Figure 14-2. *Packed form of relation in Figure 14-1*

The relation in Figure 14-2 is the *packed form* of the one in Figure 14-1, and it can be obtained from that one by means of a new relational operator called PACK, as follows:

```
PACK S_DURING ON ( DURING )
```

In effect, what this expression does is this: For each supplier represented in the current value of relvar S_DURING, it combines into a single interval any DURING values that either overlap or meet. For example, with reference to Figures 14-1 and 14-2:

- In the case of supplier S1, the intervals [*d04:d07*] and [*d05:d10*] overlap, and so they can be combined to form the interval [*d04:d10*].

- In the case of supplier S2, the intervals [*d05:d06*] and [*d07:d08*] meet, and so they can be combined to form the interval [*d05:d08*].

Note: The "other" interval for S1, viz., the interval [*d09:d09*], effectively just gets absorbed into that combined interval [*d04:d10*]. By contrast, the "other" interval for supplier S2, viz., the interval [*d03:d03*], can't be combined with any other interval in this way and thus remains unaffected.

---

[9]I'll define this notion of information equivalence more precisely later. For now, I'll just assume it makes good intuitive sense.

There's another new operator as well, UNPACK, which "goes the other way," as it were; that is, given a relation such as that shown in Figure 14-1 (or the one shown in Figure 14-2, come to that) as input, it produces a relation in which the DURING values are all of the minimum possible size (in other words, they're *unit intervals*). For example, the following expression applied to the relation shown in Figure 14-1—

```
UNPACK S_DURING ON ( DURING )
```

—produces the result shown in Figure 14-3 below. That result is the *unpacked form* of the relation shown in Figure 14-1 (also of the relation shown in Figure 14-2, as I hope should be obvious).

SNO	DURING
S1	[d04:d04]
S1	[d05:d05]
S1	[d06:d06]
S1	[d07:d07]
S1	[d08:d08]
S1	[d09:d09]
S1	[d10:d10]
S2	[d03:d03]
S2	[d05:d05]
S2	[d06:d06]
S2	[d07:d07]
S2	[d08:d08]

Figure 14-3. *Unpacked form of relations in Figures 14-1 and Figure 14-2*

The relation shown in Figure 14-3 is information equivalent to each of the relations in Figures 14-1 and 14-2. What's more, like the one in Figure 14-2, it doesn't suffer from redundancy (though like the one in Figure 14-1 it does rather obviously suffer from circumlocution).

Now, you might be thinking from what I've said so far that all we need to do to avoid those redundancy and circumlocution problems is just to make sure that relvars are always kept in packed form.[10] Unfortunately, however, packed form, though it's part of the solution, isn't sufficient to solve the problems completely, and the following example shows why. Consider Figure 14-4, which shows a sample value for a relvar called SCT_DURING, with predicate as follows: *Supplier SNO was located in city CITY and had status STATUS throughout interval DURING.*

---

[10]Keeping a relvar in packed form means imposing a constraint on the relvar in question to ensure that all of the relations that can be assigned to that relvar are themselves in packed form in turn.

SNO	CITY	STATUS	DURING
S1	London	20	[d04:d05]
S1	London	20	[d05:d06]
S1	London	30	[d07:d07]
S1	Athens	30	[d08:d09]
S1	Athens	10	[d10:d10]
S2	Paris	20	[d03:d03]
S2	Paris	10	[d05:d05]
S2	Paris	10	[d06:d06]
S2	Paris	20	[d07:d07]
S2	Paris	20	[d08:d08]

Figure 14-4. *Relvar SCT_DURING—sample value*

Let's assume now that (in contrast to earlier chapters) the FD {CITY} → {STATUS} no longer holds. Then relvar SCT_DURING is in BCNF—the sole key is {SNO,DURING}, and the only FDs that hold are ones implied by that key. (As a matter of fact, though I won't attempt to prove it, the relvar is in 5NF also.) Yet the sample value in Figure 14-4 clearly exhibits both redundancy and circumlocution. So the first lesson of this example is this: Nonloss decomposition as classically understood—i.e., nonloss decomposition based on classical projection and classical join—is of no help in avoiding those problems. We need something else.

What's more, as I've already said, packed form by itself doesn't solve the problem either. Figure 14-5 shows the packed form of the relation from Figure 14-4—and as you can see, that relation, though it doesn't suffer from redundancy, still does suffer from circumlocution. (Of course, the relations of Figures 14-4 and 14-5 are certainly information equivalent, though.)

SNO	CITY	STATUS	DURING
S1	London	20	[d04:d06]
S1	London	30	[d07:d07]
S1	Athens	30	[d08:d09]
S1	Athens	10	[d10:d10]
S2	Paris	20	[d03:d03]
S2	Paris	10	[d05:d06]
S2	Paris	20	[d07:d08]

Figure 14-5. *Packed form of relation in Figure 14-4*

So packed form isn't the solution (at least, not the whole solution); to repeat, we need something else. In order to see what that something else might be, observe now that the redundancy and circumlocution in Figure 14-4, and the circumlocution in Figure 14-5, are all really a consequence of the fact that the DURING value in any given tuple applies not to the CITY and STATUS values in that tuple individually, but rather to those CITY and STATUS values taken in combination. But as the example makes clear, a given supplier's city and that supplier's status vary independently over time; so surely what we need to do is split the original relation into two separate relations, one for supplier cities and one for supplier status values, each with a DURING attribute of its own. We can achieve this split as follows—first, unpack the original relation on DURING; second, take projections of that unpacked form on {SNO,CITY,DURING} and {SNO,STATUS,DURING}, respectively; finally, pack those two projections on DURING. Given the sample SCT_DURING value from Figure 14-4, Figure 14-6 shows the relations that result from this process—and as you can see, these relations exhibit neither redundancy nor circumlocution:

SNO	CITY	DURING
S1	London	[d04:d07]
S1	Athens	[d08:d10]
S2	Paris	[d03:d03]
S2	Paris	[d05:d08]

SNO	STATUS	DURING
S1	20	[d04:d06]
S1	30	[d07:d09]
S1	10	[d10:d10]
S2	20	[d03:d03]
S2	10	[d05:d06]
S2	20	[d07:d08]

Figure 14-6. *Relvars SC_DURING and ST_DURING—sample values*

Moreover, as the caption to the figure suggests, these two relations can be regarded as sample values of two relvars SC_DURING and ST_DURING, which, I'm suggesting, might reasonably and desirably be regarded as a replacement for the original relvar SCT_DURING.

Now, the sequence of steps involved in this example—unpack, project, pack again—turns out to be needed so frequently in practice that defining an appropriate shorthand seems like a good idea. Here then is a definition—a considerably simplified definition, please note!—of an operator (actually a generalized form of classical projection) that, for reasons that should quickly become clear, we call *U_projection*:

Definition (U_projection): Let *r* be a relation, let attribute *A* of *r* be interval valued, and let *X* be a subset of the heading of *r* that contains *A*. Then the expression USING (*A*) : *r*{*X*} denotes the U_projection (with respect to *A*) of *r* on *X*, and it's defined to be shorthand for the following:

```
PACK
   ( ( UNPACK r ON ( A ) ) { X } )
ON ( A )
```

In other words, U_projection works by first unpacking the input relation as indicated, then doing a regular projection on that unpacked intermediate result, and then (re)packing the result of that projection to obtain the final packed result. Here are a couple of examples:

```
USING ( DURING ) : SCT_DURING { SNO , CITY , DURING }
```

```
USING ( DURING ) : SCT_DURING { SNO , STATUS , DURING }
```

Given the sample value for relvar SCT_DURING from Figure 14-4, these two expressions produce the relations shown in Figure 14-6. *Exercise:* Check this claim, if you haven't done so already.

What I'm suggesting, then, is that the original relvar SCT_DURING be replaced by the two "U_projection" relvars SC_DURING and ST_DURING. For that replacement to be valid, though, it obviously needs to be nonloss. Now, if we do a regular join on the two U_projections shown in Figure 14-6 (the join will be on the basis of attributes SNO and DURING), we clearly won't obtain either the relation shown in Figure 14-4 or the one shown in Figure 14-5. In fact, all we'll get is the following:

SNO	CITY	STATUS	DURING
S2	Paris	20	[d03:d03]

Well, you might be ahead of me here (in fact, I hope you are) ... Clearly, what we need to do is, first, unpack the two input relations; then do the join on those unpacked relations; and then pack the result of that join to obtain the final result. If we do all that, then what we'll get is the packed relation shown in Figure 14-5. *Exercise:* Again, check this claim (see Exercise 14.6d).

With the foregoing example by way of motivation, therefore, here's a definition—a considerably simplified definition again, please note—of a generalized form of join that we call *U_join*:

> **Definition (U_join):** Let relations *r1* and *r2* be joinable,[11] and let them have a common attribute *A* that's interval valued. Then the expression USING (*A*) : JOIN {*r1,r2*} denotes the U_join (with respect to *A*) of *r1* and *r2*, and it's defined to be shorthand for the following:

```
PACK
  ( JOIN
      { ( UNPACK r1 ON ( A ) ) ,
        ( UNPACK r2 ON ( A ) ) }
ON ( A )
```

So, as I've more or less said already, U_join works by first unpacking both input relations, then doing a regular join on those unpacked intermediate results, and then (re)packing the result of that join to obtain the final result.

I can now also as promised make the notion of information equivalence a little more precise. To be specific, the relations of Figures 14-4 and 14-5 are information equivalent because they have the same unpacked form; in fact, they're *U_equal*. Here's a simplified definition:

> **Definition (U_equality):** Let relations *r1* and *r2* have the same heading *H*, and let them have a common attribute *A* that's interval valued. Then the expression USING (*A*) : *r1* = *r2* denotes a U_equality comparison (with respect to *A*) between *r1* and *r2*, and it's defined to be shorthand for the following:

```
( UNPACK r1 ON ( A ) ) = ( UNPACK r2 ON ( A ) )
```

To summarize so far, then: The relation of Figure 14-4 is certainly not equal to the regular join of its regular projections on {SNO,CITY,DURING} and {SNO,STATUS,DURING}. However, it *is* U_equal to the U_join of the corresponding U_projections.

---

[11]Two points here: First, recall from Chapter 5 that *joinable* just means that attributes with the same name are of the same type; second, U_join in general is an *n*-adic operator, but here for simplicity I'm defining a dyadic version only.

Now suppose this state of affairs isn't just a fluke—it isn't just a matter of the sample value I happened to choose to show in Figure 14-4—but is, rather, a property that applies to all possible values of the relvar in question (i.e., relvar SCT_DURING). Then we can say that the relvar in question is subject to a certain generalized join dependency (a *U_JD*, in fact). Here's a simplified definition:

> **Definition (U_join dependency):** Let H be a heading, and let attribute A of H be interval valued. Then a U_join dependency (U_JD for short) with respect to A and H is an expression of the form USING $(A) : \text{✿}\{X1,X2,...,Xn\}$, where $X1$, $X2$, ..., Xn (the components of the U_JD) are subsets of H whose union is equal to H.

Then, of course, we go on to say that:

- A given relation satisfies a given U_JD if and only if it's U_equal to the U_join of the pertinent U_projections.

- A given relvar is subject to a given U_JD—equivalently, the given U_JD holds in the given relvar—if and only if every relation that can be assigned to that relvar satisfies that U_JD.

In the example, therefore, the following U_JD holds in relvar SCT_DURING:

```
USING ( DURING ) :
     ✿ { { SNO , CITY , DURING } , { SNO , STATUS, DURING } }
```

Moreover, since the original relvar suffers from certain redundancies and circumlocutions that don't apply to those U_projections, the recommendation is to nonloss decompose it accordingly. And we can define a new normal form based on such considerations, in such a way that relvar SCT_DURING isn't in that new normal form but its U_projections are. Before defining that new normal form, however, there are some further important points to be made—points that I've hinted at in the foregoing but haven't yet stated explicitly:

- The first is that the generalized form of projection that we call U_projection truly is a generalization as such. In other words, regular projection is just a special case of U_projection—or to put it another way, all projections are U_projections, but some U_projections aren't projections (at least, as this latter term is usually understood). The reason is as follows (simplifying somewhat yet again):

299

a. First, we allow a U_projection of relation *r* to be taken with respect to *no attributes at all*. The definition becomes:

```
PACK
    ( ( UNPACK r ON ( ) ) { X } )
ON ( )
```

b. Second, it turns out—see the temporal book if you need further explanation—that PACK and UNPACK, when performed with respect to no attributes, both just return their input, and so the foregoing expression reduces to just *r{X}*, the regular projection of *r* on *X*.

c. Third, we allow the USING prefix and its accompanying colon to be omitted from the concrete syntax for a U_projection that's done with respect to no attributes.

It follows from the foregoing that, as claimed, regular projection is just a special case of U_projection, both syntactically and semantically.

- Analogously, regular join is a special case of U_join, both syntactically and semantically.

- Analogously, a regular JD is a special case of a U_JD, both syntactically and semantically.

It follows that we can drop those U_ prefixes, if we like (except in circumstances where we might want to retain them for emphasis), and simply understand that henceforth projection means U_projection, and similarly for join and join dependency (and similarly for relation equality too, come to that).[12] So the "new normal form" we want to define is just 6NF, except that the concepts that underpin that normal form (projection, join, etc.) now have an extended interpretation. So here's the definition (but of course it's the same as it always was):

---

[12]And similarly too for all of the other familiar relational operators. Indeed, as I hope you would expect, we can and do define "U_" versions of all of the relational operators (U_union, U_restriction, and so on)—but the regular operators are just a special case of their U_ counterpart in every case. (I mention this point merely for completeness. The details are beyond the scope of this chapter, and indeed this book.)

Definition (sixth normal form): Relvar *R* is in sixth normal form (6NF) if and only if the only JDs that hold in *R* are trivial ones; in other words, the only JDs that hold in *R* are of the form ☼{ ..., *H*, ... }, where *H* is the heading of *R*.

Exercises

14.1   6NF relvars are sometimes said to be irreducible, and I noted in the body of the chapter that this was yet another of the many kinds of irreducibility that are relevant to design theory. How many different kinds can you identify?

14.2   Suppose relvar P is replaced as discussed in the body of the chapter by its 6NF projections PN, PL, PW, and PC. Can you think of any improvements on that design?

14.3   Consider a relvar *R* representing marriages, with attributes *A*, *B*, and *C* and predicate *Person A married person B on date C.* Assume no polygamy; assume also that no two persons marry each other more than once. What keys does *R* have? Does the JD ☼{*AB,BC,CA*} hold? What's the highest normal form *R* is in?

14.4   Design a database for the following. The entities to be represented are soccer match fixtures for a certain team. For matches that have already been played, we wish to record "goals for" and "goals against"; however, these two properties clearly make no sense for matches that have yet to be played. What normal forms are your relvars in?

14.5   In the body of the chapter, I showed informally how reducing a relvar to 6NF projections corresponded to reducing a conjunctive predicate to simple predicates. Could there be such a thing as a disjunctive predicate? How might a relvar correspond to such a predicate? What would be involved in reducing such a predicate to simple predicates?

14.6   Given the sample value of relvar SCT_DURING in Figure 14-4,
       show the result of evaluating each of the following expressions:

   a. `USING ( DURING ) : SCT_DURING { SNO , DURING }`

   b. `USING ( DURING ) : SCT_DURING { CITY , DURING }`

   c. `USING ( DURING ) : SCT_DURING { STATUS , DURING }`

   d. `USING ( DURING ) :`
       `   JOIN { SCT_DURING { SNO , CITY , DURING } ,`
       `          SCT_DURING { SNO , STATUS , DURING } }`

   Note: The answer in the last case is, of course, the relation shown
   in Figure 14-5—but don't just take my word for it, please confirm
   that result for yourself (unless you've done so already).

Answers

14.1   Irreducibility of keys and FDs, and the relevance of FD
       irreducibility to 2NF, are all discussed in Chapter 4; FD
       irreducibility is discussed further in Chapter 5. Irreducible
       covers are discussed in Chapter 6. Irreducible JDs are discussed
       in Chapter 11. Irreducible (i.e., 6NF) relvars and the associated
       notion of "irreducible facts" are discussed in the present chapter.

14.2   The main point that occurs to me is that it might be nice to have
       some kind of "master" relvar whose primary purpose is just to
       record the part numbers for all parts currently represented in the
       database. If we call that relvar P, there'll be EQDs between that
       relvar P and the projection on {PNO} of each of the relvars PN, PL,
       PW, and PC (instead of EQDs between, arbitrarily, the projection
       of PN on {PNO} and the projections on {PNO} of each of PL, PW,
       and PC; indeed, one nice thing about having the master relvar is
       precisely that it avoids that slight arbitrariness).

Moreover, suppose every part always has a known name and weight but doesn't necessarily have a known color or city. Then we can combine relvars P, PN, and PW, making that combination—which I'll still call P—the master relvar, and replace those previously required EQDs by foreign key constraints from PL and PC to that master relvar P. (A part with no known color will be represented in P but not PL; likewise, a part with no known city will be represented in P but not PC.)

Incidentally, another argument in favor of including that master relvar P has to do with the shipments relvar SP—given that master relvar, we can retain the conventional foreign key constraint from SP to P; without it, life becomes rather messier (right?).

14.3 Every pair of attributes is a key. The specified JD doesn't hold, because the following is certainly a legitimate value for the relvar:

a1	b1	c2
b1	a1	c2
a2	b1	c1
b1	a2	c1
a1	b2	c1
b2	a1	c1

($a1 \neq a2$, $b1 \neq b2$, $c1 \neq c2$); that is, the tuples ($a1,b1,c2$), ($a2,b1,c1$), and ($a1,b2,c1$) most certainly don't force the tuple ($a1,b1,c1$) to appear (!). The relvar is in 6NF. Note, however, that it's subject to a certain *symmetry* constraint; to be specific, the tuple (a,b,c) appears if and only if the tuple (b,a,c) appears (see the sample value above for an illustration of this point).[13] As a consequence, the relvar is also subject to certain insertion and deletion anomalies. (In particular, therefore, it isn't in DK/NF. See Chapter 15.)

---

[13]Two questions: First, do you think that symmetry constraint is tuple forcing? Second, do you think the relvar is subject to redundancy? Justify your answers!—especially to the second question.

14.4   The thing to do here is to separate matches that have already been played from those that haven't:

```
PAST_MATCHES { DATE , OPPONENT , GOALS_FOR , GOALS_AGAINST , ... }
              KEY { DATE }

FUTURE_MATCHES { DATE , OPPONENT , ... }
               KEY { DATE }
```

These relvars are both in 5NF. PAST_MATCHES in particular probably shouldn't be replaced by 6NF projections.
Note: Alternatively, we might consider replacing FUTURE_MATCHES by a relvar FIXTURES, giving DATE and OPPONENT for all matches past and future. What constraints would apply then? Come to that, what constraints apply to the design shown above?

14.5   A disjunctive predicate is the logical OR of two or more other predicates. If some relvar *R* had a disjunctive relvar predicate, then the individual predicates that are OR'd together would have to have the same parameters (because the tuples that satisfy them would all have to be of the same type). Reducing such a relvar to ones with simple predicates would probably involve decomposition via restriction instead of projection (and recomposition via union instead of join). See Chapters 15 and 16 for further discussion.

14.6   a.

SNO	DURING
S1	[d04:d10]
S2	[d03:d03]
S2	[d05:d08]

b.

CITY	DURING
London	[d04:d07]
Athens	[d08:d10]
Paris	[d03:d03]
Paris	[d05:d08]

c.

STATUS	DURING
20	[d03:d08]
30	[d07:d09]
10	[d10:d10]
10	[d05:d06]

d.   Here first are the two U_projections (repeated from
Figure 14-6):

SNO	CITY	DURING
S1	London	[d04:d07]
S1	Athens	[d08:d10]
S2	Paris	[d03:d03]
S2	Paris	[d05:d08]

SNO	STATUS	DURING
S1	20	[d04:d06]
S1	30	[d07:d09]
S1	10	[d10:d10]
S2	20	[d03:d03]
S2	10	[d05:d06]
S2	20	[d07:d08]

The corresponding unpacked forms are as follows:

SNO	CITY	DURING
S1	London	[d04:d04]
S1	London	[d05:d05]
S1	London	[d06:d06]
S1	London	[d07:d07]
S1	Athens	[d08:d08]
S1	Athens	[d09:d09]
S1	Athens	[d10:d10]
S2	Paris	[d03:d03]
S2	Paris	[d05:d05]
S2	Paris	[d06:d06]
S2	Paris	[d07:d07]
S2	Paris	[d08:d08]

SNO	STATUS	DURING
S1	20	[d04:d04]
S1	20	[d05:d05]
S1	20	[d06:d06]
S1	30	[d07:d07]
S1	30	[d08:d08]
S1	30	[d09:d09]
S1	10	[d10:d10]
S2	20	[d03:d03]
S2	20	[d07:d07]
S2	20	[d08:d08]
S2	10	[d05:d05]
S2	10	[d06:d06]

Here's the join of these two unpacked relations:

SNO	CITY	STATUS	DURING
S1	London	20	[d04:d04]
S1	London	20	[d05:d05]
S1	London	20	[d06:d06]
S1	London	30	[d07:d07]
S1	Athens	30	[d08:d08]
S1	Athens	30	[d09:d09]
S1	Athens	10	[d10:d10]
S2	Paris	20	[d03:d03]
S2	Paris	20	[d07:d07]
S2	Paris	20	[d08:d08]
S2	Paris	10	[d05:d05]
S2	Paris	10	[d06:d06]

Packing this result on DURING yields the relation shown in Figure 14-5.

CHAPTER 15

The End Is Not Yet

Now, this is not the end. It is not even the beginning of the end.
But it is, perhaps, the end of the beginning.

—Winston Churchill:
Speech at the Lord Mayor's Day Luncheon, London
(November 10th, 1942)

Eternity's a terrible thought.
I mean, where's it all going to end?

—Tom Stoppard:
Rosenkrantz and Guildenstern Are Dead (1967)

What a long strange trip it's been ... In Part II of this book, we covered 1NF, 2NF, 3NF, and BCNF (the last at some length); in Part III we covered 4NF and 5NF (the latter at considerable length); and in the previous two chapters we've met four more normal forms, ETNF, RFNF, SKNF, and 6NF (of which the last is easily the most important). But even that's not the end of the story. In this chapter, just for completeness, I briefly describe or at least mention a few other normal forms that have been defined in the literature at one time or another.

© C. J. Date 2019
C. J. Date, *Database Design and Relational Theory*, https://doi.org/10.1007/978-1-4842-5540-7_15

Domain-Key Normal Form

Domain-key normal form (DK/NF) differs from all of the normal forms discussed in this book prior to this point in that it's not defined in terms of FDs, MVDs, and JDs, as such, at all.[1] DK/NF is really a kind of "ideal" normal form: It's desirable because, by definition, a relvar in DK/NF is guaranteed to be free of certain update anomalies; sadly, however, it's not always achievable, nor has the question "Exactly when can it be achieved?" been answered. Be that as it may, let's investigate.

DK/NF is defined in terms of *domain constraints* and *key constraints*. Key constraints are already familiar, of course (they were defined formally in Chapter 5). As for domain constraints, I remind you that *domain* is essentially just another word for *type* (see the answer to Exercise 2.4 in Chapter 2). It follows that a domain constraint ought logically to be the same thing as a type constraint; in other words, it ought simply to be a specification of the set of values that constitute the type in question (see *SQL and Relational Theory* for further discussion of this concept). However, the term is being used in the present context in a slightly special sense. To be specific, a *domain constraint*, as that term is used here, is a constraint to the effect that values of a given attribute are taken not just from some prescribed domain, but rather from some prescribed subset of that domain. For example, there might be a constraint on the suppliers relvar S to the effect that STATUS values (which are integers, i.e., values of type INTEGER) must be in the range one to a hundred, inclusive.

Here then are some definitions:

> **Definition (domain-key normal form):** Relvar R is in domain-key normal form (DK/NF) if and only if every single-relvar constraint that holds in R is implied by the domain constraints and key constraints that hold in R.

---

[1] Well ... it's defined in terms of key constraints, as we'll see, and key constraints in turn are a special case of FDs, so this remark is perhaps not quite accurate as stated. PS: Domain-key normal form is probably the only one of the various normal forms discussed in this chapter, or indeed anywhere in this part of the book, that you might see mentioned elsewhere in the computing literature—in the popular computing literature, at any rate.

Definition (single-relvar constraint): Any integrity constraint that can be tested by examining the pertinent relvar in isolation (i.e., without having to examine any other relvar in the database).[2]

Enforcing constraints on a DK/NF relvar is thus conceptually simple, since it's sufficient to enforce just the pertinent domain and key constraints, and all constraints— not just FDs, MVDs, and JDs, but *all* single-relvar constraints that apply to the relvar in question—on the relvar will then be enforced automatically.

DK/NF was first defined by Fagin in 1981,[3] and it was the DK/NF paper that first gave precise definitions for the terms *insertion anomaly* and *deletion anomaly*. I defined these notions in Chapter 10 (and referred to them again in Chapter 13), but those previous definitions and discussions were framed in terms of JDs specifically. Here for the record are the general definitions (note that they refer to single-relvar constraints in general, not just ones that happen to be FDs or MVDs or JDs):[4]

Definition (insertion anomaly): Relvar *R* suffers from an insertion anomaly if and only if there exists a legal value *r* for *R* and a tuple *t* with the same heading as *R* such that the relation obtained by appending *t* to *r* satisfies *R*'s key constraints but violates some other single-relvar constraint on *R*.

Definition (deletion anomaly): Relvar *R* suffers from a deletion anomaly if and only if there exists a legal value *r* for *R* and a tuple *t* of *r* such that the relation obtained by removing *t* from *r* violates some single-relvar constraint on *R*.

The DK/NF paper proves that a relvar in DK/NF can't suffer from insertion or deletion anomalies as just defined. (Actually it proves a stronger result: viz., that a relvar can't suffer from such anomalies if *and only if* it's in DK/NF.)

---

[2]For example, key constraints are always single-relvar constraints, by definition. By contrast, foreign key constraints are usually not. *Note:* Single-relvar constraints are usually referred to as just relvar constraints for brevity. For further discussion, see *SQL and Relational Theory*.

[3]See Ronald Fagin: "A Normal Form for Relational Databases That Is Based on Domains and Keys," *ACM Transactions on Database Systems 6*, No. 3 (September 1981).

[4]Footnote 6 in Chapter 10 applies here also. That is, the definitions that follow are very slightly suspect, in a sense, inasmuch as they talk about appending or removing individual tuples whereas (as explained in *SQL and Relational Theory*) INSERT and DELETE really "append" or "remove" entire relations, not individual tuples. However, the definitions can clearly be refined in such a way as to take care of this minor quibble.

Finally, we have the following theorem:

> **Theorem:** So long as every pertinent attribute can take on at least two distinct values, DK/NF implies 5NF.

That is (speaking a trifle loosely), every DK/NF relvar is in 5NF—though it's not necessarily in 6NF, of course. As noted in Chapter 13, in fact (in a footnote), DK/NF and 5NF coincide in the—sadly, probably unlikely—special case where the only constraints that hold are FDs and JDs specifically.

Elementary Key Normal Form

Elementary key normal form (EKNF) was introduced by Zaniolo in 1982.[5] Here's the definition:

> **Definition (elementary key normal form):** Relvar R is in elementary key normal form (EKNF) if and only if, for every nontrivial FD $X \rightarrow Y$ that holds in R, either (a) X is a superkey or (b) Y is a subkey of some elementary key—where key K is elementary if and only if there exists some attribute A of R such that the FD $K \rightarrow \{A\}$ is nontrivial and irreducible.

It's immediate from this definition that EKNF falls strictly between 3NF and BCNF; that is, BCNF implies EKNF, EKNF implies 3NF, and the reverse implications don't hold. As for an example: Well, as noted elsewhere in this book, with the normal forms it's usually more instructive to show a counterexample rather than an example per se. Suppose, therefore, that:

a.   Our usual shipments relvar SP has, instead of the usual QTY attribute, an attribute SNAME, representing the name of the applicable supplier.

b.   Supplier names are necessarily unique (i.e., no two distinct suppliers ever have the same name at the same time).

---

[5]See Carlo Zaniolo: "A New Normal Form for the Design of Relational Database Schemata," *ACM Transactions on Database Systems 7*, No. 3 (September 1982).

Then this revised version of SP has two keys, {SNO,PNO} and {SNAME,PNO}. However, these keys aren't elementary keys, because the only nontrivial FDs that hold with one of these keys as determinant are {SNO,PNO} → {SNAME} and {SNAME,PNO} → {SNO}, and these FDs are both reducible (in both cases PNO can be dropped from the determinant without loss). So the relvar is subject to two nontrivial FDs, {SNO} → {SNAME} and {SNAME} → {SNO}, in which the determinant isn't a superkey and the dependant isn't a subkey of an elementary key. So this version of relvar SP isn't in EKNF (though it is in 3NF).

The stated intent of EKNF is "to capture the salient qualities of both 3NF and BCNF" while avoiding the problems of both (namely, that 3NF is "too forgiving" and BCNF is "prone to computational complexity"). That said, I should say too that EKNF isn't much referenced in the literature.

Overstrong PJ/NF

Recall that 5NF was originally called PJ/NF, and PJ/NF meant that every JD was implied by keys (speaking rather loosely). In fact, in the paper in which he introduced PJ/NF, Fagin also introduced what he called *overstrong* PJ/NF, which meant (again rather loosely) that every JD was implied by some specific key considered in isolation. Note that this latter is what one might intuitively have expected the definition of *regular* PJ/NF (i.e., 5NF) to have been—recall the remarks in Chapters 10 and 12 concerning the parallelism among the definitions of BCNF, 4NF, and 5NF. Be that as it may, here's the definition:

> **Definition (overstrong PJ/NF):** Relvar R is in overstrong PJ/NF if and only if every JD of R is implied by some key of R.

Overstrong PJ/NF clearly implies 5NF (i.e., "regular" PJ/NF), but the reverse is false. A single counterexample suffices to demonstrate this latter fact:[6] Consider a relvar R with attributes A, B, C, and D (only) and keys {A} and {B} only. Let the only dependencies to hold in R be ones that are implied by these keys (so R is definitely in 5NF). Now consider the JD ⋈{AB,BC,AD}. Applying the membership algorithm, we see that this JD holds in R; but it's not a consequence of either of the keys considered in isolation, as can also be seen by checking the membership algorithm. So R is in 5NF (or PJ/NF) but not in overstrong PJ/NF.

---

[6]This same example was used in Chapter 13, footnote 2, in connection with the definition of tuple forcing JDs.

"Restriction-Union" Normal Form

Consider the parts relvar P from the suppliers-and-parts database. Normalization theory as I've described it up to this point tells us relvar P is in a "good" normal form; indeed, it's in 5NF, and it's therefore guaranteed to be free of anomalies that can be removed by taking projections. But why keep all parts in a single relvar? What about a design in which red parts are kept in one relvar (RP, say), blue ones in another (BP, say), and so on? In other words, what about the possibility of decomposing the original parts relvar via restriction instead of projection? Would the resulting structure be a good design or a bad one? (In fact it would almost certainly be bad unless we were very careful, as we'll see in Part V of this book; however, the point here is that classical normalization theory as such has absolutely nothing to say about the matter.)

Another direction for design research therefore consists of examining the implications of decomposing relvars by some operator other than projection. In the example, the decomposition operator is, as already mentioned, (disjoint) restriction, and the corresponding recomposition operator is (disjoint) union. Thus, it might be possible to construct a "restriction-union" normalization theory, analogous to—but orthogonal to—the projection-join normalization theory we've been considering throughout the bulk of this book. I don't want to get much more specific on such matters here; suffice it to say that some initial ideas along these lines can be found:

a. In a paper by Smith, which discusses a normal form called (3,3)NF.[7] Smith shows, first, that (3,3)NF implies BCNF; second, that a (3,3)NF relvar need not be in 4NF, nor need a 4NF relvar be in (3,3)NF. As suggested above, therefore, reduction to (3,3)NF is orthogonal to reduction to 4NF (and 5NF).

b. In Fagin's PJ/NF paper, which includes as a kind of postscript a preliminary discussion of a normal form called PJSU/NF (S for "split" and U for union). *Tentative definition:* Relvar R is in PJSU/NF if and only if it's in PJ/NF (i.e., 5NF) and there's no way to split it via restriction into relvars R1 and R2 such that the dependencies of R1 and R2 are different.

---

[7]J. M. Smith: "A Normal Form for Abstract Syntax," Proc. 4th International Conference on Very Large Data Bases, Berlin, Federal German Republic (September 1978).

Exercises

15.1   Define DK/NF. Give an example of a relvar in 6NF that's not in DK/NF.

15.2   What's the difference between SKNF and overstrong PJ/NF? In fact, *is* there a difference?

15.3   Give definitions, as precise as you can make them, of the relational operators restriction and union.

15.4   How would you fit the various normal forms mentioned in this chapter (also 6NF) into the normal form hierarchy of Figure 13-1?

Answers

15.1.   For the definition, see the body of the chapter. As for an example, suppose relvar SP is subject to a constraint to the effect that odd numbered parts can be supplied only by odd numbered suppliers and even numbered parts only by even numbered suppliers. (This example is very contrived, of course, but it suffices for the purpose at hand.) Then this constraint is clearly not implied by the domain and key constraints that hold in relvar SP, and so the relvar isn't in DK/NF; yet it's certainly in 6NF.

15.2.   There certainly is a difference, since overstrong PJ/NF implies 5NF and 5NF implies SKNF and the reverse implications don't hold. But it's easy to confuse the two, because the following superficially similar observations are both true (note the **boldface**). Let R be a relvar, and let $J = \Leftwedge\{X1,...,Xn\}$ be an irreducible JD that holds in R. Then:

- R is in SKNF if and only if, for every such J, each Xi ($i = 1, ..., n$) includes **some** key of R.

- R is in overstrong PJ/NF if and only if, for every such J, each Xi ($i = 1, ..., n$) includes **the same** key of R.

15.3. Apologies if you think these definitions a little late in coming:

- **Definition (restriction):** Let r be the relation $<H,h>$ and let bx be a boolean expression in which every attribute reference identifies some attribute of r and there aren't any relvar references. Then bx denotes a restriction condition, c say, and the restriction of r according to c, r WHERE c, is the relation $<H,x>$, where x is the set of all tuples of r for which c evaluates to TRUE.

- **Definition (union):** Let relations $r1$, ..., rn ($n \geq 0$) all have the same heading H. Then the union of $r1$, ..., rn, UNION $\{r1,...,rn\}$, is a relation with heading H and body the set of all tuples t such that t appears in at least one of $r1$, $r2$, ..., rn. (If $n = 0$, some syntactic mechanism, not shown here, is needed to specify the pertinent heading H, and the result is the unique empty relation having that heading.) Observe that union as here defined is an n-adic operator, not a dyadic operator merely.

15.4. This one isn't easy to answer! Figure 15-1 is my attempt.

1NF
2NF
3NF
EKNF
BCNF
4NF
ETNF
RFNF / KCNF
SKNF
5NF
6NF

Figure 15-1. *The normal form hierarchy (III)*

The figure is accurate as far as it goes. But:

- DK/NF needs to be added—probably on a par with 6NF (neither DK/NF nor 6NF implies the other, but "most" DK/NF relvars are in 5NF).

- Overstrong PJ/NF needs to be added—again, probably on a par with 6NF.

- (3,3)NF needs to be added—probably on a par with EKNF but off to one side, as it were (since (3,3)NF implies BCNF but neither (3,3)NF nor 4NF implies the other).

- PJSU/NF needs to be added—again, probably on a par with 6NF.

Note, however, that even if we stay in the "direct mainstream" (i.e., from 1NF to 6NF, inclusive), there are still eleven logically distinct normal forms; the others—the ones discussed in the present chapter—might fairly be described as outliers.

PART V

Orthogonality

To repeat something I said in Chapter 1, database design is not my favorite subject. The reason is that so little of design practice is truly scientific; normalization is scientific, of course, but not much else is. However, the topic of this part of the book, orthogonality, does represent another tiny piece of science in what's otherwise still, sadly, a fairly subjective field.

CHAPTER 16

The Principle of Orthogonal Design

> ***Orthogonal*** *At right angles to; independent.*
>
> —David Darling:
> *The Universal Book of Mathematics* (2004)

I've said repeatedly in earlier parts of this book that normalization is the science (or a large part of the science, at any rate) underlying database design. Thus, it's appropriate to begin this chapter with a quick review of normalization principles and a brief analysis of how well normalization meets its objectives.

Two Cheers for Normalization

Here first, then, is a simplified summary of the principles of normalization:

1. A relvar not in 5NF should be decomposed into a set of 5NF projections.[1]

2. The original relvar should be reconstructable by joining those projections back together again—i.e., the decomposition should be nonloss.

3. Every projection should be needed in the reconstruction process.

4. The decomposition should preserve dependencies (FDs and JDs), insofar as it can do so without violating the first principle.

---

[1]You can replace 5NF here by ETNF (twice), if you like, or maybe even 6NF (?).

Normalization is far from being a panacea, however, as we can easily see by considering what its goals are and how well it measures up against them. Here are those goals:

- To achieve a design that's a "good" representation of the real world (i.e., one that's logically correct and intuitively easy to understand, and is a good basis for future growth)

- To reduce redundancy

- Thereby to avoid certain update anomalies that might otherwise occur

- To simplify the statement and enforcement of certain integrity constraints

I'll consider each in turn.

- *Good representation of the real world:* Normalization does well on this one. I have no criticisms on this score.

- *Reduce redundancy:* Normalization is a good start on this problem too, but it's only a start. For one thing, it's a process of taking projections, and we've seen that not all redundancies can be removed by taking projections; indeed, there are many kinds of redundancy that normalization simply doesn't address at all. (Chapter 17 takes up this issue.) For another thing, taking projections, even when the decomposition is nonloss, can cause dependencies to be lost, as we saw in Chapter 6 and elsewhere.

- *Avoid update anomalies:* This point is, at least in part, just the previous one by another name. It's well known that designs that aren't properly normalized can be subject to certain update anomalies, precisely because of the redundancies they entail. In relvar STP, for example (see Figure 1-2 in Chapter 1), supplier S1 might be shown as having status 20 in one tuple and status 25 in another.

  Of course, this particular anomaly can arise only if a less than perfect job is being done on integrity constraint enforcement. Perhaps a better way to think about the update anomaly issue is this: The constraints needed to prevent such anomalies will be easier to state, and might be easier to enforce, if the design is properly normalized than they would be if it isn't (see the next bullet item below). Yet another way to think about it is: More single-tuple updates[2] will be logically acceptable if the design is properly normalized than would be the case if it isn't (because unnormalized designs imply redundancy—i.e., several tuples saying the same thing—and redundancy in turn implies that sometimes we have to update several things at the same time).

- *Simplify statement and enforcement of constraints:* As we know from earlier chapters, some dependencies imply others. (More generally, in fact, constraints of any kind can imply others. As a trivial example, if shipment quantities must be less than or equal to 5000, they must certainly be less than or equal to 6000.) Now, if constraint *A* implies constraint *B*, then stating and enforcing *A* will effectively state and enforce *B* "automatically" (indeed, *B* won't need to be separately stated at all, except perhaps by way of documentation). And normalization to (at least) 5NF gives us a very simple way of stating and enforcing certain important constraints; basically, all we have to do is define keys and enforce their uniqueness—which we're going to do anyway—and then all applicable JDs (and all applicable MVDs and FDs as well) will effectively be stated and enforced automatically, because they'll all be implied by those keys. So normalization does a pretty good job in this area too. (Of course, I'm ignoring here the various multirelvar constraints that the normalization process is likely to give rise to.)

Here on the other hand are several more reasons, over and above those already given, why normalization is no panacea:

- First, JDs and MVDs and FDs aren't the only kind of constraint, and normalization doesn't help with any others.

- Second, given a particular set of relvars, there'll often be several distinct nonloss decompositions into 5NF projections—see Chapter 6 for several examples—and there's little or no formal guidance

---

[2]Perhaps better, more *singleton set* updates.

available to tell us which one to choose in such cases. (To be honest, though, I doubt whether this lack is likely to cause major problems in practice.)

- Third, there are many design issues that normalization simply doesn't address. For example, what is it that tells us there should be just one suppliers relvar, instead of one for London suppliers, one for Paris suppliers, and so on? It certainly isn't normalization as classically understood.

All of that being said, I must make it clear that I don't want the foregoing comments to be seen as any kind of attack. As I said in Chapter 8, I believe anything less than a fully normalized design is strongly contraindicated. But the fact remains that normalization (what I referred to as "the scientific part of design") as such really doesn't do as much of the job as we'd like—and so it's good to be able to say that now there's a tiny piece of additional science available to us. That's what orthogonal design is all about.

Note: The concept of orthogonality has evolved over time. As a result, portions of this chapter are at odds, somewhat, with previous writings—mostly by myself—on this same subject. What's more, I very much doubt whether this chapter is the last word, either. I do believe the chapter is accurate as far as it goes; however, further refinements to the material might well be possible, and desirable, in the future. *Caveat lector.*

A Motivating Example

For simplicity, let the FD {CITY} → {STATUS} *not* hold any longer in relvar S (*and please note that I'll stay with this revised assumption throughout the present chapter*). Consider now the following decomposition of that relvar:

```
SNC { SNO , SNAME , CITY }
    KEY { SNO }

STC { SNO , STATUS , CITY }
    KEY { SNO }
```

Sample values are shown in Figure 16-1. As the figure clearly shows, this decomposition is hardly very sensible (in particular, note that the fact that a given supplier is located in a given city appears twice), and yet it abides by all of the normalization principles—both projections are in 5NF; the decomposition is nonloss; both projections are needed in the reconstruction process; and dependencies are preserved.

SNC

SNO	SNAME	CITY
S1	Smith	London
S2	Jones	Paris
S3	Blake	Paris
S4	Clark	London
S5	Adams	Athens

STC

SNO	STATUS	CITY
S1	20	.London
S2	30	Paris
S3	30	Paris
S4	20	London
S5	30	Athens

Figure 16-1. *Relvars SNC and STC—sample values*

Intuitively, the problem with the foregoing design is obvious: The tuple (s,n,c) appears in SNC if and only if the tuple (s,t,c) appears in STC; equivalently, the tuple (s,c) appears in the projection of SNC on {SNO,CITY} if and only if that very same tuple (s,c) appears in the projection of STC on {SNO,CITY}. To state the matter a trifle more formally, we can say the design is subject to the following equality dependency (EQD)—

```
CONSTRAINT ... SNC { SNO , CITY } = STC { SNO , CITY } ;
```

—and this EQD makes the redundancy explicit.

To repeat, however, the foregoing design abides by *all* of the well established principles of normalization. It follows that those principles by themselves aren't enough—we need something else to tell us what's wrong with the design (something else *formal*, that is; we all know what's wrong with it informally). To put the matter another way, the normalization discipline provides a set of formal principles to guide us in our attempts to reduce redundancy, but that set of principles by itself is inadequate, as the example plainly shows. We need another principle; in other words, as I keep saying, we need more science.

A Simpler Example

In order to see what the principle we need might look like, let's consider another, simpler (?) example. As you know, normalization as such—in particular, normalization as used in the SNC / STC example of the previous section—has to do with "vertical" decomposition of relvars (meaning decomposition via projection). But "horizontal" decomposition (that is, decomposition via restriction) is clearly possible, too. Consider the design illustrated in Figure 16-2, in which the parts relvar P has been split horizontally—in fact, partitioned—into two relvars, one ("light parts," LP) containing parts with weight less than 17.0 pounds and the other ("heavy parts," HP) containing parts with weight greater than or equal to 17.0 pounds.[3]

LP

PNO	PNAME	COLOR	WEIGHT	CITY
P1	Nut	Red	12.0	London
P4	Screw	Red	16.0	London
P5	Cam	Blue	12.0	Paris

HP

PNO	PNAME	COLOR	WEIGHT	CITY
P2	Bolt	Green	17.0	Paris
P3	Screw	Blue	17.0	Paris
P6	Cog	Red	19.0	London

Figure 16-2. *Relvars LP and HP—sample values*

The predicates are as follows:

- LP: *Part PNO is named PNAME, has color COLOR and weight WEIGHT (which is less than 17.0 pounds), and is stored in city CITY.*

---

[3] I'm assuming for definiteness here (and will continue to do so throughout this chapter) that WEIGHT values are presented to the user in terms of pounds avoirdupois. Please note, however, that I don't say they're *represented* in such terms; weights are weights, and what units they're presented to the user in is a separate issue (in fact, one that should be under user control—e.g., users might want, and should be allowed, to see the very same weight in pounds in some circumstances and in grams in others). See Chapter 2 ("Types without Inheritance") of my book *Type Inheritance and Relational Theory: Subtypes, Supertypes, and Substitutability* (O'Reilly, 2016) for further discussion of such matters, as well as a fairly detailed proposal for how such matters might be handled in practice.

- HP: *Part PNO is named PNAME, has color COLOR and weight WEIGHT (which is greater than or equal to 17.0 pounds), and is stored in city CITY.*

Note that the original relvar P can be recovered by taking the (disjoint) union of relvars LP and HP.

Why might we want to perform such a horizontal decomposition? Frankly, I'm not aware of any good logical reason for doing so, though of course that's not to say no such reason exists. Be that as it may, observe that we can, and should, state two constraints that apply to these relvars:

```
CONSTRAINT LPC AND ( LP , WEIGHT < 17.0 ) ;

CONSTRAINT HPC AND ( HP , WEIGHT ≥ 17.0 ) ;
```

(I remind you from Chapter 2 that the **Tutorial D** expression AND (*rx,bx*), where *rx* is a relational expression and *bx* is a boolean expression, returns TRUE if and only if the condition denoted by *bx* evaluates to TRUE for every tuple in the relation denoted by *rx*.)

So we have here what is at least arguably a slightly unusual situation. To be specific, for each of relvars LP and HP, part of the predicate can and should be captured formally in the shape of an explicit constraint. Indeed, the very fact that such constraints need to be stated and enforced might be seen as militating against the design. But even if horizontal decomposition is therefore contraindicated at the logical level, there are still plenty of pragmatic reasons (having to do with recovery, security, performance, and other such matters) for such a decomposition at the physical level. Hence, given that the logical and physical levels tend to be in lockstep, pretty much, in today's DBMSs—i.e., there's not nearly as much data independence in those DBMSs as there ought to be—it follows that there are likely to be pragmatic reasons, if not logical ones, for performing such a decomposition at the logical level as well, at least given the state of the art found in current implementations.

Now, regardless of what you might think of the foregoing argument, at least there's nothing obviously bad about the design of Figure 16-2 (well, let's agree as much for the sake of the example, at any rate).[4] But suppose we were to define relvar LP just a little differently; to be specific, suppose we were to define it to contain those parts with

---

[4]Actually there might be something logically bad. Consider, for example, what has to happen if the weight of part P1 is doubled.

weight less than *or equal to* 17.0 pounds (adjusting the predicate and constraint LPC accordingly, of course). Figure 16-3 is a revised version of Figure 16-2, showing what happens with this revised design.

LP

PNO	PNAME	COLOR	WEIGHT	CITY
P1	Nut	Red	12.0	London
P2	Bolt	Green	17.0	Paris
P3	Screw	Blue	17.0	Paris
P4	Screw	Red	16.0	London
P5	Cam	Blue	12.0	Paris

HP

PNO	PNAME	COLOR	WEIGHT	CITY
P2	Bolt	Green	17.0	Paris
P3	Screw	Blue	17.0	Paris
P6	Cog	Red	19.0	London

Figure 16-3. *Relvars LP (revised) and HP—sample values*

As you can see, now the design is definitely bad; to be specific, the tuples for parts P2 and P3 now appear in both relvars in Figure 16-3 (in other words, there's now some redundancy). What's more, those tuples *must* appear in both relvars! For suppose, contrariwise, that (say) the tuple for part P2 appeared in HP and not in LP. Then, noting that LP contains no tuple for part P2, we could legitimately conclude from *The Closed World Assumption*—see Chapter 2—that it's not the case that part P2 weighs 17.0 pounds. But then we see from HP that part P2 in fact does weigh 17.0 pounds, and the database is thus inconsistent (it contains a contradiction). *Note:* Inconsistency in a database is highly undesirable, of course. In fact, I'll show in Appendix B that you can never trust the results you get from an inconsistent database; indeed, you can get *absolutely any result whatsoever*—even results that effectively imply nonsensical things like 1 = 0—from such a database!

Now, the problem with the design of Figure 16-3 is easy to see: The predicates for LP and HP "overlap," in the sense that the very same tuple *t* can satisfy both of them. What's more, as we've seen, if *t* is such a tuple, and if at some given time tuple *t* represents a "true fact," then, in accordance with *The Closed World Assumption*, tuple *t* must necessarily appear in both relvars at the time in question (whence the redundancy, of course). In fact, we have another EQD on our hands:

```
CONSTRAINT ... ( LP WHERE WEIGHT = 17.0 ) =
                ( HP WHERE WEIGHT = 17.0 ) ;
```

To say it again, the problem in the example is that we've allowed two relvars to have overlapping predicates. Clearly, then, the principle we're looking for is going to say something along the lines of: Don't do that! Let's try and state the matter a little more precisely:

> **Definition (*The Principle of Orthogonal Design*, first attempt):** If
> relvars *R1* and *R2* are distinct, then there must not exist a tuple with
> the property that it appears in *R1* if and only if it appears in *R2*.[5]

The term *orthogonal* here derives from the fact that what the principle effectively says is that relvars should be independent of one another—which they won't be, if their meanings overlap in the foregoing sense. *Note:* In what follows, I'll often abbreviate *The Principle of Orthogonality* to just *the orthogonality principle*, or sometimes just to *orthogonality*.

As elsewhere in this book, I might be accused of practicing a tiny deception in the foregoing. Take another look at Figure 16-3; in particular, take a look at the tuple for part P2. That tuple appears in both LP and HP because it represents a true instantiation of the predicate for LP *and* a true instantiation of the predicate for HP. Or does it? The instantiations of those predicates for part P2 are actually as follows:

- LP: *Part P2 is named Bolt, has color Green and weight 17.0 pounds (which is less than or equal to 17.0 pounds), and is stored in city Paris.*

- HP: *Part P2 is named Bolt, has color Green and weight 17.0 pounds (which is greater than or equal to 17.0 pounds), and is stored in city Paris.*

---

[5]The "if" part of that "if and only if" is important. Consider a revised version of the suppliers-and-parts database, in which (a) attribute QTY is dropped from relvar SP and (b) another relvar, SAP, with heading {SNO,PNO} and predicate *Supplier SNO is able to supply part PNO* is added. Then there might well be a constraint to the effect that a given tuple can appear in SP only if it also appears in SAP, and such a reasonable state of affairs doesn't (and obviously shouldn't) constitute a violation of orthogonality.

These two propositions aren't the same! Of course, they're certainly *equivalent*—but in order to recognize that equivalence, we need to know that "$17.0 \leq 17.0$" and "$17.0 \geq 17.0$" are both true, and then we need to apply a little logical reasoning. (The point is, what's obvious to us as human beings isn't necessarily obvious to a machine, and for completeness I really ought to have spelled out the missing steps in my argument.).

Now, adherence to the orthogonality principle in the light vs. heavy parts example would certainly avoid the redundancies illustrated in Figure 16-3. Note, however, that the principle as stated applies only to relvars like LP and HP that have the very same heading, because of course it's impossible for the very same tuple to appear in two different relvars if the relvars in question have different headings. Thus, you might be thinking the orthogonality principle isn't much use, because it's probably unusual in practice to have two relvars in the same database with the same heading.[6] And if that were all there was to it, then I would probably agree with you; I mean, in that case life would be fairly simple and this chapter could stop right here (it might not even be worth dignifying such a very obvious rule with the rather grand label "principle"). But, of course, there's quite a lot more to be said on the matter. In order to explore the possibilities further, I first need to take a closer look at the relationship between tuples and propositions.

Tuples vs. Propositions

As you know, every tuple appearing in some given relvar *R* at some given time represents a certain proposition, the proposition in question being an instantiation of the relvar predicate for that relvar *R* that (by convention) is understood to be true at the time in question. For example, here again is the predicate for relvar HP (sample value as in Figures 16-2 and 16-3):

---

[6]In this chapter, unlike most others in this book, the fact that the heading concept includes the pertinent attribute types is sometimes going to be important; thus, the term *heading* must be (re)interpreted accordingly, where it makes any difference. By way of example, the headings {PNO CHAR, WEIGHT RATIONAL} and {PNO CHAR, WEIGHT INTEGER}, though they involve the same attribute names, aren't the same heading, precisely because the two WEIGHT attributes are of different types. All of that being said, for simplicity I'll continue to ignore attribute types as much as I can throughout the rest of the chapter.

Part PNO is named PNAME, has color COLOR and weight
WEIGHT (which is greater than or equal to 17.0 pounds), and is
stored in city CITY.

This relvar currently contains (among other things) a tuple for part P6, and that tuple represents the following instantiation of the foregoing predicate:

Part P6 is named Cog, has color Red and weight 19.0 pounds
(which is greater than or equal to 17.0 pounds), and is stored in city
London.

Loosely speaking, then, we can say the database "contains propositions" (or representations of propositions, at any rate). Now, I've said, or at least suggested, several times at earlier points in this book that the database involves some redundancy if and only if it says the same thing twice. Now I can make this statement a little more precise:

Definition (redundancy): The database involves redundancy if
and only if it contains two distinct representations of the same
proposition.

Now, given that tuples represent propositions, it's tempting to understand the foregoing definition as meaning that the database involves redundancy if and only if it contains two distinct appearances of the same tuple.[7] Unfortunately, however, this (mis)interpretation of the definition is considerably oversimplified at best. Let's examine it more carefully.

First of all, of course, it's at least true that we don't want the same tuple to appear more than once in the same relvar (at the same time, that is), because such a state of affairs would certainly constitute "saying the same thing twice." (As I once heard Codd remark: If something is true, saying it twice doesn't make it any more true.) Now, the relational model itself takes care of this particular requirement—by definition, relations never contain duplicate tuples, and the same is therefore true for relvars, and so we can ignore this possibility.

---

[7]One reviewer of this book argued rather strongly that this "temptation" wasn't tempting at all. Maybe not, but I still think it's worth discussing.

Two points here. First, given the truth of the foregoing, it could be argued that a desire to avoid redundancy was one of the motivations—albeit a minor one, perhaps (?)—for choosing sets (which can't contain duplicate elements, by definition) instead of "bags" (which can) as the right mathematical abstraction on which to found a solid database theory. SQL apologists please note!

Second, I note that now we have a precise characterization of the notion of "duplicate tuples." (People use this phrase all the time, and yet I very much doubt whether many of them would be able to define it precisely if pressed.) Strictly speaking, of course, two tuples are duplicates if and only if they're the very same tuple, just as two integers are duplicates if and only if they're the very same integer. Thus, the phrase "duplicate tuples" thus doesn't really make much sense from a logical point of view (to say two distinct tuples are duplicates is a contradiction in terms). What people are really talking about when they use that phrase is duplicate *appearances* of the *same* tuple. For that reason, the phrase "duplicate elimination," which as we all know is often encountered in database contexts, would much better be *duplication* elimination. But I digress ... Let's get back to the main discussion.

Next, then, I observe that we often don't want the same *sub*tuple to appear more than once in the same relvar (again, at the same time).[8] But classical normalization takes care of this one; e.g., it was precisely because, in earlier chapters, the FD {CITY} → {STATUS} held in relvar S—causing the same {CITY,STATUS} pair (or subtuple) to occur repeatedly, with the same meaning every time it did—that we were recommended to replace that relvar by its projections on {CITY,STATUS} and {SNO,SNAME,CITY}, respectively.

My next point is that the very same tuple can represent any number of distinct propositions, as can easily be seen. As a trivial example, let SC and PC be the projection of relvar S on {CITY} and the projection of relvar P on {CITY}, respectively. Given our usual sample values, then, a tuple containing just the CITY value London appears in

---

[8]This statement too is hugely, and in fact grotesquely, oversimplified. A slightly better one is: We don't want the same subtuple to appear more than once *if distinct appearances represent the same proposition*—but this statement isn't perfect, either. However, to try to make it more precise still would take us much further afield than I'm prepared to go at this point. See Chapter 17 for further explanation.

both SC and PC—but those two appearances represent distinct propositions. To be specific, the appearance in SC represents the proposition *There's at least one supplier in London*, and the appearance in PC represents the proposition *There's at least one part in London* (simplifying slightly in both cases for the sake of the example).

What's more—and here I have to get a little more formal on you for a moment—the same proposition can be represented by any number of distinct tuples, too. That's because, formally, the pertinent attribute names are part of the tuple (check the definition of *tuple* in Chapter 5 if you need confirmation of this point). For example, consider our usual shipments relvar SP, with attributes SNO, PNO, and QTY, and with predicate:

> *Supplier SNO supplies part PNO in quantity QTY.*

Now suppose we additionally had a relvar PS, with attributes SNR, PNR, and AMT, and with predicate:

> *Supplier SNR supplies part PNR in quantity AMT.*

Then (using **Tutorial D** syntax) the following tuples might well appear in relvars SP and PS, respectively:

```
TUPLE { SNO 'S1' , PNO 'P1' , QTY 300 }

TUPLE { SNR 'S1' , PNR 'P1' , AMT 300 }
```

These are clearly different tuples, but they both represent the same proposition, viz.:

> *Supplier S1 supplies part P1 in quantity 300.*

In fact, each of the two relvars SP and PS can be defined in terms of the other, as the following constraints (actually EQDs once again) both show:

```
CONSTRAINT ...
   PS = SP RENAME { SNO AS SNR , PNO AS PNR , QTY AS AMT } ;

CONSTRAINT ...
   SP = PS RENAME { SNR AS SNO , PNR AS PNO , AMT AS QTY } ;
```

A database that contained both relvars would thus clearly involve redundancy.[9]

The net of the foregoing discussion is this: There's a many to many relationship between tuples and propositions—any number of tuples can represent the same proposition, any number of propositions can be represented by the same tuple. Given this state of affairs, then, here's an attempt at stating the orthogonality principle a little more precisely:

> **Definition (*The Principle of Orthogonal Design*, second attempt):** Let relvars R and R2 be distinct, and let them have headings {A1,...,An} and {B1,...,Bn}, respectively. Let relvar R1 be defined as follows:
>
> `R1 = R RENAME { A1 AS B1' , ... , An AS Bn' }`
>
> where B1', ..., Bn' is some permutation of B1, ..., Bn. (Observe that R1 and R2 thus have the same heading.)[10] Then there must not exist restriction conditions c1 and c2, neither of which is identically false, such that following equality dependency holds:
>
> `( R1 WHERE c1 ) = ( R2 WHERE c2 )`

Points arising from this second attempt:

- Adherence to this version of the principle solves the problem with the design of Figure 16-3. To be specific, take R and R2 to be LP and HP, respectively, and define R1 as follows:

  `R1 = LP RENAME { PNO AS PNO , ... , CITY AS CITY }`

  (In other words, take R1 to be identically equal to R.) Now take both c1 and c2 to be the restriction condition WEIGHT = 17.0. Then the equality dependency $(R1 \text{ WHERE } c1) = (R2 \text{ WHERE } c2)$ obviously holds, and the design thus violates orthogonality.

---

[9]The example thus suggests an obvious rule of thumb: When you start the design process—which as far as I'm concerned means when you write down the predicates and other business rules—*always use the same name for the same property*; don't "play games" by using, e.g., both SNO and SNR to refer to supplier numbers, both QTY and AMT to refer to quantities, and so on. Following this rule will (among other things) make it much less likely that you'll wind up with two distinct tuples that represent the same proposition.

[10]Assuming, of course, that each attribute in R1 is of the same type as its counterpart in R2— but I remind you that I'm trying to ignore attribute types as much as I can in this chapter, for simplicity. I won't keep on repeating remarks of this same general nature from this point forward but will simply let this one footnote do duty for all.

Note: As this example demonstrates, so long as *c1* and *c2* aren't identically false, then certain tuples must exist that, if and when they represent "true facts," will necessarily have to appear in both *R1* and *R2*—and, in essence, that's the situation we want to outlaw. (By contrast, if either of *c1* and *c2* were identically false, the corresponding restriction—*R1* WHERE *c1* or *R2* WHERE *c2*, as applicable—would be empty, and so there wouldn't and couldn't be any orthogonality violation.)

- This second version of the principle subsumes the first, because we can make *R1* identical to *R*—in effect, by making the renaming a "no op," as in the previous bullet item. (As I pointed out earlier, the previous version of the principle did assume the relvars in question had the same heading. As the discussions of the present section have shown, however, we can't limit our attention to that simple case alone.) That second version also solves the SP vs. PS problem, of course—in effect, by taking each of *c1* and *c2* to be simply TRUE.

- Recall from Chapter 6 that, in logic, something that's identically false (e.g., the boolean expression WEIGHT $\geq$ 17.0 AND WEIGHT $<$ 17.0) is called a *contradiction*. Thus, the requirement that *c1* and *c2* not be identically false can be stated thus: Neither *c1* nor *c2* is a contradiction in the logical sense.

The First Example Revisited

Now let's return to our motivating example, in which relvar S was decomposed vertically into its projections SNC and STC on {SNO,SNAME,CITY} and {SNO,STATUS,CITY}, respectively.[11] (The example of light vs. heavy parts involved horizontal decomposition, of course.) Observe now that although SNC and STC are certainly of the same degree, there's no way any given tuple can appear in both: Tuples in SNC have an SNAME attribute, while tuples in STC have a STATUS attribute instead. What's more, there's no way we can simply rename (say) the SNAME attribute in SNC to STATUS and thereby produce a relvar with the same

---

[11]And in which, I remind you, the FD {CITY} $\rightarrow$ {STATUS} no longer held in relvar S.

heading as STC, because SNAME in SNC is of type CHAR and STATUS in STC is of type INTEGER. (Renaming attributes changes *names*, not types.) It follows that our second attempt at defining the orthogonality principle is still inadequate; in the case at hand, in fact, it simply doesn't apply.

Recall now what the problem was with the foregoing design: The tuple (s,c) appears in the projection of SNC on {SNO,CITY} if and only if that very same tuple (s,c) appears in the projection of STC on {SNO,CITY}. That is, the following EQD holds:

```
CONSTRAINT ... SNC { SNO , CITY } = STC { SNO , CITY } ;
```

Let's agree to ignore the question of attribute renaming for the moment, since it isn't relevant to this example. Then the crucial point about the foregoing EQD is that it holds, not between distinct database relvars as such, but rather between distinct *projections* of the *same* database relvar: to be specific, projections arising from vertical decomposition of the database relvar S. But such doesn't have to be the case, of course—I mean, SNC and STC might have been defined independently, as two completely distinct relvars, without there ever having existed (in the designer's mind, so to speak) a relvar S that's equal to their join. They might even be, not distinct relvars in their own right, but projections of two such distinct relvars. All of which leads to a third attempt at defining the orthogonality principle:

> **Definition (*The Principle of Orthogonal Design, third attempt*):**
> Let relvars *R1* and *R2* be distinct. Then:
>
> a.   There must not exist a JD ☼{*X1*,...,*Xn*} that's irreducible with respect to *R1*[12] such that
>
> b.   There exists some *Xi* $(1 \le i \le n)$ and some possibly empty set of attribute renamings on the projection, *R1X* say, of *R1* on *Xi* that maps *R1X* into *R1Y*, say, such that
>
> c.   *R1Y* has the same heading as some subset *Y* of the heading of *R2*, such that
>
> d.   The following equality dependency holds:
>
>   *R1Y* = *R2Y*
>
>   (where *R2Y* is the projection of *R2* on *Y*).

---

[12]Note that any JD that's irreducible with respect to relvar *R1* certainly holds in that relvar *R1*, by the definition of JD irreducibility (see Chapter 11).

Now, this all looks quite complex, but basically all it says is that no projection in any nonloss decomposition of *R1* can be information equivalent to any projection of *R2*. Indeed, as you can probably see, much of the complexity in the definition (what complexity there is) arises from the need to deal with the renaming issue. The following slightly simpler version of the definition, which ignores that complication, might help to make the point clearer:

> **Definition (*The Principle of Orthogonal Design*, third attempt but ignoring renaming):** Let relvars *R1* and *R2* be distinct. Then:
>
> a.   There must not exist a JD ☼{*X1*,...,*Xn*} that's irreducible with respect to *R1* such that
>
> b.   There exists some *Xi* ($1 \leq i \leq n$) that's identical to some subset *Y* of the heading of *R2*, such that
>
> c.   The following equality dependency holds:
>
> R1Y = R2Y
>
> (where *R1Y* and *R2Y* are the projections on *Y* of *R1* and *R2*, respectively).

Observe now that adherence to this third version of the principle resolves the problem with our motivating example, in which relvar S was decomposed into its projections SNC and STC on {SNO,SNAME,CITY}) and STC {SNO,STATUS,CITY}, respectively. Because suppose that decomposition is done. Then:

a.   The database now contains two distinct relvars, SNC and STC.

b.   Thanks to Heath's Theorem together with the fact that the FD {SNO} → {SNAME} holds in relvar SNC, the JD ☼{{SNO,SNAME},{SNO,CITY}} holds in—in fact, is irreducible with respect to—that relvar SNC.

c.   Thus, the projection of relvar SNC on {SNO,CITY} is part of a valid nonloss decomposition of SNC. But an equality dependency holds between that projection and the projection of STC on those same attributes. Thus, the design violates the orthogonality principle as just articulated (the "third attempt").

I now observe that this third version of the orthogonality principle lets me take care of a piece of unfinished business from Chapter 11. As you might recall, I pointed out in that chapter that the following JD held in relvar S, and in fact was irreducible with respect to that relvar:

☼ { { SNO , SNAME , CITY } , { CITY , STATUS , SNAME } }

But I also said that decomposing relvar S on the basis of this JD wouldn't be a good idea (and Exercise 11.4 asked why not). Well, we can see now that if that decomposition is done:

a.   The database now contains two distinct relvars—I'll call them SNC and CTN—with headings {SNO,SNAME,CITY} and {CITY,STATUS,SNAME}, respectively.

b.   Thanks to Heath's Theorem together with the fact that the FD {CITY} → {STATUS} holds in CTN—at least, recall that it did as far as Chapter 11 was concerned—the JD ☼{{CITY,STATUS},{CITY,SNAME}} holds in, and in fact is irreducible with respect to, that relvar CTN.

c.   Thus, the projection of relvar CTN on {CITY,SNAME} is part of a valid nonloss decomposition of CTN. But an equality dependency holds between that projection and the projection of SNC on those same attributes. In other words, the design violates the orthogonality principle once again.

The net of the example is this: Doing a nonloss decomposition on the basis of a "bad" JD is contraindicated by virtue of *The Principle of Orthogonal Design*. (The JD in the example is "bad" because attribute SNAME could be dropped from the {CITY,STATUS,SNAME} component without significant loss.) What's more, one consequence of abiding by the orthogonality principle is that the third of the normalization principles as given at the beginning of the chapter—viz., that every projection should be needed in the reconstruction process—will automatically be satisfied (and so there's a logical connection, of a kind, between orthogonality and normalization after all).

The Second Example Revisited

Unfortunately, the third version of the orthogonality principle as given in the previous section is still missing something, and revisiting the light vs. heavy parts example shows what it is: It's missing that business about restrictions. (In that example, the equality dependency wasn't between database relvars as such, nor between projections of such relvars, but rather between certain restrictions of such relvars.) In other words, the third version of the principle failed to subsume the second version. By contrast, the following formulation takes care of both the restriction issue and the projection issue:

> **Definition (*The Principle of Orthogonal Design*, fourth attempt):** Let relvars *R1* and *R2* be distinct. Then:
>
> a.   There must not exist a JD $\Leftrightarrow\{X1,...,Xn\}$ that's irreducible with respect to *R1* such that
>
> b.   There exists some Xi $(1 \leq i \leq n)$ and some possibly empty set of attribute renamings on the projection, *R1X* say, of *R1* on *Xi* that maps *R1X* into *R1Y*, say, such that
>
> c.   *R1Y* has the same heading as some subset *Y* of the heading of *R2*, such that
>
> d.   There exist restriction conditions *c1* and *c2*, neither of which is identically false, such that
>
> e.   The following equality dependency holds:
>
>   (`R1Y` WHERE `c1`) = (`R2Y` WHERE `c2`)
>
>   (where *R2Y* is the projection of *R2* on *Y*).

The Final Version (?)

Believe it or not, there's still a problem ... Consider a version of the suppliers relvar—I'll call it SCC—with attributes SNO, CITYA, and CITYB. Let SCC be subject to the constraint that for any given supplier, the CITYA and CITYB values are identical. *Result:* Redundancy! Of course, this is a crazy design, but it's a possible one, and it would be nice to extend the orthogonality principle to take care of (i.e., prohibit) such designs also. And the following final (?) formulation should do the trick (I'll leave it as an exercise for you to figure out exactly how):

> **Definition (*The Principle of Orthogonal Design,* "final" version):** Let $R1$ and $R2$ be relvars (not necessarily distinct). Then:
>
> a.   There must not exist a JD $\Join\{X1,...,Xn\}$ that's irreducible with respect to $R1$ such that
>
> b.   There exists some Xi $(1 \leq i \leq n)$ and some possibly empty set of attribute renamings on the projection, $R1X$ say, of $R1$ on Xi that maps $R1X$ into $R1Y$, say, such that
>
> c. $R1Y$ has the same heading as some subset Y (distinct from Xi, if $R1$ and $R2$ are one and the same) of the heading of $R2$, such that
>
> d.   There exist restriction conditions $c1$ and $c2$, neither of which is identically false, such that
>
> e.   The following equality dependency holds:
>
>   (R1Y WHERE c1) = (R2Y WHERE c2)
>
>   (where $R2Y$ is the projection of $R2$ on Y).

This version of the principle subsumes all previous versions.

A Clarification

I'm sorry to have to report that there's quite a lot of confusion in the literature over orthogonality, even though the basic idea is so simple. I'm even sorrier to have to say the confusion is probably my fault—some of my previous writings on this topic have been (not to put too fine a point upon the matter) flat out wrong. So let me take this opportunity to try and set the record straight. The basic point is this:

> *Orthogonality says that relvars shouldn't have overlapping meanings; it doesn't say that relvars shouldn't have the same heading (or, more generally, headings that "overlap").*

Here's a simple example, due to Hugh Darwen, that illustrates the difference. Consider the predicates *Employee ENO is on vacation* and *Employee ENO is awaiting phone number allocation*. The obvious design for this situation involves two relvars of degree one that look like this (in outline):

```
ON_VACATION { ENO }
           KEY { ENO }

NEEDS_PHONE { ENO }
           KEY { ENO }
```

Clearly, the very same tuple can appear in both of these relvars at the same time. But even if it does, those two appearances represent two different propositions, and there's no redundancy involved, and no violation of orthogonality.[13]

Observe now that there's a difference in kind between the example just discussed and the light vs. heavy parts examples (relvars LP and HP) illustrated in Figures 16-2 and 16-3, earlier in this chapter. In the latter case, as we saw earlier, we can write a formal constraint, to the effect that the pertinent WEIGHT value has to lie in a certain range, that a given tuple has to satisfy in order for it to be accepted for insertion into LP or HP or both. However, there's no formal constraint we can write that a given tuple has to satisfy in order for it to be accepted for insertion into ON_VACATION or NEEDS_PHONE or both. In other words, if the user asserts that a certain tuple is to be inserted into, say, ON_VACATION, then the system simply has to trust the user; there's no check it can perform to ascertain that the tuple does indeed belong in ON_VACATION instead of (or as well as) NEEDS_PHONE.

Here's another example, also due to Hugh Darwen, that might also mistakenly be thought to violate orthogonality but in fact doesn't. We're given three relvars that look like this (in outline):[14]

```
EARNS      { ENO , SALARY }
           KEY { ENO }

SALARY_UNK { ENO }
           KEY { ENO }
```

---

[13]But what if relvars ON_VACATION and NEEDS_PHONE each had an additional attribute, say SALARY? See Exercise 16.5 at the end of the chapter.

[14]I note in passing that the example illustrates a recommended approach (discussed in detail in *SQL and Relational Theory*) to dealing with "missing information" in relational designs.

```
UNSALARIED { ENO }
           KEY { ENO }
```

Sample values are shown in Figure 16-4.

EARNS

ENO	SALARY
E1	85,000
E3	70,000

SALARY_UNK

ENO
E2

UNSALARIED

ENO
E4

Figure 16-4. *Relvars EARNS, SALARY_UNK, and UNSALARIED—sample values*

The predicates for these three relvars are as follows:

- EARNS: *Employee ENO has salary SALARY.*
- SALARY_UNK: *Employee ENO has a salary, but we don't know what it is.*
- UNSALARIED: *Employee ENO doesn't have a salary.*

Now, relvars SALARY_UNK and UNSALARIED do have the same heading—but even if the same tuple could simultaneously appear in both, there wouldn't be any redundancy, because the appearances in question would represent two different propositions. In fact, of course, the semantics of the situation are such that no tuple should simultaneously appear in both, anyway (in other words, the relvars are disjoint). The following constraint will take care of this requirement:

```
CONSTRAINT ... IS_EMPTY ( JOIN { SALARY_UNK , UNSALARIED } ) ;
```

(As explained in the answer to Exercise 6.4 in Chapter 6, the **Tutorial D** expression IS_EMPTY (*rx*) returns TRUE if the relation *r* denoted by the relational expression *rx* is empty and FALSE otherwise.)

Note: In fact, of course, no employee should be represented in more than one of the relvars EARNS, SALARY_UNK, and UNSALARIED, so the foregoing constraint ought to be extended or revised appropriately. I'll leave the details as an exercise (part of Exercise 16.3).

Concluding Remarks

In closing, I want to make a few further (and somewhat miscellaneous) observations on the concept of orthogonality in general. First of all, the overall objective of orthogonal design, like that of normalization, is to reduce redundancy and thereby to avoid certain update anomalies that might otherwise occur. In fact, orthogonality complements normalization, in the sense that—to speak rather loosely—normalization reduces redundancy within relvars, while orthogonality reduces it across relvars.

What's more, orthogonality complements normalization in another way also. Consider once again the (bad) decomposition of relvar S into its projections SNC and STC, as illustrated in Figure 16-1. As we saw earlier, that decomposition abided by all of the usual normalization principles; in other words, it was orthogonality, not normalization, that told us the design was bad.

My next point is that, like the principles of normalization, *The Principle of Orthogonal Design* is basically just common sense—but (again like normalization) it's formalized common sense, and the remarks I made in Chapter 1 in connection with such formalization apply here also. As I said in that chapter:

> What design theory does is [formalize] certain commonsense principles, thereby opening the door to the possibility of mechanizing those principles (that is, incorporating them into computerized design tools). Critics of the theory often miss this point; they claim, quite rightly, that the ideas are mostly just common sense, but they don't seem to realize it's a significant achievement to state what common sense means in a precise and formal way.

My final point is this: Suppose we start with the usual parts relvar P, but decide for design purposes to decompose that relvar into a set of restrictions, as in the light vs. heavy parts example. Then the orthogonality principle tells us that the restrictions in question should be pairwise disjoint (also, of course, that their union—which will in fact be a disjoint union—should take us back to the original relvar).

Note: In previous writings, I've referred to a decomposition that meets the foregoing requirement as an orthogonal decomposition. However, I now think it would be better to generalize this term and use it to mean any decomposition that abides by the orthogonality principle. This revised definition includes the earlier one as a special case.

Exercises

16.1   Try stating the final version of *The Principle of Orthogonal Design* without looking back at the body of the chapter.

16.2   Consider the design of any database you happen to be familiar with. Does it involve any violations of *The Principle of Orthogonal Design*? Are there any constraints—especially "overlapping" ones—that ought to be stated declaratively but haven't been?

16.3   Consider the second example in the section "A Clarification" (the one involving relvars EARNS, SALARY_UNK, and UNSALARIED). Do you think the design illustrated in that example is redundancy free? Also try stating a formal constraint to guarantee that no employee is represented in more than one of those three relvars.

16.4   Suppose we replace the suppliers relvar S by a set of relvars LS, PS, AS, ... (one for each distinct supplier city—the LS relvar, for example, contains tuples for suppliers in London only). These relvars all have the same attributes, viz., SNO, SNAME, and STATUS (there's no need to keep the CITY attribute, because if we did its value would be constant throughout each relvar). Does this design violate orthogonality? Can you think of any other problems with it?

By the way, if we did keep the CITY attribute in relvars LS, PS, AS, etc., the design would actually violate the principles of normalization! Why so, exactly?

16.5   Suppose attribute CITY in both the suppliers relvar S and the parts relvar P is replaced by a pair of attributes CITY and STATE (sample values: Burlington, Vermont vs. Burlington, Massachusetts). Does this revised design display any redundancy? Does it violate the principles of normalization? Does it violate orthogonality?

Answers

16.1   See the body of the chapter.

16.2   *No answer provided.*

16.3   No, it isn't redundancy free (see the further remarks on examples of this kind in Chapter 17). As for the constraint, the following will suffice:

```
CONSTRAINT ... IS_EMPTY ( JOIN { SALARY_UNK , UNSALARIED } )
           AND IS_EMPTY ( JOIN { EARNS , SALARY_UNK } )
           AND IS_EMPTY ( JOIN { EARNS , UNSALARIED } ) ;
```

Note: In my book *View Updating and Relational Theory: Solving the View Update Problem* (O'Reilly, 2013), I propose support for expressions of the form DISJOINT {*r1*,...,*rn*}, which return TRUE if and only if no two of the argument relations *r1*, ..., *rn* have any tuples in common. Using this DISJOINT operator, the foregoing constraint could be simplified to just:

```
CONSTRAINT ...
DISJOINT { EARNS { ENO } , SALARY_UNK , UNSALARIED } ;
```

16.4   The design doesn't violate orthogonality, but there are several other things wrong with it. For example, how would you express the query "Get the city for supplier S1"? (There are two cases to consider: one where you do at least know what supplier cities exist, and one where you don't. In the latter case, you might want to think about this query too: "Is supplier S1 represented in the database?") Also, what's happened to the FD {CITY} → {STATUS} (assuming such an FD is supposed to hold)? And what about the {SNO} foreign key in relvar SP? (Again there are two cases to consider—the same two as before, in fact.)

If we do keep the CITY attribute in relvars LS, PS, etc., then:

a. If the FD {CITY → {STATUS} held in the original suppliers relvar S, then it certainly still holds in relvars LS, PS, etc., and so those relvars aren't in BCNF.

b. What's more, the FD { } → {CITY} also holds in each of those relvars. Since this FD isn't "an arrow out of a key," that's another reason why the relvars wouldn't be in BCNF. (See the answer to Exercise 4.6 in Chapter 4, where an essentially similar example is discussed.)

Finally, if the FD {CITY → {STATUS} held in the original suppliers relvar S, then—regardless of whether we keep the CITY attribute in relvars LS, PS, etc., or not—the FD { } → {STATUS} also holds in each of those relvars, and so yet again the relvars wouldn't be in BCNF. Note, therefore, that the FD {CITY} → {STATUS}, if it holds at all (which it can do only if the CITY attribute is retained, of course), is in fact reducible, under the suggested horizontal decomposition.

16.5   If there exist two distinct tuples, both in S or both in P or one in each, that contain the same CITY / STATE pair (say Burlington, Vermont), then clearly there's some kind of redundancy involved. But there's no violation of the principles of normalization—both relvars are still in 5NF. And there's no violation of orthogonality either!—more evidence, if evidence is still required, that we need more science in this area.

Note, incidentally, that {CITY,STATE} in relvars S and P might very well be foreign keys, referencing a {CITY,STATE} key in some other relvar. I'll leave the implications of this possibility as something for you to think about.

Now recall the example of relvars ON_VACATION and NEEDS_PHONE from the body of the chapter. Suppose we extend both of those relvars to include an employee salary attribute (SALARY). Then (like the {CITY,STATE} example) this revised design certainly suffers from redundancy, and yet it doesn't

violate either normalization principles or orthogonality. This
time, however, we can at least write a formal constraint that makes
the redundancy explicit. Let me abbreviate ON_VACATION and
NEEDS_PHONE to OV and NP, respectively. Then we have:

```
CONSTRAINT ... WITH ( X := JOIN { OV { ENO } , NP { ENO } } ) :
                 JOIN { X , OV } = JOIN { X , NP } ;
```

This constraint requires that if ENO *e* appears in both relvars, then
e's salary must be the same in both.

PART VI

Redundancy

Throughout this book, we've been concerned with getting redundancy out of the design. But what *is* redundancy?

CHAPTER 17

We Need More Science

What I tell you three times is true.

—Lewis Carroll:
The Hunting of the Snark (1876)

What does it mean to say something's redundant? It turns out, rather surprisingly—or perhaps it's not so surprising, given all of the difficulties we've experienced in connection with the concept in prior chapters—to be quite difficult to come up with a precise answer to this question. The best *Chambers Twentieth Century Dictionary* (usually so good and pithy in its definitions) is able to come up with is the following:

> **redundant** copious: over-copious: superfluous

However, *Chambers Twentieth Century Thesaurus* (a companion to the dictionary) does give the following splendid list of synonyms or near synonyms:

> **redundant** *de trop*, diffuse, excessive, extra, inessential,
> inordinate, padded, periphrastic, pleonastical, prolix, repetitious,
> supererogatory, superfluous, supernumerary, surplus,
> tautological, unemployed, unnecessary, unneeded, unwanted,
> verbose, wordy

It also gives the following nice list of antonyms:

> concise, essential, necessary

Be all that as it may, we've seen that design theory in general can be regarded among other things as a set of principles and techniques for reducing redundancy (and thereby reducing the potential for certain inconsistencies and update anomalies that might otherwise occur). To repeat, however, what exactly is redundancy? We don't seem to

© C. J. Date 2019
C. J. Date, *Database Design and Relational Theory*, https://doi.org/10.1007/978-1-4842-5540-7_17

have a very precise definition of the term—we just have a somewhat vague idea that it can lead to problems, at least if it isn't managed properly. This chapter takes a closer look at such matters.

In order to get a slightly better handle on the question of what constitutes redundancy, we first need to distinguish clearly between the logical and physical levels of the system. Obviously the design goals are different at the two levels. At the physical level, redundancy will almost certainly exist in some shape or form. Here are a couple of reasons why:

- Indexes and other such "fast access path" structures necessarily entail some redundancy, because certain data values are stored both in those auxiliary structures and in the structures to which they provide that "fast access."

- Derived relvars and/or derived relations that are physically stored in some way—what are known variously as *snapshots* or *summary tables* or *materialized queries* or *materialized views*[1]—also obviously involve some redundancy.

The reason for redundancy at the physical level is performance, of course. But physical redundancy has, or should have, no effect on the logical level—it's managed by the DBMS, and it isn't, or shouldn't be, seen by the user. I mention it here only to get it out of the way, as it were. From this point forward, I'll be concerned only with redundancy at the logical level.

At the logical level, then, it's tempting just to say that redundancy is always bad. But of course this statement is much too simplistic, owing to the availability of the view mechanism if nothing else. Let me digress for a moment to elaborate on this latter point. It's well known, but worth stating explicitly nevertheless, that views (like normalization, in fact, though for very different reasons) serve two rather different purposes:

1. The user who actually defines view *V* is, obviously, aware of the expression *X* in terms of which *V* is defined. That user can use the name *V* wherever the expression *X* is intended, but such uses are basically just shorthand (much like the use of macros in a programming language).

---

[1]This last term is strongly deprecated, by the way, because the construct in question isn't a view. Views are virtual, not materialized (at least as far as the relational model is concerned), and *materialized view* is simply a contradiction in terms. *Snapshot* is a better term.

2.   By contrast, a user who's merely informed that view *V* exists and
     is available for use is supposed not to be aware of that defining
     expression *X*; to that user, in fact, *V* is supposed to look and feel
     just like a base relvar.[2]

As an example of Case 1, suppose the user perceives the database as containing two
relvars *R1* and *R2* and goes on to define their join as a view; clearly, then, that view is
redundant so far as that user is concerned, and it could be dropped without any loss of
information. For definiteness, therefore, I'm going to assume from this point forward
(barring explicit statements to the contrary) that no relvar in the database is defined
in terms of any others, so that at least this particular kind of redundancy isn't present.
With this possibility ruled out, then, it's tempting to set a stake in the ground and say
again that redundancy at the logical level is always undesirable. In order to adopt such
a position, however, we need to be able to say what we mean by the term, for otherwise
the position can't possibly make sense. And even if we manage to come up with a good
definition, is the position (i.e., that redundancy at the logical level is always bad) really
tenable? Is it possible to eliminate all redundancy? Is it even desirable?

These are questions of considerable pragmatic importance, of course. Indeed, I
think it's noteworthy that Codd called his very first (1969) paper on the relational model
"Derivability, *Redundancy*, and Consistency of Relations Stored in Large Data Banks"
(my italics). And his second (1970) paper, "A Relational Model of Data for Large Shared
Data Banks"—this is the one that's usually regarded as the seminal paper in the field,
though that characterization is a little unfair to its 1969 predecessor—was in two parts
of almost equal length, the second of which was called "Redundancy and Consistency"
(the first was called "Relational Model and Normal Form"). Codd thus clearly regarded
his thoughts on redundancy as a major part of the contribution of his relational work:
rightly so, in my opinion, since he did at least provide us with a framework in which we
could begin to address the issue precisely and systematically.

Now, I showed in the previous chapter that one putative definition of redundancy
that doesn't work is this: The database involves redundancy if and only if it contains two
distinct appearances of the same tuple. But we can validly say the following:[3]

---

[2]Emphasis on *supposed*—I'm describing an ideal situation here. Today's reality is rather messier,
as I'm sure you know.

[3]The definition that follows is a deliberately, albeit only slightly, expanded version of one from
Chapter 16.

Definition (redundancy in the database, generic version): The database involves redundancy if and only if it contains, directly or indirectly, two distinct representations of the same proposition.

The trouble is, although this definition is clearly correct, it doesn't help much with the practical problem of reducing redundancy. But it does at least imply the following, which is a little better:

Definition (redundancy in the database, preliminary detailed version): Let *D* be a database design and let *p* be a proposition. Then:

a.   If there exists a database value (i.e., a set of values for the relvars mentioned in *D*), *DB*, that conforms to *D*, such that

b.   There exists within *DB* some specific appearance of some tuple or combination of tuples that represents *p*, either explicitly or implicitly, and

c.   There exists within *DB* some distinct appearance of some tuple or combination of tuples that also represents *p*, either explicitly or implicitly, then

d.   *DB* contains, and *D* permits, redundancy.

The principles of normalization and *The Principle of Orthogonal Design* are aimed precisely at reducing redundancy in the foregoing sense. Observe, however, that all the definition says is *if*—not *if and only if*—certain tuples appear, *then* there's redundancy. In other words, it's not a complete definition. Indeed, we'll see examples of designs later in this chapter that clearly involve redundancy, even though they don't contain distinct tuples or tuple combinations that represent the same proposition. What's more, the examples in question are fully normalized and fully orthogonal, for the most part. Thus, the principles of normalization and orthogonality, though necessary and undoubtedly important, are a long way from being sufficient.

A Little History

Before I get into a discussion of just how and why normalization and orthogonality are insufficient, I'd like to say a little more about Codd's attempts in his very first two papers to address the issue of redundancy. In his 1969 paper, he said this:

> A set of relations is *strongly redundant* if it contains at least one relation [that] is derivable from the rest of the [relations in the set].

And he tightened up this definition slightly in his 1970 paper:

> A set of relations is *strongly redundant* if it contains at least one relation that possesses a projection [that] is derivable from other projections of relations in the set.

I should explain that when Codd says a relation *r* is *derivable* from a set *S* of relations, he means *r* is equal to the result of applying some sequence of relational operations (join, projection, and so forth) to relations from *S*. I do have a few comments on his definitions, however:

- First, the term *relation* should be replaced by the term *relvar* throughout. (Of course, this latter term wasn't introduced until several years later, and Codd never used it at all.) In fact, I think it's fair to say that what Codd meant by the term *relation* in these quotes wasn't just a relvar as such but, more specifically, a *base* relvar.

- Second, we can ignore the qualifier *strongly*. Codd was distinguishing between "strong" redundancy and what he called *weak* redundancy, but weak redundancy is irrelevant as far as we're concerned. The reason is that weak redundancy has to do merely with equality dependencies that don't hold at all times but do happen to be satisfied at particular times, given the relation values that happen to exist at the times in question.

Actually, it seems to me that what was going on here was precisely that Codd was struggling with the logical difference between relations and relvars!—see the previous bullet item. "Strong" redundancy applies to relvars (it's what we usually mean by *redundancy* when we talk about database design). "Weak" redundancy, by contrast, applies to relations, not relvars (it's just an artifact of the values the relvars happen to have at some particular time, and it's not particularly interesting).

- The 1969 definition is subsumed by the 1970 definition, of course, because (as we know from Chapter 6) every relvar *R* is identically equal to a certain projection of *R*—namely, the corresponding identity projection.

- More to the point, the 1970 definition is still deficient as a definition of redundancy in general for at least the following two reasons:

  a. It includes certain possibilities that we normally wouldn't regard as redundancies at all. For example, suppose the suppliers-and-parts database is subject to the constraint that every part must be supplied by at least one supplier. Then the projection of relvar SP on {PNO} will necessarily be equal to the projection of relvar P on {PNO}, and we'll have a "strong redundancy" on our hands.

     Note: Perhaps a more realistic example to illustrate the same point would be a constraint on a personnel database to the effect that every employee must be in a department and every department must have at least one employee.

  b. At the same time, it excludes many possibilities that we certainly would regard as redundancies—see, e.g., the example of light vs. heavy parts in Chapter 16 (second version, as illustrated in Figure 16-3). Several further examples are given in later sections of the present chapter.

- Even more to the point, the first reference (at least) to *projections* in the 1970 definition should be replaced by references to *projections that correspond to components of irreducible JDs*. (The first of the two objections in the previous bullet item, objection a., would then go away.)

One last comment on Codd's definitions: Codd did at least say (in both papers) that "we shall associate with [the database] a collection of statements [that] define all of the redundancies" in that database. The "statements" Codd is referring to here are **Tutorial D** CONSTRAINT statements (or something logically equivalent to such statements), of course. In other words, Codd certainly wanted the system to be aware of the redundancies, and he wanted those redundancies to be managed accordingly. Unfortunately, however, he then went on to say:

> The generation of an inconsistency ... could be logged internally, so that if it were not remedied within some reasonable time ... the system could notify the security officer [*sic*]. Alternatively, the system could [inform the user] that such and such relations now need to be changed to restore consistency ... Ideally, [different remedial actions] should be possible ... for different subcollections of relations.

Note: "Inconsistencies" (or, as I would prefer to call them, integrity violations) can certainly be caused by redundancy—more precisely, by redundancy that's inadequately managed—but not all integrity violations are caused by redundancy, of course. More to the point, I believe the database should *never* be allowed to contain any inconsistencies, at least as far as the user is concerned; as I said in Chapter 16, you can never trust the results you get from an inconsistent database. In other words, "remedying inconsistencies" needs to be done immediately, at the level of individual statements (not even at the transaction level).[4] See the section "Managing Redundancy" later in this chapter.

---

[4]See Appendix B, also *SQL and Relational Theory*, for a defense of this possibly rather unorthodox position. Let me add, with little by the way of elaboration, that the position does imply a requirement for the system to support *multiple assignment*, which is a form of assignment that allows several variables—in particular, several relvars—to be updated "simultaneously" (in other words, within the confines of a single statement).

Predicates vs. Constraints

Although I've had a lot to say about both predicates and constraints in previous chapters, I haven't explicitly called out the logical difference between these concepts; so let me remedy that deficiency now. First, then, the predicate—sometimes referred to more explicitly as the relvar predicate, for definiteness—for a given relvar R is the *intended interpretation*, or *meaning*, for R. Of course, every user of a given relvar R is supposed (or assumed!) to understand the corresponding predicate. Note, however, that—at least in today's implementations—predicates are stated in natural language and are therefore somewhat informal in nature, necessarily.

So predicates are informal. By contrast, constraints are *formal*. In essence, a constraint is a boolean expression, expressed in some formal language like SQL or **Tutorial D** and normally containing references to relvars in the database, that's required to evaluate to TRUE at all times. Let R be a relvar. Then it's convenient to think of the logical AND of all of the constraints that mention R as *the* constraint for R. Note, therefore, that whereas the predicate for R is understood only by the user, the constraint for R is "understood" by both the user *and the system*. In fact, the constraint for R might be regarded as the system's approximation to the predicate for R. Ideally, of course, we would like R to be such that it always satisfies its predicate; the best we can hope for, however, is that it always satisfies its constraint.[5]

Given now that a database is supposed to be a faithful representation of the semantics of what might be called "the microworld of interest," it follows that predicates and constraints are highly relevant to the business of database design. We could say that predicates are the informal, and constraints the formal, representation of those semantics. Overall, therefore, the database design process as I see it goes like this:[6]

1. First we pin down the relvar predicates (and other business rules) as carefully as possible.

2. Then we map those predicates and rules into relvars and constraints.

---

[5]As an aside, I remark that *The Closed World Assumption* applies to predicates, not constraints. That is, (a) if tuple t appears in relvar R at time T, then t certainly satisfies both the predicate and the constraint for R at time T; (b) if tuple t could plausibly appear in relvar R but doesn't, then t certainly doesn't satisfy the predicate for R at time T, but it still has to satisfy the constraint for R (because if it doesn't, then it couldn't "plausibly appear" in the first place).

[6]See Appendix A for an elaboration of this brief overview.

As a consequence of the foregoing, we can see that another way to think about design theory—normalization and so forth—is as follows: *It's a set of principles and techniques for helping with the business of pinning down predicates* (and hence constraints). This perspective underpins much of what follows in this chapter.

As an aside, I note that the foregoing goes a long way toward explaining why I'm not much of a fan of E/R ("entity / relationship") modeling and similar pictorial methodologies. (You might have noticed the total absence of E/R diagrams and the like in previous chapters!) The problem with E/R modeling and suchlike schemes is that they're less powerful—much less powerful—than formal logic. In particular, they don't include anything like adequate support for the quantifiers (EXISTS and FORALL)[7]— which is a serious omission, because the formulation of constraints *always* at least tacitly requires such support, or something equivalent to such support.[8] As a consequence, those schemes and those diagrams are completely incapable of representing all but a few (admittedly important, but limited) constraints. Thus, while it might be acceptable to use such diagrams to explicate the overall design at a high level of abstraction, it's misleading, and in some respects quite dangerous, to think of such diagrams as actually *being* the design in its entirety. *Au contraire:* The design is the relvars, which the diagrams do show, plus the constraints, which they don't.[9]

Example 1

It's my claim that design theory as a field of investigation is, in general, still wide open. To bolster this claim, in this section and the next few I want to give some examples of designs that (a) are fully normalized and fully orthogonal (at least in most cases) and yet (b) still suffer from various redundancies (again, in most cases).

---

[7]Since the quantifiers were invented by Frege in 1879, this omission makes E/R diagrams and the like (as a friend of mine once put it to me) "a pre 1879 kind of logic." *Note:* A tutorial on quantifiers and related matters in the database context can be found in *SQL and Relational Theory* and many other places.

[8]**Tutorial D** has no explicit quantifier support either, but anything expressible in terms of the quantifiers can nevertheless be expressed in **Tutorial D**; that is, **Tutorial D** does at least have something equivalent to quantifier support.

[9]Two qualifications here: First, the diagrams do show *some* constraints (basically key and foreign key constraints), as already noted. Second, they might not in fact show all of the relvars—some E/R modeling schemes don't include in their diagrams relvars (like SP in our running example) that correspond to many to many relationships.

For my first example, consider the following simple relvar, which represents a set of names and addresses (the predicate is *Person NAME resides at address ADDR*):

```
NADDR { NAME , ADDR }
      KEY { NAME }
```

Suppose attribute ADDR in this relvar is *tuple valued*, where the tuples in question have attributes STREET, CITY, STATE, and ZIP. (Yes, tuple valued attributes or TVAs are legal, just as relation valued attributes or RVAs are legal—see Chapter 4—and for much the same reasons.) A sample value for this relvar is shown in Figure 17-1.

NADDR

NAME	ADDR /* tuple valued */			
Jack	STREET	CITY	STATE	ZIP
	1 Main St.	SFO	CA	94100
Jill	STREET	CITY	STATE	ZIP
	2 Main St.	SFO	CA	94100

Figure 17-1. *Relvar NADDR (attribute ADDR tuple valued)—sample value*

Assume now for the sake of the example, as we did in Exercise 6.2, that whenever two ADDR values have the same ZIP component, they also have the same CITY and STATE components. Then the foregoing design clearly involves some redundancy. Yet there's no violation of normalization here. In particular, the functional dependency

```
{ ZIP } → { CITY , STATE }
```

does *not* hold. (Why not? *Answer:* Because FDs are defined to hold among attributes, not among components of attributes.)

That said, let me now point out that the foregoing FD does hold in the result of replacing NADDR by the result of the following expression:

```
NADDR UNWRAP ( ADDR )
```

The **Tutorial D** UNWRAP operator effectively replaces some tuple valued attribute by a set of attributes, one for each component of that TVA; thus, the foregoing expression returns a result with attributes NAME, STREET, CITY, STATE, and ZIP. Of course, that result is still only in 2NF, not even BCNF, and it still suffers from redundancy.

We might be tempted to conclude from this example that unwrapping TVAs is a good idea. But is it enough of a good idea to be enshrined as a *principle* of good design, as opposed to a mere recommendation or rule of thumb?[10]

Example 2

Codd would probably have argued against the design of Example 1 on the grounds that values of attribute ADDR aren't "atomic" (though I'm not aware that he ever explicitly addressed the question of tuple valued attributes, as such, in any of his writings). Now, I don't agree with this position myself, for reasons explained in detail in Chapter 4 of the present book and elsewhere—but the point isn't worth fighting over, because we can obviously replace that tuple valued attribute by an attribute of type CHAR as shown in Figure 17-2. And Codd would surely have allowed that revised design, and yet it suffers from redundancies precisely analogous to those in Example 1.

```
NADDR

┌────────┬──────────────────────────────┐
│ NAME   │ ADDR    /* type CHAR */       │
├────────┼──────────────────────────────┤
│ Jack   │ 1 Main St., SFO, CA 94100     │
│ Jill   │ 2 Main St., SFO, CA 94100     │
└────────┴──────────────────────────────┘
```

Figure 17-2. Revised relvar NADDR (attribute ADDR text valued)—sample value

And if you don't like this example, consider what could happen if attribute ADDR were of some user defined type (ADDRESS, say) instead of type CHAR.

---

[10]In his book *An Introduction to Relational Database Theory* (Ventus, 2010), Hugh Darwen suggests that it might be, and that we might consider a *wrap-unwrap normal form* in this connection (WRAP and UNWRAP being the TVA analogs of the RVA operators GROUP and UNGROUP, respectively--see the answer to Exercise 4.14 in Chapter 4). He also suggests in that same book that ungrouping RVAs is a good idea, too, and that we might thus also consider a *group-ungroup normal form* accordingly.

Example 3

Redundancies similar to those in Example 2 can arise in connection with attributes of type DATE, if those attributes include—as they frequently do—the day of the week as well as a calendar date (as in, for example, "Friday, January 18th, 2019").

Example 4

My next example is an extremely simple version of the familiar employees-and-programmers database, in which all programmers are employees but some employees aren't programmers (as in Exercise 5.7 in Chapter 5). I note in passing that some people would say that employees and programmers in this example correspond to an *entity supertype* and an *entity subtype*, respectively.[11] Be that as it may, here's the conventional design:

```
EMP   { ENO }
      KEY { ENO }

PGMR { ENO , LANG }
      KEY { ENO }
```

I'm assuming for simplicity that:

a. Employees in general have no attributes of interest apart from ENO (because even if they do, it doesn't materially affect the situation).

b. Programmers have just one additional attribute, LANG (programming language skill—e.g., "Java" or "SQL" or **"Tutorial D"**).

---

[11]Please note, however, that if the terms "subtype" and "supertype" are indeed used in this way, then they're definitely *not* being used in the way I use them in the inheritance model described in my book *Type Inheritance and the Relational Model: Subtypes, Supertypes, and Relational Theory* (O'Reilly, 2016). In fact they're being used in a sense rather close to that of the terms "subtable" and "supertable," terms that *are* used—somewhat deprecatingly—in that book in connection with SQL in particular.

Now we have a choice: Record all employees in EMP, or record just the nonprogrammers in EMP? Which is better? Well, if we record just the nonprogrammers in EMP, the processing involved when an employee becomes or ceases to be a programmer is slightly nontrivial (in both cases we have to delete a tuple from one relvar and insert a tuple into the other). We also need to state and enforce the following constraint:

```
CONSTRAINT ... IS_EMPTY ( JOIN { EMP , PGMR } ) ;
```

Note too the implication if we want some other relvar to include a reference to employees; normally such a reference would be a simple foreign key, but if employees are split across two relvars as above it can't be (at least, not with foreign keys as conventionally understood).[12]

The net of such considerations is that this particular design is probably not recommended—instead, we would probably want to record all employees in EMP.[13] Either way, however, the example displays no redundancy.[14]

Example 5

Now I'd like to modify Example 4 slightly in order to make an additional point. Suppose relvar EMP does include at least one additional attribute, JOB; suppose further that a given employee is a programmer, and is represented in relvar PGMR, if and only if the JOB value in that employee's tuple in EMP has the value Programmer (perhaps other values of JOB—Janitor, for example—correspond to other relvars in the same kind of way). This kind of situation is not at all uncommon in practice, by the way. Now there's definitely some redundancy, because the fact that some given employee *e* is a programmer is represented

---

[12]Though it could be if we allowed foreign keys to reference views, as **Tutorial D** does, and we defined the (disjoint) union of EMP{ENO} and PGMR{ENO} as a view.

[13]I note in passing that SQL's "subtable and supertable" support agrees with this position.

[14]In the first edition of this book I said I thought the recommended design did involve some redundancy, but that was a mistake on my part. In fact I've changed my mind on several of the examples discussed in this chapter ... and I hereby apologize to anyone who might have been misled accordingly by that previous edition. But it seems to me that this very fact—the fact of my being able to change my mind in this way, I mean—is itself evidence in support of my repeated claims that redundancy as a concept still isn't properly understood, and hence that we need more science in this area.

twice—once by the fact that a tuple for *e* appears in PGMR, and once by the fact that *e*'s tuple in EMP has the JOB value Programmer. In fact the design is subject to the following equality dependency (as well as many similar ones, possibly):

```
CONSTRAINT ...
   PGMR { ENO } = ( EMP WHERE JOB = 'Programmer' ) { ENO } ;
```

Note, however, that there's no violation of orthogonality in this example, even though, given that all employees (programmers included) are represented in EMP, it's certainly the case that the projection of PGMR on {ENO} is equal to a certain subset—it's not a restriction as such—of the projection of EMP on {ENO}.[15] But neither of those projections corresponds to a component of any irreducible JD that holds in the pertinent relvar.[16] (Check the final version of *The Principle of Orthogonal Design* in Chapter 16 if you need to refresh your memory on this point.) Thus, a database can be fully orthogonal and yet still exhibit some redundancy.

Example 6

In his 1979 paper "Extending the Database Relational Model to Capture More Meaning" (*ACM Transactions on Database Systems 4*, No. 4, December 1979), Codd proposed a certain design discipline, which—simplifying slightly—can be described as follows:

- Let *E* be an "entity type," and let *ID* be a data type such that every entity of type *E* has exactly one *primary identifier* (my term, not Codd's), of type *ID*. For example, *E* and *ID* might be the entity type "suppliers" and the data type "character string," respectively.

- Let *P1*, ..., *Pn* be a set of "property types" such that every entity of type *E* has at most one property of each of the types *P1*, ..., *Pn*. For example, in the case of suppliers, *P1*, *P2*, and *P3* might be the property types "name," "status," and "city" (so *n* = 3 in this example).

---

[15]Why isn't it a restriction as such? *Answer:* Because it's a projection of a restriction, as opposed to a restriction of a projection, and a projection of a restriction and a restriction of a projection are different things—the latter is indeed a restriction but the former isn't, in general.

[16]In fact relvars EMP and PGMR are both in 6NF, and the only irreducible JDs that hold are trivial ones.

Note: I'm assuming for the sake of the present discussion (only) that a given supplier can have any subset of the three properties, including the empty subset in particular.

- Corresponding to each entity type *E*, then, the database should contain:

    a.   Exactly one *E-relvar*, with *ID* values for those entities of type *E* that exist at some time, and

    b.   Exactly one *P-relvar* for each *Pi* (i = 1, ..., *n*), with {*ID* value, *Pi* value} pairs for each entity of type *E* that exists at some time and has a property of type *Pi* at that time.

I'll refer to this discipline as *the RM/T discipline*, since it's part of what Codd referred to, in that 1979 paper, as "the extended relational model RM/T" (T for Tasmania, where Codd first presented his ideas for that extended model). Applying the discipline to the case of suppliers specifically, we obtain a design that looks like this (I ignore here for simplicity the fact that throughout much of this book the FD {CITY} → {STATUS} was supposed to hold in relvar S):

```
S  { SNO }
   KEY { SNO } ;

SN { SNO , SNAME }
   KEY { SNO }
   FOREIGN KEY { SNO } REFERENCES S ;

ST { SNO , STATUS }
   KEY { SNO }
   FOREIGN KEY { SNO } REFERENCES S ;

SC { SNO , CITY }
   KEY { SNO }
   FOREIGN KEY { SNO } REFERENCES S ;
```

Each of these relvars is in 6NF.[17] Figure 17-3 shows a set of sample values. *Note:* The values shown aren't meant to correspond exactly to our usual sample values, though they're close. Observe in particular that (a) supplier S3 has no status, (b) supplier S4 has no status and no city, and (c) supplier S5 has no name, no status, and no city.

S		SN			ST			SC		
SNO		SNO	SNAME		SNO	STATUS		SNO	CITY	
S1		S1	Smith		S1	20		S1	London	
S2		S2	Jones		S2	30		S2	Paris	
S3		S3	Blake					S3	Paris	
S4		S4	Clark							
S5										

Figure 17-3. *An RM/T design for suppliers—sample values*

As a matter of fact, this kind of design actually has quite a lot to recommend it (at least, it would do, given a well architected DBMS). For present purposes, however, all I want to do is call your attention to the following: So long as every entity of type E has at least one of the n properties, then such a design certainly involves some redundancy—arguably, in fact, *strong* redundancy as defined by Codd himself in his 1970 paper—because, at any given time, the value of the E-relvar will be equal to the union of the projections of the P-relvars over the identifier attribute. In the case of suppliers, for example, there would be a constraint (an EQD, of course) that looks like this:

```
CONSTRAINT ... S { SNO } = UNION { SN { SNO } ,
                                   ST { SNO } ,
                                   SC { SNO } } ;
```

Note: This particular redundancy doesn't apply to Figure 17-3, though—i.e., the constraint isn't satisfied, given the values shown in that figure—because there's one supplier (supplier S5) who doesn't have any of the three properties name, status, and city.

Observe now that the foregoing kind of design becomes "even more redundant," as it were, in the (common?) special case in which every entity of type E in fact has all of the n properties. Figure 17-4 is a revised version of Figure 17-3 that illustrates this situation:

---

[17]In the interest of historical accuracy, I note that P-relvars as described by Codd in his RM/T paper weren't necessarily in 6NF, because he didn't insist that each P-relvar involve just a single "property."

S
SNO
S1
S2
S3
S4
S5

SN	
SNO	SNAME
S1	Smith
S2	Jones
S3	Blake
S4	Clark
S5	Adams

ST	
SNO	STATUS
S1	20
S2	30
S3	30
S4	20
S5	30

SC	
SNO	CITY
S1	London
S2	Paris
S3	Paris
S4	London
S5	Athens

Figure 17-4. *A revised version of Figure 17-3*

Observe that now—speaking a trifle loosely—{SNO} is now a foreign key in each of the relvars that references the sole key {SNO} in each of the others; equivalently, the projection on {SNO} of any of the relvars is equal to the projection on {SNO} of any of the others. Well ... to be more precise about the matter, there's an equality dependency interrelating every pair of the four relvars:

```
CONSTRAINT ...
   IDENTICAL { S { SNO } , SN { SNO } , ST { SNO } , SC { SNO } } ;
```

IDENTICAL is an operator proposed by Hugh Darwen and myself, in our book *Database Explorations: Essays on The Third Manifesto and Related Topics* (Trafford, 2010) and elsewhere, as an addition to **Tutorial D**. You can think of it as a kind of *n*-adic "=" operator. The semantics as follows: The expression

```
IDENTICAL { rx1 , ... , rxn }
```

returns TRUE if the relations *r1*, ..., *rn* represented by the expressions *rx1*, ..., *rxn*, respectively, are all equal; otherwise it returns FALSE.

Even in the extreme case illustrated in Figure 17-4, however, the design doesn't violate orthogonality. What's more, I say again that this kind of design would have quite a lot to recommend it, given a well architected DBMS. In particular, the equality dependencies, and therefore the redundancy, would be "automatically" managed and maintained in such a system (see the section "Managing Redundancy," later).

Example 7

Consider a company in which every employee is required to be in exactly one department and every department is required to have at least one employee. Figure 17-5 shows sample values (in outline) for an RM/T design for this situation:

EMP	DEPT	EMPDEPT	
ENO	DNO	ENO	DNO
E1	D1	E1	D1
E2	D2	E2	D2
E3	D3	E3	D2
E4		E4	D3
E5		E5	D3

Figure 17-5. Employees and departments—sample values

By the way, do you think relvar EMPDEPT here is a P-relvar for employees, or for departments, or for both? Justify your answer! (In fact, to pursue the point a moment longer, an RM/T design might not be the best option in this example, because there's necessarily a one to one correspondence between EMP and EMPDEPT, and there seems little reason not to collapse those two relvars into one.)

Anyway, with reference to the sample values in the figure, we see that there are exactly five employees and exactly three departments. Since every employee must be in exactly one department and every department must have at least one employee, why not define one department—D3, say—to be the "default" one, and adopt a rule that says that any employee mentioned in EMP and not in EMPDEPT is in that default department? In terms of Figure 17-4, this rule would allow us to omit the tuples (E4,D3) and (E5,D3) from EMPDEPT. Note that if we don't adopt such a rule, then the design clearly involves some redundancy once again—to be specific, it's subject to the following equality dependencies:

```
CONSTRAINT EVERY_EMP_HAS_A_DEPT EMP { ENO } = EMPDEPT { ENO } ;

CONSTRAINT EVERY_DEPT_HAS_AN_EMP DEPT { DNO } = EMPDEPT { DNO } ;
```

There seem to me to be at least two factors that militate against adopting such a "default department" design, however. The first is that the choice of which department to make the default is likely to be arbitrary. The second is that now we need to be extremely careful over the meaning of relvar EMPDEPT! The obvious predicate *Employee ENO is in department DNO* doesn't work. Why not? Because, under that predicate (and assuming department D3 is the default), omitting the tuple (E5,D3), say, would mean—thanks to *The Closed World Assumption*—that employee E5 *isn't* in department D3! So the predicate has to be something like this:

> *Employee ENO is in department DNO (which is not the default department number D3).*

Now, this predicate does work (I think!), but it's pretty tricky. Suppose the tuple (E1,D1) appears in the relvar, as shown in Figure 17-5. Then the corresponding proposition is:

> *Employee E1 is in department D1 (which is not the default department number D3).*

And of course this proposition evaluates to TRUE. OK so far. However, now suppose there's no tuple in the relvar for employee E5. The intended interpretation is, of course, that employee E5 is in department D3; but what does *The Closed World Assumption* actually say? Well, first of all, observe that, e.g., the specific tuple (E5,D1) doesn't appear. By *The Closed World Assumption*, then, the following must be a true proposition:

> ***It's not the case that*** *employee E5 is in department D1 (which is not the default department number D3).*

Or a little more formally:

NOT (E5 *is in* D1 AND D1 ≠ D3)

By De Morgan's laws, this expression is equivalent to:

E5 *is not in* D1 OR D1 = D3

Since D1 = D3 is false, this expression reduces to just "E5 is not in D1," which is what we want (I mean, it's a true proposition).

A similar analysis shows that we can infer that E5 certainly isn't in any department that's not the default one, D3. But what about that default one? Well, the tuple (E5,D3) doesn't appear, and so the following must be a true proposition:

NOT (E5 *is in* D3 AND D3 ≠ D3)

Equivalently:

```
E5 is not in D3 OR D3 = D3
```

And since D3 = D3 is true, this expression reduces to just TRUE. Note, however, that the fact that this proposition is true certainly doesn't tell us is that E5 is in D3! Now, perhaps we can infer this latter fact, given that E5 does exist and certainly isn't in any department not equal to D3 (?). But I seriously doubt whether users would want to have to deal with such convoluted, logic-chopping arguments in practice.

Example 8

Consider the design illustrated in Figure 17-6 (a slightly revised, somewhat RM/T-like version of Figure 16-4 from the previous chapter):

EMP

ENO
E1
E2
E3
E4

EARNS

ENO	SALARY
E1	85,000
E3	70,000

SALARY_UNK

ENO
E2

UNSALARIED

ENO
E4

Figure 17-6. *An RM/T design for employees and salaries—sample values*

The predicates for these relvars are as follows:

- EMP: *Employee ENO is employed by the company.*
- EARNS: *Employee ENO has salary SALARY.*
- SALARY_UNK: *Employee ENO has a salary, but we don't know what it is.*
- UNSALARIED: *Employee ENO doesn't have a salary.*

Observe now that either relvar SALARY_UNK or relvar UNSALARIED is redundant—any employee represented in relvar EMP and not in relvar EARNS must be represented in exactly one of the other two; so we could drop, say, relvar SALARY_UNK without any loss of information.[18] Yet there doesn't seem to be any good reason for choosing either of SALARY_UNK and UNSALARIED over the other as the one to be dropped, and considerations of symmetry would argue in favor of retaining both, and living with the redundancy (?).

Symmetry is usually another good design principle. To quote Polya:[19] "Try to treat symmetrically what is symmetrical, and do not destroy wantonly any natural symmetry." But Example 8 and others like it—Example 7 too, perhaps—show that symmetry and nonredundancy can sometimes be conflicting objectives.

Example 9

This example is due to Hugh Darwen. It's based on a real life situation that arises in connection with the Open University in the U.K. We're given a relvar that looks like this:

```
SCT { SNO , CNO , TNO }
    KEY { SNO , CNO , TNO }
```

The predicate is: *Student SNO is enrolled on course CNO and is tutored on that course by tutor TNO* (or, more briefly, *Tutor TNO tutors student SNO on course CNO*). Figure 17-7 shows a sample value for this relvar. The redundancies are obvious: For example, the fact that student S1 is enrolled on course C1, the fact that course C1 is tutored by tutor T1, and the fact that tutor T1 tutors student S1 are all represented more than once in the sample value shown in the figure.[20]

---

[18]And we can write a constraint to express that redundancy, too—viz., CONSTRAINT ... SALARY_UNK = (EMP MINUS EARNS{ENO}) MINUS UNSALARIED. Or perhaps better: CONSTRAINT ... EMP = D_UNION {EARNS{ENO}, SALARY_UNK, UNSALARIED}. (D_UNION here stands for disjoint union. See *SQL and Relational Theory*.)

[19]G. Polya: *How To Solve It* (2nd edition, Princeton University Press, 1971).

[20]You might not agree that those repetitions constitute redundancy. If you don't, however, I ask you to hold your objections for now—I'll be taking a much closer look at this example later in the chapter.

SCT

SNO	CNO	TNO
S1	C1	T1
S1	C1	T2
S2	C1	T1
S2	C1	T2
S1	C2	T1
S2	C2	T1

Figure 17-7. *Relvar SCT—sample value*

Now, one tactic we might consider for reducing redundancy in examples like this one is to make use of surrogate keys (surrogates for short).[21] For example, we might introduce an attribute XNO, say, whose values serve as surrogates for (SNO,CNO) pairs, as illustrated in Figure 17-8. (Observe from that figure that I've made {XNO} the primary key for relvar XSC. However, the combination {SNO,CNO} is a key too, of course.)

XSC

XNO	SNO	CNO
x1	S1	C1
x2	S2	C1
x3	S1	C2
x4	S2	C2

XT

XNO	TNO
x1	T1
x1	T2
x2	T1
x2	T2
x3	T1
x4	T1

Figure 17-8. *Using surrogates for {SNO,CNO} combinations*

One difficulty with this approach is as follows: On what basis do we decide to use surrogates for {SNO,CNO} combinations and not for {CNO,TNO} combinations or {TNO,SNO} combinations? Whichever choice we make is asymmetric. Moreover, surrogates are not without problems of their own. Here are some of them:[22]

---

[21]As a matter of fact, Codd advocated the use of surrogates in his RM/T discipline in connection with *all* entity types. In this recommendation he was following the pioneering work of Patrick Hall, John Owlett, and Stephen Todd in their paper "Relations and Entities," in G. M. Nijssen (ed.), *Modelling in Data Base Management Systems* (North-Holland/Elsevier Science, 1975).

[22]These problems are elaborated in the paper "Composite Keys" in my book *Relational Database Writings 1989-1991* (Addison-Wesley, 1992).

- Surrogates can make updating more complicated (in essence, users have to do their own foreign key checking).

- To add insult to injury, the system's foreign key checking—which almost certainly still has to be done—(a) will never fail and (b) will therefore be pure overhead.

- Queries and updates become longer, more tedious to write, more error prone, harder to debug, and harder to maintain.

- More integrity constraints become necessary.

For present purposes, however, the real question is this: Does introducing surrogates really serve to reduce redundancy? I don't want to try to address this question here; I'll come back to it later, in the section "Refining the Definition."

Example 10

Another tactic we might consider for reducing redundancy in examples like that of Figure 17-7 is to introduce some relation valued attributes or RVAs. Figure 17-9 gives an example.

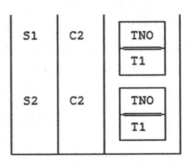

Figure 17-9. *Using an RVA for tutors*

One obvious problem with this approach—quite apart from all of the usual problems that always attend the use of RVAs, of course, as described in Chapter 4—is again asymmetry: On what basis do we decide to use an RVA for tutors and not for students or courses? And in any case, does this tactic really reduce redundancy? Again I'll come back to this question later, in the section "Refining the Definition."

Example 11

This one is just a placemarker. In our book *Time and Relational Theory: Temporal Databases in the Relational Model and SQL* (Morgan Kaufmann, 2014), Hugh Darwen, Nikos Lorentzos, and I show that certain "new" kinds of redundancy can arise in connection with temporal data, and we propose a number of new design principles and techniques for dealing with them.[23]

Example 12

My last example is typical of a common practical situation. It's loosely based on an example in Fabian Pascal's book *Practical Issues in Database Management: A Reference for the Thinking Practitioner* (Addison-Wesley, 2000). We're given two relvars that look like this (and I assume until further notice that they're base relvars specifically):

```
PAYMENTS { CUSTNO , DATE , AMOUNT }
        KEY { CUSTNO , DATE }

TOTALS { CUSTNO , TOTAL }
        KEY { CUSTNO }
```

Attribute TOTAL in relvar TOTALS is an example of what's often called *derived data*; its value for any given customer is derived by summing all of the payments for the customer in question. In fact, the following equality dependency holds[24] (and note that for once I've given the constraint a name, viz., C12, because I'm going to want to refer to it later):

```
CONSTRAINT C12 TOTALS = SUMMARIZE PAYMENTS BY { CUSTNO } :
                            { TOTAL := SUM ( AMOUNT ) } ;
```

---

[23]That book ("the temporal book," as I called it in Chapter 14) is, of course, the source of the "new" normal form 6NF (again see Chapter 14), but there's a great deal more to database design in the temporal context than just making sure all relvars are in 6NF—in particular, there's a great deal more to reducing redundancy—and I refer you to that book for an exhaustive discussion of the issues.

[24]Actually another EQD also holds in this example—viz., PAYMENTS {CUSTNO} = TOTALS {CUSTNO}—but we can ignore this one for present purposes.

Note: SUMMARIZE is **Tutorial D**'s analog of SQL's SELECT with a GROUP BY (speaking *very* loosely!).[25] However, in case you feel more comfortable with SQL than **Tutorial D**, let me also give an SQL version of the foregoing:

```
CREATE ASSERTION C12 CHECK
      ( NOT EXISTS
          ( SELECT *
            FROM    TOTALS
            WHERE   NOT EXISTS
                 ( SELECT *
                   FROM ( SELECT CUSTNO , SUM ( AMT ) AS TOTAL
                          FROM    PAYMENTS
                          GROUP   BY CUSTNO ) AS TEMP1
                   WHERE   TOTALS.CUSTNO = TEMP1.CUSTNO ) )
        AND
        NOT EXISTS
          ( SELECT *
            FROM ( SELECT CUSTNO , SUM ( AMT ) AS TOTAL
                   FROM    PAYMENTS
                   GROUP   BY CUSTNO ) AS TEMP2
            WHERE   NOT EXISTS
                 ( SELECT *
                   FROM    TOTALS
                   WHERE   TOTALS.CUSTNO = TEMP2.CUSTNO ) ) ) ;
```

Now, derived data is redundant by definition—though once again there are no violations of either normalization or orthogonality in the example (in particular, relvars PAYMENTS and TOTALS are both in 6NF). I'll analyze this example in more detail in the section immediately following.

---

[25]Actually SUMMARIZE might be dropped from the next version of **Tutorial D**, because expressions involving SUMMARIZE can always be formulated more simply, and arguably more comprehensibly, in terms of the relational EXTEND operator and what are called *image relations*. For example, the SUMMARIZE expression in the example could be replaced by the following: EXTEND PAYMENTS{CUSTNO}: {TOTAL := SUM (IMAGE_IN (PAYMENTS),AMOUNT). For further information regarding SUMMARIZE and EXTEND and image relations, I refer you to *SQL and Relational Theory*.

Managing Redundancy

The fact that the design of Example 12 from the previous section is redundant is clearly shown by the fact that the specified equality dependency holds (Constraint C12). And there are, at least in principle, four basic approaches to dealing with the kind of redundancy illustrated by that example:

1. Raw design only

2. Declare the constraint

3. Use a view

4. Use a snapshot

Let's take a closer look.

1. Raw Design Only

This is perhaps the approach most likely to be encountered in practice, given the limited functionality provided by most of today's DBMSs. The idea is simply that:

a. Relvars PAYMENTS and TOTALS are defined exactly as shown in the previous section.

b. Constraint C12 is *not* declared to the DBMS.

c. Maintaining the derived data is 100% the user's responsibility. (Or some user's responsibility, at any rate; the maintenance might be done by means of a triggered procedure, but some user still has to write the code for that procedure.)[26]

In effect, this approach trades off (a) the extra work involved on the part of the user—or some user, at any rate—in executing certain updates (as well as the associated performance hit) against (b) the improved performance obtained when executing certain queries. But there are no guarantees; if the user makes a mistake during some update that (in effect) causes Constraint C12 to be violated, well, tough.

---

[26]Note that relvar TOTALS should never be updated at all, except for the updates that are needed to keep the two relvars "in synch," as it were; ideally, therefore, some kind of control needs to be in place in order to enforce this rule. (An analogous observation applies to the other three approaches as well.)

2. Declare the Constraint

In this approach Constraint C12 is explicitly declared to the DBMS and the DBMS takes the responsibility for enforcing it. Maintaining the derived data is still the user's responsibility, though, exactly as it was under the previous approach. What's more, if the user carries out this task reliably and correctly, the constraint checking will never fail, and it will thus, in effect, constitute pure overhead on the user's updates. But we can't dispense with the constraint, precisely because we do need the system to check that the user *is* carrying out the maintenance task reliably and correctly.

3. Use a View

Clearly it would be better if, instead of simply declaring the constraint, we could actually inform the system of the rule by which the derived data is defined and have the system perform the derivation process automatically. And we can; that's exactly what the view mechanism does. To be specific, we can replace the base relvar TOTALS by a view (or "virtual relvar") of the same name, thus:

```
VAR TOTALS VIRTUAL
  ( SUMMARIZE PAYMENTS BY { CUSTNO } :
          { TOTAL := SUM ( AMOUNT ) } ) ;
```

Now the user no longer has to worry about maintaining the derived data; moreover, there's now no way that Constraint C12 can possibly be violated, and there's no need even to state it any more, except perhaps informally (as a means of telling the user the semantics of the view, perhaps). Note, however, that the user does have to be explicitly told not to try to maintain the totals! This fact doesn't mean the user has to be told that relvar TOTALS is a view, though; it just means the user has to be told that the maintenance task will effectively be performed by the system and the user shouldn't interfere.

4. Use a Snapshot

The drawback to the view solution, however, is that the derivation process is performed every time the view is referenced (even if no updates have been done since the last time it was referenced). Thus, if the whole object of the exercise is to do the derivation work at update time in order to improve subsequent query performance, the view solution is clearly inadequate. In that case, we should use a snapshot instead of a view:

```
VAR TOTALS SNAPSHOT ... /* hypothetical syntax */
  ( SUMMARIZE PAYMENTS BY { CUSTNO } :
          { TOTAL := SUM ( AMOUNT ) } )
  REFRESH ON EVERY UPDATE ;
```

The snapshot concept has its origins in a paper by Adiba.[27] Basically, snapshots, like views, are derived relvars; unlike views, however, they're real, not virtual—that is, they're represented not just by their definition in terms of other relvars, but also (at least conceptually) by their own separately materialized copy of the data. In other words, defining a snapshot is much like executing a query, except that:

a.   The result of the query is kept in the database under the specified name (TOTALS in the example) as a *read-only relvar* (read-only, that is, apart from the periodic refresh—see point b. immediately following).

b.   Periodically (ON EVERY UPDATE in the example) the snapshot is *refreshed*—that is, its current value is discarded, the query is executed again, and the result of that new execution becomes the new snapshot value.

The general form of the REFRESH clause is

```
REFRESH [ ON ] EVERY <now and then>
```

where *<now and then>* might be, for example, MONTH or WEEK or DAY or HOUR or *n* MINUTES or MONDAY or WEEKDAY (and so on). In particular, the specification REFRESH ON EVERY

---

[27]Michel Adiba: "Derived Relations: A Unified Mechanism for Views, Snapshots, and Distributed Data," Proc. 1981 International Conference on Very Large Data Bases, Cannes, France (September 1981).

UPDATE means the snapshot is kept permanently in synch with the relvar(s) from which it is derived—which is presumably just what we want, in the case of Example 12.

Now, in this section so far I've concentrated on Example 12 and the specific kind of "derived data" illustrated by that example. However, the fact is that *all* forms of redundancy can be thought of as derived data—if *x* is redundant, then by definition *x* can be derived from something else in the database. (Limiting use of the term *derived data* to the kind of situation illustrated by Example 12 is thus misleading, and not recommended.) It follows that the foregoing analysis—in particular, the four different approaches—can be generalized to apply to all kinds of redundancy, at least in principle. Note in particular that the third and fourth of those approaches, using views and snapshots respectively, both constitute examples of what's sometimes called *controlled* redundancy. Redundancy is said to be controlled if it does exist (and the user is aware of it), but the task of "propagating updates" to ensure that it never leads to any inconsistencies is managed by the system, not the user. Uncontrolled redundancy can be a problem, but controlled redundancy shouldn't be. In fact, I want to go further—I want to say that while it's probably impossible, and might not even be desirable, to eliminate redundancy completely, any redundancy that isn't eliminated ought at least to be controlled. In particular, we need support for snapshots.[28]

Refining the Definition

Note: I've deliberately left this somewhat lengthy section to the very end of the chapter (almost).

Consider the shipments relvar SP, with its predicate *Supplier SNO supplies part PNO in quantity QTY*. Consider also the relation shown as the value of that relvar in Figure 1-1 in Chapter 1. Observe that:

a.   Two of the tuples in that relation are (S1,P5,100) and (S1,P6,100).

b.   Both of those tuples include (S1,100) as a subtuple.

---

[28]Fortunately, many commercial products do now support snapshots, albeit under the strongly deprecated name *materialized views* (see footnote 1).

What do those two appearances of that subtuple mean? Well, the appearance in (S1,P5,100) means the following (I've numbered this proposition—note that it is indeed a proposition—for purposes of future reference):

1. *Supplier S1 supplies some part in quantity 100.*

And the appearance in (S1,P6,100) means exactly the same thing! So don't we have here a situation in which the database contains two distinct appearances of some (sub)tuple that represent the very same proposition? In other words, in accordance with the definition I gave in the introduction to this chapter, doesn't the database contain some redundancy?

Before I try to answer this question, I want to offer a simpler illustration of the same point. With reference to Figure 1-1 again, consider the six shipment (SP) tuples shown in that figure for supplier S1. Clearly, those tuples all contain the subtuple (S1), of degree one. And those six appearances of that subtuple all mean the same thing:

2. *Supplier S1 supplies some part in some quantity.*

We could even take the argument one step further and consider the fact that *every* SP tuple—in fact, every possible tuple, no matter what attributes it has—always has the 0-tuple as a subtuple. Thus, there are twelve "appearances" (if you see what I mean!) of that subtuple in the shipments relation of Figure 1-1, and they all represent the following proposition:

3. *Some supplier supplies some part in some quantity.*

So do we have redundancy on our hands here, or don't we? Well, notice that propositions 1-3 all involve some *existential quantification*. Here then are slightly more formal versions of those same propositions with that quantification made explicit and highlighted:

1. ***There exists some part PNO such that*** *supplier S1 supplies part PNO in quantity 100.*

2. ***There exists some part PNO such that there exists some quantity QTY*** *such that supplier S1 supplies part PNO in quantity QTY.*

3. ***There exists some supplier SNO such that there exists some part PNO such that there exists some quantity QTY*** *such that supplier SNO supplies part PNO in quantity QTY.*

In these propositions, SNO in the third, QTY in the second and third, and PNO in all three aren't parameters—of course not, since propositions never contain parameters!—but, rather, what the logicians call *bound variables*, owing to the fact that they're all "existentially quantified" by the phrase *There exists some ... such that.*[29] *Note:* If you're unfamiliar with these notions (viz., bound variables and existential quantification), you can find a tutorial treatment in *SQL and Relational Theory*. However, I think the present discussion should be easy enough to follow even if you don't have any prior knowledge of such matters.

In contrast to the foregoing, the propositions represented by tuples in the underlying relvar SP don't involve any existential quantifiers. That's because they're all just instantiations of the relvar predicate (i.e., they're all obtained just by substituting arguments for the parameters of that predicate), and that predicate in turn, which is as follows, involves no such quantifiers either:

Supplier SNO supplies part PNO in quantity QTY.

To summarize to this point, then, it looks as if the following observations apply:

a.   What might be called the *given* propositions—the ones represented by tuples in the given relvars—are quantifier free.

It might not be quite true to say that such "given propositions" are always quantifier free; consider, e.g., a relvar with attributes WEIGHT and HEIGHT and predicate *Some person has weight WEIGHT and height HEIGHT*. However, we can effectively eliminate the quantifiers in such a situation by a process known as *skolemization* (after the logician T. A. Skolem). In the example, that process involves replacing the original predicate by a predicate of the form *Person p has weight WEIGHT and height HEIGHT* (where *p* denotes some person or persons unknown). This latter predicate is quantifier free.

---

[29]In the section "Predicates vs. Constraints" earlier, I said there were two quantifiers, EXISTS and FORALL (known more formally as the existential and the universal quantifier, respectively). However, EXISTS is the only one that's relevant for present purposes. Moreover, we can assume without loss of generality that—as indeed the examples we've already seen strongly suggest—the quantification always appears as the opening part of the proposition in question. In other words, what I'll be referring to from this point forward as *quantified propositions* can always be assumed to be in what's called "prenex normal form," meaning they take the form *There exists ...such that there exists ... such that ...* (and so on), followed by *p*, where *p* in turn is a (sub)proposition that's quantifier free.

b. By contrast, *derived* propositions—at least, derived propositions
    that correspond to tuples obtained by taking projections of tuples
    in the given relvars—do involve at least one existential quantifier,
    and possibly more than one.

Now, we surely don't want to think of our usual shipments relvar SP as being
intrinsically redundant. So it looks as if what we might want to say is something along the
lines of the following:

> (*Warning: Tentative!*) If the same proposition is represented twice,
> but that proposition is existentially quantified, then that repetition
> doesn't count as redundancy.

But wait a minute—what about the suppliers relvar S, with its FD {CITY} → {STATUS}
(which I now want to assume does hold again)? An argument precisely analogous to the
foregoing would seem to suggest that, e.g., the tuple (London,20), which appears as a
subtuple in two of the supplier tuples depicted in Figure 1-1, represents the proposition:

> ***There exists some supplier SNO such that there exists some***
> ***name SNAME such that*** *supplier SNO is named SNAME, has*
> *status 20, and is located in city London.*

Clearly this proposition is existentially quantified; yet it's represented twice, and we
do want that repetition to count as redundancy. (As we know, relvar S, with its FD {CITY}
→ {STATUS}, isn't in BCNF.) So what's going on?

As is so often the case, I believe the answer to this question can be found by taking a
closer look at the predicates. First, recall from Chapter 14 that a predicate is *simple* if and
only if it involves no connectives, and *conjunctive* if it consists of a set of other predicates
connected by AND (and I'll assume for present purposes that those other predicates are
all simple ones).[30] Now, the predicate for relvar SP, *Supplier SNO supplies part PNO in
quantity QTY*, is simple in the foregoing sense. By contrast, the predicate for relvar S is
conjunctive—it can be decomposed into a set of simple predicates. I can make this latter
fact more immediately obvious by stating the predicate in the following slightly stilted
but actually more logical form:

---

[30]Since propositions are a special case of predicates in general—see the answer to Exercise 2.14 in
Chapter 2—we can say a proposition too is simple if and only if it involves no connectives (i.e., if
and only if it's an instantiation of a simple predicate).

Supplier SNO is named SNAME **AND**

Supplier SNO is located in city CITY **AND**

City CITY has status STATUS.

From this version of the predicate, then, it should be clear that:

a. Relvar S is subject to the nontrivial, irreducible JD ⋇{SN,SC,CT}, where the names SN, SC, and CT denote the headings {SNO,SNAME}, {SNO,CITY}, and {CITY,STATUS}, respectively. (By contrast, the only JDs that hold in relvar SP are trivial ones, and SP is in 6NF. Relvar S, to repeat, isn't even in BCNF.)

b. Relvar S can therefore be nonloss decomposed in accordance with that JD. The predicates for the corresponding projections are as follows:

SN: *Supplier SNO is named SNAME.*

SC: *Supplier SNO is located in city CITY.*

CT: *City CITY has status STATUS.*

These predicates involve no existential quantification, and so the corresponding propositions don't, either.[31]

c. Relvar S certainly contains subtuples corresponding to SN, SC, and CT; however, those corresponding to SN and SC are never repeated because {SNO} is a key. By contrast, those corresponding to CT are repeated, at least potentially (as we know from Figure 1-1), and such repetition does constitute redundancy.

---

[31]In connection with the lack of quantification in the predicate for CT in particular, you might want to take another look at the section "Normalization Serves Two Purposes" in Chapter 3.

With all of the foregoing by way of motivation, then, I offer the following as a putative "final" definition of what it means for a database to exhibit redundancy:

> **Definition (redundancy in the database, "final" detailed version):** Let D be a database design and let proposition p be both simple and unquantified. Then:
>
> a. If there exists a database value (i.e., a set of values for the relvars mentioned in D), DB, that conforms to D, such that
>
> b. There exists within DB some specific appearance of some tuple or combination of tuples that represents p, either explicitly or implicitly, and
>
> c. There exists within DB some distinct appearance of some tuple or combination of tuples that also represents p, either explicitly or implicitly, then
>
> d. DB contains, and D permits, redundancy.

Of course, the foregoing definition can also be expressed more succinctly thus:

> **Definition (redundancy in the database, "final" succinct version):** Let D be a database design; let DB be a database value (i.e., a set of values for the relvars mentioned in D) that conforms to D; and let p be a simple unquantified proposition. If DB contains two or more distinct representations of p (either implicitly or implicitly), then DB contains, and D permits, redundancy.

Observe in particular that a database can still display redundancy by this definition, even if it fully conforms to *The Principle of Orthogonal Design* and all normalization principles. Note, however, that the definition still says that *if*—not *if and only if*—a certain condition holds, *then* there's redundancy; I'd like to replace that *if* by *if and only if*, but I don't quite have the courage of my convictions here. Not yet.

Be that as it may, let's consider Examples 1-12 from earlier sections of this chapter and see what the implications of the foregoing definition are for those examples specifically. *Please note carefully:* Throughout the following analysis, the unqualified term *proposition* should be taken to mean a simple proposition that's not existentially quantified, unless the context demands otherwise. (However, I often use the more explicit term *simple unquantified proposition* anyway, for emphasis.)

Examples 1 and 2

Both of these examples display redundancy because the simple unquantified proposition *San Francisco, California is the city corresponding to zip code 94100* is represented twice.

Example 3

Suppose two distinct tuples both contain the DATE value "Friday, January 18th, 2019"; then the database clearly displays redundancy because the simple unquantified proposition *January 18th, 2019 is a Friday* is represented twice, explicitly. In fact, there's redundancy even if that DATE value appears just once! The reason is that even in that case, the proposition *January 18th, 2019 is a Friday* is represented both explicitly and implicitly. The explicit representation is obvious; the implicit representation is a consequence of the fact that one part of the value, viz., the day of the week (Friday, in the example), can be computed from the rest of the value (January 18th, 2019, in the example).[32]

Example 4

There's no redundancy in this example.

Example 5

Let employee *e* be represented in relvar EMP and let the JOB value for *e* be "Programmer" (so employee *e* is represented in relvar PGMR as well). As pointed out earlier, then, the simple unquantified proposition *Employee e is a programmer* is clearly represented (explicitly!) in two different ways.

---

[32]If we were to represent the day of the week and the rest of the date as two separate attributes—DAY and DATE, say—then the FD {DATE} → {DAY} would hold.

Example 6

For a supplier *s* who doesn't have all three properties (i.e., name, status, and city), this example is essentially similar to Example 4, q.v. For a supplier *s* who has all three, we could say the E-relvar tuple for *s* is redundant—*if* we accept that the predicate for that E-relvar takes the form *SNO is a supplier* and the predicates for the P-relvars take the form *SNO is a supplier and ...* (etc, etc.), meaning the unquantified propositions that are represented more than once are *S1 is a supplier, S2 is a supplier*, and so on. Debatable, maybe. What do you think?

Example 7

I said earlier that there seem to be good arguments against adopting the "default department" design here (and there are). But if we do adopt that design, then we might say the proposition *Employee E4 is in department D3* (for example) is represented twice: once by an explicit tuple, and once by the *lack* of a tuple corresponding to the proposition *Employee E4 is in department Dj* for any department *Dj* not equal to D3. But that's a pretty tortuous argument! What's more, the (missing) proposition "*Employee E4 is in department Dj for some department Dj not equal to D3*" isn't really unquantified—it's an abbreviation for something like this:

> **There doesn't exist a department Dj such that** employee E4 is in department Dj and Dj ≠ D3.[33]

So what do you think?

Example 8

The proposition *Employee E4 is unsalaried* is represented both explicitly by a tuple in UNSALARIED and implicitly by the lack of a tuple for employee E4 in either EARNS or SALARY_UNK. (This example has points of similarity with both Example 6 and Example 7.)

---

[33]Or equivalently: **For all departments Dj** employee E4 is not in department Dj or Dj ≠ D3. Observe that not only is this proposition quantified, it's—unlike all of the other quantified propositions discussed thus far—*universally* quantified.

Examples 9 and 10

Under the earlier discussion of Example 9, I said the following:

> The redundancies ... are obvious: For example, the fact that
> student S1 is enrolled on course C1, the fact that course C1 is
> tutored by tutor T1, and the fact that tutor T1 tutors student S1
> are all represented more than once in the sample value shown in
> [Figure 17-7].

I also said the predicate was *Tutor TNO tutors student SNO on course CNO.* But if
the redundancies really are as stated, it can't be quite that simple—instead, it has to
look like this:

> *Student SNO is enrolled on course CNO* **AND**
> *Course CNO is tutored by tutor TNO* **AND**
> *Tutor TNO tutors student SNO* **AND**
> *Tutor TNO tutors student SNO on course CNO.*

A more complete design would thus involve relvars as follows:

- S {SNO,...}, C {CNO,...}, and T {TNO,...}, representing students,
  courses, and teachers, respectively;

- SC {SNO,CNO,...}, CT {CNO,TNO,...}, and TS {TNO,SNO,...}, showing
  which students are enrolled on which courses, which courses are
  tutored by which tutors, and which tutors tutor which students,
  respectively;

- SCT {SNO,CNO,TNO}, as in the original version of the example.

Observe now that:

1. Relvar SC is equal to some subset of the join (actually the
   cartesian product) of S{SNO} and C{CNO}, and similarly for CT
   and TS.

2. More importantly, relvar SC is also equal to the projection of SCT
   on {SNO,CNO} (and, again, similarly for CT and TS). At least, SC
   is equal to SCT projected on {SNO,CNO} so long as the following
   assumption is valid: *No student can be enrolled on a course*

without being assigned a tutor for that course. (I focus on SC for definiteness, but of course analogous remarks apply to CT and TS once again.) But:

    a.   If that assumption is valid, then SC can be dropped (and similarly for CT and TS).

    b.   Alternatively, if that assumption isn't valid, then SC *mustn't* be dropped—a design consisting of SCT only is invalid.[34] (Once again a similar remark applies to CT and TS.)

3.   Relvar SCT is also equal to some subset of the join of SC, CT, and TS, and that join in turn is some subset of the join (actually the cartesian product) of S{SNO}, C{CNO}, and T{TNO}.

Now, if SC, CT, and TS aren't dropped, then there's clearly redundancy. For example, given the sample values from Figure 17-7, the simple unquantified proposition *Student S1 is enrolled on course C1* is represented (a) by an explicit tuple in relvar SC and also (b) as one of the conjuncts in the following (also unquantified, though not simple) proposition, which is represented by an explicit tuple in relvar SCT:

> *Student S1 is enrolled on course C1* **AND**
> *Course C1 is tutored by tutor T1* **AND**
> *Tutor T1 tutors student S1* **AND**
> *Tutor T1 tutors student S1 on course C1.*

Even if SC or CT or TS is dropped, however, there's still redundancy. For example, that same proposition *Student S1 is enrolled on course C1* is represented as one of the conjuncts in the foregoing (compound) proposition **and** as one of the conjuncts in the following (also compound) proposition:

> *Student S1 is enrolled on course C1* **AND**
> *Course C1 is tutored by tutor T2* **AND**
> *Tutor T2 tutors student S1* **AND**
> *Tutor T2 tutors student S1 on course C1.*

Both of these compound propositions are represented by explicit tuples in SCT. Thus, although my earlier characterization of the redundancies in this example might perhaps have been slightly misleading, it seems to me that redundancies of some

---

[34]Again I refer you to the section "Normalization Serves Two Purposes" in Chapter 3.

kind do exist. What's more, if you agree with this position, I think you also have to agree that the use of either surrogates (see the discussion of Example 9 earlier in the chapter) or—perhaps more obviously—relation valued attributes (see the discussion of Example 10 earlier in the chapter) makes no essential difference! That is, it's still the case, with both surrogates and RVAs, that certain propositions are represented more than once, in general. In other words, I think the redundancies in this example are intrinsic.

Now, I admit that these claims on my part might be open to debate. However, if you don't agree with them, then I think you need to justify your position rather carefully; in particular, I think you need to come up with a replacement for—in fact, an improvement on—my proposed "final" definition of redundancy.

As a kind of appendix to all of the above, let me add that I believe a similar analysis applies to certain other examples from earlier in this book. For example, consider relvar CTXD from Chapters 9 and 12, with its attributes CNO, TNO, XNO, and DAYS. When I first introduced that example, I said the predicate was *Teacher TNO spends DAYS days with textbook XNO on course CNO*. But it would be more accurate to say it's as follows:

*Course CNO can be taught by teacher TNO **AND***

*Course CNO uses textbook XNO **AND***

Teacher TNO spends DAYS days with textbook XNO on course CNO.

Similarly, consider relvar SPJ from Chapters 9 and 10, with its attributes SNO, PNO, and JNO. When I first introduced that example, I said the predicate was *Supplier SNO supplies part PNO to project JNO*. As noted in Chapter 14, however, it would be more accurate to say it's as follows:

*Supplier SNO supplies part PNO **AND***

*Part PNO is supplied to project JNO **AND***

*Project JNO is supplied by supplier SNO **AND***

Supplier SNO supplies part PNO to project JNO.

Example 11

A few of the issues raised by temporal data were discussed in Chapter 14. Further discussion of such matters is beyond the scope of this book.

Example 12

Let c be a customer and let the sum of payments for customer c be (say) $10,000. Then that very proposition—*The sum of payments for customer c is $10,000*—is represented explicitly by the appearance of a tuple for customer c in relvar TOTALS and implicitly by the appearance of the set of tuples for that same customer in relvar PAYMENTS.

Concluding Remarks

I've claimed that a database certainly involves redundancy if it contains two distinct representations of the same simple unquantified proposition. In particular, we don't want the same tuple to appear in two different places if those two appearances represent the same proposition. (Obviously we'd like to prohibit duplicate propositions as such; unfortunately, however, the DBMS doesn't understand propositions as such.) But it's all right for the same tuple to appear in two different places if those two appearances *don't* represent the same proposition—and in any case we can have redundancy without any tuple appearing twice at all, as we've seen.

Normalization and orthogonality seem to be all we have by way of a scientific attack on the redundancy issue at the present time. Unfortunately, we've seen that normalization and orthogonality don't go very far toward solve the problem—they can certainly reduce redundancy, but they can't eliminate it entirely. To be specific, we've seen several examples of designs that fully conform to the principles of normalization and orthogonality and yet display some redundancy, and those discussions were certainly far from exhaustive. We need more science! (Now I've told you that at least three times, and what I tell you three times is true.)

Given the foregoing state of affairs, it seems that redundancy will definitely exist in most databases. If it does, then:

- It should at least be controlled, in the sense that the DBMS should take responsibility for guaranteeing that it never leads to inconsistency.

- If it can't be controlled, then appropriate constraints should at least be declared, and enforced by the system, to ensure (again) that it never leads to inconsistency.

- If it can't be controlled and constraints can't be enforced by the system (or perhaps can't even be formally declared), then you're on your own—and woe betide you if you make any mistakes.

Sadly, this last scenario is the one most likely to obtain in practice, given the state of today's commercial implementations.

Exercises

17.1   I claimed in the body of the chapter that if database *DB* contains (either explicitly or implicitly) two or more distinct representations of some simple unquantified proposition *p*, then *DB* contains some redundancy. Can you think of a database that doesn't contain two or more such representations of any such proposition and yet in your opinion still displays some redundancy?

Answers

17.1   If you have a good answer to this exercise, please communicate it to me at PO Box 1000, Healdsburg, CA 95448, USA (regular mail only, please).

PART VII

Appendixes

APPENDIX A

What Is Database Design, Anyway?

Official designs are aggressively neuter,
The Puritan work of an eyeless computer

—John Betjeman:
The Newest Bath Guide (1974)

An early version of this appendix appeared as a foreword to the book Oracle SQL Developer Data Modeler for Database Design Mastery, by Heli Helskyaho (Oracle Press, 2015), and a revised and considerably expanded version of that foreword subsequently appeared on the O'Reilly website (`http://www.oreilly.com/data/free/what-is-database-design-anyway.csp`). But it struck me that it would serve very well in the present book as a kind of broad overview of what database design is all about. Since it's much less formal in tone than most of this book, however, I decided to relegate it to an appendix. My thanks to Heli, Oracle Press, and O'Reilly for allowing me to republish the material here in its present form.

Note: There's naturally some overlap between what follows and material in the body of the book, but I've done my best to keep that overlap to a minimum.

Databases lie at the heart of so much we do in the IT world that it's surely obvious that they need to be properly designed. Yet design theory—meaning database design theory specifically, of course—doesn't seem to be very well understood in the industry at large, and the same goes for design best practice also. You only have to look at the

© C. J. Date 2019
C. J. Date, *Database Design and Relational Theory*, https://doi.org/10.1007/978-1-4842-5540-7_18

Wikipedia entry on database design to see the truth of these claims! In fact, before going any further, I'd like to offer a few quotes from that Wikipedia piece (with commentary by myself) as evidence in support of these claims.[1] Here's the first:

- **Database design** is the process of producing a detailed *data model* of a *database*. This *logical data model* contains all the needed logical and physical design choices and physical storage parameters needed to generate a design ...

Comment: So the "logical data model" contains "physical design choices" and "physical storage parameters"? Clearly, somebody's confused here, and I don't think it's me. Note too the circular nature of the foregoing "definition" (doing database design apparently consists of producing the things needed for doing database design). The fact that the Wikipedia piece actually opens with the foregoing extract doesn't bode well for what's to come—but I suppose it might at least be argued that we've been given fair warning.

- The term database design can be used to describe many different parts of the design of an overall *database system*. Principally, and most correctly, it can be thought of as the logical design of the base data structures used to store the data. In the *relational model* these are the *tables* and *view* [sic "view," singular].

Comment: I'm going to argue later in this appendix that database design *isn't* "principally and most correctly" about "the logical design of the base data structures" (at least, not exclusively), so I won't comment further on that particular issue for the moment. I'm also going to say something later about the idea that "tables and views" are "used to store the data," so I won't comment further on that issue at this point either. But I do want to say something here about that phrase "tables and view(s)."

Sadly, the phrase "tables and views," or one very much like it, appears all over the place in the database literature.[2] In particular, it appears throughout SQL books, SQL journals, SQL product documentation, and the like (it even appears, albeit only briefly but still unfortunately, in the SQL standard itself). But, clearly, anyone who talks this

---

[1] I've replaced the links in the original Wikipedia entry by italicized words and phrases, as in (e.g.) *data model* and *database*. Otherwise the extracts are quoted verbatim.

[2] Since as I've said this appendix is deliberately fairly informal, I've decided to stay with the SQL terminology of tables, rows, and columns throughout in place of the relational terminology of relations, tuples, and attributes.

way is under the impression that tables and views are different things, and probably also that "tables" always means base tables specifically, and probably also that base tables are physically stored and views aren't (see my comments on the next quote below). But the whole point about a view is that it *is* a table—just as, in mathematics, the whole point about, say, the union of two sets is that it is a set. Thus, in mathematics we can perform the same kinds of operations on the union of two sets as we can on a regular set, because a union *is* a regular set. And in exactly the same kind of way, in the relational model we can perform the same kinds of operations on a view as we can on a regular table, because a view *is* a "regular table." So it's very important not to fall into the common trap of thinking that the term *table* always means a base table specifically. People who fall into that trap aren't thinking relationally, and they're likely to make mistakes as a consequence—mistakes in their database designs, and mistakes in applications, and even, to some extent, mistakes in the design of the SQL language itself.

To pursue the point just a moment longer: In fact, it could be argued that the very names of the SQL operators CREATE TABLE and CREATE VIEW are and always were at least a psychological mistake, in that they tend to reinforce both (a) the idea that the term *table* means a base table specifically and (b) the idea that views and tables are different things.

- Once the relationships and dependencies amongst the various pieces of information have been determined, it is possible to arrange the data into a logical structure which can then be mapped into the storage objects supported by the *database management system*. In the case of *relational databases* the storage objects are *tables* which store data in rows and columns.

Comment: Tables in the relational model—even base tables—are most categorically *not* "storage objects"![3] The relational model deliberately has nothing to say regarding what's physically stored; in fact, it has nothing to say about physical storage matters at all. In particular, it does *not* say that base tables are physically stored and views aren't. The only requirement is that there must be some mapping between whatever's physically stored and the base tables, so that those base tables can somehow be obtained

---

[3]Given the context, it's reasonable to assume that (a) by *storage*, the writer here means physical storage specifically, and (b) by *tables*, he or she means base tables specifically. Whether these terms ought to have these meanings is a very different matter!

when they're needed (conceptually, at any rate). If the base tables can be obtained from whatever's physically stored, then so can everything else. For example, we might physically store the join of the employee and department base tables, instead of storing them separately; then those base tables could be obtained, conceptually, by taking appropriate projections of that join.

To repeat, the relational model has nothing to say about physical storage matters, and of course that omission was deliberate. The idea was to give implementers the freedom to implement the model in whatever way they chose—in particular, in whatever way seemed likely to yield good performance—without compromising on physical data independence. Unfortunately, most SQL product vendors seem not to have understood this point (or not to have risen to the challenge, at any rate); instead, they do map base tables fairly directly to physical storage, and their products thus provide far less physical data independence than relational systems are or should be capable of.[4] But this state of affairs needs to be recognized for what it is: namely, a (major) defect in the products in question. It's not, and should not be taken to be, something that's intrinsic to the relational model as such.

- Each table may represent an implementation of either a logical object or a relationship joining one or more instances of one or more logical objects. Relationships between tables may then be stored as links connecting child tables with parents. Since complex logical relationships are themselves tables they will probably have links to more than one parent.

Comment: I have quite a lot to say about this one! To be specific:

- First of all, the writer is certainly playing pretty fast and loose with the language. For example, an employee might perhaps be considered as a "logical object"; but then the employees table will "represent an implementation," not of that "logical object" as such, but rather of the set of all such "logical objects" ("instances"?) currently existing in

---

[4] I say this knowing full well that today's SQL products do provide a variety of options for hashing, partitioning, indexing, clustering, and otherwise organizing the data as represented in physical storage. Despite this state of affairs, I still consider the mapping from base tables to physical storage in those products to be fairly direct. For that very reason, in fact, elsewhere I've labeled those products "direct image systems." For further explanation of this term, and much further discussion of such matters, see my book *Go Faster! The TransRelational™ Approach to DBMS Implementation* (Ventus, 2002, 2011; available as a free download from http://bookboon.com).

the enterprise. And the term "joining" as used in the first sentence is inappropriate, to say the least ("associating" might be better).

- Second, with respect to that phrase "logical object or a relationship": Well, it's one of the very great strengths of the relational model that it recognizes that what might be seen as a "relationship" by one person (or one application) is seen as a "logical object" by another, and vice versa. In other words, "relationships" *are* "logical objects" in the relational model, and they're represented in exactly the same way as all other "logical objects"—namely, as rows in tables.

- Third, it follows that to talk of "relationships between tables" being "stored as links" is misleading in the extreme; in fact, it's totally wrongheaded. I mean, there's no such thing as a "link" in the relational model—there are only tables.

- Fourth, the (unexplained) terminology of "child and parent tables" is highly deprecated, for more reasons than I care to go into here.

- Fifth, what's a "complex logical relationship"? More specifically, what would be an example of a relationship that's not "complex," or one that's not "logical"? As I've had occasion to write elsewhere, it's truly distressing in the relational context above all others—where precision of expression, not to mention precision of thought, was always a key objective—to find such dreadfully sloppy phrasing.

Note: The foregoing list of criticisms of this particular quote isn't meant to be complete. For example, what exactly does it mean to say, as the final sentence does, that "complex logical relationships are tables"? But I don't think any further deconstruction of the text is needed here. I think I've made my point.

- The physical design of the database specifies the physical configuration of the database on the storage media. This includes detailed specification of ... data types ... and other parameters ... .

Comment: I'm sorry, but data types are most definitely a logical consideration, not a physical one! Unless—and this thought has only just crossed my mind, because it's almost beyond belief that someone could be so deeply muddled—by "data types" here the writer really means *representations*? (Well, I suppose I shouldn't be so surprised. In fact, I now recall that confusion over types vs. representations wasn't exactly unknown in certain earlier writings by certain other parties, some very highly respected names among them ... But that was then and this is now, and I would have hoped that our understanding of such matters might have improved since then.)

Logical vs. Physical Design

Enough of Wikipedia; I think I've shown that I'm justified in complaining that design theory and design best practice seem not to be very well understood in the industry at large. In the rest of this appendix, therefore, what I'd like to do is try to inject some clarity into the debate; more specifically, I'd like to try to clarify exactly what database design really is, or at least ought to be. I'll start with some definitions.

> **Definition (database design):** Either logical database design or physical database design, as the context demands—though the unqualified term *database design*, or sometimes just *design*, is usually taken to mean logical database design specifically, unless the context demands otherwise.

> **Definition (logical database design, or logical design for short):** The process, or the result of the process, of deciding what tables some database should contain, what columns those tables should have, and what integrity constraints those tables and columns should be subject to.

The goal of the logical design process is to produce a design that's independent of all considerations having to do with either physical implementation or specific applications (this latter objective being desirable for the very good reason that it's generally not the case that all uses to which the database will be put are known at design time). And it follows from the foregoing definition that the process overall can be summed up as one of:

1. Pinning down the table predicates and other business rules as carefully as possible, albeit necessarily somewhat informally, and then

2. Mapping those informal predicates and rules to formally defined tables, columns, and integrity constraints—preferably in such a way as to ensure that the result of the process involves no uncontrolled redundancy.

I'll explain later in this appendix what I mean by the terms *table predicate, business rule,* and *uncontrolled redundancy.* Meanwhile, here's one more definition:

> **Definition (physical database design, or physical design for short):** The process, or the result of the process, of deciding, given some logical design, how that design should map to whatever physical constructs the target DBMS happens to support.

Observe carefully that (as the foregoing definition indicates) the physical design should be derived from the logical design and not the other way around. Ideally, in fact, it should be derived automatically, though I realize this might be a bit of a pipedream as far as most of today's commercial products are concerned.[5]

For the remainder of this appendix, I'll concentrate on logical design specifically (which from this point forward I'll usually abbreviate to just *design*).

The Role of Theory

The main thing I want to say here is just that there does exist some science, or theory, that can help with the logical design process. I refer, of course, to such matters as the principles of further normalization and *The Principle of Orthogonal Design.* In other words, if you're a designer, you owe it to yourself—as well as to your clients, which is to say the people who are going to have to live with the databases you design—to be thoroughly familiar with those principles and to know how and when to apply them. (I note in passing that there's quite a bit more to the theory than many people seem to realize. It's certainly not just a matter of making sure the tables are all in some particular normal form. However, this isn't the place to go into details.[6])

The second thing I want to say is that although the science is important, there are, sadly, numerous aspects of design that the science doesn't address at all. And that's where practical experience comes in. If you do have a lot of personal experience in the design field, well, good for you—you'll have learned (possibly the hard way!) what works and what doesn't. But if you don't have much experience of your own to fall back on

---

[5]But see the book mentioned in footnote 4, *Go Faster! The TransRelational™ Approach to DBMS Implementation,* for a description of a system in which that automatic derivation does in fact occur.

[6]Of course, the body of this book *is* that place!

(and maybe even if you do), then you'll need sound advice you can follow, advice from someone who does have such experience. A good book on design, by a suitably qualified professional, can help meet that need. A word of caution, though: Books on database technology, as opposed to books on design specifically, might *not* be what you need here. Such books do often describe theoretical design concepts (e.g., the various normal forms), but they don't usually give much guidance on how to apply those concepts to the practical task of design. *Caveat lector.*

Predicates

Let me now elaborate as promised on those terms *table predicate, business rule,* and *uncontrolled redundancy.* I'll discuss predicates in this section and rules and redundancy in the next two.

First of all, then, predicates. The *table predicate* for a given table is simply a reasonably precise, but informal, statement in natural language of what the table in question means—in other words, it's a statement of how that table is supposed to be understood by users. For example, suppose we have a table called EMP ("employees"), with columns called ENO, ENAME, DNO, and SALARY. Then the predicate for that table EMP might look something like this:

> *The person with employee number ENO is an employee of the company, is named ENAME, works in the department with department number DNO, and is paid salary SALARY.*

ENO, ENAME, DNO, and SALARY are the *parameters* to this predicate, and of course they correspond to the columns of the table with those same names.

Let me take a few moments to explain where this terminology of table predicates comes from.[7] In logic, a predicate is basically just *a truth valued function.* Like all functions, it has a set of parameters; it returns a result when it's invoked; and (because it's truth valued) that result is either TRUE or FALSE. Here's a trivial example:

$x > y$

For this predicate, the parameters are x and y, and they stand for values of—let's agree for the sake of the example—type INTEGER. When we invoke this function, we

---

[7]A more detailed explanation can be found in Chapter 2.

substitute arguments of the appropriate types for the parameters. Suppose we substitute the integers 8 and 5, respectively. We obtain the following statement:

8 > 5

This statement is in fact a *proposition*, which in logic is something that's unequivocally either true or false. In the case at hand, of course, it's true; but if we substituted, say, 3 and 7 instead of 8 and 5 as the pertinent arguments, the resulting proposition would be false.

Now let me get back to the predicate for table EMP. For that predicate the parameters are, as previously stated, ENO, ENAME, DNO, and SALARY, and they stand for values of (again let's agree for the sake of the example) types CHAR, CHAR, CHAR, and MONEY, respectively. (See the next section for more on the question of data types.) Now suppose we invoke this function—i.e., suppose we *instantiate this predicate*, as the logicians say— and substitute the arguments E4, Evans, D8, and 70K, respectively, for the parameters. We obtain the following proposition:

> *The person with employee number E4 is an employee of the company, is named Evans, works in the department with department number D8, and is paid salary 70K.*

And—here comes the point—*the corresponding row (E4, Evans, D8, 70K) will appear in the EMP table if and only if this particular proposition is true*. From a logical point of view, in fact, that's exactly what a "table" is: It's a set of rows, where the rows in question consist of all and only those rows whose column values form the arguments to a true instantiation of some specified predicate—and that specified predicate is, precisely, the "table predicate" for the table in question.

Another way of saying the same thing is this (the following constitutes what's usually known as *The Closed World Assumption*):

- If row *r* appears in table *T*, then the proposition corresponding to *r* is true.

- If row *r* could appear in *T* but doesn't, then the proposition corresponding to *r* is false.

Note: By "the proposition corresponding to *r*" in the foregoing, I mean, of course, the instantiation of the table predicate for *T* that's obtained by substituting column values from *r* for the parameters of that predicate.

Rules

Now I turn to the second of those terms I promised to explain, *business rule*. Like a table predicate, a business rule too is a reasonably precise but informal statement in natural language. However, it differs from a table predicate in its purpose, which is to capture some aspect of how the data in the database needs to be constrained:[8]

- To start with, there'll certainly be rules that specify what type of information is denoted by the parameters to those table predicates. In the case of employees, for example, there'll be a rule to the effect that the SALARY parameter ("salaries") denotes money values, expressed in, let's say, euros or U.S. dollars.[9]

- Second, there'll be rules that constrain the values those parameters can take for a given employee considered in isolation. For example, there might a rule that says salaries mustn't be negative and must be less than some specified upper limit.

- Third, there'll be rules that constrain the set of employees taken as a whole, independent of other "entities" such as departments, that might be represented in the same database. For example, there might be a rule to the effect that employee numbers must be unique.

- Finally, there'll be rules that constrain employees considered in combination with other entities represented in the database. For example, there might be a rule to the effect that every employee must be assigned to some known department, or a rule to the effect that no employee can have a salary greater than that of the manager of the department the employee in question is assigned to.

---

[8]I note in passing that some writers regard table predicates as just a special case of business rules—there's no consensus on the point. But there's certainly much more to business rules in general than just the table predicates as such.

[9]Actually I'm not sure that money values in general should be represented (at least as far as the user is concerned) in any particular currency—rather, I think it should be possible for the user to deal with such values in whatever currency he or she chooses (see Chapter 16, footnote 3). On the other hand, given that currency conversion rates can and do fluctuate, the same value in one currency might correspond to different values in another at different times. More study is required.

I'd like to say a bit more about this issue of business rules, because it's important—also because in practice it does tend to get somewhat overlooked. As the foregoing discussion should be sufficient to suggest, business rules can get quite complicated (as complicated as you like, in fact). As I've said, however, they're necessarily somewhat informal. Their formal counterpart—i.e., the thing they map to in the logical design—is *integrity constraints* (constraints for short), which thus need to be stated in some formal language and enforced by the DBMS. In other words, I depart here from certain other writers in stating categorically that database design isn't just about choosing data structures—integrity constraints are crucial as well. (Of course, it's true that other writers usually do at least talk about key and foreign key constraints—sometimes cardinality constraints too—but these particular constraints are really nothing more than important special cases of a much more general phenomenon.) In this connection, I'd like to draw your attention to the following remarks (somewhat paraphrased here) from *The Business Rule Book* (2nd edition), by Ron Ross (Business Rule Solutions Inc., 1997):

> Even though business rules (like the data itself) are "shared" and universal, traditionally they haven't been captured in database design. Instead, they've usually been stated vaguely (if at all) in largely uncoordinated analytical and design documents, and then buried deep in the logic of application programs. Since application programs are notoriously unreliable in the consistent and correct application of such rules, this has been the source of considerable frustration and error.

I couldn't agree more. Moreover, note the implicit but strong criticism of DBMS products that fail to provide adequate support for integrity constraints! (Interestingly, the support provided in this area by the SQL standard is actually not too bad. Unfortunately, however, SQL products have been rather slow, to say the least, in implementing this aspect of the standard.)

Redundancy

The third term I promised to explain is *uncontrolled redundancy*. Now, we often say, loosely, that the database is redundant if and only if "it says the same thing twice." We also often say, again loosely, that we don't want the database to involve any redundancy in this sense. However, it would be more accurate to say we don't want it to involve any *uncontrolled* redundancy. Uncontrolled redundancy can be a problem, but controlled redundancy shouldn't be. Let me explain ... First, here are some more definitions:

> **Definition (controlled redundancy):** Redundancy in the database is controlled if the user is aware of it, but it's guaranteed never to lead to any inconsistencies.

> **Definition (uncontrolled redundancy):** Redundancy in the database is uncontrolled if it has the potential to lead to inconsistencies.

> **Definition (inconsistency):** The database is inconsistent (at least from a formal point of view) if and only if there's some integrity constraint it's supposed to conform to but doesn't.

So if controlled redundancy means no inconsistencies, it must also mean no constraints are violated—or at least, and more precisely, no constraints having to do with data redundancy as such. Of course, not all constraints do have to do with data redundancy as such; for example, a constraint to the effect that salaries mustn't be negative doesn't. Thus, if the database were to show some employee as having a negative salary it would certainly be inconsistent, but that particular inconsistency wouldn't be one that arises from redundancy.[10] (It would, however, mean the database was incorrect, in the sense that it didn't faithfully reflect the state of affairs in the real world. Inconsistent implies incorrect, though the converse is false—the database can be incorrect without being inconsistent. For example, if it showed some employee as earning a salary different from that employee's true salary, it would be incorrect, but probably not inconsistent.)

To say it again, then, constraints don't always have to do with redundancy. But redundancy does always have to do with constraints.[11] For example, suppose—very unrealistically!—that there's a constraint to the effect that all employees in the same department must earn the same salary. Suppose further that the database shows Heli and Chris as being in the same department. Then if it were also to show Heli and Chris, separately, as earning the same salary, it would be redundant; by contrast, if it were to show Heli and Chris as earning different salaries, it would be inconsistent (and incorrect).

---

[10]It would be, rather, an inconsistency—in the normal English sense of that word—between the data in the database, on the one hand, and the pertinent constraint, on the other.

[11]By redundancy here I mean, more specifically, redundancy that's *understood by the system* to be redundancy.

So to say the database involves some redundancy is to say some constraint is supposed to apply. The constraint in question, in the case of the "same salary" example, might be formulated in SQL as follows:[12]

```
CREATE ASSERTION AX1 CHECK
    ( ( SELECT COUNT ( DISTINCT DNO ) FROM EMP ) =
      ( SELECT COUNT ( * ) FROM
              ( SELECT DISTINCT DNO , SALARY FROM EMP ) AS POINTLESS ) ) ;
```

Stating this constraint serves to inform the user that the redundancy exists; enforcing it serves to ensure that it won't lead to any inconsistencies, thereby guaranteeing that the redundancy in question is controlled. Note, therefore, that we see once again, not incidentally, how important it is to be able to state constraints formally and how important it is for the DBMS to be able to enforce them.

"Eventual Consistency"

There's one more topic I want to cover in this appendix. Some readers, I'm sure, will have found the remarks in the previous section concerning consistency and redundancy a little puzzling, especially in view of the recent interest in what has come to be known as *eventual consistency* (in the context of so called "NoSQL" systems in particular). So let me try to clarify those remarks.

First of all, to repeat, to say that a database is consistent merely means, formally speaking, that the database conforms to all stated constraints. Now, it's crucially important that the database *always* be consistent in this formal sense; indeed, a database that's not consistent in this sense, at some particular time, is like a logical system that contains a contradiction. Well, actually, that's exactly what it is—a logical system with a contradiction. And in a logical system with a contradiction, you can prove *anything*; for example, you can prove that 1 = 0.[13] What this means in database terms is

---

[12]As you can see, the constraint in question is defined by means of a CREATE ASSERTION statement in SQL. For some reason, SQL sometimes (but not always!) calls constraints assertions. As for that AS *POINTLESS* specification, it's pointless, but it's required by the rules of the SQL standard. PS: It might help to point out that "all employees in the same department earn the same salary" means that table EMP is subject to a functional dependency (FD) from department number to salary.

[13]In fact, you can *prove* that you can prove that 1 = 0! See Appendix B.

that if the database is ever inconsistent in the foregoing formal sense, you can never trust the answers you get to queries—they might be false, they might be true, and you have no way in general of knowing which they are. In other words, all bets are off. That's why consistency in the formal sense is so crucial. It's also why, contrary to popular opinion, integrity checking must always be immediate—i.e., it must be done at the end of any update operation that has the potential to violate the integrity constraint in question. (In other words, so called "deferred checking," meaning integrity checking that's deferred to the end of the pertinent transaction, is a violation of the principles of the relational model; in fact, it's a logical error.)

But consistency in the formal sense isn't necessarily the same thing as consistency as conventionally understood, meaning consistency as that term is typically used outside the world of databases in particular. Suppose items X and Y in the database are meant to represent quantities x and y in the real world, and suppose further that x and y are supposed always to be equal. (They might, for example, both be the selling price for some commodity, represented twice in the database because replication is being used to improve availability.) If X and Y in fact have different values at some given time, we might certainly say, informally, that there's an inconsistency in the data as stored at that time. But that "inconsistency" is an inconsistency as far as the system is concerned *only if the system has been told that X and Y are supposed to be equal*—i.e., only if "$X = Y$" has been declared as a formal integrity constraint. If it hasn't, then (a) the fact that $X \neq Y$ at some time doesn't in itself constitute a consistency violation as far as the system is concerned, and (b) importantly, the system will never rely on an assumption that X and Y are equal.

Thus, if all we want is for X and Y to be equal "eventually"—i.e., if we're content for that requirement to be handled in the application layer—all we have to do as far as the database system is concerned is omit any declaration of "$X = Y$" as a formal constraint. No problem, and in particular no violation of the relational model.

APPENDIX B

More on Consistency

You may be consistent or inconsistent,
but you shouldn't switch all the time between the two.

—Anon., quoted in Edsger W. Dijkstra:
Selected Writings on Computing: A Personal Perspective (1982)

The following is a lightly edited extract from Appendix A:

> To say the database is *consistent* means it conforms to all stated
> constraints. Now, it's crucially important that the database always
> be consistent in this formal sense; indeed, a database that's
> not consistent in this sense, at some particular time, is like a
> logical system that contains a contradiction. Well, actually, that's
> exactly what it is—a logical system with a contradiction. And in
> a logical system with a contradiction, you can prove *anything*;
> for example, you can prove that $1 = 0$. (In fact, you can *prove* that
> you can prove that $1 = 0$!) What this means in database terms is
> that if the database is ever inconsistent in the foregoing formal
> sense, you can never trust the answers you get to queries—they
> might be false, they might be true, and you have no way in
> general of knowing which they are. In other words, all bets are
> off. That's why consistency in the formal sense is so crucial. It's
> also why, contrary to popular opinion, integrity checking must
> always be immediate—i.e., it must be done at the end of any
> update operation that has the potential to violate the integrity

© C. J. Date 2019
C. J. Date, *Database Design and Relational Theory*, https://doi.org/10.1007/978-1-4842-5540-7_19

constraint in question. In other words, so called "deferred checking," meaning integrity checking that's deferred to the end of the pertinent transaction, is a violation of the principles of the relational model; in fact, it's a logical error.

Well, it occurred to me on reviewing that previous appendix that the message contained in the foregoing text could do with some elaboration. I mean, it raises various questions—rather important questions—that any competent database professional really ought to be able to answer, and yet don't seem to have received very much attention in the literature.[1] For that reason, I'd like to address those questions in the this appendix (which can thus be seen as a kind of postscript to the previous one—an appendix to an appendix, if you like).

The Database Is a Logical System

Let D be a database design and let DB be a corresponding database value (i.e., a set of values for the relvars mentioned in D). As we know, then, the tuples in the relations[2] in DB can be regarded as representing certain propositions, propositions that are assumed by convention to be true ones. By way of example, let's assume until further notice that D is our usual design for suppliers and parts and DB accordingly is our usual sample value (shown again for convenience in Figure B-1). Then all of the following are "true facts":

> *Supplier S1 is named Smith, has status 20, and is located in city London.*
>
> *Part P1 is named Nut, has color Red and weight 12.0, and is stored in city London.*
>
> *Supplier S1 supplies part P1 in quantity 300.*

And so on.

---

[1]I've written about most of those questions myself in various books and papers elsewhere, but I think it's worth bringing them together in one place and airing them all at least one more time.

[2]Throughout this appendix the term *relation* can be harmlessly taken to mean a base relation specifically.

S

SNO	SNAME	STATUS	CITY
S1	Smith	20	London
S2	Jones	30	Paris
S3	Blake	30	Paris
S4	Clark	20	London
S5	Adams	30	Athens

P

PNO	PNAME	COLOR	WEIGHT	CITY
P1	Nut	Red	12.0	London
P2	Bolt	Green	17.0	Paris
P3	Screw	Blue	17.0	Paris
P4	Screw	Red	14.0	London
P5	Cam	Blue	12.0	Paris
P6	Cog	Red	19.0	London

SP

SNO	PNO	QTY
S1	P1	300
S1	P2	200
S1	P3	400
S1	P4	200
S1	P5	100
S1	P6	100
S2	P1	300
S2	P2	400
S3	P2	200
S4	P2	200
S4	P4	300
S4	P5	400

Figure B-1. *The suppliers-and-parts database—sample value*

What I didn't mention previously, though, is that the integrity constraints that any given database value is supposed to satisfy can be understood as propositions too (again, propositions that are assumed to be true ones). For example, consider the following expression, which might be used to represent the fact that there's a foreign key constraint between shipments (SP) and suppliers (S):

SP { SNO } ⊆ S { SNO }

("the projection of SP on SNO is a subset—not necessarily a proper subset—of the projection of S on SNO"). The symbols SP and S are relvar names, of course, but in logical terms they can be understood as *designators*, where a designator is simply something that denotes, or designates, some specific object. As far as the database value *DB* is concerned, of course, those particular designators denote the current value of the suppliers relvar and the current value of the shipments relvar, respectively, and the constraint becomes (paraphrasing):

> *Every supplier number in the shipments relation also appears in the suppliers relation.*

And this latter statement is indeed a proposition. Thus, *DB* overall (data plus constraints) can be regarded (a trifle loosely) as a collection of propositions, propositions that are—to say it one more time—supposed to be true ones.

But we can go further. The fact is, a database value like *DB*, together with the operators that can be applied to the propositions in that database, can be regarded as *a logical system*. That is, it's a formal system—like euclidean geometry, for example—that has *axioms* ("given truths") and *rules of inference* by which we can prove *theorems* ("derived truths") from those axioms. Indeed, it was Codd's very great insight, when he first invented the relational model back in 1969, that a database isn't really just a collection of *data* (despite the name); rather, it's a collection of *facts*, or what the logicians call true propositions. Those propositions are represented by the tuples in the relations and the associated constraints, and they constitute the axioms of the logical system under discussion. And the inference rules are essentially the rules by which new propositions can be derived from those given ones; in other words, they're the rules that tell us how to apply the operators of the relational algebra. So when the system evaluates some relational expression—in particular, when it responds to some query—what it's really doing is deriving new truths from given ones; in effect, it's proving a theorem!

Once we recognize the truth of the foregoing, we see that the whole apparatus of formal logic becomes available for use in attacking "the database problem." In other words, questions such as

- What should the data look like to the user?

- What should the constraints look like?

- What should the query language look like?

- How should results be presented to the user?

- How can we best implement queries (or, more generally, evaluate database expressions)?

- How should we design the database in the first place?

all become, in effect, questions in logic—i.e., questions that are susceptible to logical treatment and can be given logical answers.

Of course, it goes without saying that the relational model supports the foregoing perception of what databases are all about very directly—which is why, in my opinion, the relational model is rock solid, and "right," and will endure.

Proving that 1 = 0

In the text quoted at the beginning of the appendix, I said this, more or less:

> In a logical system with a contradiction, you can prove *anything*;
> for example, you can prove that 1 = 0. In fact, you can *prove* that
> you can prove that 1 = 0!

All right, so here's the proof:

- Suppose the system in question is such that it states, either
  implicitly or explicitly,[3] that both p and NOT p are true (there's the
  contradiction), where p is some proposition.

- Let q be an arbitrary proposition.

- From the truth of p, we can infer the truth of p OR q.

- From the truth of p OR q and the truth of NOT p, we can infer the
  truth of q.

- But q was arbitrary!—it could, for example, be the proposition 1 = 0.
  QED.

It follows more generally that *absolutely any proposition whatsoever* can be shown to
be "true" in an inconsistent system.

---

[3]As far as databases are concerned, a proposition is stated explicitly if it corresponds either to a
"base tuple" (i.e., a tuple in the current value of some base relvar) or to some stated constraint. A
proposition is stated implicitly if it's not stated explicitly but is a logical consequence of the ones
that are.

Wrong Answers

The foregoing argument should be sufficient to show the crucial importance of integrity constraints. To be specific, if the database is in violation of some constraint, then the logical system that's the database is inconsistent—and (as we now know) we can get absolutely any answer at all from an inconsistent system.[4]

That said, however, the skeptic might still say "Really? I'm not convinced. Come on, show me a realistic example, not one of your abstract p and q arguments." So let me see if I can rise to this challenge.

I'll start with a really simple example. Suppose the current value of the suppliers-and-parts database is such that (a) there's at least one supplier; (b) there's a constraint to the effect that there must always be at least one part; but in fact (c) right now there aren't any parts at all (there's the inconsistency). Now consider the relational calculus expression:[5]

```
S WHERE EXISTS P ( TRUE )
```

Or if you prefer SQL:

```
SELECT  *
FROM    S
WHERE   EXISTS
    ( SELECT  *
      FROM    P )
```

Now, if either of these expressions is evaluated directly, the result will be empty, because the expression in the WHERE clause evaluates to FALSE. Alternatively, if the system (or the user, come to that) observes that there's a constraint that says that EXISTS P (TRUE) must evaluate to TRUE—or, in SQL, that SELECT * FROM P must return

---

[4]Perhaps I should rephrase the first part of this sentence. As should be clear from the text quoted at the beginning of the appendix, I'm interested here in consistency in its formal sense only. (See Appendix A for a brief discussion of the difference between formal and informal consistency.) And a database is inconsistent in that formal sense if *and only if* it's in violation of some stated constraint—and that *and only if* is important.

[5]I'm using a dialect of relational calculus here that allows a relvar name to be used to denote a range variable that ranges over the tuples of the relation that's the current value of the relvar with that name (just as SQL does, in fact).

a nonempty result—then that WHERE clause can be replaced by one saying simply WHERE TRUE, and the result will then be all suppliers.[6] At least one of these answers must be wrong! In a sense, in fact, they're both wrong; given an inconsistent database, there simply isn't—there can't be—any well defined notion of correctness, and any answer is as good (or bad) as any other. Indeed, this state of affairs should be self-evident: If I tell you some proposition p is both true and false, and then I ask you whether some proposition that relies on p in some way is true, there's simply no right answer you can give me.

In case you're still not convinced, consider the following slightly more realistic SQL example:

```
SELECT CASE
          WHEN EXISTS ( SELECT * FROM P )
             THEN ( x )
             ELSE ( y )
          END AS Z
FROM    S
```

Under the same assumptions as before—i.e., at least one supplier but no parts, despite a constraint saying there should be a part—this expression will return either x or y (more precisely, it will return a table containing a row containing either x or y), depending, in effect, on whether or not the EXISTS invocation is replaced by just TRUE. Now consider that x and y can each be essentially anything at all ... For example, x might be the SQL expression SELECT SUM (WEIGHT) FROM P while y might be the literal 0.0—in which case executing the query could easily lead to the erroneous conclusion that the total part weight is null instead of zero. (The total part weight should be zero, of course, if there are no parts. What makes the wrong answer particularly galling in this example is that the user has clearly gone out of his or her way to formulate the query in such a way as to obtain the logically correct answer, zero, if indeed there are no parts.)

---

[6]Using an integrity constraint in this way in the evaluation of some expression is known as *semantic transformation*. As the text suggests, such transformations can be done—indeed are done, all the time—by the user or the DBMS or both.

Generalizing the Argument

One reviewer of an early version of this appendix, still not convinced, tried a different question. He asked, in effect, how we might express the query "Get the total shipment quantity, taken over all shipments" in such a way as to obtain some specific incorrect answer, say 5000, from a certain inconsistent database. Well, before I try to answer that question, let me try to generalize the argument as presented in the previous section.

First of all, then, we know that a database value is, abstractly, a collection of propositions. Let *DBP* be the collection of propositions constituting database value *DB*. Let *LA* be the logical AND—i.e., the conjunction—of all of the propositions in *DBP*. Further, let some query against *DB* return a result *R*, where *R* is a relation that's derived from the relations in *DB* by evaluating the relational expression representing the given query. Of course, *R* in turn can be understood as another collection of propositions *RP*; so we can say that "*LA* implies *RP*" is true, or in other words that the propositions in *RP* are a logical consequence of those in *LA*. But if *DB* is inconsistent (i.e., if *DBP* involves a contradiction), *LA* evaluates to FALSE—and the implication "FALSE implies *p*" evaluates to TRUE for all possible propositions *p*,[7] regardless of whether that proposition *p* is true or false in itself. If *DB* is inconsistent, therefore, we have no way (in general) of knowing whether the individual propositions in *RP* are true or false.

Now I return to the reviewer's question: How might we express the query "Get the total shipment quantity, taken over all shipments" in such a way as to obtain the answer 5000 from a certain inconsistent database? In fact I don't think the way this question is stated makes very much sense. In **Tutorial D**, the obvious way of expressing the query as such (i.e., ignoring for the moment the requirement that it has to return the value 5000 against a certain inconsistent database) is as follows:

```
EXTEND TABLE_DEE : { TOTQ := SUM ( SP , QTY } }
```

Or if you prefer SQL:

```
SELECT SUM ( QTY ) AS TOTQ
FROM   SP
```

---

[7]Sometimes stated in the form "If you'll believe a falsehood, you'll believe anything."

Evaluating either of these expressions yields a result that looks like this:

TOTQ
x

The corresponding proposition is "The total shipment quantity TOTQ, taken over all shipments, is *x*." Now, it doesn't matter what the actual value of *x* is (it might or might not be 5000); what matters is that if the database is inconsistent, we have no way of knowing whether the corresponding proposition is true or false (i.e., whether *x* is the true total quantity). In other words, it's not *how we write the query* that's the point at issue—it's *how we interpret the result*. More specifically, we can't assume that the result we've been given is correct. As I said earlier, if the database is inconsistent, then all bets are off.[8]

Why Integrity Checking Must Be Immediate

In the text quoted at the beginning of the appendix, I said this, more or less:

> Contrary to popular opinion, integrity checking must always be immediate—i.e., it must be done "at statement boundaries," meaning the end of any update operation that has the potential to violate the integrity constraint in question. In other words, so called "deferred checking," meaning checking that's deferred to the end of the pertinent transaction, is a violation of the principles of the relational model; in fact, it's a logical error.

---

[8]But in case you're still not convinced, of course I *could* write an expression that apparently represents the query "Get the total shipment quantity, taken over all shipments" but in fact returns the value 5000 (at least potentially) if the database happens to be inconsistent. I'll leave the details as an exercise.

Actually there are at least five reasons for insisting that database constraints must be checked at statement boundaries, but the first and biggest one is simply that (as I've tried to show in previous sections) we can *never* tolerate any inconsistencies in the database, not even within the bounds of a single transaction. That is, while it might be true, thanks to the so called isolation property of transactions, that no more than one transaction ever sees any particular inconsistency, the fact remains that the particular transaction in question does see the inconsistency and can thereby produce wrong answers. *Note:* The book *SQL and Relational Theory* contains a detailed discussion of the foregoing issue, as well as of the other four reasons—the other four reasons, that is, for insisting that database constraints must always be checked at statement boundaries.

APPENDIX C

Primary Keys Are Nice but Not Essential

Life is rather like a tin of sardines—
we're all of us looking for the key.

—Alan Bennett:
Beyond the Fringe (1960)

Recall this text from Chapter 1:

> I said it's *usual* to choose a primary key. Indeed it is usual—but
> it's not 100% necessary. If there's just one candidate key, then
> there's no choice and no problem; but if there are two or more,
> then having to choose one and make it primary smacks a little
> bit of arbitrariness, at least to me. (Certainly there are situations
> where there don't seem to be any really good reasons for making
> such a choice. There might even be good reasons for not doing
> so. Appendix C [*i.e., the present appendix*] elaborates on such
> matters.)

Now, the position articulated in this extract clearly flies in the face of conventional wisdom; indeed, it might even be said to contravene certain widely accepted precepts of the relational model, or of relational theory in general. To be specific:

- Out of the necessarily nonempty set of keys possessed by a given relvar, the relational model as originally defined ascribes a primal role to an arbitrarily chosen member of that set called the *primary* key.

417

© C. J. Date 2019
C. J. Date, *Database Design and Relational Theory*, https://doi.org/10.1007/978-1-4842-5540-7_20

- Relational design methodologies—though not the relational model per se—tend to suggest, again a trifle arbitrarily, that a given "entity" should be identified and referenced throughout the database by the same (primary) key value everywhere it's represented.

As indicated, however, these recommendations—some might even call them *prescriptions*—both involve a certain degree of arbitrariness. The first in particular has always been the source of some slight embarrassment to relational advocates (myself included). One of the strongest arguments in favor of the relational model is and always has been its claim to a solid logical foundation. However, whereas this claim is clearly justified for the most part, the distinction between primary and alternate keys[1]—i.e., the idea of having to choose one member from a set of equals and make it somehow "more equal than the others"—has always seemed to rest on grounds that don't enjoy the same degree of theoretical respectability. Certainly there doesn't seem to be any *formal* justification for the distinction; it seems to smack more of dogma than logic, which is why as I said I find the situation embarrassing. This appendix grew out of my own increasing dissatisfaction with the seeming lack of solid justification for the orthodox relational position on these matters. (As a friend of mine once said to me, these are the areas where in live presentations "You talk very quickly and hope no one will notice.")

What's more, not only does there seem to be no formal justification for the primary vs. alternate key distinction, there doesn't seem to be any formal way of making the choice, either. Indeed, Codd himself is on record as saying "The normal basis [for making the choice] is simplicity, *but this aspect is outside the scope of the relational model*" (my italics).[2] But why should it be necessary to make the choice in the first place?—i.e., why, in those cases where a genuine choice does exist, should it be necessary, or desirable, to introduce such an element of arbitrariness?

Furthermore, the relational model as originally defined goes on to insist that all references via foreign keys, anywhere in the database, to (tuples in) a given relvar must always be via that relvar's primary key specifically, never via some alternate key. Thus we see that a decision that was essentially arbitrary in the first place—the choice of which

---

[1]The term *alternate key* was defined in Chapter 1, but I repeat the definition here for convenience: Let relvar *R* have two or more keys and let one be chosen as primary; then the others are *alternate* keys. (The term isn't used much in practice, but I do need to use it in this appendix.)

[2]The quote is from Codd's paper "Domains, Keys, and Referential Integrity in Relational Databases," *InfoDB 3*, No. 1 (Spring 1988).

key is to be primary—can lead to arbitrary restrictions on subsequent decisions as well; that is, it might constrain the set of decisions as to what can and can't be a legal foreign key, in ways that might not have been foreseen when that first decision (i.e., the primary key decision) was made.

I claim, then, that the idea that a distinction should be made, in the relational model as such, between primary and alternate keys—hereinafter referred to as *the PK:AK distinction*—introduces an unpleasant note of arbitrariness, artificiality, awkwardness, and asymmetry into what is otherwise a formally defined system (viz., the relational model). I claim further that it can also serve to introduce an unpleasant degree of arbitrariness, artificiality, awkwardness, and asymmetry into the database itself. And I claim still further that it can also lead to an undesirable and unnecessary distinction between base and derived relvars, as I'll show.

All of that being so, can the PK:AK distinction truly be justified? This appendix offers what I consider to be strong arguments in support of the position that the answer to this question must be *no*.

Arguments in Defense of the PK:AK Distinction

Before I consider consequences of the PK:AK distinction in detail, I should first examine the arguments in its defense. Since I'm on record as a defender of that distinction myself,[3] perhaps I should begin by summarizing, and with hindsight responding to, my own arguments! The principal ones were as follows:

1. Dropping the PK:AK distinction would imply among other things that "the entity integrity rule" would have to be extended to apply to all candidate keys (all candidate keys in base relvars, at any rate). *Note:* Refer to Chapter 1 if you need to refresh your memory regarding the term *candidate key*.

As I expect you know, the entity integrity rule is a rule to the effect that attributes participating in the primary key of a base relvar don't allow nulls. Now, I've argued for a long time that this rule should be dropped anyway, partly because it has to do with nulls (a concept I categorically reject), and partly because it draws a distinction between base

---

[3]In "Why Every Relation [*sic*] Should Have Exactly One Primary Key," in *Relational Database: Selected Writings* (Addison-Wesley, 1986); "Referential Integrity and Foreign Keys," in *Relational Database Writings 1985-1989* (Addison-Wesley, 1990); and elsewhere.

and other relvars and thereby violates *The Principle of Interchangeability* (i.e., of base relvars and views); thus, I now find this first argument in favor of the PK:AK distinction to be irrelevant.

Note: In case you're unfamiliar with *The Principle of Interchangeability*, I should explain that basically what it says is that there shouldn't be any unnecessary distinctions between base relvars and views—views should "look and feel" to the user just like base relvars.

2. The discipline of using the same symbol to identify a given entity everywhere it's referenced allows the system to recognize the fact that those references do all refer to the same thing.

This argument is clearly valid as far as it goes, but I now feel the discipline referred to should be treated as an informal guideline rather than a hard and fast requirement. See the discussions later in this appendix—in particular, the applicants and employees example—for examples of situations in which it might be desirable not to follow such a guideline in practice. In any case, the guideline in question really has to do with design (in other words, with how to apply the relational model in some specific situation), not with the relational model as such; in particular, therefore, it has nothing to do with whether the relational model as such should insist on primary keys. I must have been a little confused when I advanced this argument originally.

3. "Metaqueries"—i.e., queries against the catalog—can be more difficult to formulate if entities are identified in different ways in different places. For example, consider what's involved in formulating the metaquery "Which relvars refer to employees?" if employees are referred to sometimes by employee number and sometimes by social security number.

The idea here is basically that the discipline referred to under point 2 above can be beneficial for the user as well as the system. Again, however, it seems to me that we're really talking about informal guidelines, not absolute requirements.

4. My next point wasn't exactly an argument for the PK:AK distinction, but rather a criticism of an argument against it. This latter argument went as follows: Suppose some user is prevented, for security reasons, from seeing some primary key; then that user needs access to the data by some alternate key instead; so why make the PK:AK distinction in the first place?

I still don't find "this latter argument" very convincing, but of course criticizing an argument against some position doesn't prove the contrary position is correct!

5. My final point was an appeal to Occam's Razor ("Concepts should not be multiplied beyond necessity"). In effect, I was arguing that to treat all candidate keys as equals was to complicate the relational model's tuple level addressing scheme unnecessarily. But it might well be argued (and now I would argue) that Occam's Razor actually applies the other way around, and that it's the concepts of primary key and alternate key that are unnecessary!— i.e., all we really need is candidate keys, or in other words just keys *tout court*.

In a nutshell, the foregoing arguments no longer seem to me very compelling; the only one that still appears to have any validity is the one summarized under points 2 and 3 above, which (as I've said) isn't really an argument for making the PK:AK distinction in the relational model as such, anyway. As I've also said, I now feel the position supported by that particular argument should be seen more as a guideline than as an inviolable rule (again, see later for examples to justify this position).

I note in passing, though, that I did hedge my bets somewhat when I first discussed this issue ... Here's another extract from the pertinent paper (I've reworded it just slightly here):

> Note that if we can agree on retaining the PK:AK distinction for now, there's always the possibility of eliminating that distinction if desirable at some future time. And note moreover that this argument doesn't apply in the opposite direction: Once we're committed to treating all candidate keys equally, a system that requires a distinguished primary key will forever be nonstandard.

Although I didn't say as much at the time, this quote effectively constitutes an appeal to *The Principle of Cautious Design*, a principle I do still strongly believe in.[4] Indeed, it seems to me that the very fact that I'm able to shift my position on

---

[4]*The Principle of Cautious Design* says: Given a design choice between options *A* and *B*, where *A* is upward compatible with *B* and the full implications of *B* aren't yet known, the cautious decision is to go with *A*.

the PK:AK distinction now—which is indeed what I'm doing—can be seen as a vindication of that principle.

Before closing this section, I remark that Codd himself is also on record, in the same paper where he said there was no formal basis for choosing the primary key, as a defender of the PK:AK distinction (not surprisingly, since he originated it):

> Severe problems would arise ... if any relvar whatsoever were permitted to have more than one primary key [*sic*] ... The consequences of permitting more than one primary key ... for a single base relvar [would be] disastrous.

(I've taken the liberty of replacing Codd's term *relation* by the term *relvar* twice in this extract.) He goes on to give an example involving employees with "several distinct responsibilities"—project management, department management, inventory management, etc.—and then says:

> Comparing for equality of identifiers ... is intended to establish that one and the same employee is involved ... This objective is dealt a severe blow if the types of identifiers used for employees can be different depending on which pair of employee-identifying [attributes] is selected for the comparison.

Well, I think you can see this argument is essentially the same as the one given under points 2 and 3 above, which (a) as I've already indicated, is slightly confused, and (b) as we'll see later in this appendix, doesn't fully stand up under close scrutiny anyway.

Relvars with Two or More Keys

Now let's consider some reasonably realistic examples of relvars with two or more keys. The first concerns a relvar EXAM, with attributes S (student), J (subject), and P (position), and predicate *Student S was examined in subject J and achieved position P in the class list*. For the sake of the example, let's assume there are no ties (that is, no two students obtained the same position in the same subject). Then, clearly, given a student and subject, there's exactly one corresponding position; equally, given a subject and position, there's exactly one corresponding student. So the FDs $\{S,J\} \to \{P\}$ and $\{J,P\} \to \{S\}$ both hold, and $\{S,J\}$ and $\{J,P\}$ are both keys (or both candidate keys, if you prefer):

```
EXAM { S , J , P }
    KEY { S , J }
    KEY { J , P }
```

Exercise: What normal form is this relvar in?

Here's another example (it's basically Exercise 14.3 from Chapter 14): We're given a relvar representing marriages, with attributes A, B, and C and predicate *Person A married person B on date C*. Assuming no polygamy, and assuming also that no two persons marry each other more than once, every pair of attributes here is a key:

```
MARRIAGE { A , B , C }
        KEY { A , B }
        KEY { B , C }
        KEY { C , A }
```

And here's yet another example, based on a simple airline application (the predicate is *Pilot PILOT takes a flight out from gate GATE at hour HOUR on day DAY*):

```
ROSTER { DAY , HOUR , GATE , PILOT }
       KEY { DAY , HOUR , GATE }
       KEY { DAY , HOUR , PILOT }
```

How do we choose the primary key in cases like the foregoing? What grounds are there for choosing one key over another? Codd's criterion of "simplicity" doesn't seem to help. Note too that whichever one we choose, we wind up with an unpleasant asymmetry; e.g., in the marriage example, we might find ourselves treating one spouse as "more equal than the other" (and thereby certainly offending someone). Why should we be forced to introduce such asymmetry? Asymmetry is usually not a good idea. Here again, repeated from Chapter 17, is that quote from Polya: "Try to treat symmetrically what is symmetrical, and do not destroy wantonly any natural symmetry."

Now, in all of the foregoing examples the keys were not only composite, they all overlapped one another (i.e., they had an attribute in common). Lest it be thought that it's only when keys overlap that there might be difficulty in choosing the primary key, therefore, let me give a counterexample. Suppose we have a relvar ELEMENT representing the periodic table (i.e., the table of chemical elements).[5] Then every

---

[5]Actually, ELEMENT might more realistically be a relation constant, not a relation variable, but it still has to satisfy certain key constraints. (The same goes for the PLUS example in Chapter 16, incidentally, q.v.)

element has a unique name (e.g., lead), a unique symbol (e.g., the symbol for lead is Pb), and a unique atomic number (e.g., the atomic number for lead is 82). The relvar thus clearly has three distinct keys, all of which are simple (i.e., they each involve just one attribute), and there's obviously no overlap at all. On what grounds do we choose one of these three keys as the primary key? It seems to me a good case could be made for any of them, depending on circumstances.

Here's another familiar (perhaps all too familiar) example of a relvar with several keys, all of which are simple:

```
TAX_BRACKET { LOW , HIGH , RATE }
          KEY { LOW }
          KEY { HIGH }
          KEY { RATE }
```

Of course, I'm assuming here that no two taxable income ranges (LOW to HIGH) are subject to the same tax rate. *Note:* I suggested in Chapter 14 that tax brackets might better be represented as a single interval valued attribute (RANGE, say) instead of separate LOW and HIGH attributes. Even if it were, however, there would still be two nonoverlapping keys, RANGE and RATE.

I could give many more examples, but by now my point is presumably clear: Not only are there no formal criteria for choosing one key over another, in those cases where there's a choice, but sometimes there don't appear to be any informal criteria either. Thus, it really doesn't seem appropriate to insist that such a choice must always be made, even if it's appropriate in some cases (perhaps even in most cases).

There's another important point that needs to be mentioned, a more formal one than most of those I've been making so far. Over the past 50 years a great deal of research has been carried out on dependency theory and further normalization, view updating, optimization (including semantic optimization in particular), and many other matters. And in all of this research it's candidate keys, not primary keys, that play the crucial role. (Indeed, it must be, precisely because the research in question is formal. The candidate key concept is formally defined. The primary key concept isn't.) Since this is so, it really doesn't seem appropriate to insist *formally* on the PK:AK distinction—though, to repeat, it might be appropriate to recommend it *in*formally.

Yet another point I want to make is that the PK:AK distinction seems to lead to an undesirable and unnecessary differentiation between base relvars and other relvars (at least according to Codd). That's because, according to Codd, the relational model:

- *Requires* primary keys for base relvars;

- *Permits* but does not require them for views and snapshots; and

- Considers it *"completely unnecessary* for primary keys to be declared or deduced" for any other relvars (italics in the original).

These statements are paraphrased (but only slightly) from the paper in which Codd said there was no formal basis for choosing the primary key.[6] As a matter of fact, that paper goes so far as to suggest that relvars other than base ones might not even possess a primary key, a suggestion that if true surely raises serious questions about the concept in the first place (remember *The Principle of Interchangeability*). Be that as it may, my position on these matters is rather different. To be specific, I would say that:

- First, every relvar, base or derived, does have at least one key (because, of course, no relation, and a fortiori no relvar, ever permits duplicate tuples).

- Second, every base relvar must have at least one key explicitly declared. Preferably, of course, all such keys should be explicitly declared. (In fact, a base relvar key that's not explicitly declared simply isn't a key so far as the system—or the relational model itself, come to that—is concerned.)

- Often a base relvar will have an explicitly declared primary key in particular, but I don't insist on this state of affairs as a hard requirement.

- For reasons explained in detail in *SQL and Relational Theory*, I believe the system should be able to deduce keys for derived relvars.

- The previous point notwithstanding, I believe it should also be possible to declare keys, explicitly, for derived relvars (for views and snapshots in particular). Again, see *SQL and Relational Theory* for further discussion.

---

[6]I.e., the paper mentioned in footnote 2.

The Invoices and Shipments Example

I now turn my attention to a more elaborate example. The example (which is based on a real world application) concerns invoices and shipments, and there's a one to one relationship between these two entity types: Each shipment has exactly one invoice, each invoice has exactly one shipment. Here then is the "obvious" database design (for the sake of the example, I use a hypothetical syntax that explicitly distinguishes between primary and alternate keys):[7]

```
INVOICE  { INVNO , SHIPNO , INV_DETAILS }
         PRIMARY KEY { INVNO }
         ALTERNATE KEY { SHIPNO }
         FOREIGN KEY { SHIPNO } REFERENCES SHIPMENT

SHIPMENT { SHIPNO , INVNO , SHIP_DETAILS }
         PRIMARY KEY { SHIPNO }
         ALTERNATE KEY { INVNO }
         FOREIGN KEY { INVNO } REFERENCES INVOICE
```

So the database structure is as shown in Figure C-1 (note that the arrows in that figure, in contrast to arrows in figures elsewhere in this book, represent foreign key references, not functional dependencies):

Figure C-1. *The invoices-and-shipments database*

Now, each relvar in this example actually has two keys, {INVNO} and {SHIPNO}. However, I assume we can agree for the sake of argument that the "natural" primary key for INVOICE is {INVNO} and the "natural" primary key for SHIPMENT is {SHIPNO}; then

---

[7]One reviewer asked why a design consisting of three relvars (one each for invoices and shipments and one for the association between them) wasn't the "obvious" design. Well, it's probably a better design, and it might be the obvious one. But that association relvar still has two keys (INVNO and SHIPNO), and the major conclusion of the argument that follows—viz., that those two keys need to be treated as equals—still stands.

{SHIPNO} in INVOICE and {INVNO} in SHIPMENT are alternate keys. Furthermore, of course, each of those alternate keys is also a foreign key (as Figure C-1 indicates), referring to the primary key of the other relvar.

One problem with the foregoing design is as follows. Clearly, the database is subject to the constraint—actually it's an equality dependency, and I'll call it Constraint CIS— that if the INVOICE relvar shows invoice i as corresponding to shipment s, then the SHIPMENT relvar must show shipment s as corresponding to invoice i (and vice versa):[8]

```
CONSTRAINT CIS
    INVOICE { INVNO , SHIPNO } = SHIPMENT { INVNO , SHIPNO } ;
```

In other words, the tuple ($i,s,...$) appears in INVOICE if and only if the tuple ($s,i,...$) appears in SHIPMENT. But the design illustrated in Figure C-1 doesn't capture or enforce this constraint (for example, the configuration of values shown in Figure C-2 is permitted by that design and yet violates the constraint). The constraint thus needs to be separately stated (as above) and separately enforced.

INVOICE

INVNO	SHIPNO	...
i1	s1	...
i2	s2	...

SHIPMENT

SHIPNO	INVNO	...
s1	i2	
s2	i1	

Figure C-2. *"Legal" INVOICE and SHIPMENT values that violate constraint CIS*

It might be thought that if we pretended the primary key for each relvar was the *combination* {INVNO,SHIPNO}, and if we further defined each of those fake "primary keys" to be a foreign key referencing the other, then Constraint CIS would be taken care of automatically. (In fact, I've actually seen such a subterfuge explicitly recommended, by people who really ought to know better.) But the relational model requires primary keys—in fact, keys in general—to be irreducible, meaning they mustn't contain any attributes that are irrelevant for unique identification purposes (and there are good reasons for that requirement, too, as we know from Chapter 4). In other words, {INVNO,SHIPNO} just *isn't* a key (and so it certainly can't be the primary key)

---

[8]Observe, therefore, that—why, exactly?—the design violates orthogonality (see Chapter 16).

for either relvar, and we'd be lying if we told the system otherwise. Indeed, if {INVNO,SHIPNO} were truly a key, then the relationship between invoices and shipments would be many to many, which it isn't.

Precisely because Constraint CIS holds, the design of Figure C-1 clearly involves some redundancy: Every pair of {INVNO,SHIPNO} values appearing in either relvar also necessarily appears in the other. Now, we could avoid that redundancy by combining the two relvars into one ("INV_SHIP"), as follows:

```
INV_SHIP { INVNO , SHIPNO , INV_DETAILS , SHIP_DETAILS }
        PRIMARY KEY { INVNO }
        ALTERNATE KEY { SHIPNO }
```

By eliminating the redundancy in this way, we've also eliminated the need to state and enforce Constraint CIS. Furthermore, we could now define the original INVOICE and SHIPMENT relvars as views—specifically, projection views—of INV_SHIP, thus allowing the user still to regard invoices and shipments as distinct entities.[9] This revised design thus does enjoy certain advantages over the "obvious" version.

On the other hand, there are some disadvantages too. Observe first that we've had to make an asymmetric decision once again, choosing {INVNO} over {SHIPNO}—arbitrarily—as the primary key for relvar INV_SHIP.[10] Second, suppose further that shipments have certain subsidiary information that invoices don't; e.g., suppose shipments are containerized, each shipment involving several containers. Then a new CONTAINER relvar is needed:

```
CONTAINER { CONTNO , SHIPNO , ... }
          PRIMARY KEY { CONTNO }
          FOREIGN KEY { SHIPNO } REFERENCES INV_SHIP { SHIPNO }
```

---

[9]There might be some difficulty over updating those views, of course, given the state of today's commercial products—but this is a separate issue, beyond the scope of this appendix (and this book). See my book *View Updating and Relational Theory: Solving the View Update Problem* (O'Reilly, 2013) for further discussion.

[10]In fact, which key is chosen as primary might depend on the user's point of view! That is, users principally interested in invoices might want {INVNO} to be the primary key, whereas users principally interested in shipments might want {SHIPNO} to be the primary key.

And now we have a foreign key referencing an alternate key!—which the relational model as originally defined explicitly prohibits, as we know.

Now, can we avoid this apparent violation of the prescriptions of the original model? Well, of course, the answer is *yes*. There are various ways in which this might be done:

1. We could go back to the two-relvar design (thereby reintroducing the data redundancy and the need for the additional constraint, however).

2. We could replace SHIPNO by INVNO in the CONTAINER relvar. However, this approach seems very artificial (containers have nothing to do with invoices per se), and moreover introduces an unpleasant level of indirection into the design (the shipment for a given container would be accessible only via the corresponding invoice).

3. We could leave the CONTAINER relvar as it is, but replace the foreign key specification by an explicit declaration to the effect that every SHIPNO value in CONTAINER must also appear in INV_SHIP (using a language like SQL or **Tutorial D** that permits the definition of arbitrarily complex constraints). But it does seem a pity to have to deal with a constraint that's so similar to a "true" foreign key constraint in such a roundabout manner; indeed, it could be argued that the effect is again to introduce an undesirable asymmetry, foreign keys that reference primary keys being treated in one manner and "foreign keys" that reference alternate keys being treated in quite another.

4. We could introduce a surrogate primary key ({ISNO}, say) for INV_SHIP, and use that as the foreign key in the CONTAINER table— which would still involve a level of indirection, as in paragraph 2 above, but would at least reintroduce the symmetry that was lost when we arbitrarily chose {INVNO} as the primary key for INV_SHIP.

To summarize: None of these four "workaround" approaches seems totally satisfactory. The example thus seems to show that—if we wish to avoid redundancy and arbitrariness and artificiality and asymmetry and indirectness—then we need to be able to treat primary and alternate keys as equals, and we need to be able to have foreign keys that reference alternate keys. In other words, we need to ignore the differences between primary and alternate keys, and simply consider them all as just keys. Please note carefully, however, that I'm *not* saying the apparent need in this example to violate certain precepts of the original relational model can't be avoided; what I'm saying is I don't see a good way to avoid it, nor a good reason for adopting a bad way. I would therefore like to suggest that the precepts in question be treated as strong (?) guidelines but not as inviolable rules.

One Primary Key per Entity Type?

I turn now to the second of the two issues mentioned in the introduction to this appendix: viz., that entities of a given type are supposed to be identified in exactly the same way everywhere in the database. What this means, loosely speaking, is that there'll typically be:

- A single "anchor" relvar for the pertinent entity type, having some particular primary key, together with

- Zero or more subsidiary relvars giving further information about entities of that type, each having a foreign key that refers back to the primary key of that anchor relvar.

(Does this state of affairs remind you of the RM/T design discipline discussed in Chapter 17?) But several obvious questions arise:

- Might there not be good reasons to have more than one anchor relvar for a given entity type, perhaps corresponding to different "roles"— see the discussion of applicants and employees in the next section— for that entity type?

- If there are several such anchor relvars, might there not be good reasons to have different primary keys in different anchor relvars— thus implying that the same entity might be identified in different ways in different contexts?

- Hence, might there not be good reasons to have different foreign keys in different relvars that, again, identify the same entity in different ways in different contexts?

- Finally, might there not even be good reasons to have several distinct identifiers, all of equal weight, for the same entity in the *same* relvar?

We've already seen several examples in this appendix (in the section "Relvars with More than One Key") in which the answer to the last of these questions is clearly *yes*. In order to examine the other questions, let's consider another example.

The Applicants and Employees Example

This example (which, like the invoices and shipments example, is based on a real world application) concerns applicants for jobs in a certain enterprise. Relvar APPLICANT is used to keep a record of such applicants:

```
APPLICANT { ANO , NAME , ADDR , ... }
        PRIMARY KEY { ANO }
```

The applicant number (ANO) is assigned at the time the applicant applies for the job; it's unique to the applicant, and {ANO} thus constitutes the obvious primary key (in fact, it's the only key).

Next, several further relvars are used to keep subsidiary applicant information (previous jobs held, list of references, list of dependants, etc.). I consider just one of these here, the "previous jobs held" relvar (APPLICANT_JOBS):

```
APPLICANT_JOBS { ANO , EMPLOYER , JOB , START , END , ... }
            PRIMARY KEY { ANO , START }
            ALTERNATE KEY { ANO , END }
            FOREIGN KEY { ANO } REFERENCES APPLICANT
```

Observe, incidentally, that once again we seem to be faced with an arbitrary choice of primary key, but that's not the point I want to examine here.[11]

Now, when a job applicant is successful and becomes an employee, he or she is assigned an employee number (ENO, unique to the employee), and information regarding the new employee—job title, department number, phone number, etc.—is recorded in an EMP relvar:

```
EMP { ENO , JOB , DNO , PHONENO , ... }
    PRIMARY KEY { ENO }
```

---

[11]Once again, as with the tax bracket example, it might be desirable to use an interval valued attribute—replacing, in the present case , the pair of attributes START and END—in which case there'll be just one key after all and the choice issue goes away. As I've said, however, choosing the primary key isn't the issue I want to examine here.

Now we have two distinct anchor relvars, APPLICANT and EMP, such that the very same entity (i.e., a successful applicant) is identified by an ANO value in one of the two and by an ENO value in the other. Of course, it's true that the two relvars represent different *roles*—a tuple in APPLICANT represents a person in an applicant role and the corresponding tuple in EMP (if there is one) represents the same person in an employee role—but the fact remains that there's just a single entity involved.

The foregoing isn't the end of the story. Clearly, relvar EMP needs to refer back to relvar APPLICANT somehow (I'm assuming for the sake of the example, though the assumption might be a little unrealistic, that every employee was once an applicant). Thus, we need to add an ANO attribute to the EMP relvar and define a foreign key accordingly:

```
EMP { ENO , ANO , JOB , DNO , PHONENO , ... }
   PRIMARY KEY { ENO }
   ALTERNATE KEY { ANO }
   FOREIGN KEY { ANO } REFERENCES APPLICANT
```

Now we have two candidate keys once again!—namely, {ENO} and {ANO}. This point will be relevant in a few moments; for now, however, I'll ignore it.

Next, of course, we'll need additional relvars to carry subsidiary information for employees (salary history, benefit details, etc.). Here's the salary history relvar:

```
SAL_HIST { ENO , DATE , SALARY , ... }
        PRIMARY KEY { ENO , DATE }
        FOREIGN KEY { ENO } REFERENCES EMP
```

Now we have the very same entity being not only *identified*, but also *referenced*, by an ENO value in one relvar (SAL_HIST) and by an ANO value in others (APPLICANT_JOBS, EMP). In other words, the database structure is as shown in Figure C-3.

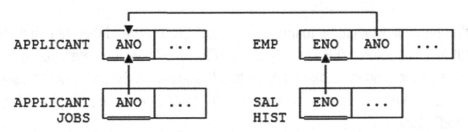

Figure C-3. *The applicants-and-employees database*

Now, we might avoid the apparent need for two different identifiers (ANO and ENO) for the same entity type by regarding EMP as a *subtype* of APPLICANT;[12] after all, every employee is or once was an applicant (loosely speaking), while the converse isn't true. In this way we could use {ANO} as the primary key for EMP, treating {ENO} as an alternate key (or even dropping it altogether), and replace ENO by ANO in the SAL_HIST relvar. The database structure is now as shown in Figure C-4:

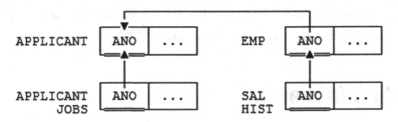

Figure C-4. *Using {ANO} as the primary key for EMP*

However, note the implications of this state of affairs: It's not just the database design that's changed, it's the way the enterprise has to operate. (For a start, it now has to identify employees by applicant number instead of employee number.) Why should the enterprise change its way of doing business, just because of a piece of relational dogma ("one primary key per entity type")? To be specific, why shouldn't it be allowed to identify applicants by applicant number and employees by employee number—even though applicants and employees are all persons, and indeed every employee is (or once was) also an applicant?

---

[12]But see Chapter 17, footnote 11, in this connection.

Another possibility would be to introduce a PERSON relvar and then regard both APPLICANT and EMPLOYEE as subtypes of PERSON. I leave the details as an exercise for the reader; I simply remark that this approach basically doesn't solve anything, even if we invent a "person number" (PNO) and make {PNO} the primary key of PERSON.

To summarize: The foregoing example strongly suggests there might be occasions on which it's indeed desirable (a) to have several different anchor relvars for the same entity type; (b) to have a different primary key in each of those anchor relvars; and (c) to have different foreign keys referring to those different primary keys in different subsidiary relvars. Again, please note that I'm *not* saying the apparent need here to violate the rule "one primary key per entity type" can't be avoided; what I'm saying is I don't see a good way to avoid it, nor do I see a good reason for adopting a bad way. Again, therefore, I would like to suggest that the "one primary key for one entity type" precept be treated as a strong (?) guideline, but not as an inviolable rule.

Concluding Remarks

In this appendix I've presented a number of pragmatic arguments for:

- Relaxing the commonly accepted rule that every base relvar have a distinguished key called the primary key

- Relaxing the (perhaps less commonly accepted) rule that every foreign key refer specifically to a primary key instead of to an alternate key[13]

- Relaxing the commonly accepted rule that there be exactly one anchor relvar for each entity type

---

[13]The reason I say *less commonly accepted* here is because—to its credit—the SQL standard, at least, does allow foreign keys to reference any candidate key.

Of course, I'm well aware that if we do relax these rules, then we open the door to the possibility of bad designs. That's why I recommend retaining recommendations such as "one primary key per entity type" as rules of thumb, or good design guidelines. In other words, the rules in question should be violated only if there's some really good reason for doing so. But what I've tried to show in this appendix is that sometimes such good reasons do exist.

APPENDIX D

Historical Notes

History is not what you thought.
It is what you can remember.

—W. C. Sellar and R. J. Yeatman:
1066 and All That (1930)

This appendix presents a brief and not unbiased survey of some of the seminal research publications in the field of design theory. The publications in question are listed in chronological order, more or less.

The relational model as such has its origins in two landmark papers by Codd:

- E. F. Codd: "Derivability, Redundancy, and Consistency of Relations Stored in Large Data Banks," IBM Research Report RJ599 (August 19th, 1969) and elsewhere

- E. F. Codd: "A Relational Model of Data for Large Shared Data Banks," *Communications of the ACM 13*, No. 6 (June 1970) and elsewhere

The first of these papers has nothing to say about design per se. The second, however, has a section with the title "Normal Form" that includes the following tantalizing remarks:

> Further operations of a normalizing kind are possible. These are not discussed in this paper.

These remarks appear following an example that shows how to eliminate relation valued attributes or RVAs (see the answer to Exercise 12.8 in Chapter 12). *Note:* The "further operation" in question—there's really only one of them—is what **Tutorial D** calls UNGROUP. See the answer to Exercise 4.14 in Chapter 4.

© C. J. Date 2019
C. J. Date, *Database Design and Relational Theory*, https://doi.org/10.1007/978-1-4842-5540-7_21

Design theory as such began with Codd's introduction of FDs, 2NF, and 3NF in:

- E.F. Codd: "Further Normalization of the Data Base Relational Model," in Randall J. Rustin, ed., *Data Base System: Courant Computer Science Symposia Series 6* (Prentice Hall, 1972)

Two brief comments here: First, the title of the paper is misleading—further normalization isn't something that's done to the relational model, it's something that's done to relvars, or rather to relvar designs. (To paraphrase something I said in the answer to Exercise 1.1 in Chapter 1, the relational model as such doesn't care what normal form the relvars are in, just so long as those relvars are indeed relvars—i.e., relation variables—as such and not something else). Second, a preliminary version of some of the material in this paper can be found in two earlier papers of Codd's. The first is:

- E.F. Codd: "The Second and Third Normal Forms for the Relational Model," internal IBM memo (October 6th, 1970)

The second is:

- E.F. Codd: "Normalized Data Base Structure: A Brief Tutorial," Proc. 1971 ACM SIGFIDET Workshop on Data Description, Access, and Control, San Diego, Calif., (November 11th-12th, 1971)[1]

Heath's Theorem was presented (though not under that name) in the same workshop as this latter paper.[2] See:

- I. J. Heath: "Unacceptable File Operations in a Relational Data Base," Proc. 1971 ACM SIGFIDET Workshop on Data Description, Access and Control, San Diego, Calif. (November 11th-12th, 1971)

---

[1] However, this paper isn't concerned so much with 2NF and 3NF per se as it is with the idea that relations can represent anything that other data structures—hierarchies, networks, etc.—can. It does discuss 2NF and 3NF very briefly, but its coverage of those topics is essentially limited to giving a single fairly informal example in each case.

[2] In fact Codd's contribution to that workshop references Heath's, while Heath's in turn references Codd's as yet unpublished 1972 paper on 2NF and 3NF. By the way, it's pertinent to point out that Heath's paper certainly appeared before Codd's 1974 paper that defined what's now called BCNF (see Chapter 5 for further elaboration of this point).

BCNF was defined in the following paper (though it was referred to therein as "an improved version" of *third* normal form):

- E. F. Codd: "Recent Investigations into Relational Data Base Systems," Proc. IFIP Congress, Stockholm, Sweden (North-Holland, 1974) and elsewhere

That same IFIP meeting also saw the first presentation of Armstrong's axioms for FDs:

- W. W. Armstrong: "Dependency Structures of Data Base Relationships," Proc. IFIP Congress, Stockholm, Sweden (North-Holland, 1974)

MVDs and 4NF and what in Chapter 12 I referred to as Fagin's Theorem were all defined in:

- Ronald Fagin: "Multivalued Dependencies and a New Normal Form for Relational Databases," *ACM Transactions on Database Systems 2*, No. 3 (September 1977)

The axiomatization of MVDs was defined in:

- Catriel Beeri, Ronald Fagin, and John H. Howard: "A Complete Axiomatization for Functional and Multivalued Dependencies," Proc. 1977 ACM SIGMOD International Conference on Management of Data, Toronto, Canada (August 1977)

The theory of dependency preservation had its origins in:

- Jorma Rissanen: "Independent Components of Relations," *ACM Transactions on Database Systems 2*, No. 4 (December 1977)

The next paper is generally credited with being the first to point out that relvars can exist that aren't equal to the join of any two of their projections but are equal to the join of three or more (though in fact, as mentioned in Chapter 9, Codd had effectively made the same observation in his original 1969 paper):

- A. V. Aho, C. Beeri, and J. D. Ullman: "The Theory of Joins in Relational Databases," Proc. 19th IEEE Symposium on Foundations of Computer Science (October 1977); subsequently republished in *ACM Transactions on Database Systems 4*, No. 3 (September 1979)

The foregoing paper is also the source of the chase algorithm—at least for FDs and MVDs, though not for JDs in general, because JDs in general hadn't yet been defined. In fact, they were first defined in:

- Jorma Rissanen: "Theory of Relations for Databases—A Tutorial Survey," Proc. 7th Symposium on Mathematical Foundations of Computer Science, Springer-Verlag Lecture Notes in Computer Science *64* (Springer-Verlag, 1979)

The next paper introduced the concept of projection-join normal form (PJ/NF), also called 5NF (it can be regarded as the definitive statement of what might be called "classical" normalization theory—i.e., the theory of nonloss decomposition based on projection as the decomposition operator and natural join as the corresponding recomposition operator, and the normal forms BCNF, 4NF, and 5NF):

- Ronald Fagin: "Normal Forms and Relational Database Operators," Proc. 1979 ACM SIGMOD International Conference on Management of Data, Boston, Mass. (May/June 1979)

The next paper presents a sound and complete set of inference rules—in other words, an axiomatization—for inclusion dependencies (INDs):[3]

- Marco A. Casanova, Ronald Fagin, and Christos H. Papadimitriou: "Inclusion Dependencies and Their Interaction with Functional Dependencies," Proc. 1st ACM SIGACT-SIGMOD Symposium on Principles of Database Systems, Los Angeles, Calif. (March 1982)

The next three papers define ETNF, RFNF, and SKNF, respectively:

- Hugh Darwen, C. J. Date, and Ronald Fagin: "A Normal Form for Preventing Redundant Tuples in Relational Databases," Proc. 15th International Conference on Database Theory, Berlin, Germany (March 26th-29th, 2012)

---

[3]Using "$X \subseteq Y$" to represent the IND "X is included in Y," the rules in question can be stated as follows:

1. $X \subseteq X$.
2. If $XY \subseteq ZW$, then $X \subseteq Z$ and $Y \subseteq W$.
3. If $X \subseteq Y$ and $Y \subseteq Z$, then $X \subseteq Z$.

Note that these rules are obviously valid if "$\subseteq$" is replaced by "$=$" (i.e., if the INDs are in fact EQDs).

- Millist W. Vincent: "Redundancy Elimination and a New Normal Form for Relational Database Design," in B. Thalheim and L. Libkin (eds.), *Semantics in Databases*, Vol. 1358 of *Lecture Notes in Computer Science* (Springer, 1998)

- Ragnar Normann: "Minimal Lossless Decompositions and Some Normal Forms between 4NF and PJ/NF," *Information Systems 23, No. 7* (1998)

6NF was originally defined in:

- C. J. Date, Hugh Darwen, and Nikos A. Lorentzos: *Temporal Data and the Relational Model: A Detailed Investigation into the Application of Interval and Relation Theory to the Problem of Temporal Database Management* (Morgan Kaufmann, 2003)

However, this book has since been superseded by:

- C. J. Date, Hugh Darwen, and Nikos A. Lorentzos: *Time and Relational Theory: Temporal Databases in the Relational Model and SQL* (Morgan Kaufmann, 2014)

Domain-key normal form was defined in:

- Ronald Fagin: "A Normal Form for Relational Databases That Is Based on Domains and Keys," *ACM Transactions on Database Systems 6*, No. 3 (September 1981)

As for orthogonality, the concept was first discussed, though not by that name, in:

- C. J. Date and David McGoveran: "A New Database Design Principle," *Database Programming & Design 7*, No. 7 (July 1994); republished in C. J. Date, *Relational Database Writings 1991-1994* (Addison-Wesley, 1995)

Note, however, that orthogonality as described in the present book is significantly different from the version discussed in the foregoing paper. (I accept full responsibility for this state of affairs; although the concept was originally due to David McGoveran, I wrote the bulk of the referenced paper, and I realize now that I must have been rather confused when I did so.)

Index

For alphabetization purposes, (a) differences in fonts and case are ignored; (b) quotation marks are ignored; (c) other punctuation symbols—hyphens, underscores, parentheses, etc.—are treated as blanks; (d) numerals precede letters; (e) blanks precede everything else.

Symbols

→ (FD arrow), 32
→→ (MVD double arrow), 244
✿ (JD star), 188
⋈ (bow tie), 188
∈ (set membership), 111, 188, 243
⇒ (logical implication), 263
⊆ (subset of), 38
⊂ (proper subset of), 38

Numerals

0-tuple, *see* empty tuple
1NF, *see* first normal form
2NF, *see* second normal form
3NF, *see* third normal form
3NF procedure, 129–133
(3,3)NF, 312
4NF, *see* fourth normal form
5NF, *see* fifth normal form
6NF, *see* sixth normal form

A

Abbey, Edward, 29
Abbott, Bud, 241

Abiteboul, Serge, 236
Adamson, Chris, xix, 170
Adiba, Michel, 376
Aho, A.V., 439
ALL BUT, 48
all key, 75
alternate key, 12, 418
AND (aggregate operator), 34, 89, 325
arity, 27
Armstrong, Louis, 3
Armstrong, W.W., 146, 439
Armstrong's axioms, 146
"arrow out of," 73
"atomic fact," 289
atomicity (data), 94
attribute
    attribute-name / type-name pair, 26
    relation valued, *see* relation valued
        attribute
    tuple valued, *see* tuple
        valued attribute
attribute renaming, *see* RENAME
axiomatization
    FDs, 147
    MVDs, 250
    not for JDs, 236

B

Bacon, Francis, 145
base relvar, 25
BCNF, *see* Boyce/Codd normal form
BCNF procedure, 133–134
Beeri, Catriel, 439
Bennett, Alan, 417
Betjeman, John, 393
body
 relation, 26, 98
 relvar, 99
bound variable, 379
Boyce, Raymond F., 81
Boyce/Codd normal form,
  68, 79–80, 102–105
 explanation of name, 81
Brown, Robert R., 15
business rule, 120, 402–403

C

candidate key, 10, 74
canonical form, 61
cardinality, 27
Carroll, Lewis, 287, 349
Casanova, Marco A., 440
catalog, 71, 91, 420
chase algorithm, 231–235
Churchill, Winston, 307
*Closed World
  Assumption*, 30, 256
closure
 relational algebra, 43
 set of attributes, 85, 151–153
 set of FDs, 147
Codd, E. F., *passim*
commalist, 10
common sense, 14–15

completeness, 146
component (JD), 187
composite key, 11
compound
  predicate, 289
connection trap, 191
connective, 289
consistency (database), 404–416
consistency (dependencies), 282
CONSTRAINT, 33
constraint, 57
 checked immediately, 415–416
 see also single-relvar constraint;
  multirelvar constraint
contain vs. include, 38
contradiction, 136, 326, 333
Costello, Lou, 241
cover (FDs), 130
CWA, *see Closed World Assumption*
cyclic rules, 194

D

D, 31
D_UNION, 369
da Vinci, Leonardo, 15
Darling, David, 319
Darwen, Hugh, *passim*
Darwen's Theorem, 153
data model
 first sense, 7–8
 second sense, 7–8
database
 logical system, 408–410
database professional, 23
Date, C. J., *passim*
DB2, 167
DBMS, xviii

Printed in the United States
By Bookmasters